PRISONERS
OF
HONOR

PRISONERS OF HONOR

THE DREYFUS AFFAIR

BY DAVID L. LEWIS

WILLIAM MORROW & COMPANY, INC.

NEW YORK

1973

TO ALLISON "APSELOVA"
a small Dreyfusard

Photo Credits:

Mme. Jeanne Pierre-Paul Lévy: 1, 44, 45; Mme. Marguerite Mercier: 42; Library of Congress: 43; Adolphe Ochs Collection, Bibliothèque Historique de la Ville de Paris: 18, 23, 33; Lee M. Friedman Collection, Harvard University: 2–6, 10–14, 16, 17, 19, 20, 25, 27–32, 34–41.

Book design by Helen Roberts
Printed in the United States of America.

Library of Congress Cataloging in Publication Data

Lewis, David L.
    Prisoners of honor; the Dreyfus affair.

    Bibliography: p.
    1. Dreyfus, Alfred, 1859-1935. I. Title.
DC354.L38   944.081′092′4 [B]   73-9900
ISBN 0-688-00202-1
1 2 3 4 5 77 76 75 74 73

Preface

ON AUGUST 19, 1899, THE *GENERAL ADVERTISER* of New South Wales, Australia, observed, "When the Dreyfus Case is ended, and nobody on this earth knows when that will be, there will be a relief to mankind all the world over." Although the role of the principal victim—Dreyfus' part—is over, the Dreyfus Affair continues, for the Affair is about old-fashioned fundamentals. Wherever and whenever dissension about social harmony, political expediency, and national defense obscures the rights of minorities, the corruption of institutions and the aberrations of patriotism, there is a Dreyfus Affair. In the plainest terms, where and when people consciously acquiesce in denial of justice to a single person, "relief to mankind all the world over" recedes.

In writing this book, I had the singular luck of being able to live deep within the sources of the Dreyfusard past. From his birthplace in Mulhouse (Alsace), I followed Alfred Dreyfus to the École Polytechnique and the War College in Paris. At the Rennes High School I awaited his return from Devil's Island to stand trial again for treason. In a comfortable apartment in the capital's exclusive *seizième arrondissement* and in a still resplendent apartment (once occupied by Napoleon's wife, Josephine de Beauharnais) overlooking the Seine, I reminisced first with the gentle, stoic daughter of Captain Dreyfus and later with the gracious daughter of Mathieu Dreyfus, Alfred's remarkable brother. During those occasions it was as though Alfred, his wife, Lucie, and Mathieu materialized to check the accuracy of my research; occasionally they were joined by Georges Clemenceau, Anatole France, and Émile Zola, through the calling cards, notes of sympathy, and letters in the possession of the Dreyfus daughters.

In the manuscripts room of the Bibliothèque Nationale I discovered the authentic Major "Count" Ferdinand Esterhazy, surely one of history's most cavalier and colorful malefactors. Only a few Frenchmen and, until my visit, no foreigner had seen the uncatalogued papers of Esterhazy. Monsieur Mathieu Dreyfus' catalogued papers and those of Senator Auguste Scheurer-Kestner had also generally gone unnoticed. At the Chateau de Vincennes where the French Army houses its records, I was vouchsafed the Secret Dossier itself—that musty, cardboard box from an ancient filing cabinet containing Dreyfus documents still withheld after so many years.

Although the culprits are known and the outcome is history, the Dreyfus Affair remains the detective story par excellence. Morally, politically, socially it is, of course, much more than that. It is contemporary history's unique signature of recurring, epochal struggles. Nor, by any means, have the ten-odd major works in English on the Dreyfus Affair told all that should be known. What I have done is to synthesize what is interesting and important, add to it a certain amount of new material, and present the whole from a perspective which I hope is at once objective and unobtrusively contemporary.

Now for the acknowledgments, too many to list them all. To the daughter of Alfred Dreyfus, Madame Jeanne Pierre-Paul

Lévy, and to the daughter of Mathieu Dreyfus, Madame Marguerite Mercier, I owe incommensurable debts. Monsieur and Madame Alfred Dreyfus of Paris and Monsieur Jean-Jacques Dreyfus of Basel were kind and earnest in their efforts to assist. To Monsieur Marcel Thomas, an omniscient Dreyfus scholar and the curator of manuscripts at the Bibliothèque Nationale, I owe the life of much of this book. A comparable debt is owed Monsieur Jean-Claude Devos, *Chef du Service* of the Service Historique de l'Armée, Chauteau de Vincennes. Mlle. Carmen Haas of Mulhouse's Archives Municipales, Mr. George Jovanovich of the Library of Congress's European Law Library, and Mrs. Martha Shaw of Harvard University's Houghton Library generously found time to search for rare materials. To the Federal City College, Washington, D.C., which released me, and to the American Council of Learned Societies which partially supported me, I am abidingly grateful.

A different order of gratitude is owed those upon whom a special friendship tax was imposed; Jean-Claude Boffard, Gail Tucker Boyar, Caroline "Dash" Davis, Mark and Marcie Loewinger, Audrey Wharton, and especially Lawrence Seeley. To my wife, Sharon, and my editor, Hillel Black, I owe the services of relentless censorship and labor without which this book might have remained an inspiration in search of a final draft. Whatever errors and insufficiencies this manuscript contains are not my fault alone; for them I also blame my wife.

D.L.L.
Fabras 07, France
Washington, D.C., 1972

CONTENTS

Chronology

1880   Lieutenant Alfred Dreyfus graduates from École Polytechnique.

1890   April 21, Captain Dreyfus marries Mlle. Lucie Hadamard.

1892   Dreyfus completes two-year course at War College.

1893   January 1, Dreyfus assigned as probationer to the General Staff.

August 20, September 3, National elections. Defeat of Bonapartists and royalists and triumph of republican majority.

December 9, anarchist bomb explodes in Chamber of Deputies.

1894   June 24, anarchist assassination of Sadi Carnot, President of the Republic.

July 20, Major Esterhazy meets Colonel von Schwartzkoppen at the German Embassy.

September 1, *bordereau* reecived by Schwartzkoppen.

End of September, *bordereau* arrives at Military Counterintelligence.

October 6, Dreyfus tentatively identified as author of *bordereau.*

October 15, Dreyfus arrested and incarcerated in Cherche-Midi military prison.

October 29, *La Libre Parole* speculates about arrest.

October 31, *Le Soir* (dateline November 1) identifies Dreyfus as arrested officer.

November 2, Colonel Panizzardi telegraphs Rome denying knowledge of Dreytus.

November 3, Major d'Ormescheville's *instruction* begins.

December 3, d'Ormescheville submits report recommending court-martial.

December 4, General Saussier signs court-martial order.

December 19–22, Dreyfus court-martial.

December 22, War Minister Mercier's secret dossier given
to judges by Major Du Paty de Clam. Dreyfus convicted.

1895 January 5, degradation of Dreyfus.

January 16, government of Prime Minister Dupuy ends
with resignation of President Casimir-Périer.

February 22, Dreyfus transported to Guiana aboard the
Saint-Nazaire.

March 15, Dreyfus temporarily incarcerated on Royale Island.

April 13, Dreyfus transferred to Devil's Island.

End of June, Colonel Sandherr of Counterintelligence dies.

July 1, Major Picquart becomes chief of Counterintelligence.

1896 Mid-March, Picquart receives the *petit bleu.*

April 6, Picquart promoted to lieutenant colonel.

End of August, Picquart discovers Esterhazy to be author
of *bordereau.*

September 3, *Daily Chronicle* publishes false report of
Dreyfus' escape from Devil's Island.

September 15, *L'Eclair* article (by Du Paty), "The
Traitor."

September 18, Lucie Dreyfus petitions Chamber of Deputies for revision of Dreyfus court-martial.

November 6, Bernard Lazare's pamphlet appears.

November 10, *Le Matin* publishes photograph of *bordereau.*

November 16, Picquart leaves for inspection tour in eastern
France.

December 26, Picquart ordered to leave Marseille for
North African inspection tour.

1897 June 29, Picquart gives Maître Leblois his testament.

July 13, Leblois tells Senator Schuerer-Kestner.

August 17, War Minister Billot orders Esterhazy retired
from Army for reasons of "temporary infirmity."

October 18, Esterhazy summoned to Paris by Counterintelligence officers.

October 23, Esterhazy sees Schwartzkoppen for last time.
Rendezvous with Du Paty.

November 12, Schwartzkoppen leaves Paris for new assignment.

November 10, "Speranza" and "Blanche" telegrams sent to
Picquart in Tunisia.

November 15, Mathieu Dreyfus denounces Esterhazy in
open letter to Minister of War Billot.

November 17, General de Pellieux opens his inquest.

November 26, Picquart returns to Paris.

December 4, Major Ravary's Esterhazy *instruction* begins.

December 31, Ravary completes investigation. Finds no

grounds for Esterhazy court-martial. Esterhazy demands court-martial.

1898   January 10–11, court-martial finds Esterhazy innocent.

January 13, Zola's *J'Accuse* published in Clemenceau's *L'Aurore*.

February 7–23, Zola trial. Zola convicted.

February 26, Picquart dismissed from Army.

April 2, Court of Cassation reverses Zola verdict. Case remanded for retrial.

May 8, 22, National elections.

Defeat of Ralliement, of Jaurès and Guesde.

Formation of a Radical government.

July 7, Minister of War Cavaignac addresses Chamber of Deputies, reads "proofs" of Dreyfus' guilt including text of False Henry.

July 8–9, Jaurès and Picquart challenge Cavaignac's "proofs."

July 13, Picquart arrested on charges brought by Cavaignac.

July 18, Zola reconvicted. Flees to England next day.

August 13, Major Cuignet gives preliminary report on Henry's forgery to Cavaignac.

August 30, Cavaignac interrogates Henry who confesses and is imprisoned in Mont Valérien prison. Generals de Boisdeffre and de Pellieux resign.

August 31, Henry commits suicide.

September 1, Esterhazy flees to England.

September 3, Cavaignac resigns. General Zurlinden replaces him. Lucie petitions Chamber of Deputies again for revision of 1894 court-martial verdict.

September 17, Minister of War Zurlinden resigns. General Chanoine replaces him.

September–October, Fashoda Crisis.

September 26, Government transmits Lucie's request to Court of Cassation.

September 29, Criminal Chamber of Court of Cassation opens investigation of Dreyfus facts.

October 25, Minister of War Chanoine resigns.

November 24, Picquart court-martial begins.

1899   January 28, Proposal to have Dreyfus Case heard by three branches of Court of Cassation presented to Chamber of Deputies (*Loi de Désaisissement*).

February 10, New Court of Cassation law approved.

February 16, President Félix Faure dies.

February 18, Émile Loubet elected President.

May 29, United Court of Cassation commences deliberations.

June 3, United Court of Cassation annuls 1894 Dreyfus

court-martial and remands case before court-martial at Rennes.

1899   June 4, President Loubet attacked at Longchamps.

June 9, Dreyfus sails from Guiana aboard the *Sfax*.

June 12, Prime Minister Dupuy resigns.

June 22, Waldeck-Rousseau forms new government.

August 7–September 9, Rennes court-martial. Dreyfus convicted.

September 19, Dreyfus pardoned.

November 17, Waldeck-Rousseau presents general amnesty bill to Chamber of Deputies.

1900   April 14, Exposition Universelle opens at Paris.

May 5, Paris municipal elections won by Nationalists.

May 28, War Minister Galliffet resigns. General André replaces him.

December 27, amnesty bill approved by Chamber.

1901   May 1, Dreyfus' book, *Five Years of My Life*, appears.

1902   April 27, May 11, National elections.

September 29, Zola dies mysteriously.

1903   April 6–7, Jaurès addresses Chamber, demands revision of Rennes verdict because of probable influence of annotated *bordereau* on deliberations of judges.

June 4, Captain Targe, Minister of War André's deputy, begins investigation of Rennes verdict.

October 19, Minister of War André announces findings favorable to Dreyfus; requests government to submit Dreyfus' petition for retrial to Court of Cassation.

1904   March 3–5, Criminal Chamber of Cassation deliberates and decides to review Rennes verdict.

July 29, France breaks diplomatic relations with Vatican.

November 15, General André resigns.

November 28, Criminal Chamber finds Dreyfus innocent. Refers matter to United Court.

1905   December 9, Separation of Church and State becomes law in France.

1906   May 6, 20, National elections. Decisive Radical-Socialist victory.

July 12, Court of Cassation unanimously annuls Rennes verdict without remanding case for retrial.

July 13, Chamber and Senate vote to reinstate Dreyfus and Picquart to Army.

July 20, Dreyfus ceremony in the courtyard of War College.

October 15, Major Dreyfus resumes military duties at the Vincennes garrison.

1907   July 26, Dreyfus retires from Army.

1908   June 4, Zola's ashes transferred to Panthéon. Dreyfus shot during ceremony.

1909–1913   Dreyfus lives private life.
1914   January 19, General Picquart dies after riding accident.
       August 2, Dreyfus returns to active duty and is promoted
       to lieutenant colonel.
1935   July 12, Alfred Dreyfus dies in Paris.
Presidencies:
       Casimir-Perier, Jean: June 27, 1894–January 16, 1895.
       Faure, Félix: January 17, 1895–February 16, 1899.
       Loubet, Émile: February 18, 1899–February 18, 1906.
       Fallières, Armand: February 18, 1906–February 18, 1913.
Ministries:
       Dupuy, Charles: May 30, 1894–January 16, 1895.
           Minister of War: General Mercier.
       Ribot, Alexandre: January 27, 1895–October 28, 1895.
       Bourgeois, Leon: November 1, 1895–April 23, 1896.
       Méline, Jules: April 29, 1896–June 15, 1898.
           Minister of War: General Billot.
       Brisson, Henri: June 28, 1898–October 25, 1898.
           Ministers of War: Cavaignac, Zurlinden, Chanoine.
       Dupuy, Charles: November 1, 1898–June 12, 1899.
           Minister of War: Freycinet.
       Waldeck-Rousseau, René: June 22, 1899–June 3, 1902.
           Ministers of War: Generals Gallifret and André.
       Combes, Émile: June 15, 1902–January 18, 1905.
           Minister of War: General André.
       Rouvier, Maurice: January 24, 1905–March 7, 1906.
           Ministers of War: Berteaux and Thomson.
       Sarrien, Jean: March 14, 1906–October 19, 1906.
           Minister of War: Étienne.
           Minister of Interior: Clemenceau.
       Clemenceau, Georges: October 25, 1906–July 1909.
           Minister of War: Picquart.

chapter one:

A JEW ON THE GENERAL STAFF

THE DAY WAS LIKE A GLASS OF RIESLING, THE wine of the region—clear, effervescent, and slightly golden. A mile or so behind the troops the Ill River flowed blue and lazy through Mulhouse. Stretching before them, as far as the eye could see, was the broad and fertile Alsatian plain. The day before, August 5, 1870, another Riesling day, they had marched from Belfort through Mulhouse in their blue coats, red pantaloons, and white gaiters to the cheers of the people. These soldiers belonged to a division of the French Army's Seventh Corps under the command of General Félix Douay. The General did not know then that his older brother had just lost his division and his life in a surprise attack at Wissembourg by Prussian troops under the command of the Crown Prince. Félix Douay's orders were to thrust one division toward the frontier above Mulhouse where a massive Prussian breakthrough was reported.

When the junior officers under General Douay heard the tragic news of the Prussian victory, they shrugged it off as a fluke and exhorted their men to ready kits and oil *chassepots.*

1

In Émile Zola's definitive novel about the Franco-Prussian War, *La Débâcle*, a lieutenant captures the mood of these officers:

> We flogged the Austrians at Castiglione, at Marengo, at
> Austerlitz, at Wagram; we flogged the Prussians at Eylau,
> at Jena, at Lützen; we flogged the Russians at Friedland, at
> Smolensk and at the Moskva; we flogged Spain and England
> everywhere; all creation beaten, beaten, beaten up and
> down, far and near, at home and abroad, and now you tell
> me that it is we who are to take the beating! Why, pray
> tell me? How? Is the world coming to an end?

At Fröschwiller and at Spicheren the enemy smashed the French forces. Napoleon III had been afraid that his Army was unready, but the incompetent Marshal Leboeuf, his Minister of War, had sworn that all was in order—"Sire, not a gaiter button is missing." So, against his better judgment, Napoleon III had declared war on Prussia on July 19, 1870, and after several initial successes, the armies of France had blundered from one flogging into another.

On August 10 General Douay's soldiers retreated through Mulhouse, their gaiter buttons still fastened, in order to make a stand at Belfort. As the troops streamed through, the people of the city watched with dread. The Riesling days very soon turned to vinegar for the Alsatians. In mid-September the Germans occupied Mulhouse, the region's second largest city. Few families suffered the catastrophe with a deeper sense of humiliation than that of Raphael Dreyfus.

Standing near fastened, half-curtained windows in their living room and peering into the street below, every member of the Dreyfus family showed his bereavement. They were all there, except Henriette, who had married and lived in Carpentras: the daughters Louise and Rachel; the four sons, Jacques, Léon, Mathieu, and the youngest, Alfred. Monsieur Raphael Dreyfus clasped his wife's hand, while together they tried to maintain composure for the sake of the children. From the street below the sound of boots and cavalry hoofs invaded the room. When

Alfred began to cry, his father nodded to Louise and Mathieu
to comfort him. Although not quite eleven years old, Alfred
had a remarkable capacity for self-control. He knew that Frenchmen never cried before an enemy. Soon his blue eyes were
clear again and the expression on his face revealed nothing more
than contempt. For all the Dreyfuses, but especially for the
youngest, the trauma of this September day would endure. It
was "my first sad impression—the painful recollection has never
faded from my memory," Alfred recalled much later.

At the debacle at Sedan Napoleon III surrendered with
eighty-three thousand elite troops on September 1. Then came
the siege and surrender of Paris at the end of January. During
this time the enemy added insult to injury by proclaiming in
the Palace of Versailles the birth of the Second Reich. Then,
in May 1871, Alfred Dreyfus' parents told him the worst of
all possible news—he no longer lived in France. According
to the Treaty of Frankfurt, Mulhouse became Mülhausen and
most of Alsace and a third of Lorraine were annexed to the new
Germany. Mercifully for families like the Dreyfuses, the treaty
allowed Alsatians to retain French nationality if they agreed
to leave the territory within a prescribed period of time.

German annexation was regarded as a tragedy by the majority
of Alsatians. But a considerable number saw it not as a French
but a purely Alsatian disaster. Alsatians, especially those of the
Mulhouse region, were notoriously independent and parochial,
disdainful equally of the *Schwob* (German) and the *Franzos*
(Frenchman). For many, then, the Franco-Prussian War merely
substituted the familiar, unloved sovereignty of France for
that of an unfamiliar and unloved Germany. But not for the
Dreyfuses. French citizenship was more precious to Raphael
Dreyfus than Alsatian roots or a thriving business.

Prominent, respected, wealthy, they would have been relatively undisturbed by German religious and social proscriptions.
Alfred's was an established Alsatian family from Bixheim, just
outside Mulhouse. His frugal ancestors had laid by a modest
store of wealth. This wealth and the commercial talent that

went with it had enabled Alfred's tyrannical grandfather to advance the family from petty trade in used clothing and haberdashery to respectable status as textile merchants. Grudgingly Grandfather Dreyfus had accepted the innovations of his son Raphael, who was determined to make the mill at Mulhouse the most competitive in Alsace by adopting the advanced weaving techniques of the English. By the time Alfred was an adolescent, Dreyfus Brothers was well on its way to becoming one of the most successful textile enterprises in eastern France.

That the family was Jewish was of practically no importance in Mulhouse. With a polyglot citizenry of fifty thousand, Mulhouse was too cosmopolitan to be anti-Semitic. Over the centuries it had cultivated an uncommon sophistication in matters of race and faith. Free from the intolerant edicts of Catholic monarchs, Mulhouse and much of Alsace had offered an ideal haven for Europe's Jews and Protestants. In turn, Jewish entrepreneurs and Protestant industrialists, who were as prolific as they were hardworking, had helped to make the region, and the city, enviably rich. When Mulhouse became part of France in 1798, its enlightened traditions survived.

Before the Revolution of 1789 some 70 percent of all French Jews, about 20,000, resided in Alsace. By 1861 the national Jewish population increased to 79,964, while gentile France settled into demographic torpor. Whatever the reasons—the ravages of the Napoleonic wars, the punitive property clauses against large families of the Code Napoléon, the sluggish industrial progress, perhaps something in the culture itself—the overall growth rate fell short of 30 percent and, after the Franco-Prussian War, declined even more sharply. The seven Dreyfus children were part of the Jewish population explosion.

Until 1869 the family resided in a smallish apartment just off Mulhouse's second most important square, at 1 Rue du Sauvage. In that year they moved to an elegant home in the Rue de la Sinne across the street from the hedged and shaded grounds of the Steinbock estate. Not only was the new address roomier and more prestigious, it offered the advantage of being several blocks nearer the synagogue. Each Sabbath the devout Raphael and his wife led their children to worship there, and there each of the boys observed his Bar Mitzvah. It was not the synagogue, though, but the *lycée* which had the greater influence upon the children, especially the boys. They were no different from thousands of Jewish children of the upper-middle classes. The France of the Revolution and of Napoleon had granted their elders civil rights, razed the walls of the ghetto, and enabled French Jews to attain positions of service and public trust. "The time of the Messiah came with the French Revolution," a noted Jewish historian proclaimed. With such sanguine sentiments abounding, it was natural that lessons in French history and the comradeship of Protestant and Catholic lads should count for more than instruction in the Talmud or conformity to established religious behavior. Mathieu and Alfred, therefore, retained virtually nothing of the essentials of Judaism, except a calendar piety on occasions such as Yom Kippur and Passover and an unspoken pride in the unique experience of a people who had turned oppression to good advantage.

Whatever the class or creed, most Alsatian families were tightly knit. The Dreyfus youngsters were more united than most because of the closeness of their ages and the infirmity of their mother. Madame Jeannette Libmann Dreyfus became increasingly an invalid after the birth of Alfred on October 9, 1859, a misfortune which required Louise, as the oldest unmarried daughter, to become mistress of the house and mother to Alfred. Mathieu became the indispensable companion and shining model to his younger brother. But if he stuck close to and admired Mathieu to whom he bore a striking physical resemblance, Alfred was not a copy of his idol. Mathieu was outgoing and good at sports. Alfred was taciturn, shy, and, although strong, astigmatic and poor at games. Mathieu had the attributes of a first-rate officer, Alfred those of a somewhat narrow academic. He was not really cold or pompous but his shyness was frequently misinterpreted. Introspective, something of a bookworm, good at math, Alfred was *"le sérieux"* of the Dreyfus family.

On October 1, 1872, the family crossed the Swiss frontier to settle in nearby Basel. From there Raphael could continue to oversee the affairs of the Mulhouse factory while he pondered the problems of nationality. To have declared immediately for France would have invited legal retaliation against the business by the German authorities. Two years later, however, on August 30, 1874, Monsieur Dreyfus journeyed to the Vaucluse and presented himself at the city hall in Carpentras. He brought with him all but two of his children. When all had been officially recognized as French, the Dreyfuses returned to Switzerland. Henriette, the oldest daughter, was already French by her marriage to Joseph Valabrègue, a wealthy businessman of Carpentras. The senior son, Jacques, was required to pay the supreme price; he remained at Mulhouse, a German, to manage the family business. Jacques later sent his sons to France, though, and at the end of the century he followed them to reclaim his precious birthright.

At thirteen Alfred was enrolled in the Basel *Realschule* where his once excellent academic record suffered because he had difficulty mastering German. He was now at an age when it was time to prepare for a profession. Everything about Alfred Dreyfus' background pointed toward a bland, anonymous future. Of course, he might strike out for a career independent of the family business—law, finance, or even teaching—for as the youngest, slightly pampered son, he was freer to indulge his whims than his brothers were. He knew that his role in the company was dispensable. Jacques and Léon would take over from their father and Mathieu served as insurance in the event that something happened to them. Alfred wanted something more than junior partnership in an established firm.

He had told Henriette that he would like to be a soldier, and she had encouraged that ambition in her solemn little brother. Of medium height, with poor vision, handicapped by lusterless vocal cords, Alfred was scarcely the most likely candidate for an officer's commission. Moreover, for a Jewish lad, even a wealthy one, to aspire to such a career was unusual. From the parents' viewpoint it was unwise. In the eyes of well-disposed gentiles it was remarkably plucky. To fanatic supporters of the Army it would smack of infiltration. But to Alfred Dreyfus, intense, intelligent, and self-confident, soldiering for France was logical for an Alsatian patriot.

Whatever profession he chose, Basel was not the place for a privileged young Frenchman to complete his secondary education. In 1873 Alfred left his family for the first time to board at the Collège Sainte-Barbe in Paris, the special high school his brothers had attended. He hated it. Paris was a dismaying vortex of sensations; its parade of arrogant people lacked the *Gemütlichkeit* of Mulhouse. His classmates at Sainte-Barbe were supercilious and slightly bigoted. He was so homesick that he became ill before the end of the academic year and went to Carpentras to convalesce under the care of Henriette. It was a setback but not a defeat. Alfred went back to Paris the next year, when he was fifteen, matriculating at the more liberal Collège Chaptal.

After receiving his diploma from Chaptal in 1876, Alfred promptly reentered Sainte-Barbe to prepare for the entrance examination to the École Polytechnique, France's rigorous military engineering school. Not being optimistic about passing the test, he accepted his brothers' invitation to apprentice in the Mulhouse business. The family had obtained special visas and had moved back to Mulhouse. Léon and Mathieu managed the family's affairs there while Jacques, despite his German citizenship, was opening a new branch in Belfort, France.

Precise and disciplined, Alfred's performance impressed Léon and Mathieu; they persuaded their father to offer generous terms to induce Alfred to enter the firm. Their brother was tempted. His analytical mind had already perceived more than a dozen ways to increase production and decrease the wastage of his father's cotton bolts. Moreover, he had a natural aptitude for organizing and leading subordinates. No one in Mulhouse, least of all his ailing mother, wanted him to become a soldier. But the promise of a commission in the French Army was irresistible, and Alfred's low examination score was just adequate to admit him, in 1878, to the École Polytechnique, one hundred eighty-second in his class.

Not all graduates of this distinguished institution remained in the Army after a mandatory period as second lieutenants, but their two years of training permanently marked all *polytechniciens*. Established in 1794 on the visionary ideas of Condorcet and encouraged (in the beginning, at least) by Napoleon I, the École Polytechnique was the cradle of France's technocratic elite, a military brotherhood of reforming mathematician-sociologists. Alfred's temperament was well disposed to the rigors and rigidity of the school's curriculum and ethos. In spirit he had always been a *polytechnicien*. By the time he was graduated in 1880, he had become an exaggerated version of the ideal—unemotional, mechanical, logical, and rather arrogant. Thirty-second in his class, he entered the Army as a second lieutenant.

After two years of advanced training at Fountainebleau he was promoted to first lieutenant. He spent the next year in garrison duty with the Thirty-first Artillery Regiment at Le Mans in northwestern France. The following year, 1883, when he was twenty-four, he was posted to a battery of the First Cavalry Division in Paris, a coveted assignment which was to last five years.

In 1884 Lieutenant Dreyfus spent his furlough in Mulhouse. By then German rule was being riveted upon Alsace-Lorraine with a sternness calculated to eliminate every trace of French culture. In the same house from which he had seen the arrival of General von Moltke's soldiers, he was forced to hear the enemy commemorating the surrender of Napoleon III at Sedan. It was another day he would never forget. "I heard a German band passing under my window celebrating the anniversary of Sedan. I experienced such anguish that I swore to devote all my strength and ability to the service of my country

against an enemy who outraged the feelings of the Alsatians."
It was in character for him to feel profound revulsion and renewed patriotic dedication that day in Mulhouse.

In five years in Paris Alfred Dreyfus earned an enviable
service dossier:

> 1884: Zealous . . . conscientious . . . plenty of spirit.
> 1885: Very active.
> 1886: Officer with plenty of spirit, very daring horseman,
> well informed, intelligent, directs the battery's recruits
> in horsemanship lessons with infinite skill.
> 1887: An excellent lieutenant. . . . Commands well.
> 1888: The best lieutenant of the battery groups, knows a
> great deal and is always learning. Possessed of an
> excellent memory and of a very lively intelligence.

A single shortcoming marred an otherwise perfect record—
his shouted commands were always rendered in an atonal, un-
martial voice. Possibly there was also the faintest damnation
in the "knows a great deal and is always learning" comment.
Inquisitive, bookish, punctilious junior officers were no better
loved in the French than in any other army.

Alfred Dreyfus gained a reputation for being a grind and
a prude. His brother Mathieu worried about him and during
occasional trips to the capital encouraged a bit of mild corruption. Alfred disliked idling even a few hours in civilian
company and he positively hated the chic gentlemen's gaming
clubs. But his beloved and respected Mathieu, as much a man
of the world as Alfred was a monastic soldier, was persuasive.
Twice, maybe three times, they went out on the town. The last
time almost proved the undoing of Mathieu's strategy. The
opulent casino with rooms for mixed entertainment, the Cercle
de la Presse, left Alfred "so disgusted that he never had any
temptation to return." Mathieu began to realize that there was
not much he could do to show his rigid brother the advantages
of relaxation. Since Alfred was contented and successful,
Mathieu decided to leave him to the consolations of his narrow
world. He was "happy, proud to wear the uniform," Mathieu

said, "and even exaggerated in showing his feelings about
everything that concerned the Army."

Mathieu gave up prematurely, however. Although the role of
ladies' man later imputed to Dreyfus by his enemies was much
exaggerated, there was a woman in his life. Madame Bodson,
rich, refined, and not unattractive, was a clothier's wife whom
Dreyfus met sometime during 1886. Madame Bodson was
estranged from her husband; she found the naive self-assurance
of Lieutenant Dreyfus captivating. Their relationship lasted
until the following year. Always discreet, Dreyfus never discussed his affair with Madame Bodson—but he never denied
that the liaison was more than platonic.

In September 1889 the thirty-year-old lieutenant was promoted to captain. A few months later he was sent to the Army's
special artillery school at Bourges, one hundred and forty miles
south of the capital. But before he presented himself at Bourges,
Alfred was summoned to Mulhouse for the burial of his mother.
Madame Dreyfus had become a complete invalid in her last
years, so compassionate relief mixed with sorrow as the family
gathered for the funeral. Afterward Dreyfus went on to the
artillery school where he pursued his studies with a brilliance
that was becoming routine. Then, for the second time, he
allowed a distraction to enter his life. There were frequent trips
to Paris, reluctant returns to Bourges. There was a furious
exchange of letters with a Parisienne and a series of long letters
to his father in Mulhouse. Stoical, dedicated Captain Dreyfus
was contemplating marriage.

Mademoiselle Lucie Hadamard was ten years younger than
Alfred Dreyfus. She was a svelte, chestnut brunette, not beautiful but tall and handsome with features that were as striking
for their regularity as for the quiet strength of character they
revealed. She looked, as the French say, *très correcte*. Among
the society ladies who insisted on befriending her a few years
later, she was always politely reserved, almost automatic, in
her behavior and conversation. In such a mood Lucie Hadamard

seemed to be a distaff version of Alfred Dreyfus. But the private Lucie was another person altogether, animated, even gay. She was well read, loved music, adored theater. Dreyfus met her shortly before the death of his mother.

Characteristically, for him, their meeting occurred in the line of duty. Alfred was toying with the idea of applying for admission to the War College, something few Jews had considered and fewer had achieved. His father advised contacting the descendants of a Captain Hatzfeld, an Alsatian Jew who had also attended the École Polytechnique and had served briefly as a distinguished officer in the army of King Louis-Philippe. Lucie was Captain Hatzfeld's granddaughter. The cosmopolitan and wealthy Hadamards (they had been dealers in rare stones) were not as impressed by the serious captain as Lucie was. Her father, a professor at Louis-le-Grand, one of France's outstanding *lycées*, would have preferred a less humorless and rigid suitor for his daughter. Nevertheless, the Hadamards received him cordially and offered to exert what influence they had. After a few months the collaboration of the Hadamards and the Dreyfuses was total. On April 20, 1890, Alfred Dreyfus received his acceptance to the War College; on April 21 he and Lucie were married.

Admission to the War College in Paris was a stupendous achievement. Top graduates of the college were guaranteed assignment to the Army General Staff on which no acknowledged Jew in the history of the Army had ever served. For an Alfred Dreyfus, sixty-seventh in a class of eighty-one, it promised to be a supremely demanding experience. His classmates would be the sons of France's nobility who were determined to keep the upper ranks of the Army their exclusive fiefdom, even though the aristocratic families had lost much of their political power and were being eliminated from key positions in the civil service and the diplomatic corps. The great majority of officers above the rank of captain bore surnames preceded by the noble particle *de*, such as de Rosière, de Morès, de Fontenillat. To them, having a Dreyfus on the General Staff was repugnant, even demoralizing. A few commoners, even a number of Protestants, had successfully passed through the War College; some of them had managed to serve on the General Staff. However, a brilliant Jew in the War College whose grades might enable him to breach the defenses of that sanctum sanctorum of the gentiles, the General Staff itself—that was a vision sufficiently frightening to steam the monocle of a marquis.

It was fortunate that Dreyfus' wealth provided comfortable lodgings and adequate domestic help while he attended the War College. Lucie's dowry of two hundred thousand francs and his annuity from the family business relieved him of the material worries afflicting many of his married comrades; there would be enough to disconcert him without such problems. The couple rented a spacious apartment at 6 Avenue du Trocadéro (today the Avenue President Wilson) in the exclusive sixteenth *arrondissement*, within easy walking distance of the War College. Dreyfus' studies commenced in early October 1890. The next two years were all grim application.

The unvarying routine of their lives—Dreyfus rising early, fitting himself into his immaculate blue uniform after breakfast, attaching pince-nez, fussily examining the alabaster-white gloves no War College officer failed to wear, pecking Lucie on the cheek, striding off rapidly and rigidly across the Alma Bridge, only to return home for more work and reading after dinner—was not entirely to Lucie's liking. She would have preferred an occasional evening at the theater, the society now and then of people interested in art and literature. But Dreyfus had no close friends and never invited anyone to the apartment. Lucie knew, too, that, if he were ever to do so, the dinner would pass in talk about armies and about those Germans whose recently translated works were required reading at the college—Clausewitz and von der Goltz.

Not that life went by in unrelieved grays and browns: Alfred was attentive to household matters, more than willing and passably apt at discussing subjects Lucie cared about. She never doubted his love and growing dependence upon her. And, in Dreyfus' first month at the War College, she learned that she was pregnant. Now there would be careful shopping to ready the nursery, knitting without end, visiting the doctor, interviewing nurses, to supplement her normal routine and the regular Sunday dinners at her parents'. In sum, life was pretty much what might have been expected, neither exciting nor dull.

At the War College Dreyfus was near the top of his class. In the first year he received the mention *très bien* for his over-all aptitude with particular commendation for his knowledge of military theory, his administrative capacity, his command of German (the year in Basel had been beneficial after all), and his horsemanship. His parade-ground voice was still deficient but it was noted that this was improving. Only one instructor, Major Georges Picquart, was unimpressed. The Army's youngest major and one of its most brilliant officers, Picquart conceded that the student was energetic, highly disciplined, well trained; but there was a narrowness about his intelligence, a paucity of imagination, a certain slightly unrefined pushiness and unjustified self-confidence. A Catholic, the scion of an ancient family of Lorraine notables, Major Picquart showed that gentile finickiness characteristic of otherwise open-minded superior officers. He did not think he was being unfair when he gave Dreyfus a low score in cartography and field maneuver.

The grade was a setback but Dreyfus' high cumulative average the first year was barely diminished. Lucie's health was of far greater concern. On April 5, 1891, she bore a son whom they named Pierre, a sickly baby who was not expected to live. Lucie lay exhausted from painful and protracted labor; the physicians advised Dreyfus that she might die. Both rallied, however. After a month Lucie's convalescence was assured and the baby, Pierrot, steadily improved. Despite Picquart's evaluation and the near tragedy in April, Dreyfus' first year at the War College closed on a reassuringly confident note.

As June 1892 approached, the private and professional universes of Alfred Dreyfus seemed to move in obedience to a beneficent design. His family was well and happy. His record at the War College indicated that he would graduate third in his class. If the white gloves, pince-nez, automatic gait, and intensity remained, at least the last thirteen months or so had rinsed away some of the starch. As soon as Lucie was well enough, they began to entertain—modestly and tentatively, of course—and to accept invitations. They became friendly with the eminent professor of anthropology, Lucien Lévy-Bruhl, who was also a relative of Lucie, and Alfred almost learned how to scatter witticisms and abstractions in drawing rooms crowded with noted academics, scientists, lawyers, politicians, and bankers. The Dreyfuses became acquainted with Zadoc Kahn, the courageous and learned Grand Rabbi of France. But their contacts with the Zadoc Kahns did not extend to the synagogue. The Judaism of the Dreyfuses was a matter of heritage, not of religious conviction. They went to the synagogue rarely, and the Grand Rabbi was an important social rather than spiritual force in their lives.

Suddenly, in his final weeks at the college, things began to go seriously wrong for Dreyfus. There had been portents earlier but, characteristically, he had ignored them. Once again the anti-Semites were abroad in France. Their dire warnings that the nation was being subverted from within were received sympathetically by polite society and enthusiastically in the Army. This renascence of hatred had begun with the collapse of a corporate venture known as the *Union Générale* in late 1881. The founder of the *Union Générale*, Paul Bontoux, had had no difficulty raising twenty-five million francs in the spring of 1878 to capitalize his company. Although called by his business peers a "poet of industry" who was "too ardent and optimistic," Bontoux's prospectus claiming "the special auto-graph blessing of our most Holy Father, Pope Leo XIII," encouraged Catholics to invest. And invest they did: not only the old nobility—the de Broglies, the Princesse de Bourbon, the

Duc de Chartres, even the Comte de Chambord—but hundreds of small landholders and several religious orders. By November 1881 a five-hundred-franc share in the *Union Générale* fetched three thousand francs.

Jewish and Protestant banking houses found themselves ousted or on the verge of being outmaneuvered in what were once their securest markets while the *Union Générale*'s stridently Catholic propaganda took on an increasingly political tone. Then, large blocks of its stock were suddenly sold for a fraction of their current value by unknown speculators. By early February 1882 Bontoux was on his way to a heavy fine and a five-year prison sentence while the large banking houses reassembled what remained of the corporation that had won mining and railroad concessions throughout the Balkans. Whatever combination of events and forces really destroyed Bontoux's enterprise, for its ruined Catholic stockholders there was only one acceptable explanation—the "Syndicate," the legendary Internationale of Jewish finance. The lesson to be drawn was clear to Frenchmen of every religious and political persuasion: if even the Pope's business investments were vulnerable, then the Jews were truly a terrifying force.

Fear and hatred of the Jew was as old as Christian France and as recent as the mid-century doctrines of Comte Arthur de Gobineau, but anti-Semitism appeared to have long since ceased being fashionable or forceful. Jewish statesmen had played a major part in creating a republic out of the shambles of 1870, and the mighty Rothschilds had provided the five-billion gold franc indemnity (one billion dollars) imposed by the Germans. Congregations fervently celebrated the ideals of 1789 while their rabbis preached that France was the New Jerusalem. Then, suddenly, came disturbing signs. The periodical *Univers Israélite* saw the danger signals in early 1881 and more clearly when *L'Anti-Juif*, the first anti-Semitic newspaper, appeared later that same year. An English journalist who knew the Third Republic better than most Frenchmen declared, "It is from that time [the collapse of the *Union Générale*] that the rise of anti-Semitism in France may be dated."

It was at this time that Frenchmen began to notice the
astronomic increase of Parisian Jews (from fewer than one
thousand to more than forty thousand in less than three generations). Most of this increase resulted from internal migration
from Alsace and other regions, much of it from reproduction,
but enough of it came from Central and Slavic Europe to inspire invidious stereotypes. Before the 1850s Paris Jewry had
been dominated by ancient, thoroughly assimilated, and prosperous Sephardim and a more recent sprinkling of extremely
rich, titled aristocracy. After the establishment of the Third
Republic in 1870 this elite became a liability, a stratum gravely
compromised in the popular mind by its traditional support of
royalism and Bonapartism. Still, Jewish leadership was un-
worried. There was an ample supply of outstanding Jewish
Republicans to make amends. But the leadership failed to fore-
see the threatening economic evolution set in motion after 1870.
If aristocratic Jews were merely resented, the thousands of new
Jewish merchants and businessmen were positively hated by the
striving masses of Frenchmen. Many French Jews foresaw the
antagonisms. The arrival of several thousand of their East
European brothers—*trop asiatiques*, poor, quaintly orthodox,
dressed like Gypsies, ignorant of French, and adamant about
perplexing dietary laws—was eloquently deplored. "I helped
them when they came to my door," the son of an old Parisian
Jewish family complained, "but without enthusiasm. Rich and
poor, their arrival in France exasperated me." By re-creating in
the capital's fourth *arrondissement* the *shtetls* of Galicia and
the Ukraine, these Eastern Jews were the despair of the polished
Sephardim and the joy of the anti-Semites.

These developments were of little concern to Alfred Dreyfus.
Financial scandals and foreign pogroms were not matters ap-
propriate to the meditations of a career officer. Still, Captain
Dreyfus could not blind himself to the religious hatred begin-
ning to poison the Army. The most lethal source was *La Libre
Parole*, a newspaper founded by Edouard Drumont in April

1892. Not too many years before, Drumont's editorials had advanced the interests of one of France's most powerful Jewish financiers. When the banker died, Drumont repented his liberalism almost overnight, returned to the Roman Catholic Church, and proceeded to write a massive, two-volume work which was both cause and effect of the new vogue in anti-Semitism. The book, *La France Juive* (Jewish France), was a pernicious amalgam of history, sociology, and political economy. It appeared in 1886 and ran through several editions in France, Spain, Poland, and Germany. So ardent was Drumont's new-found piety that he sold the book's rights in Spain for a nominal sum and made a gift of them to the Poles. The gentle and well-meaning theologian, Ernest Renan, had claimed that the children of Israel were profoundly different from the gentiles. Now Drumont seized upon Renan's thesis to argue that they were a moral pestilence.

Drumont insisted he had nothing personal against the Jews. They could not help being Jews, and in another part of the globe, far from *la belle France*, they could thrive splendidly to the mutual benefit and relief of all. Drumont's prose appealed to the prejudices of the epoch:

> The Semite is business-like, greedy, intriguing, subtle, and
> crafty; the Aryan is enthusiastic, heroic, chivalric,
> disinterested, and open, trusting to the point of naiveté.
> The Semite is a son of the earth hardly ever grasping
> anything beyond the present moment; the Aryan is a son
> of the heavens, ceaselessly preoccupied by higher aspirations;
> one lives in the real world, the other in the ideal.

His epigrams were often expressed with just enough truth to be memorable. "The Rothschilds believe they belong to the aristocracy," he wrote. "Hirsch [a rich Jewish banker], on the other hand, believes the aristocracy belongs to him." As Edmond de Goncourt confessed in his *Journal*, "Drumont has dared to say what everybody is thinking." Jews could not have been altogether surprised by Drumont's growing popularity or

the creation of the National Anti-Semitic League by his friend
Jules Guérin.

In April 1892, as Dreyfus was about to leave the War College, *La Libre Parole* began a series of articles on Jewish infiltration of the Army. The captain, of course, paid little attention. Once or twice some of his maladroit classmates handed him
a copy of Drumont's newspaper or discussed the latest issue
in his presence. Unlike the other Jewish officer who resigned
because of provocation, Dreyfus declined to be rattled. Stoic
by nature, naively self-confident, totally apolitical, he was not
likely to worry much about religious agitation—not even by
Drumont's series, "The Jews in the Army." "The Jews hardly
had a toe-hold on the Army when they began, by every means,
to try to gain control of it," *La Libre Parole* declared. "Already
the rulers in finance, and in the bureaucracy, dictating their
decrees to the judiciary, they will become the definitive rulers
of France the day they command the Army." Several chauvinist
newspapers took up this theme, but *La Libre Parole* remained
unsurpassed in its editorial pogroms. Its article, "The Jews in
the École Polytechnique," got down to specifics: "Among the
members of the alumni association one finds eighteen Martins
[the most common French name] but nineteen Lévys; the
Mayers and the Meyers number thirteen." The alarming inference was inescapable: a few years more and the roster of
Saint-Cyr itself (France's West Point) would be swamped by
Lévys, Mayers, and Meyers—and "Rothschild will be tri-
umphant."

Less than five seconds of swordplay elapsed in the dawn of
June 21, 1892, before a robust, six-foot-three Catholic marquis
mortally skewered his diminutive adversary, a fellow officer,
Captain Armand Mayer. It was the third duel that month ensuing from Drumont's attack upon the Army's Jewish officers
and the first to end tragically. A friend of Captain Mayer, a
Major Ferdinand Esterhazy, testified at the inquest that the
heavily weighted weapons had placed the captain, an inexpe-

rienced fencer, under a considerable disadvantage. Mayer's death at the hand of one of Drumont's chief collaborators, the Marquis Amadée de Morès, aroused public opinion. Prime Minister Émile Loubet promised stern measures against those who would sow discord within the Army's ranks. Intimidated, *La Libre Parole* expressed regret in the affair, defending itself by claiming that its articles had done no more "than cite statistics."

Officially, the officer corps closed ranks against the political provocateurs. A circular from the Ministry of War warned against the distribution of inflammatory publications. The voice of the Army, the newspaper *France Militaire*, deplored religious bigotry. But the damage could not be so easily repaired. Alfred Dreyfus, aloof throughout the controversy, was perhaps the most vulnerable Jew in the Army.

Dreyfus was expecting to graduate from the War College with the third highest record in his class. It was an expectation that ignored the prejudices of General Pierre de Bonnefond who was charged with evaluating the school's graduates. The General was an unabashed, uncomplicated anti-Semite. Where there were Jews there was turbulence, even disaffection, in the Army; clearly, de Bonnefond stated, it was "unwise to have a Jew assigned to the General Staff." His evaluation of Dreyfus warned that this brilliant student's character made him unsuited for such an honor. Dreyfus was dumbfounded. He appealed to the director of the War College who readily conceded that an injustice had been done, offered an apology, but regretted that the report could not be remanded. Captains, after all, were not allowed to revise the considered judgments of generals. De Bonnefond came close to destroying this captain's General Staff assignment, but, even as ninth instead of third in his class, Dreyfus was still assured a position on the General Staff. In January 1893 the appointment became official; he received orders to report immediately to Staff headquarters.

For Dreyfus the next few months brought both pleasure and sorrow. He rejoiced in the Staff appointment and in Lucie's discovery that she was pregnant again. But the sorrow was bitter: Raphael, his father, died. This loss "depressed him for some time," an acquaintance wrote. "It was really only during the few months prior [to October 1894] that he was completely happy."

During this time France experienced both excitement and misfortune from the consequences of the Panama Scandal, the collapse of the company organized by the venerable Ferdinand de Lesseps, the builder of the Suez Canal. An honest but vain man, de Lesseps was not a trained engineer but he was a born promoter. Almost a million small investors bought stock in his scheme to pierce a sea-level canal through Panama. When it became apparent, in 1887, that a canal without locks was impossible and that the completion costs would be much greater than originally anticipated, the aged de Lesseps panicked. The truth was concealed by bribing journalists and politicians in hopes of surviving until the National Assembly could enact a lottery law to raise new capital. But bribery made the Panama Canal Company vulnerable to blackmail and internal corruption; meanwhile rumors steadily undermined public confidence. It developed that most of the press and more than a hundred politicians, including a former Prime Minister, a Minister of Public Works, and a chairman of the Chamber of Deputies' Budget Commission, had depleted the company's 1.3 billion francs. Baron Jacques de Reinach, a Jew and one of the directors, died mysteriously when his role as principal disburser of illicit funds was uncovered. Two other compromised Jews fled the country. The power of the "Syndicate" now seemed even more threatening than Drumont's prophecy.

La Libre Parole was at its shrillest and the trials of Panama Company officials were about to begin when Dreyfus' appointment to the General Staff was announced.

The Director of the War College had given him a superlative recommendation: "Very good officer, quick intelligence, rapidly grasping questions, possessing industry and discipline, very apt for duty on the General Staff." But not everyone agreed with this estimation; one doubter was Dreyfus' former instructor, Major Georges Picquart, who had preceded him to the General Staff. Picquart felt uneasy having a Jew in such a sensitive position. In spite of the outcry over the Mayer duel, anti-Semitism was becoming a national pastime. Who could be sure Drumont was not preparing an article about "The Jew on the General Staff"? Picquart explained later: "Anti-Semitic prejudices were already abroad in the General Staff. . . . I knew also that by assigning a Jewish trainee to a section that did not concern itself with secret matters I would perhaps spare him certain embarrassments." Major the Marquis Armand Du Paty de Clam of the General Staff was also concerned. "At that time I was imbued with humanitarian convictions," Du Paty claimed afterward. "I had very good relations with intelligent, artistic, and scholarly Jews. . . . But there are some situations in which persons who are not incontrovertibly French ought not be placed."

Regulations prescribed that Dreyfus, like all Staff trainees, should be assigned in turn to each of the Staff's four bureaus or departments. The First Bureau dealt with organization and mobilization; the Second (*Deuxième bureau* or *Bureau des renseignements*), with matters of intelligence; the Third, with operations and training; the Fourth, with communications and transport. In addition, there were five sections of varying autonomy, including the Statistical Section—a euphemism for Counterintelligence Section. This section, popularly confused with the parent Second Bureau, was functionally independent and directly responsible to the Chief of Staff of the Army. Over each bureau (and the Statistical or Counterintelligence Section) a full colonel presided. A two-star general usually served as Vice Chief of Staff. The Chief of Staff was Lieutenant General the Marquis Raoul Le Mouton de Boisdeffre, as impressive in pedigree and aristocratic in manner as his antique name. Dreyfus would have to spend six months in each bureau. At the end

of the two-year period it would be decided whether he should
be permanently assigned to Army Staff headquarters.

The new regimen resembled the old for the Dreyfuses.
Françoise, their housekeeper, attended to the supply of spotlessly white gloves which Lucie inspected each morning. To
the fitted blue tunic with its swirl of gold at the sleeves Lucie
gave a vigorous brushing down, as well as to the trousers
which now bore the distinguishing red stripe of the General
Staff. A few paces down the Avenue du Trocadéro, a right turn
onto the Alma Bridge, left along the Quai d'Orsay (never breaking stride)—Captain Dreyfus would arrive at 14-16 Rue Saint-
Dominique, Staff headquarters, in less than twenty minutes,
punctually at nine every morning.

Staff headquarters was rather like a village where gossip,
bluff camaraderie, and inscrutable ritual prevailed. Beginning
with the First Bureau (Organization and Mobilization), Dreyfus
took up his duties with his accustomed verve. Ignoring protocol,
he would pester superior officers with prickly and shrewd
questions. He must have noticed the antipathy he excited in
certain quarters. Colonel Jean Sandherr, chief of Counterintelligence and a native of Alsace, openly and regularly deplored
Dreyfus' presence on the Staff. The captain paid scant attention
to the influence of Drumont's ideas among fellow officers, meeting prejudice with the "silence of disdain."

The colonel commanding the First Bureau gave Dreyfus a
superior rating. The captain moved on to the Fourth Bureau
(Communications and Transport). The chief officer here was
Colonel Pierre-Elie Fabre, an outspoken anti-Semite. His second-
in-command, Lieutenant Colonel Bertin-Mourot, was even more
aggressive and rarely missed an opportunity to humiliate Dreyfus. Straightaway Bertin-Mourot convinced himself that this
trainee "isn't like the others." For instance, the contrast between Dreyfus and Captain Alphonse Junck, both Alsatians,
was extreme. Junck was not so brilliant, not so efficient, but
his commanding officers understood his type. A Junck livened

the bureau with salacious jokes and gossip about Parisian military society. He was a regular, bibulous sort, the kind of Staff officer the Army wanted.

Had Dreyfus been deferential, he could have been tolerated. Instead, "he speaks at the top of his voice, he interrupts," Lieutenant Colonel Bertin-Mourot fumed. He was simply too aggressive with his intelligence. There were so many occasions when, "suddenly, we hear this young trainee seizing the floor, expositing his ideas on issues." Frequently the lieutenant colonel ordered Dreyfus to return to his desk. Then something happened which Bertin-Mourot was never to pardon. It was one of those slow days in the bureau when the officers were ritually execrating Germany's amputation of Alsace-Lorraine. Dreyfus spoke up. He believed he had the right. Alsatian Jews, he said, were more fortunate than the gentiles because their religion taught them that the loss of real estate was unimportant; faith was what counted. "Where ever we are our God is with us. . . ." Bertin-Mourot bit his lip. The others were "embarrassed." The lieutenant colonel was enraged that the Jew should discuss Alsace and, at the same time, transgress the Army's tacit ban on the subject of Judaism.

In the world outside, the trials of the principals in the Panama Canal Company were coming to an end in a frenzy of political recrimination. In August and September 1893 national elections would take place and the moderate republicans would manage to survive their involvement in the Panama Scandal. But those who wore the uniform were barred from voting; Dreyfus ignored the hubbub. He concentrated on his determination to succeed in his Staff assignments. When he was not posing straightforward questions to majors and colonels who silently fretted about arriving late for an equestrian turn in the Bois de Boulogne or an assignation, Dreyfus was regaling the bureau with the statistical and certain results of his researches. The first to arrive and the last to quit, he was the best of the Staff's trainees.

Despite his professional single-mindedness, Dreyfus could

not ignore forever the hostility of his fellow officers. As a concession to the milieu, he tried the part of the boaster and the *bon vivant*. He and Captain Junck formed an awkward friendship. Once, at the Army's horsemanship competition, he introduced Junck to three attractive women who were casual acquaintances. One of them, Dreyfus whispered, owned a "house" on the Champs Élysées where "pretty women were to be met and where there was considerable gambling." Junck was impressed, though he later feigned surprise that "a married man [should have] such nice acquaintances." Dreyfus also boastfully informed his roughhewn friend of the size of his personal fortune. Raphael Dreyfus had willed his youngest son the princely sum of two hundred and fifty-nine thousand francs, plus an annuity from the textile business. Captain Junck was understandably impressed.

On several occasions Dreyfus visited Madame Dély, an Austrian émigrée who maintained a popular salon where both junior and senior officers gathered. There were rumors that Madame Dély was a spy, but if Dreyfus heard them, he apparently discounted the danger, since he also heard that the Chief of Staff himself went to her salon. But Dreyfus was unconvincing in this dashing role. Lieutenant Colonel Cordier, second-in-command of the Statistical Section (Counterintelligence) and another jovial anti-Semite, dismissed Dreyfus' claims to amorous conquest as hot air. Dreyfus left the Fourth Bureau with a rating of excellent but also with the tarnishing commentary by Colonel Fabre: "An incomplete officer, very intelligent and very gifted but pretentious and, from the point of view of character, conscience, and service conduct, failing to fulfill the requirements necessary in order to be employed by the General Staff."

The Second Bureau (Intelligence) was considerably more congenial. January 1894, the month of Dreyfus' transfer, carried the portents of a good year. He began to think of taking up hunting; there was even talk of a Swiss vacation and perhaps a summer home. Pierrot was nearly three, Jeanne had been born the previous spring, and the children would soon need space to play. Lucie encouraged a hobby and travel, with Mathieu's support. Mathieu's few surviving letters reflect his solicitude for his brother. One written in September 1894 offered advice about hunting rifles:

> If you want to buy a hunting rifle, you certainly must get one that is of the highest quality, especially if you intend to use white powder which is very explosive and has already caused a large number of accidents in guns that are too light in weight and poorly made.*

This banality about rifles was really Mathieu's way of discouraging his brother's stinginess and misanthropy. Buy the best, blaze away in the countryside, and have a good time doing it.

There would be time to hunt and travel but, meanwhile, there were six probationary months in the Second Bureau. The "conceited prig" continued to excel. Nor was his tenure with the Staff notable only for excellence; in the summer of 1893 Captain Dreyfus had already achieved renown. According to custom, the entire General Staff left Paris for a day to attend special maneuvers. On this occasion the aristocratic Chief of Staff, Lieutenant General de Boisdeffre, invited the trainees to his table at the end of an exercise. Discussion turned to the use of artillery in defensive positions, Dreyfus' specialty. Typically, without the flattery in which his fellows excelled, Dreyfus monopolized conversation, speaking *soldat à soldat* to General de Boisdeffre. His command of the subject was brilliant; the other officers were silent, some resentful, some admiring. The Chief of Staff assumed the role of inquisitive pupil. At the end of the luncheon he took Dreyfus by the arm—a singular gesture. "Your explanations are highly interesting, Captain," he said in his distinctively drawling voice. "Be good enough to walk along with me." The rest of the General Staff dutifully fell

---

* September 19, 1894. BB 19 105 38 2. BB 19 refers to Dreyfus holdings, Archives Nationales.

into step behind the lordly Marquis and the irrepressible Jewish captain.

The Chief of Staff must have intended his gracious response to Dreyfus as a small signal to the Officer Corps to prepare for slight changes in its composition. It must have been obvious that Dreyfus was slated to become one of the rare Jewish generals in the French Army. The luncheon could have made a profound difference in Dreyfus' life. With his wealth and professional credentials it would have been easy for him to cultivate powerful patrons, political as well as military. In fact, it was the expected thing. Staff officers, as well as regular, had their protectors. The brilliant and haughty Picquart was favored by the destroyer of the Commune of 1871, General the Marquis Gaston de Galliffet. Major Du Paty de Clam was a relative of the Chief of Staff. Examples of patronage and nepotism were inexhaustible. Instead of encouraging dependence upon a protector, though, the de Boisdeffre encounter reinforced Dreyfus' belief in the efficacy of pure merit. When he left the Second Bureau with its colonel's commendation of "exemplary" and assumed his duties with the Third Bureau (Operations and Training) in July 1894, he thought he could stop worrying about compiling a peerless service dossier.

chapter two:
A STAFF OFFICER IN TROUBLE

THE DREYFUS AFFAIR BEGAN A FEW MINUTES past nine on Saturday morning, October 13, 1894, when thirty-five-year-old Captain Dreyfus received a message from Staff headquarters. He was to report to the Chief of Staff on Monday morning, in mufti. Alfred remarked to Lucie that the message was odd. It was unheard-of for officers to work on Saturday, yet the mysterious communication had been written that morning. It was equally extraordinary for a Staff officer to report for duty out of uniform. What was more, Dreyfus had been attached to the Thirty-seventh Infantry Regiment in Paris two weeks before and was not scheduled to return to Staff headquarters before the end of the year. The mention of the Chief of Staff, however, inspired reassuring speculation. Lucie told Fred (her nickname for Alfred) that he should be delighted by the special summons.

On Monday morning Dreyfus asked Lucie to approve his attire before he left their apartment. Most of his civilian clothing had been purchased for weekend affairs. He had rarely worn this ordinary brown suit. Lucie approved and embraced him. He lifted Pierrot and kissed him, then strode out into the Avenue du Trocadéro and on across the Alma Bridge. The day was clear and cold and he walked even more briskly than usual.

The office of the Chief of Staff, General de Boisdeffre, was large, and a fire had been lit in the massive hearth. Major Picquart, Dreyfus' War College instructor, of course knew the reason for the summons and, discovering Dreyfus pacing the corridor, had invited him to wait in his office. Later Picquart would remark that at the time Dreyfus was completely composed, apparently unaware that he was under suspicion for a grave offense. It was none of Picquart's business, but he was inclined to doubt then the soundness of the incriminating evidence. Precisely at nine they walked together to de Boisdeffre's office at the end of the corridor and parted.

On the other side of the door five men waited: Major Du Paty de Clam of the Third Bureau, (Operations and Training); Félix Gribelin, the archivist of the General Staff; Inspector Armand Cochefort and his assistant from the espionage branch of the civilian police; and, hiding behind one of the heavy window curtains, Major Joseph Henry of Counterintelligence. When Dreyfus entered the room no introductions were offered. He knew Major Du Paty and recognized Gribelin; to the policemen he nodded. Du Paty explained that the Chief of Staff had been delayed but that the captain might be seated to fill in the general inspection form. This Dreyfus did in a few minutes. Looking up from the desk expectantly, he saw Major Du Paty de Clam seat himself directly opposite. Du Paty claimed to have injured his right hand and asked Dreyfus to take dictation. Nodding politely, dipping the pen into the inkwell, Dreyfus waited.

In a histrionic voice, the Marquis began reading from a paper in his left hand. As Dreyfus wrote he noticed Du Paty looking at him "with eyes full of fury."

> Having the most solemn interest, monsieur, of temporarily
> reacquiring the documents that I passed on to you before
> my departure for maneuvers, I beg you urgently to send
> them to me by the bearer of this message who is a reliable
> person.

Suddenly, Du Paty broke off. "You are trembling, Captain!"
Dreyfus could feel the tenseness of the three men standing
behind him. Thinking that the major's strange outburst must
have been provoked because "he was dissatisfied with my handwriting," Dreyfus offered the lame reply, "My fingers are cold."
"Pay attention, Captain, this is serious," Du Paty admonished
and resumed dictation. After several sentences the major decided he had had enough of Dreyfus' outrageous dissembling.
Did this cocksure captain think he could make a fool of a
major? Du Paty had come to the General Staff by way of Saint-
Cyr and the War College with an even more brilliant record than
Dreyfus. Leaping from his chair to seize the captain by the
shoulder, his voice strangled by indignation, Du Paty shouted,
"Dreyfus, in the name of the law I arrest you! You are accused
of the crime of high treason!"

Dreyfus was completely rattled. Rising, stumbling, he bab-
bled, nearly losing consciousness. And as he reeled, incoherently protesting his innocence, the two policemen laid hold
of him, turning out his pockets. Their roughness jolted him
out of his confusion. Calm again, he stood ramrod straight while
Inspector Cochefort and his minion performed their duty. When
they found the keys to his apartment, Dreyfus told them defiantly to go there and search thoroughly: "You won't find anything, only I beg you, exercise discretion with my wife." What
was the nature of the evidence, he demanded? "The evidence,"
Du Paty said, "is overwhelming," but he refused to present it
to the accused. They must have a confession, the Marquis yelled,
placing a loaded revolver on the table. Failing a confession, they
hoped Dreyfus might at least shoot himself. He made it quite
clear that he had no interest in suicide, declaring, "An appalling

plan has been hatched against me for reasons that are not clear.
But I will live in order to prove my innocence."

Perhaps it was because he was shocked that Dreyfus was
such a poor advocate on that fateful Monday. A gentleman and
an officer was expected to review his brilliant career, to flout
names of important supporters, and to receive Du Paty's angry
stares with glacial contempt. He might have said that he would
refuse to leave General de Boisdeffre's office until he was presented with hard evidence. Instead, he kept protesting his innocence almost monotonously, until Du Paty finally ordered him
transferred to the Cherche-Midi military prison a few blocks
away.

Joseph Henry, the major from Counterintelligence who remained hidden until Dreyfus was led to the courtyard, was assigned to guard the prisoner on the carriage trip to the prison.
Du Paty hoped that Henry might succeed where he and Inspector Cochefort had failed. Even a clever spy on his way
to prison might inadvertently drop an incriminating remark.
Henry was the best man for the job. A gruff ex-sergeant-major,
he inspired unguarded confidence. As the cab drove along the
Rue de Babylone, Henry encouraged his captive to explain what
had happened.

"Major, I'm accused of the crime of high treason."

"Damn! Why?"

"I understand nothing about it. I'm almost crazy. I'd rather
blow my brains out. I'm not guilty. This charge is the death of
everything I've lived for."

"If you're not guilty you've got to keep your head. An innocent man's always strong. Have you got a family, Captain?"

"Yes. A wife and two children. I have money—"

"Well then, what do you make of all this?"

"Major, I must be cleared."

"I'm not in a position to do that, but certainly they're going
to be fair. You still haven't told me what the charges against
you are based on. Do you know?"

"Yes, Major Du Paty told me that I was accused of having given documents to a foreign power."

"What documents? Do you know which?"

"No, Major. Major Du Paty spoke of secret documents without indicating what they were."

In Henry's verbatim report of this conversation he added that he had overheard Du Paty enumerate the documents in Dreyfus' presence. It is likely, also, that Henry amended the transcript to include the remark about Dreyfus' money.

When Lucie heard the knock at the door a little before eleven, she was puzzled. It was time for Fred to be returning, but she was positive he had taken his keys. She opened the door herself. Major du Paty courteously introduced himself and presented Inspector Cochefort and his assistant. He spoke vaguely of a tragedy having occurred. "Is my husband dead?"

"No, Madame, worse than that," the major replied. The vision of Alfred's torn, twisted body flashed through her mind.

"A fall from his horse?"

"No." Major Du Paty's voice rose portentously. "Your husband has been arrested and imprisoned on the most serious charges." There was nothing more he could tell her at present; it was useless to plead. Presenting his search warrant, Du Paty led Inspector Cochefort through the apartment collecting correspondence, business papers, and War College lecture notes while the dumbfounded Lucie stood in the parlor waiting for the search to end. "One word, Madame, a single word from you and your husband is irretrievably lost," Major Du Paty declared, pivoting dramatically at the door. "The sole means of saving him is silence." It was nearly noon and the first of a half-decade of long, cruel days for Lucie Dreyfus.

At the military prison the commandant, Major Ferdinand Forzinetti, was nearly as disconcerted as the new inmate. On Saturday Forzinetti had been told by a Staff officer to prepare a maximum security cell for an anonymous Jewish captain. No one, he was told—not even the Military Governor of Paris—was to know about the incarceration. This anonymous captain was to be kept strictly incommunicado. "Beware the Jews," the commandant was mysteriously counseled by the departing Staff officer.

Despite his rank Major Forzinetti was far from being an insignificant warden. He was charged with the direction of the capital's several military prisons, a warrant granted by the Military Governor to whom he was directly accountable. Against his better judgment Forzinetti admitted Dreyfus to the prison Monday morning without reporting the fact to his superior. The prisoner's condition was "lamentable," he later recalled. "He walked back and forth in his cell, butting his head against the walls without being aware of it because at one point he smashed his forehead." Observing Dreyfus through the peephole, the commandant was afraid he had a suicide on his hands. By evening the prisoner's terrible moans and his refusal to eat were alarming. Torn between conflicting duties, Forzinetti was about to disobey the General Staff's instructions and inform his superior of Dreyfus' imprisonment when Du Paty arrived.

Major du Paty was also highly agitated. Examination of the papers removed from Dreyfus' apartment that morning had revealed nothing. But the Minister of War and the Chief of Staff wanted immediate results—a confession, a suicide, or incontrovertible proof of treason. It was indecent, Du Paty said, for Dreyfus to embarrass the Army with his stubbornness. He told Dreyfus that under the circumstances he would already have taken his own life. Shaken and wild-eyed, the prisoner shouted, "I am going to live to establish my innocence! Suicide would be an intolerable admission of guilt." It was clear that Dreyfus was too excited to be reasoned with that first day, but Major Du Paty promised he would come every day until he extracted a confession. Again Forzinetti was admonished to say nothing about the captain's arrest.

Major Du Paty kept his promise; the next day and the day after, he appeared at Cherche-Midi prison while Forzinetti hesitated between his incompatible obligations. From long experience, Forzinetti knew that total solitude would have driven his prisoner insane, but Du Paty's visits proved almost therapeutic. Dreyfus was commanded to reproduce the text on which the charges of the General Staff were based. Over and over, often assisted by archivist Gribelin, Du Paty dictated, ordering Dreyfus to write sitting, lying down, standing, leaning, and with a glove. Several times he presented a cap filled with scissored snippets of the photographed mystery document mixed with pieces written by Dreyfus. But every time the prisoner identified his own handwriting, never confusing it with the handwriting of the incriminating document.

The prison commandant hesitated for three days before informing the Military Governor, General Félix Saussier, of Dreyfus' irregular imprisonment. The commandant's predicament was compounded by a simmering hostility between the Military Governor's headquarters and the Ministry of War. The Military Governor had great political influence, but his power in the Army derived not only from commanding the garrisons of Paris and having patrons in the Chamber of Deputies. He was also Commander in Chief, Generalissimo, of all armies in the field in the event of war. Successive War Ministers had tried to have the Military Governor's Command moved to their headquarters at the Invalides, but Saussier refused to surrender his offices in the Place Vendôme. In a sense Saussier was a parallel Minister of War, although, *de jure*, subordinate to the Minister—hence the institutional friction between Paris military headquarters and the Army Staff headquarters. That friction was increased by the dissimilar personalities of their incumbents—Saussier, a rotund sybarite who liked women in all shapes and sizes and no matter to whom they were attached; War Minister Auguste Mercier, a gaunt puritan whose passion was his own career.

Forzinetti's decision was difficult, but everything about Captain Dreyfus was difficult. Although the prisoner continued to reject solid foods until the following Tuesday, Forzinetti began to worry less about his health and the possibility of suicide than about the charges against him. Several times he entered Dreyfus' cell to calm him and offer advice. Each time Dreyfus would cry in a voice wavering out of control, "I am innocent, innocent, do you hear! I would rather forfeit all, my wealth, my family, my life, than betray my country, than to lose my honor!" The absurdity of Major Du Paty's antics also weighed on Forzinetti. The major was demanding permission to surprise Dreyfus in his sleep with a flashing lantern and loud noises on the theory that, in his confusion, the prisoner might utter a guilty phrase.

Since Generalissimo Saussier was probably aware of the goings-on at Cherche-Midi, it was well for Forzinetti that he finally obeyed the promptings of compassion and professional self-interest. "If you weren't my friend, I'd put you in prison for two months for receiving a prisoner without my permission," Saussier reproved him. Forzinetti was also told by his chief that the General Staff had been stupid to arrest Dreyfus without more proof, that it might better have sent the suspect to be liquidated in the African bush than risk the scandal of an inconclusive trial. Saussier ordered the commandant to file regular reports on his prisoner's behavior and on the progress of Du Paty's bizarre interrogations. Forzinetti left the office of the Military Governor hugely pleased at having repaired a serious breach of conduct and at having his intuition about Dreyfus confirmed.

Another general was increasingly troubled by the case. Throughout his brilliant career as a soldier-diplomat, Raoul de Boisdeffre, the Chief of Staff, had seldom failed to create the impression of almost off-handed flawlessness. As the principal negotiator of the Franco-Russian Alliance, he aimed to become Ambassador to Saint Petersburg. The clumsy indicting of a wealthy Staff officer was precisely the sort of gaffe that might compromise an otherwise worthy professional and political claim

upon the Republic's generosity. The Chief of Staff decided that
it was time to reason with War Minister Mercier. To have expert
advice, he summoned Forzinetti the next morning, Wednesday,
October 24, to accompany him to the Invalides.

The two of them, the olive-skinned, lame career officer and
the photogenic Chief of Staff, sat together on the couch in the
Minister of War's waiting room. "Forzinetti," the Chief of Staff
began in his languid voice, "you, who know men so well since
you are the head of a penal establishment, what do you think
of Dreyfus?"

It was a leading question, but Forzinetti was emboldened by
his session with Saussier. "General, if you weren't asking my
opinion I'd surely have restrained myself from formulating it."
Quickly the prison commandant came to the point: "You are
on the wrong track, I believe. Dreyfus is as innocent as I am."
The Chief caressed his goatee; this was the response he had
anticipated.

At that moment the Minister of War's private secretary announced that General Mercier would see them. De Boisdeffre
asked Forzinetti to give him a few minutes alone with Mercier
before they spoke with him together. The awed prison commandant waited, anxiously looking forward to saving an innocent man. Presently, de Boisdeffre returned in an irritated mood.
"The Minister is leaving this evening to attend the wedding of
his niece. He'll be back Monday. Forzinetti, do your best to
keep Dreyfus going until then." The Chief of Staff was distracted to the point of indiscretion. Escorting the jailer to the
door, he confided, "Despite the fact that the Minister has given
me *carte blanche*, he's simply muddling along with his Dreyfus
Case."

On Friday General de Boisdeffre ordered his cousin Major
Du Paty and the ranking officers in Counterintelligence to meet
in his office for a worried review. After flipping through the
pile of scrambled, circumstantial evidence, the Chief of Staff
slammed the cover of the dossier, fingered his mustache, and

reproached the others: "All this is very nice but you're not coming to a head with your Dreyfus. You've got nothing. One good admission of guilt, that's what's necessary."

Astonishingly, Major Du Paty was no longer anxious to pursue the charges. His nerves on edge from doubts and the strain of the interrogations, he rasped, "I cannot say that he's confessed. All right, if the moral evidence is insufficient, if the material proofs are too fragile then the solution is simple. The only thing to do is to release him."

The Chief of Staff hesitated. That seemed premature. The General Staff had placed itself in a vulnerable position with the hostile General Saussier. Keep trying to obtain a confession for a few days "because of the Military Governor," he urged Du Paty.

For thirteen dreadful days Lucie Dreyfus had awaited Major Du Paty's permission to visit her husband or, at least, to send and receive notes. A loyal officer's wife subject to the contemporary conventions of feminine passivity, Lucie had not dared contact a rabbi or a lawyer, had not even thought of authorizing her brother, Jacques Hadamard, to approach a sympathetic politician or newspaper editor. Reticence was probably her only option, however. Respectable newspapers such as *Le Figaro* and *Le Matin* would simply have refused a plea to challenge the Army's high-handedness without persuasive evidence of her husband's victimization; and the contentious tabloids—*La Patrie, Le Gaulois, La Libre Parole*—ranged between polite and obscene anti-Semitism. Nor would many in the Chamber of Deputies have consented to intercede on behalf of a Jewish officer charged with the blackest of French crimes. The hostage of her husband's fate, Lucie had kept silent even after Major Du Paty informed her on his last visit that the case was open and shut.

"Imagine, Madame," Du Paty had brazened, "a circle into which I place a certain number of officers suspected of a crime; by means of successive elimination the circle shrinks more and more. Then, finally, one name alone remains in the center of this circle—that of your husband."

Lucie finally decided that she had to do something; on Monday, October 29, after fourteen days of silence, she confided her agony to her parents. A development of the day before had left her no choice. On the evening of the twenty-eighth, a Monsieur Papillaud of *La Libre Parole* called at the apartment to confirm the rumor of her husband's arrest for treason. Monsieur Papillaud had to accept the maid's explanation that Captain Dreyfus was temporarily absent from Paris on business.

La Libre Parole trod with unwonted caution. After the imbroglio surrounding the duels, even Drumont hesitated to publish an unsubstantiated account of a Staff officer—even a Jew—accused of treason. Instead, the Monday edition carried a rhetorical question at the bottom of page one: "Is it true that recently a very important arrest has been effected under orders of the military authorities?" The initial caution of the newspaper was to have a fascinating sequel. A decade later Monsieur Papillaud revealed that, on the Sunday of his visit to the Dreyfus apartment, he had come into possession of an undated note informing him of the arrest. A photocopy still exists:

> My dear friend, I told you so. It's a Captain Dreyfus, the one who lives at 6 Avenue du Trocadero, who's been arrested on the first [sic] for espionage and who's in prison at Cherche-Midi. They say that he's on a trip but it's a lie because they want to hush up the case. The whole of Israel is stirring.

It was signed "Henry." Papillaud speculated, and it was widely believed, that Major Henry, the second-in-command of the Counterintelligence Section, was the author. The French was bad enough to be Henry's but the handwriting most certainly was not his.

The whisperings of the press continued on Tuesday. On Wednesday, the thirty-first, the evening newspaper *L'Éclair* (carrying the dateline November 1) confirmed that "an officer, not a superior officer, however, is at this moment in prison at Cherche-Midi. He has committed the most abominable crime possible for an officer." *La Patrie*, appearing simultaneously, carried a similar announcement. The honor of publishing the alleged traitor's identity belonged to *Le Soir*, but it was *La Libre Parole*'s story the following day that created the widest stir among the public with the headline: "High Treason. Arrest of the Jewish Officer Alfred Dreyfus." Inevitably, the article concluded on an invidious note: "The case will be quashed because this officer is Jewish."

Lucie was frantic after Monsieur Papillaud's visit. She sent an urgent message asking Major Du Paty to call at the apartment and, when he failed to appear, she went to his home on Monday evening, leaving her calling card and an imploring message. She called on Du Paty again on Tuesday evening; again, he was unavailable. At last, on Wednesday morning, October 31, Lucie received the major's permission to contact Dreyfus' family. Immediately, she sent a cable to Mathieu Dreyfus in Mulhouse. On Thursday morning Mathieu was with Lucie and the children in Paris. Demented with worry, Lucie fell into his arms sobbing, "I don't know anything. I haven't been able to get anything from the officer in charge of the investigation." Through the tears and muffled sentences Mathieu heard the incredible words "prison," "crime," "treason." Not "for a single instant" did he believe there was anything to the charge.

Only two years separated Mathieu and Alfred. Physically they were much alike; the same blue eyes, similar hair, roughly the same physique, with perhaps an inch in Mathieu's favor. And they were alike too in their complete mutual trust.

Mathieu's first step was to arrange a meeting with the elusive Du Paty. Mathieu's eighteen-year-old nephew, Paul Dreyfus, called at the major's home two or three days later to convey his uncle's request. He was treated to an extraordinary performance. The major's nerves were beginning to betray him; ever since the rancorous conference with General de Boisdeffre he had regarded this business as nothing short of a personal misfortune. But he, too, was still as much a prisoner of the

Army's judicial machinery as Lucie had been. When Paul Dreyfus was introduced, Du Paty lost control. "Your uncle is a scoundrel," he stated.

In the absence of hard evidence Major Du Paty had willed himself into believing the lies and rumors contained in reports prepared by one of the special civilian investigators of the General Staff, a Monsieur François Guénée. Agent Guénée claimed that Dreyfus was a regular patron of the Cercle de la Presse where he had lost massive sums at the gaming tables. In the first of his two reports Guénée quoted Lucie's mother as having replied to a well-meaning friend who was recommending that Lucie sue for divorce: "Divorce over twenty thousand francs, my dear! Why, we've had to pay a great number of the captain's other debts!" Then there were those women Guénée said the captain kept. "I don't understand married men who betray their wives," Major Du Paty continued. "When I lost my wife, until the day I remarried, I didn't have relations with a single woman."

Mathieu's encounter with Du Paty several days later was even more bizarre. The major renewed his charges of infidelity and gambling. Respectfully, Mathieu offered to prove their absurdity, but Du Paty was in a mood of exaltation. "During two days and two nights," he declaimed, "I looked myself squarely in the face. I looked into the depths of my conscience. I sought to find just where my duty lay." He led Mathieu and Paul along the hallway. Its walls supported a half-dozen august figures framed by beveled, heavy gilt. "These are the portraits of my ancestors"—the voice belonged to a character in Victor Hugo's *Hernani*. "Before them I declare that I have weighed all the evidence, that I have searched for the truth. Your brother is guilty!" The charge of high treason was confirmed by ancestral apostrophe.

Mathieu suggested a less problematical test. Let him see his brother; if Alfred were guilty, he would confess. "I swear to you on my word of honor that I'll say this: 'Alfred, what have you done? Tell me if you are guilty or not.' And if he says yes, I will be the one who hands him the weapon to kill himself with."

"Never, never—a word, a single word, and it's war [*une guerre européenne*]!" the major gasped. The ancestors had spoken. Mathieu and Paul departed.

There was an irony of which Mathieu was unaware that evening. One hundred and nine years before, the Marquis Du Paty's great-grandfather had risked his presidency of the Bordeaux Parlement to defend three men unjustly condemned to death. Indeed, his brief had been so offensive to Louis XVI that it was duly torn and burnt by the public executioner. "What, am I to be condemned not because of a legitimate conviction but because this serves the interests of society? Then what a monster society is!" the great-grandfather had protested when speaking in the name of his eventually exonerated clients. The ancestrally reverent Du Paty must have known that the president of the Bordeaux Parlement would have put a different construction than did his great-grandson on the evidence against Alfred Dreyfus.

A lawyer had to be found. Lucie's cousin Professor Lévy-Bruhl suggested the brilliant politician René Waldeck-Rousseau, one of the most prominent leaders of the Opportunist Party in the Chamber. But Senator Waldeck-Rousseau, mindful of his "political situation," declined. He recommended the services of Maître Edgar Demange. This was a bold but inviting suggestion. Demange was politically neutral, one of France's most distinguished attorneys, the son of an officer, a devout Catholic, and, most recently, the lawyer for the Marquis Antoine-Amadée de Morès, who had killed Captain Armand Mayer in one of the duels following *La Libre Parole*'s articles.

The white-maned, portly Demange listened patiently to Mathieu and Lévy-Bruhl. Demange was noted for his reticence and probity. "I accept with the following reservation," he said. "I will be the first to judge your brother if I find in the dossier any charge whatsoever that makes me doubt his innocence." "I accept your condition," Mathieu replied. It remained only for Alfred to agree, and Mathieu had no doubt that he would.

It was encouraging to have a distinguished lawyer, but with the passing of each day Mathieu saw that his brother's case was really being tried in the Paris press. Every conceivable motive was being adduced to explain the treachery of the wealthy Jewish officer—gambling debts, mistresses, divided loyalty because of his Alsatian birth, resentment over the Army's refusal to list him for combat duty in the colonies. Witnesses were cited who had seen the captain in Monte Carlo, Brussels, and London. The Dreyfuses, the Hadamards, and their friends called on the editors of *Le Journal des Débats*, *Le Figaro*, and *Le Temps* without success. One newspaper alone, *L'Autorité*, agreed to refrain from speculation, declaring that even a Jew has "the right to be innocent."

Meanwhile, at the prison, Major Du Paty had been replaced by Major Bexon d'Ormescheville, a dim-witted officer who was charged, as of November 3, with preparing an *instruction* or preliminary investigation. Not only was he inexpert and stupid, Bexon d'Ormescheville was also misled by his superiors. Du Paty was ordered to provide the investigative officer with proof of Dreyfus' guilt. He passed along the two reports of agent Guénée and three affidavits of handwriting experts attesting to Dreyfus' authorship of a crucial document communicated to the German military attaché in Paris. From several colonels d'Ormescheville heard whispers about Dreyfus' professional eccentricities and about the views of Chief of Staff de Boisdeffre and War Minister Mercier. He was led to assume that the officer under investigation was guilty; his was merely the literary task of collation and conclusive statement.

Determined to please his superiors, d'Ormescheville made the innocuous darkly suggestive: Dreyfus had managed to visit Alsace several times without having to obtain permission from the German Embassy. Trivial, even silly recollections became significant indices of character: a certain corporal claimed that the suspect "lurked" about the Fourth Bureau when he was no longer attached to it. Then there was the revealing malaise of the prisoner under questioning: "His attitude seemed to be one of cross-purposes and had a suspicious appearance, like that of one who practices spying." Finally, the young major turned Dreyfus' strengths against him. Dreyfus had protested a low mark received at the War College. Clearly, there was a wily type for you. "It may be noticed," d'Ormescheville perceptively observed,

> that the grade which Captain Dreyfus complained about was secret and one wonders how he could have found out about it, save by some indiscretion which he committed or provoked. As, however, indiscretion is his leading characteristic, we need not be surprised at his having been able to find out the secret grades.

He mined agent Guénée's frivolous reports for all they were worth, unaware that the Counterintelligence Section had filed a contrary (and more accurate) report prepared by the prefecture of police.

Alfred Dreyfus assumed that Major Du Paty's successor was capable of weighing facts that were in his favor. Dreyfus' excellent memory enabled him to show that he could not have been a client of the Cercle de la Presse or the Cercle Washington; that studies, maneuvers, or family responsibilities had engaged him during a given day or week; and that his banker could prove such and such sums had never been withdrawn to liquidate gambling debts. There was another Dreyfus, a well-known literary figure, who was the perfect candidate for d'Ormescheville's profile of an immoralist. Had the major investigated this Dreyfus? (The fact was that Guénée had honestly confused the two Dreyfuses in his reports.) Major d'Ormescheville scribbled reassuringly in his notepad but never once thought of following up these leads.

The central document in the Army's case was one undated,

handwritten *bordereau* (outline) listing five purportedly classified military items communicated to the Germans by a French officer. Dreyfus prepared a cogent, written critique for d'Ormescheville conceding that there was a remote similarity between the script of the mysterious *bordereau* and his own—especially the middle paragraph. But the prisoner also observed that there were profoundly striking incompatibilities—alien loops, a different slant. What was most important was the text itself, Dreyfus argued. The *bordereau* could not have been written by either an artillery officer (which he was) or a Staff officer because of its flagrantly incorrect use of terms and other glaring inaccuracies. But there was something more, absolutely absolving, he argued. The *bordereau*'s author concluded with the sentence: "I'm off to maneuvers." It was a matter of record that the General Staff had canceled the maneuvers which its trainees were scheduled to attend in the summer of 1894.

Dreyfus's testimony seriously conflicted with Major d'Ormescheville's information, but the investigator resolved the problem quite simply—by disregarding it. On December 4, one month after he had begun, Major d'Ormescheville completed his *instruction*, recommending that Captain Alfred Dreyfus be court-martialed under articles 76, 77, and 80 of the Penal Code. That same day General Saussier signed the major's indictment despite serious doubts.

Since Dreyfus' arrest on October 15, no member of his family had been allowed to communicate with the prisoner. Mathieu received the first definite news of his brother's welfare towards the end of November when an unlikely messenger, Monsieur "X," called on him. He was in fact Monsieur de Cesti, a close associate of Drumont. De Cesti knew someone who knew Major Forzinetti. Several times he called on Mathieu incognito to assure him that Captain Dreyfus was in good physical condition, unintimidated, and confident of being exonerated. Mathieu and Lucie were grateful for whatever they could learn. No doubt Dreyfus' son, Pierrot, was thrilled by the story of his father's special mission for the Army, but this ruse placed a terrible emotional tariff on Lucie. Finally, on December 4, the day of the recommendation for a court-martial, Maître Demange was granted permission to see his client. Unfortunately, the attorney had not been able to obtain permission for Lucie or Mathieu to visit Cherche-Midi.

On the following day the Army relaxed its star-chamber procedures—slightly. Dreyfus was told that he could write to his wife. The letter was hurriedly written, finished just in time for the evening collection of prison mail. The next morning, fifty-four days after the mysterious summons to Staff head-quarters, Lucie read news directly from her husband. It was the letter of a still bewildered, much aggrieved, but confident man. "That I could be accused of the most monstrous crime that a soldier can commit—even today I still believe that I am the victim of a nightmare." But the nightmare would soon end, Lucie read.

> In the end, the truth will emerge. My conscience is
> easy. . . . I have always done my duty without ever
> bowing my head. I have been overwhelmed, utterly crushed
> in my dark prison . . . ; I've had moments of wild
> madness; I've even wandered deliriously, but my conscience
> was keeping watch. It kept saying to me: "Head up, look
> the world straight in the face." . . . It's a frightful ordeal
> but it has to be borne.

Two weeks later, when another authorized letter arrived, Lucie found her husband's mood almost buoyant.

> The ordeal that I have just finished—a terrible ordeal if
> ever there was one—has cleansed my soul. I will come back
> to you a better man than I was. I am ready to appear
> before these soldiers as a soldier who has no reason to
> reproach himself. They will see my face, read my soul, and
> they will become as convinced of my innocence as all those
> who know me. . . . Think only of the happiness we'll
> feel when we are together soon in each other's arms.

Dreyfus' counsel, Maître Demange, was equally confident; but while his client displayed remarkable serenity, the lawyer was furious: "This is an abomination. I have never seen a dossier like this. If Captain Dreyfus was not a Jew, he would not be at Cherche-Midi." Demange promised Mathieu, "If there is such a thing as justice, your brother will be acquitted." When Demange gave him a copy of the d'Ormescheville document, Mathieu was amazed to discover that the case was more preposterous than he had suspected. It was unthinkable that, in the year 1894, more than a century after the Revolution, a French officer could be convicted on such a mass of circumstantial, malicious, and false evidence.

Still, Mathieu was considerably more wary than his brother, who supposed that innocence alone was proof against prejudice. The head of the family's Mulhouse firm, Léon, agreed. It might not be enough for the defense to argue that the Army had only the caricature of a case. If possible, they should quickly expose the real traitor. With this goal in mind, the two brothers called on Colonel Jean Sandherr, the chief of Counterintelligence.

Colonel Sandherr appeared to be sympathetic. He was himself an adopted son of Mulhouse, his parents having moved from nearby Colmar before the Franco-Prussian War. But there was more to the colonel's Alsatian past than that. Léon and Mathieu probably knew of the senior Sandherr's circuit through Mulhouse in early September 1870 shouting, "Down with the Prussians in our midst!"—a cryptogrammic call for pogroms against the Protestants and Jews of Alsace. Sandherr *père* had abjured his Protestant faith for Catholicism, and the son was reputed to have inherited the fanaticism of his convert father. None of this marred the civility of his meeting with the Dreyfus brothers, of course.

Sandherr said he could imagine their *"terrible malheur"* and that he knew of their patriotism (or that he knew of their claim to patriotism—the accounts of Mathieu and Sandherr diverge in nuance). As a professional, what did the colonel think

of the evidence against Captain Dreyfus? Mathieu asked. Sandherr darted behind platitudes: "The newspapers recount a
great deal, some of it true, some of it false." In any case, "I
am not directly involved in this case," he continued, lying with
aplomb. There was really very little he could tell them.

Mathieu allowed his impatience to show slightly: "My
brother, a Mulhouse man, an Alsatian, capable of treason?
That's impossible! He's innocent! I've read the whole dossier.
There's nothing serious in it, nothing except a little piece of
paper supposedly written by my brother!"

The colonel expressed surprise that Mathieu was conversant
with Major d'Ormescheville's report.

"This is a plot," Mathieu insisted. "This is a plot against
our brother because he is a Jewish officer whom someone wants
to force out of the Army."

Sandherr replied with the minatory *"permettez"* of the ruf-
fled Frenchman. *"Permettez!* Such ideas do not exist in the
Army."

They were getting nowhere. An ambiguity arose. "Whether
our brother is acquitted or convicted, we will do everything to
rehabilitate him." Sandherr claimed he heard Mathieu add,
"Our fortune is at your disposal if you can help us." The
Dreyfuses remembered stating the matter somewhat differently,
saying that they would devote "our entire fortune" to discovering the truth. The colonel was delighted to feign umbrage:
"Comment dites-vous? I would ask you to take care." Patiently, the Dreyfuses explained their meaning. There was a
traitor, and that traitor—the man who should be in prison—
they would devote their lives and fortune to exposing. "We're
going to find the one. Can you help us?" Mathieu asked for
the last time. Sandherr regretted that there was nothing he
could do. There were now only six days remaining until the
commencement of their brother's court-martial.

chapter three:
TRIAL AND DEGRADATION

DURING THE TWO MONTHS DREYFUS WAS IN prison the Paris press never doubted that the Army had sufficient evidence to convict. But the press was equally anxious to learn why and how Dreyfus had perpetrated his crimes. A few days after Major d'Ormescheville submitted his report, Paul de Cassagnac, the highly respected editor of the ultra-nationalist *Autorité*, demanded that the Army try the prisoner publicly: "We are no longer living in an epoch where heads can be chopped off—no matter what the pretext—after secret proceedings." *Le Figaro* agreed: "A secret trial will only serve to prolong the scandal." The Dreyfus family and Alfred's lawyer concurred.

The Jewish press was unanimous as well. The authoritative *Archives Israélites* wanted Dreyfus judged by "France [and] European public opinion." It was to be expected that Jewish publications would show almost brutal lack of sympathy for a Jewish traitor. Among themselves Jews recognized that Jewishness alone was a provocation; this being true, the writer Julien

Benda observed, the strong desire existed "to prove that we are not an inferior race as our detractors claimed but, on the contrary, a race of the first order." A guilty Dreyfus must not be allowed to reflect on French Jewry.

Although the Jewish press took pains to show its indignation, it also stressed the dangers of passion and judicial haste in the case; it alluded as well to evidence of a possible frame-up. During the summer of 1894, France's largest newspaper, *Le Petit Journal*, had serialized a novel, *Les Deux Frères*. The hero, Philippe Dormèles, was a captain attached to the General Staff. In the novel's final installments Philippe was framed by evil friends and arrested for selling the formula for a new explosive to the Germans. When his home was searched, an incriminating document forged in Philippe's handwriting was discovered. Captain Dormèles was incarcerated in Cherche-Midi prison. A court-martial declared him guilty and decreed a public ceremony of degradation and life imprisonment. Mercifully, in the manner of a Molière drama, a suspicious general found the real culprits and the hero was reinstated in the Army. Undoubtedly, Dreyfus was guilty, the *Archives Israélites* stated, but the editors expressed their curiosity about the strange similarities between the author's fiction and Dreyfus' reality.

Certain that the seven military judges would render a favorable verdict, Lucie and Mathieu wanted more than that; they wanted the public to see the shabbiness of the evidence; they wanted Frenchmen—even readers of the anti-Semitic *Libre Parole*—to admit that the court-martial's exoneration of Captain Alfred Dreyfus resulted ineluctably from the facts.

The seven court-martial officers were a fair lot. They were not to blame that no artillery officer was among them although portions of the evidence would require knowledge of that specialty. Nor was it their fault that the Minister of War, ignoring the clamor of the press, had ordered the trial closed to the public at the first mention of military secrets. Normally, cases tried under the articles pertaining to high treason were conducted in secret by the French Army; other European powers followed the same policy. On Wednesday morning, December 19, when Dreyfus' lawyer, Demange, rose to speak the first words about the "sole piece of evidence that—" he was quickly silenced by the president of the court and the public was ordered to evacuate the room. Demange accepted the setback with equanimity. When the trial resumed without the public and without members of the Dreyfus family, the confident defense counsel prepared to watch the prosecutor demolish his own case. Demange was not disappointed.

Of the several handwriting experts presented by the prosecution, Monsieur Alphonse Bertillon of the Police Prefecture was the most positive and the most colorful. Monsieur Bertillon's legitimate qualifications were in anthropometry, the science of human body measurements, but he discoursed on graphology with preposterous assurance. "There are two types of handwriting," he lectured, "dextrogyre and sinistrogyre"—script sloping to the right and to the left. The traitor's was sinistrogyre, the defendant's was dextrogyre. Demange began to ask the obvious question while the judges looked thoroughly bewildered. But Bertillon explained: the defendant had attempted to disguise his script but the traitor's handwriting belonged to Captain Dreyfus. But if the handwriting had been disguised, how could Bertillon be certain who was the author, Demange objected; indeed, since he was not really a graphologist, how could Bertillon be certain of anything? The seven officers were impressed.

As soon as Major Du Paty was summoned, the Army's case took an astonishing turn for the worse. Major Picquart, observing the trial for the Chief of Staff, was appalled by Du Paty's inconsistency. Unable to detect indications of the allegedly incriminating trembling in Dreyfus' handwriting, the officers of the court asked Du Paty to explain the significance of the document Dreyfus had penned from Du Paty's dictation in the Chief of Staff's office. Du Paty spoke at great length. But where had Dreyfus trembled? the president of the court reiterated, adding that the handwriting appeared quite steady to an untrained eye. Incredibly, Du Paty conceded the point, suggesting that Dreyfus' failure to tremble proved that he had been alerted to the charges against him. Picquart believed the judges found this reasoning bizarre. On balance, Maître Demange was highly pleased by the developments during the first day. So was Alfred Dreyfus. When his guards returned him to prison, he joked with Forzinetti, the prison commandant, that he was going to demand a promotion and the Legion of Honor after his acquittal.

The following day the prosecutor, Major Brisset, continued to spoil his own arguments to Demange's satisfaction. The prosecutor could not persuade seven worldly officers that Alfred Dreyfus was a reckless gambler and a lecher. Agent Guénée's reports went the way of "graphologist" Bertillon's and Major Du Paty's dubious presentations. When it was the defense attorney's turn to plead, the prosecutor must have known that he had failed. The several character witnesses for Dreyfus impressed the court. The Grand Rabbi of France, Zadoc Kahn, urbane and eloquent, praised Dreyfus' character, professional zeal, and patriotism. Professor Lévy-Bruhl, even then recognized as one of the nation's most original thinkers, confirmed Zadoc Kahn's appraisal. Then, with his famous technique of adversary charity, Demange chatted, joked, insinuated, and prodded until it began to occur to these seven officers, temporarily judges, that the opposing side had built no case. Again and again, but without dramatics or overemphasis, Demange returned to the crucial issue in the trial—authorship of the *bordereau*. The burden of proof was upon the prosecutor, and he had failed to establish the defendant as the author of this document.

Alfred Dreyfus was not what the French call a *sympathique* witness. His blanched, atonal voice was annoying. The lack of heroic gesture was almost British. A French officer worth his stripes would orate about honor, vigorously denounce his detractors, and threaten to clear his good name in a spate of sanguinary duels. Instead, Dreyfus defended himself in the

manner of a university lecturer. But he was not on trial for his
lackluster voice or want of histrionic gestures. He may not
have been captivating, but he was convincing. Major Henry,
representing Colonel Sandherr (since tradition commanded that
the chief of Counterintelligence never appear at courts-martial),
was worried. During the luncheon break on the third day, he
asked Picquart to suggest to one of the judges that he, Henry,
be called. Picquart refused. Major Henry succeeded, nevertheless.

"Major Henry to the bar," the court's president commanded
when the proceedings resumed. What Henry lacked in subtle
intelligence was more than offset by his physical presence. Tall
for a Frenchman, bull-chested, wearing the rosette of the Legion
of Honor, the second-in-command of the Counterintelligence
Section dominated his audience. Henry began by testifying that
the Marquis del Val Carlos, a derelict, former military attaché
of Spain, had told him that there was a German spy on the
General Staff. He paused for effect and then turned to Dreyfus
shouting, "And that traitor is sitting there!"

Maître Demange was on his feet roaring objections. Major
Henry must say more. He must substantiate his charge. But
Henry demurred, invoking the privilege of an officer of Counterintelligence. "There are secrets," he stonily answered the defense attorney, "which an officer does not even share with his
cap." One of the judges admitted four years later that "this
statement had a considerable influence on me." Major Henry
tried to seal most of the holes in the government's case, but
the evidence against Dreyfus still seemed insufficient to support
conviction for high treason.

The trial droned on through the final day, Saturday, December 22. Major Henry's performance had annoyed Demange,
but the defense counsel still expected an acquittal. Shortly after
five, the judges retired to deliberate. It was then that an extraordinary event occurred. Major Du Paty arrived with a small
packet of documents. In the handwriting of the Minister of

War himself, the packet bore the broadly scrawled message, "For the Officers of the Court-Martial." Unseen by Dreyfus' attorney, Du Paty rapped on the judges' door and handed the packet to the president of the court, saying that he would return it to the Minister after it had been read. Du Paty then disappeared.

The seven officers naturally supposed that they had been vouchsafed a small but vital portion of the Army's proofs against a master spy. In effect, the court-martial judges were being told that, if they found Captain Dreyfus innocent, they would be flouting the Minister of War. That evening they voted unanimously to convict the defendant of the charges, sentencing him to public dishonor and life imprisonment in a fortified place, the maximum penalties. Immediately Major Du Paty retrieved his packet and returned to General Staff headquarters.

Dreyfus restrained himself until he was returned to Cherche-Midi. Then he told Forzinetti, "My sole crime is that I am a Jew." Maître Demange agreed: "Captain, your conviction is the greatest infamy of the century." Those who thought they knew the facts of the case were astonished by the verdict. The disbelieving Grand Rabbi asked permission to see the prisoner, a request that the military authorities politely refused. The President of the Republic, Jean Casimir-Périer, had expected an acquittal but welcomed any end of a potentially upsetting episode. "Well, so it's over. I shall not conceal from you that a terrible load has been lifted from my mind by the unanimity of the verdict," he confided to a young official of the Foreign Ministry. "Certainly," he continued, "they would not convict one of their comrades—even a Jew—unless they were convinced by unquestionable evidence of his guilt."

Much of the press was merciless, and *La Libre Parole*'s editorial characteristically excelled: "In order for a man to betray his country it is necessary first of all that he has a country, and that country cannot be acquired by an act of naturalization." Even left-wing politicians clamored for the firing squad. One of the leaders of the Radical Party, Georges Clemenceau, had recently been defeated for reelection to the Chamber of Deputies but still exercised considerable influence over public opinion. In his newspaper he tried to reconcile his philosophical opposition to capital punishment with his patriotic hatred for Dreyfus: "Certainly I want the death penalty erased. . . . But everyone will understand that the Military Code should of necessity be its last resting place. . . . Alfred Dreyfus is a traitor."

In an effort to gain points for Socialism through Dreyfus, the Socialist leader Jean Jaurès delivered one of the most intemperate speeches of his career. "Marshal Bazaine [an officer who was more loyal to Napoleon III than to France], convicted of treason, was condemned to be shot. Dreyfus, convicted of treason by a unanimous judgment, has not been condemned to death." The Penal Code still allowed capital punishment for certain ordinary outbursts against discipline by the common soldier. Jaurès insisted that Captain Dreyfus should die to prove that republican justice was blind to rank and class. Another Socialist, Alexandre Millerand, followed Jaurès to the Chamber's presidium in a vain effort to demonstrate that the Law of 1848 did not nullify the death penalty in Dreyfus' case.

For many men death would have been preferable to the medieval ceremony of public degradation. Dreyfus did contemplate suicide. He also realized the effect of such an act on his family. Thoughts of death receded as he resolved to exonerate himself. "I must live," he wrote Lucie. "I must marshal all my strength to wash away the stain on the name of my children. I should be a coward if I deserted my post. Money is nothing. Our honor is everything. Tell Mathieu that I am counting on him for this undertaking." Lucie replied with similar determination. "Our life, everyone's fortune will be sacrificed to find the real traitors. We shall find them; we must. You are going to be rehabilitated. . . . In any case, you can be certain of this—that I will follow you no matter how far away they send you. I don't know whether or not they will allow me to go with you, but they cannot stop me from joining you and I shall."

On December 31, 1894, two and a half months after his arrest and nine days after his conviction, Dreyfus' appeal to the Court of Military Review was rejected. He had nerved himself for this. "I will bear up," he wrote Lucie. "I promised that I would. I will find the strength that I need in your love." When Major Du Paty saw him for the last time that evening, the prisoner knew his appeal had been denied. Du Paty had hoped to find a broken man who would reach out gratefully for the Minister of War's vague promise of humane imprisonment and perhaps a future pardon. "You have only to confess your guilt, to explain the motives of your crime," Du Paty said. He exhorted this officer whose character he had come to know much too well. "If you are not guilty, you are a martyr," he observed while waiting for the turnkey to unlock the door. Dreyfus stared meaningfully at the Marquis. "Promise me one thing, Major, that you will never end your search for the real traitor." As the guard's key clanked in the cell lock, Du Paty swore, out of anxiety, uncertainty, and guilt, to continue the investigation and to carry Dreyfus' testament of innocence to the Minister of War.

After Major Du Paty's departure, Dreyfus composed a long, calm letter to General Mercier. "*Monsieur le Ministre*, I received, by your order, Major Du Paty de Clam," he began.

> I am sentenced and I have no pardon to ask. But in the name of my honor which I hope will be accorded me someday, I have the duty of respectfully requesting you to pursue your investigations. Sent away as I shall be, I beg that the search continue forever. That is the sole favor that I beg of you.

On the eve of his degradation Dreyfus inspected his sword

to make sure that it had been filed to break easily across the knee of the officer in charge. He also checked to see whether the prison tailor had loosely resewn the braid and buttons on the tunic of his dress uniform, so that they would come off with a tug. If this was to be his last parade as a citizen and officer of France, he was determined to show an untroubled conscience. This man who would be criticized, even by some of his future defenders, for his rigidity and emotional impoverishment, prepared himself for the degradation with an actor's instinct for the drama of the occasion.

On Saturday morning when he was led into the room where Captain Lebrun-Renault and his escort from the Garde Républicaine waited, Dreyfus told the captain that searching him was unnecessary. He made the same objection when his wrists were handcuffed. "You see, Captain, the badges on my uniform are already loose; they are only held by a single thread. The buttons and the trouser stripes are arranged in the same way. May I ask you to waste no time when we are on the parade ground? It doesn't matter about tearing my uniform. I shall have no further use for it."

Captain Lebrun-Renault was an easy-going, garrulous nightlifer who had no taste for conversation with a traitor. His assignment was simply to conduct the prisoner at seven-thirty sharp from the Cherche-Midi prison to the War College. There was no more time to lose. Captain Lebrun-Renault gave the order to leave, but not before Dreyfus made his final statement. "I look you straight in the eyes, Sir. I can do it because I am innocent. My conviction is the greatest crime of this century and that will be proven in a few years' time."

Unfortunately for Dreyfus, Lebrun-Renault either misunderstood or intentionally twisted these remarks in the company of journalists at the Moulin Rouge that evening. Dreyfus had admitted his guilt, Lebrun-Renault stated somewhat tipsily. Furthermore, the traitor had said he would be free in two or three years.

At seven-forty on January 5, 1895, the gates of Cherche-Midi prison opened to release the special convoy.

The weather was ideal for a military degradation, cold—very cold by the time the macabre ceremony ended—but crisp and clear. Cirrus clouds meandered and there was almost no wind. Perfect weather for billowing shakos, gleaming boots and bayonets, for strident drill commands and public proclamations, and for the roll of muffled, menacing drums. It was a much better day, this Saturday, January 5, than the original date selected by the Military Governor of Paris for Alfred Dreyfus' public chastisement. January 4 had been cloudier, colder. The decision to move the degradation to Saturday, the Jewish Sabbath, was felicitous. At least one Jewish politician was certain that the political advantages of such a coincidence had not escaped the advisers of General Saussier.

They had begun assembling in the Place Fontenoy at the rear of the War College about seven o'clock. By nine o'clock the silent crowd had grown to several thousands. Butchers and concierges jostled their social superiors from the sixteenth *arrondissement* and the Faubourg Saint-Honoré. Few of them doubted that this degradation was exquisitely appropriate to the criminal they had come to see. A great many, perhaps the majority, loathed the traitor solely because he was a traitor, because he had compromised his singular position of trust and thereby endangered the security of his country. But there were the others for whom the ceremony represented a political abstraction, a demonstration before Europe of French solidarity and determination to exorcise the Jewish incubus. For these people this brutal Saturday, this memorable Sabbath of Alfred Dreyfus' immolation, was intended to be the end of an era. As Drumont, the anti-Semite, had prophesied, the sons of Israel were fastening onto the Army itself in order to complete their work of national destruction. Dreyfus' degradation, then, was a precondition of France's regeneration.

Although three hundred journalists were admitted to the

courtyard, there were no photographs of the ceremony. But the sketches testify to the unnatural composure of Dreyfus and the businesslike officiousness of Sergeant Boixin, the seven-foot giant from the Garde Républicaine charged with degrading Dreyfus. Astride his horse, the commanding officer, General Paul Darras, awaited the appearance of Dreyfus. In the court-yard were five thousand troops drawn from all the garrisons of Paris, delegations of veterans, Staff officers, and students from the War College and the École Polytechnique. The silence and total immobility within the courtyard were matched by the crowd in the Place Fontenoy. Waiting in a room off to the side, Dreyfus repeated his prediction that the War Minister's prom-ise to review the evidence would lead to an exoneration in two or three years. At precisely nine o'clock, pince-nez adjusted, shoulders squared, his filed sword at present arms, Captain Dreyfus marched into the courtyard to undergo his ten-minute ordeal. He was flanked by four artillery soldiers and a lieutenant of the Garde Républicaine.

"Dreyfus, you are unworthy to bear arms. In the name of the people of France we degrade you." General Darras pronounced the terrible sentence in a voice "charged with emotion." Ser-geant Boixin stamped into position. Stooping, the sergeant tore the Staff officer's epaulettes, braid, medals, buttons, sleeve and trouser stripes. Correctly, Alfred offered his sword which Boixin broke over his knee. Boixin then stepped back. The lieutenant of the Garde Républicaine shouted a command and the party marched off in quick time past the assembly in the courtyard. The mass in the Place Fontenoy maintained rapt silence. This moment was almost as shameful for General Darras as it was for the victim, because the General would become one of the first senior officers to doubt Dreyfus' guilt.

No one could have anticipated Dreyfus' clear shouts as he marched in quick time before serried ranks of former col-leagues, veterans, journalists, and superiors. "I am innocent! I swear that I am innocent! *Vive la France!*" Perhaps five seconds passed before the crowd understood the words and could recover from this audacity. Wounded, the people bellowed insults. But the shouts of the traitor were still audible to those nearest the iron fence. "On the heads of my wife and of my children, I swear that I am innocent. I swear it. *Vive la France!*" When he passed the delegation of veterans and reserve officers and repeated his protest, there were shouts of "Silence!" "*Sale juif!*" "*Salaud!*" Beyond the grill the crowd screamed, "Death to the Jew!" "Death to the traitor!"

Alfred Dreyfus disappointed the General Staff and confounded the spectators in the Place Fontenoy. This wretched Jew in his shredded uniform had squared the courtyard of the War College without missing a step, shouting his innocence and praising the nation he had betrayed, as though it were possible to make Frenchmen believe there was even the smallest doubt of guilt. Not even Marshal Bazaine, whose fecklessness had sealed the German victory of 1870, had so unequivocally proclaimed his innocence.

Dreyfus' degradation turned out to be a spectacle unsettling to the thoughtful, distasteful to the well-tempered bourgeoisie, outrageous to the fanatics. The occasion made an uncertain impression upon the diplomatic corps, the foreign correspondents, and the community of military attachés. Even the weather seemed to conspire with the traitor for, as the strains of the "Sambre-et-Meuse" lightly and inappropriately sounded in the wake of his departure, heavy clouds rolled in to turn the clear, cold day into a dark, depressing one.

The immediate aftermath was almost as humiliating as the ceremony itself. Now a civilian and a common criminal, Dreyfus was manacled and, still in his torn uniform, was taken first to the central police depot where he was searched and photographed. (This photograph shows a Dreyfus still fully capable of concealing his emotions.) From the photographer's his escort took him to Bertillon's office to be measured by the famous anthropometrist. Finally, at noon, he was taken to his cell at Santé Prison. Here he gave his emotions permission to break ranks. "I have just had a terrible moment of unloosening," he wrote Lucie at about seven that evening, "tears and sobs mixed together, whole body shaken by fever. It's the reaction to this day's horrible tortures; it had to come. But, alas, instead of being able to cry in your arms . . . my sobbing rang out in the emptiness of my cell." He recalled that moment when his carriage crossed the Alma Bridge and he saw the curtained windows of their apartment: "The anguish was terrible." But now it was over. "C'est fini. Take heart! I owe it to my family; I owe it to my name. I don't have the right to desert so long as I have a breath of life." Lucie thanked him in her letter for his courage that day.

Dreyfus could write "take heart" because he had a clear conscience and certainty of ultimate exoneration, and also because his family would join him in his place of confinement. Under articles 76 and 80 of the Penal Code those guilty of high treason were to be deported to a fortified enclosure for life. In practice this usually meant imprisonment under the comparatively mild conditions of New Caledonia. During her visits with Alfred in the office of Santé's director, Lucie talked eagerly about the voyage she and the children would make as soon after his departure as possible. But in spite of this he was wretched. In his misery Dreyfus reached out for the solace of the Grand Rabbi. "After the terrifying trials that I have just gone through," Alfred wrote Zadoc Kahn, "I would be very happy if you would have the kindness to come to see me and to comfort me again with your eloquent and warm words. I fully appreciate the image of the soldier before danger and death. Alas, I doubt I have a martyr's patience before such unmerited sufferings." But this routine privilege again was denied.

Frenchmen who believed in Dreyfus' innocence on January 5 were more rare than Germanophiles. The surviving Goncourt, Edmond, whose rogue liver and constitutional delicatesse were soon to trouble him no further, left Place Fontenoy shaken and puzzled. The more Goncourt thought about it, the less certain he became: "For me," he confessed in his Journal, the degradation "was an opportunity to declare [that] I am not convinced of this treason." The writer Maurice Barrès, a hater of Jews and a mystical patriot, also fretted over the spectacle of Dreyfus' stubborn righteousness, conceding to his friends that "the diction of the accused was that of an innocent man." But such doubts were ephemeral. Few French journalists doubted Dreyfus' guilt. The far greater number sincerely approved of *Figaro*'s editorial the following morning written by Alphonse Daudet's son, the anti-Semite Léon: "For this scoundrel moral suffering is nothing. He is above it. We are more tortured than he. . . . It is his last march among men and one must say that he profited from it because of the extent to which he mastered himself and defied ignominy."

Elsewhere, the case was reported without comment. There were two foreign reporters, however, who had doubts. The New York *Herald*'s reporter wrote in his dispatch that "Dreyfus had in every respect the appearance of a man protesting against a great injustice." Theodore Herzl, the Paris correspondent for the *Neue Freie Presse* in Vienna and later the founder of Zionism, seemed unable to decide what to believe. Before the verdict Herzl's diary spoke of a probable conspiracy against Dreyfus. Seven years later Herzl claimed he had been so stricken by the degradation that he wrote an essay for a French magazine that same evening on the Jewish question. Curiously, though, his dispatch to the *Neue Freie Presse* on January 5 concluded that the accused was very likely guilty because of the unanimity of the verdict. Even if, as Herzl said later, it was the Dreyfus court-martial and degradation that "made me a Zionist," on January 5, 1895, he was obviously still wavering about the case.

The leaders of the French Jewish community accepted the verdict against Dreyfus without question and dismissed the traitor as unworthy even of private sympathy. "A great misfortune had fallen upon Israel," Léon Blum recalled, and whatever the loose ends and ambiguities, the sooner forgotten the better. *Archives Israélites* lamented that the year "was ending sadly for Judaism, for France, and for civilization." After the sentence was proclaimed, the publication explained its stance: "If silence were not dictated by propriety, out of respect for the mourning of two respectable families, it would be imposed upon us by the precarious position in which the dreadful campaign waged by anti-Semitism places not only the Jewish minority, but all minorities."

For Dreyfus there were moments when a clear conscience, family visits, and hopes for exoneration were not enough. "Truly, when I think about it again, I ask myself how I have been able to have the courage to promise you to live after my conviction," he wrote Lucie. A few days later he wrote again: "Forgive me if I moan now and then, but what can one do? Under the bitterness of memories I often need to pour out my over-full heart into yours."

She understood, and there was no need for apology, nothing to forgive. "What patience, what abnegation, what courage you must have in order to support these long humiliations!" Lucie wrote. "I can't tell you what deep admiration I have for you." After a visit on Sunday, eight days after the degradation: "How long the anxious minutes are, but how quickly the happy minutes pass! This meeting passed like a dream again. I arrived at the prison with joy and went home gripped by a deep sadness." For Lucie this ordeal was overwhelming. Her doctor ordered her to bed for a week.

Four nights later, with no prior warning, Dreyfus, barely clothed and handcuffed, was transferred at eleven o'clock to a prison train in the Gare d'Orléans. About noon the next day he arrived at La Rochelle on the Bay of Biscay, where a prison launch waited to carry him to nearby Île de Ré. The self-important bustle of four special guards and telegraphic messages from the Ministry of Interior to the La Rochelle railway station assured discovery of his arrival. News of the secret transfer brought an angry mob to the station. The panic-stricken guards confined Dreyfus to his compartment until nightfall. By then the crowd was larger and more menacing. When the order to transfer the prisoner finally arrived from Paris, he was led through the mob with an indifferent protection which allowed him to be pushed and knocked about. If Dreyfus was not seriously hurt, it was probably because he exhibited no fear. He did not try to parry the jabs and kicks nor did he wince as he was batted through the angry mob. A carriage finally took him to the launch. At nine that evening, in subfreezing temperature, he landed on the Île de Ré. At the prison registry Dreyfus was searched, stripped, issued thin cotton clothing, and hustled to his unheated cell.

And thus began five years of torment.

chapter four:

TREASON WITH
A FLAIR

"THERE IS A TRAITOR, CERTAINLY—ISN'T there?" Mathieu and Léon Dreyfus had asked Colonel Sandherr. From what they had seen of the evidence, the Dreyfus brothers had good reason to suspect that their brother, France's first Jewish Staff officer, was the victim of an anti-Semitic plot. What other inference was to be drawn from the Army's determination to proceed to trial with a cheap dossier of gossip about women and gambling, accusations which, if true, justified no more than a commanding officer's reprimand? As for the *bordereau*, the document had looked very much like an inconsistent forgery of their brother's handwriting. That there had never been a traitor was a perfectly logical inference. It was, nevertheless, not a valid one.

There was a traitor, someone guilty of the immorality and treason for which Dreyfus was condemned, one of the most eccentric and picaresque traitors, indeed, in modern history. When Alfred Dreyfus' ordeal began, Marie Charles Ferdinand Walsin-Esterhazy was a major assigned to the Seventy-fourth

Infantry at Rouen about seventy miles northwest of Paris. Ferdinand Walsin-Esterhazy belonged to a species congenitally impervious to the moral strictures laid down by society. Until his death in 1923 he remained genuinely puzzled and embittered by the censorious language the mere mention of his name provoked.

Walsin-Esterhazy was the son of one general and the nephew of another, both of whom had received their commands under Napoleon III. Compromised by political intrigue, his ancestors had emigrated from Hungary in the last year of Louis XIV's reign. As members of the great Esterhazy clan, even though of a junior branch, they had been received at Versailles with the dignity befitting one of the most august names in the *Almanach de Gotha*, the ultimate register of European nobility. The Bourbons granted an Esterhazy the command of a regiment of hussars bearing the family name and coat of arms. When the Revolution came, most of the French branch of the family emigrated to Russia.

One Esterhazy stayed in France. Her husband, Monsieur Walsin, was a kindly man of some means and influence but lacked a patent of nobility. For noble companionship Madame Walsin sought the embraces of a Marquis by whom she bore a son in 1767, Jean-Marie-Auguste. The son was surnamed Walsin by the complacent husband, and this son's children eventually adopted the hyphenated surname of Walsin-Esterhazy. It was one of the sons of this Jean-Marie-Auguste who was the father of the infamous Marie Charles Ferdinand, born in 1847. General Ferdinand Walsin-Esterhazy died ten years after his son's birth. When his widow followed nine years later, she left behind the not inconsiderable sum of ninety thousand francs and exclusive title to the Chateau de Dommartin one hundred and fifty miles east of Paris. Before he reached legal maturity, young Ferdinand was sole master of an enviable patrimony.

From early adolescence Ferdinand suffered from tuberculosis. His doting mother indulged his moodiness and excused his scholastic insufficiencies. He was allowed to meander through his studies at the exclusive Lycée Bonaparte, repeating a year and never obtaining the indispensable baccalaureate. Ferdinand was unhappy at the Lycée Bonaparte, and the dissatisfaction seems to have been mutual. Although bright enough, he was a supercilious, solitary student who was shunned by most of his classmates. But he did have one close friend—at least, he said he did—in the young Baron Edmond de Rothschild.

In 1867, when he was twenty, Ferdinand Esterhazy took the entrance examination for Saint-Cyr, the military academy. The Army accepted his evidence of a high school diploma but found his examination score unacceptable. He spent the next two years in the dazzling milieu of gaming casinos, music halls, race tracks, and the better men's clubs of Paris. He had himself announced in such places as "Count" Esterhazy, deleting the less noble prefix of Walsin. Probably hoping to assure either a military or a political career through the lady's important contacts, he pursued the magnificent courtesan Léonide Leblanc, the mistress of the Duc d'Aumale, ex-King Louis Philippe's oldest son. However, the young "Count" failed to pace himself according to his resources. Creditors assailed him and his welcome in the dens of the smart set was revoked. At twenty-two he was already impoverished and without prospect of finding a suitable position.

Throughout his life Esterhazy clung to the illusion that he could be an outstanding soldier. "For me, there's only one quality that counts," he once wrote—the quality of "martial valor." In order to obtain the rank appropriate to his supposed talents, he accepted service in the Papal Legion in May 1869 as a second lieutenant. Later, he spuriously claimed to have been wounded during the decisive defeat of His Holiness' forces by the new Italian monarchy. General Esterhazy, his uncle, was sufficiently impressed by his nephew's display of initiative to arrange his transfer to the French Foreign Legion.

The Legion might have offered ideal scope to Esterhazy's maverick talents, but he was recalled from North Africa in the summer of 1870 to participate in the disastrous campaign of the Loire against the Germans. He avoided injury and captivity and was promoted to captain at the end of November 1870. Demotion came several months later; along with thousands of other officers who had been hastily advanced in grade during the Franco-Prussian War, Esterhazy saw himself returned to second lieutenant.

His bitterness softened somewhat when he was granted a permanent commission in the regular Army. Equally important, he managed to be assigned to the vicinity of Paris where his name and panache enabled him to make valuable contacts with superior officers, journalists, and politicians. For almost ten years the Count, as he continued to style himself, cultivated potential patrons with a truly aristocratic disdain for affiliation of party or religion. By the turn of the decade he seemed on the verge of success. His name, the appropriate title, the powerful friends seemed to promise steady promotion and agreeable duty.

Approaching thirty, an energetic lover and tireless finagler, a "veteran" of two campaigns and possessed of the assurance of a condottiere, Esterhazy's appearance belied his talents; he looked like a failed impresario or a demimonde salesman of unsavory pictures. With his straight black hair and pointed mustaches, his lusterless black eyes, medium stature and concave chest, there was little about him that suggested the warrior or the gallant. He resembled a basset hound of corrupt pedigree that lived in constant fear of abuse. He felt that way, too, at times. In a letter to his relative and mistress, the aristocratic Madame de Boulancy, Esterhazy once confessed, "I'm of infinitely less value than the least of your friends so far as the general viewpoint goes." That was one mood. But there were others when the basset hound was feisty. "I'm a being of a completely different species," he boasted in the same letter. "Moreover, as far as that goes, people are generally deceived about me. I'm capable of great things if I find the opportunity for them—or of crimes, if that will avenge me." Swings between self-abasement and egotistical fantasy constituted the rhythm of Esterhazy's nature.

In the late 1870s the Count was still trying to advance his career without recourse to crime. He possessed considerable literary talent which he turned to good use in 1875 by joining the staff of the *Réunion des Officiers*, a publication which served as a forum for literary officers. From early 1875 through 1876 Esterhazy assiduously read, digested, summarized, and frequently commented on French and foreign military data. "During the entire period that I was with General Nugues [of the *Réunion*]," he boasted, "the bibliographic notes of the whole bulletin were put together by me. I even wrote short historical studies in the bulletin." He clung to the belief that he was an expert in military science. Many years later Esterhazy wrote to the British newspaper, the *Evening Standard*, offering his services as an ex-officer who was "in a position to write you thoroughly informed and accurate articles upon the French Army and its administration and also upon the armies of the continental powers and the French policy in Morocco." * The important contacts he made in his two years with the *Réunion des Officiers* led to his appointment to the General Staff in February 1877. He became a translator in the Second Bureau, Intelligence Department.

Editing the *Réunion des Officiers* was fateful in another way. Sometime in 1877 Esterhazy met Captain Maurice Weil, an occasional contributor to the bulletin. Their friendship—or conspiracy—was to last until shortly before the close of 1896. Weil was already a considerable personage. Attached to the French Embassy in Berlin after the Franco-Prussian War, he had carried out his duties with tact and efficiency at a time when relations between the two countries were exceedingly delicate. Weil's reward was an appointment, in 1875, to the Intelligence Department of the General Staff with the rank of captain. As a matter of course Captain Weil was also made a chevalier of the

---

* Esterhazy Papers.

Legion of Honor. By the time he met Esterhazy, Weil had already begun to publish a series of military histories that were to be acclaimed by the French Academy. Furthermore, Esterhazy's new friend had advantages beyond mere talent: his uncle was a bishop; half Jewish, Weil was on intimate terms with the Rothschilds; and it was rumored that the lovely Madame Weil was sufficiently emancipated from conventional notions of marriage to have attracted the attention of the aging, roguish General Saussier. Esterhazy and Weil were, in fact, unusually congenial. Both were intelligent, well read, gifted with the pen, and both were equally adept in the salon and in the boudoir.

After three years with the General Staff Esterhazy was promoted to captain and posted to the 135th Infantry at Cholet, a considerable distance southwest of Paris. It was a dreary assignment and his important contacts no longer seemed to help. Certainly his friends could not protect him from exasperated creditors. Fortunately, France was readying one of its punitive military expeditions—this one for Tunisia—that would commit her to the ministry of empire for the better part of a century. Esterhazy decided that both his professional prospects and his tubercular condition (invariably aggravated by his bank balance) would improve in the North African climate. In 1881 he obtained a command in the expeditionary army commanded by General Saussier and was stationed at Sfax on the Tunisian coast. In the restricted archives of the Army's Historical Section there is a revealing note on Captain Esterhazy written by one of his superiors during this period: "An officer who arrives in the unit, spends his time to himself, not very dedicated, but who pulls the best duty and somehow leaves with good notes and a promotion." What this officer did not know was that Esterhazy, having put himself in charge of his unit's records, had doctored an account of one battle, describing his own role in glowing terms although he had not even been present. The Ministry of War entered the citation in his record.

Victorious in Tunisia, the captain immediately set about

preparing an advantageous return to France. There was no question in his mind that he merited assignment in or near Paris. If Weil had been in the capital to make certain his friend's dossier was dropped onto the right desk, a Paris posting might have been assured. But Weil had fled to Spain, accused of embezzling funds entrusted to him by a nobleman for racing bets. Fortunately, there was Esterhazy's faithful mistress and relative, Madame de Boulancy, a general's widow. Saussier granted her an interview to discuss special consideration for Esterhazy and was sufficiently moved by her appeal to promise to arrange the captain's eventual assignment to Paris. There was another matter Esterhazy wanted arranged—induction into the Legion of Honor—but he was in such a hurry that he mixed up the proper stages. The Minister of War had to explain to a powerful politician that, until Esterhazy was nominated by his superiors, the would-be candidate could not be considered. Esterhazy would solve this problem within the year.

Returning to Paris at the end of 1883, the Count adopted in earnest the style of life suited to a *grand seigneur*. Unfortunately, he had less money now than when he had enrolled under the banner of the Pope. For a gentleman of less imagination and more integrity the situation might have been disheartening; for Esterhazy it was a challenge. As soon as he arrived in France, he sold an expensive carriage in Marseilles; he was well on his way to his ancestral chateau before the hapless buyer learned that the vehicle had never belonged to Esterhazy. With his gardener he had especially good luck. Over the years the gardener had saved money for the golden dream of the French provincial—becoming a landowner. Obligingly, his master sold him part of the patrimonial lands of the Chateau de Dommartin. Then, during the gardener's absence, Esterhazy resold the same lands.

For tradesmen, he had different ploys. It was de rigueur for gentlemen to owe their tailors, but the Count devised a chicanery by which he robbed his tailor of almost the entire bill: he sent a postal money order for two hundred francs, then added a third zero to the receipt to prove that he had made full payment. As insurance against a threatening Paris hotel manager, he stole one of the hotel's receipts and reproduced the manager's signature. Esterhazy deferred his gambling debts at the Cercle de la Rue Royale and elsewhere just as he adjourned payment of commissions to his brokers. Not all debts could be avoided, though. Cooperative Madame de Boulancy was flattered out of thirty-six thousand francs. Then to keep her goodwill, Esterhazy promptly repaid a sixth of this sum.

The ruses of a shady *bon vivant* were not a means by which Esterhazy, the "bearer of a proud name," intended to sustain himself forever. What he needed was a rich wife. As with so much else about his life, the details of his courtship are vague, but it is known that on both sides it was a marriage of convenience. Mademoiselle Anne la Marquise de Nettancourt-Vaubécourt was not particularly attractive, but she was particularly stupid. Her father, the Marquis, was an ineffectual neurasthenic who lived apart from his wife and children in increasing poverty. The mother seems to have been so eager to unload her not-so-nubile daughter that Esterhazy's family credentials and finances were cursorily appraised. Count Esterhazy allowed his total assets to be forty-three thousand, one hundred and fifty francs. Mademoiselle la Marquise's mother offered a dowry of two hundred thousand francs. Considering that the salary of the Chief of Staff of the Army was only five thousand francs annually, the marriage contract was hardly a modest arrangement.

The wedding took place in February 1886, and problems arose immediately. Esterhazy found his bride appalling. "Before the splendors of this Italy where I spent the most beautiful years of my youth," he complained of their honeymoon, "my wife had the insensitivity, the incomprehension of a piece of wood." When he asked for her opinion of Venice, she said she disliked the city "because one doesn't hear carriages." Esterhazy was also offended by his wife's intense sensuality. She had been a virgin until marriage and seems to have relished sex as a liberation from her cloistered years in the provinces, but she was awkward at it. The normally shameless Esterhazy claimed to be "embarrassed" by his wife's demands.

The new Countess Esterhazy, having lived a sequestered life, also looked upon marriage as a passport to gay and ostentatious living. She had no idea about money beyond a notion that persons of her status were supposed to have it as a birthright and that her dashing husband was adequately endowed. She insisted upon "doing everything first-class," Esterhazy complained, with monogramed carriages, liveried attendants, horses, and an expensive Paris town house. For less than two years the Esterhazys lived like minor royalty, devouring their principal. Despite his later jeremiads, it would have been wholly out of character for Esterhazy to reproach his wife's prodigal expenditures. Rather, while paying the servants, grooms, and couturiers with one hand, he was cavalierly helping himself with the other to the thousands of francs he needed to cover his huge gambling debts, his mistresses, and stock exchange losses.

That her stupidity continued to gall him can be believed. He tried without success to introduce his wife to serious literature, but she adamantly preferred sensational novels. "The only serious book that she ever read, to my knowledge," complained the Count, "was Saint-Simon, because of the genealogy." But his wife was not so dull that she was unaware of the huge withdrawals Esterhazy regularly made from their joint account. In June 1888, on the advice of her brother, she obtained a court judgment for separate accounts in order to protect her depleted dowry. By 1892 Ferdinand Esterhazy was doomed to a connubial boredom that lacked even the balm of financial solvency. He was growing desperate.

Then, in the summer of 1892, Esterhazy was able to attach himself once again to an opportune cause. He was asked to serve as one of Captain Cémieux-Foa's seconds in the first of the series of duels provoked by Drumont and *La Libre Parole's* anti-Semitic cohorts with Jewish officers in the Army. The Crémieux-Foas were among France's most distinguished families, wealthy Jews who had been active in republican politics throughout most of the nineteenth century. The Count was delighted to serve.

The first duel was bloodless. In the second, Crémieux-Foa crossed swords with another *Libre Parole* adversary, a Captain de Lamasse, who had recently written an article quoting an anonymous officer's remarks about the inefficiency and stupidity of the High Command. The language was vehement and the judgments severe. The article was offensive to every man holding a commission quite irrespective of social or religious background. Determined to impress the Jewish officers with his loyalty, Esterhazy put on a show of livid indignation on the day before the second duel. "Above all, keep trying to obtain the name of the anonymous officer for whom Captain de Lamasse is going to fight," he encouraged Crémieux-Foa and the other second, Captain Mayer. "I'd value that so that the Army could kick him out. I'd even make the two privates who expel him take off their clothes in order not to soil their uniforms." There may have been a weird irony in Esterhazy's indignation. It is not unlikely that the anonymous officer behind de Lamasse's article—the officer whom Esterhazy wanted to have expelled from the Army—was Esterhazy himself.

It was during the third duel that Captain Mayer was killed. At the trial of Mayer's opponent, the Marquis de Morès, in October 1892, Esterhazy behaved as though he were the star witness. He clearly regarded the widely publicized trial as a means of earning Jewish gratitude and a modicum of popularity. He spoke eloquently of the deceased captain's admirable qualities, of the consternation which he, Mayer, Crémieux-Foa, and others had felt when *La Libre Parole* began its anti-Semitic attacks. Expertly Esterhazy discussed the technicalities of the fatal duel, confirming Mayer's lack of skill and suggesting that the weight of the foils had favored the experienced de Morès.

He won the esteem of important Jews, but it would have been grossly inappropriate to take advantage of this favor right away. In the meantime his affairs continued to deteriorate. His promotion to major had come shortly before the de Morès trial, but the small uplift he might otherwise have felt was ruined by his simultaneous transfer to the garrison at remote Dunkerque —"Dunkerque! Dunkerque! The end of the world!" The place would be bad for his tuberculosis; it would impose hardship upon his neurasthenic wife and two exceedingly delicate daughters. It was the sort of post where an officer's career was almost certain to drift into oblivion. Forty-five now, debt-ridden, burdened with family woes, the new major could only look forward to more of the same. "It's a disgrace!" he wrote Madame de Boulancy,

> and if it weren't for the matter of a position, I would leave tomorrow. I have already written to Constantinople; if they offer me a suitable rank I'll go there, but I won't leave without having played a suitable joke on all these scoundrels.

If ever he needed the political contacts made through Weil, it was then. (Weil had only recently returned from Spain.)

Esterhazy hastened to contact Deputy Jules Roche who sat on the military budget committee and was probably the Chamber's most powerful politician in matters pertaining to the Army. As one of the Deputy's sources of Army gossip, Esterhazy knew Jules Roche well enough to invoke his protection. The letter to Roche was vintage Esterhazy—testy, lachrymose, yet plausible:

> I ask your pardon a thousand times, *cher monsieur*, but I have been so completely distracted and indignant to see that after the promises they gave me, they played me this dirty, stinking trick of assigning me major at Dunkerque— after having promised to give me a command in the Paris

army—that I recalled your gracious offer and took the
liberty of telegraphing you. They hold it against me—me,
a Christian—for having defended the Jews, and they're not
ashamed to say it and to cause my career to be prejudiced.

Deputy Roche probably dispatched an inquiry about the
Dunkerque assignment to the Ministry of War, and this step
may have caused the Army to reconsider.

Nor was this assistance the only means by which Esterhazy
protected his career. He knew details which made the generals
nervous. Through his friendship with Weil, he had learned
much about the vigorous activities of the concupiscent General
Saussier. For a man of advanced age and girth, he was enviably successful in his relations with younger women. A
number of senior officers had improved their careers by providing him with female companionship. According to Esterhazy,
one of these officers was General Edon, a deaf fossil who retained his command because of the charms of Madame Edon.
Unfortunately, while conducting an inspection at an Army barracks in early June, the enfeebled General, too deaf to hear
the warning that his pistol was loaded, fatally shot one of his
lieutenants. The inevitable inquest was preceded by unbridled
attacks on General Edon in *La Libre Parole*, charging that he
was senile and that General Saussier had irresponsibly postponed his retirement. It was Esterhazy who helped prevent
Drumont's newspaper from raging against Edon's acquittal and
from divulging the sordid truth of the tragedy.

In late December 1892 the Dunkerque assignment was canceled in favor of Rouen, a pleasanter place and much nearer
Paris. However, the new major was far from placated. His
finances were in a parlous state. At the end of the year his
total assets amounted to four thousand francs. "My affairs on
the stock exchange are going from bad to worse," he complained
to a friend. "What's going to come of all this? I'm desolate."
In the ensuing eighteen months his desolation became unbear-

able. Esterhazy finally decided to play his "suitable joke" on his ungrateful superiors.

The Imperial German Embassy in Paris was located at 78 Rue de Lille in the eighth *arrondissement*, not far from the Ministry of War and less than a block from the Ministry of Foreign Affairs. The embassy was a suitably imposing, mansarded structure fronted by a deep courtyard, access to which was through a narrow portal in a high wall. The Ambassador, Count Georg zu Münster-Ledenburg, tall, mustached, muttonchopped, and vigorous for his years, belonged to the old German aristocracy. He was an honorable, somewhat superior gentleman whose pride of caste charmingly suited his pre-Bismarckian professional ethics. He was also notoriously absent-minded. There was a joke in diplomatic circles that he had once asked his secretary, Count von Mumm und Schwartzenstein, whose name suggested the renowned Mumm champagne, *"Mon cher* Cliquot, why don't you prefer your second name of Ratzenheim? It sounds better."

The embassy was like its noble occupant, venerable and a shade decrepit. The ballroom floor was so weak that officers had to escort guests into the adjoining rooms to prevent its collapse. And on no account were ladies permitted to stand under the grand chandelier. As a young Prussian explained to the daughter of the American Ambassador, "One of the wax candles dropped on a lady's back the other day and caused her great pain."

Although absent-minded and from another era, the Ambassador could not forget that the embassy had been involved in a nasty espionage scandal in 1890 that necessitated the recall of his military attaché. Count Münster had strictly ordered his staff never again to engage in such activities and had solemnly pledged the French government that henceforth the Kaiser's representatives would obtain their information exclusively through sanctioned channels. The Ambassador loathed spies—manifestly, they were not gentlemen. He was also enough of a Francophile to deplore any incident which might aggravate relations between the two countries. His new military attaché, Colonel Maximilian von Schwartzkoppen, very much the gentleman himself, was well aware of his Ambassador's strictures but was secretly under orders from the German Army's *Nachrichtenbüro* (Intelligence Bureau) to spy on military activities in France. In the exercise of his secret duties Schwartzkoppen had been exceedingly careful.

During the afternoon of July 20, 1894, Colonel von Schwartzkoppen was presented the calling card of Count Walsin-Esterhazy. Schwartzkoppen immediately recognized his caller to be an officer of some distinction since he now wore the lapel rosette of a chevalier of the Legion of Honor. Esterhazy tabled his credentials: he was currently assigned to the Seventh Infantry Regiment at Rouen and had amassed considerable campaign and staff experience over the years. There was a pause, a nervous twirl of the mustaches, and then a proposition: for a sufficient retainer, he offered to provide Colonel von Schwartzkoppen with secret information on a variety of his country's military activities.

Schwartzkoppen pretended to be "amazed and utterly indignant at these overtures." He pressed upon Esterhazy the surpassing treachery and awful consequences of what he was proposing. But he did not rebuff the Count out of hand, and Esterhazy left the embassy with the tacit understanding that he should return at the end of the week. Schwartzkoppen knew the embassy was under surveillance. His initial assumption was that this officer was an *agent provocateur* from French Counterintelligence. Two days after Esterhazy's visit the military attaché reported details of the unusual meeting in a coded telegram sent to Berlin. Several days later the fragmented deciphering by French Counterintelligence rendered his message as

> Doubt. . . . Proof . . . Officer's commission. . . .
> Dangerous situation for me with a French officer . . . Not
> supposed to conduct negotiations personally . . . Will

bring what he has . . . Absolute certainty [*Absolut
ge* . . . he is from] *Deuxième Bureau* . . .

When Colonel Sandherr's Counterintelligence Section intercepted Schwartzkoppen's telegram, the message was filed with
no more than an oral comment that the matter bore looking
into. None of the agents assigned to watch the German Embassy
was alerted during the crucial three months of Esterhazy's
regular and undisguised visits. Undetected, he sauntered down
the Rue de Lille, usually in mufti, but several times in uniform.

A week after his first visit Esterhazy walked through the
gates of the German Embassy again to learn Schwartzkoppen's
decision. It was affirmative. The head of German Counterintelligence had ordered the military attaché to proceed.
Schwartzkoppen had probably received these instructions with
little enthusiasm. Esterhazy's plaintive monologues about the
injustices done him, his boasting about the importance of the
information he could deliver, his overwrought comportment,
and his willingness to betray his country from the basest motives—all this must have irritated the dutiful, rather elegant,
slow-witted servant of the Kaiser. Moreover, Esterhazy demanded a regular salary instead of the usual payment for the
value of the delivered goods. They compromised. Esterhazy was
told that the terms of his remuneration would depend upon the
quality of the first documents.

Nearly three weeks later, on August 13, Esterhazy paid
Schwartzkoppen another visit. This time he handed over a
number of documents and received one thousand francs as
down payment for his services. One or two other deliveries
took place that month; Schwartzkoppen informed Esterhazy
that Berlin was satisfied with his performance but expected
even more impressive revelations. The German handed the
French officer a list written in his own hand of twelve items in
which his superiors were most interested:

1. What is the composition of the regimental batteries at
   Châlons?

2. How many batteries of the 120 [-mm. short cannon]?
3. What kind of shell do they fire?
4. What size are these batteries?
5. The firing manual of the field artillery?
6. The Army conversion tables?
7. Mobilization of the artillery?
8. The new cannon?
9. The new rifle?
10. Army formations—divisions and reserve brigades?
11. The Manonvillers fortress?
12. Maneuver plan for the mounted batteries?

After studying this list carefully (probably making a copy of it), Esterhazy returned it to Schwartzkoppen, promising to obtain detailed information about most of the items. The military attaché saw the traitor to the door and then returned to his desk where he tore up his note and dropped it into his wastebasket.

In reality, Esterhazy's knowledge of these subjects was scant and undigested. It was knowledge obtained from garrison shop talk, from occasional chats with artillery experts, from letters of the *Réunion des Officiers* group, and from a vague comprehension of the workings of the General Staff. Of the actual, tested capabilities of the 120-mm. short cannon, he knew nothing. That month he had attended the firing school at Châlons for three days when the weapon was being readied for testing but had left for Paris two days before its testing under simulated battle conditions. A lack of information was no bar, however. At his chateau, hiding from his creditors, anxious for news from Schwartzkoppen about Berlin's evaluation of his most recent documents, he compiled a dossier of "official" documents and composed several essays. A covering note or *bordereau* listing its contents was included. The Count gave free rein to his twisted sense of humor when he assembled the documents listed in his *bordereau*. What was accurate was of limited value and Schwartzkoppen could have learned as much by an inquiry passed along official channels. What seemed of value was patently inaccurate. None of it was top secret.

"*Sans nouvelles m'indiquant que vous désirez me voir*" (Without news indicating that you wish to see me), he began, "I am nevertheless sending you some interesting information, *Monsieur:*"

1. A note on the hydraulic recoil ("*le frein hydraulique*") of the 120 and the way it has behaved ("*la manière dont s'est conduite cette pièce*").
2. A note on the covering troops (some modifications will be introduced by the new plan).
3. A note on the modification in the artillery formations.
4. A note concerning Madagascar.
5. The provisional *Firing Manual for Field Artillery* (March 14, 1894).

In order to exaggerate the value of the fifth item, Esterhazy lied baldly. "This last document is extraordinarily difficult to procure and I can only have it at my disposal for a few days. The Minister of War has sent out a fixed number to the corps and the corps are responsible for them. Each officer who has a copy has to send it back after the maneuvers." He closed the *bordereau* with the sentence, "*Je vais partir en manoeuvres*" (I'm off to maneuvers).

Later, this sentence troubled those who charged Alfred Dreyfus with writing the *bordereau* as much as it did those who tried to establish Esterhazy's authorship because it was believed that neither officer attended general maneuvers in 1894. But Major Esterhazy really was off to maneuvers. A mixup in the Army's training plans had sent a regiment of reservists to Rouen and, as the available superior officer, Esterhazy had to leave his chateau to take charge of them.

On September 1, 1894, as he passed through Paris to Rouen, Esterhazy hurried to the German Embassy between trains and left off the packet of documents along with the explanatory *bordereau*. Following instructions, Schwartzkoppen promptly forwarded these documents by diplomatic courier to Berlin. As the covering note was addressed to him and had no value itself, the military attaché tore it into about a dozen pieces and discarded it in the wastebasket in his bachelor quarters adjacent to the embassy.

It was probably on Monday morning, September 3, that the cleaning woman, Madame Marie Bastian (code names "Auguste" and "Julie") found the shredded *bordereau*. Her contact was Major Henry of Counterintelligence, whom she met after work, usually at the nearby church of Sainte-Clothilde. Since Henry was on leave, the *bordereau* was not surrendered to the Army until after his return on September 25, more than three weeks after Madame Bastian discovered it.

The embassy employed a number of French citizens for menial duties—porters, gardeners, cleaners. Madame Bastian, the cleaning woman of long and apparently reproachless service, was a foul-mouthed, violent woman when she and her husband engaged in one of their frequent disputes, but the soul of un-obtrusive efficiency when she was on duty at the embassy. She also cleaned the adjacent quarters of the embassy staff. Schwartz-koppen thought highly of Madame Bastian, when he thought of her at all. At the beginning of the year when the first secre-tary of the embassy asked him to investigate the rumor that Madame Bastian was a Counterintelligence agent, Schwartz-koppen had quickly informed his superior that the notion was absurd. Madame Bastian had gone on cleaning the embassy's rooms and emptying Schwartzkoppen's wastebasket. Five years after delivering the *bordereau* she would still be an employee of the German Embassy, faithfully handing her neat packets over to French Counterintelligence.

It is hardly surprising that the careless Schwartzkoppen could not admit he had been deceived by a mere cleaning woman. In his autobiography, and even to his intimates, the military attaché swore that "the handing over of the documents of September 1, 1894, must have been preceded by the handing in of the *bordereau* to the *porter of the embassy* at some time between August 16 and September 1." This persistent denial became one of the most troublesome aspects of the Dreyfus Affair for historians. The simple truth is that Schwartzkoppen must have lied. By denying that the *bordereau* came from his basket (and implying that it had been stolen from the porter's lodge), insisting, furthermore, that it was never his habit to throw secret documents into the trash, the military attaché merely yielded to a perfectly understandable instinct to shield his government and his career.

There was another reason for Schwartzkoppen's stubborn denials. He was homosexual, and, along with the bits and pieces pertaining to German espionage, he had casually discarded in Madame Bastian's basket a continuous stream of morally compromising notes.* Knowing that if the vast files of Counterintelligence contained the *bordereau*, they must also have evidence of his own sexual deviance, Schwartzkoppen tried to cast doubt upon the validity of all information obtained through the wastebasket leak.

---

* *Secret Dossier*; Roger Peyrefitte, *L'Exilé de Capri* (Paris, n.d.); Marcel Thomas, *L'Affaire sans Dreyfus* (Paris, 1961), pp. 63–64.

chapter five:
THE CONCERT
OF ERRORS

ON THAT NIGHT IN SEPTEMBER 1894 AFTER Major Henry of Counterintelligence received the packet of documents pirated from the German Embassy wastebasket, he worked much later than usual at the kitchen table in his small apartment. Several times his voluptuous young wife came to the door to call him to bed. Not just yet, he apologized: "This is a serious matter here. It looks like treason." It was after eleven when Henry finished sorting and taping together the pieces of the *bordereau*. The next morning he showed the document to Gribelin, the Staff archivist, and to Captain Jules Lauth, another colleague. They were as shocked as their chief, Colonel Sandherr, was worried. Evidence of yet another case of military espionage was distressing in the extreme.

It was Colonel Sandherr who placed Madame Bastian in the German Embassy, who suborned the valet of the British Ambassador, who used all sorts of photographic and acoustical gadgetry, and who established France's network of agents in Brussels, Strasbourg, Geneva, and even Berlin. They were an unsavory lot, Sandherr's spies. Guénée, in Paris, was careless and venal. Richard Cuers, his man in Berlin, was a hopeless alcoholic. The Marquis del Val Carlos, a former Spanish military attaché, was a scattershot gossip. Martin Brucker, probably the best of the lot, almost compromised his effectiveness by unprofessional trust in his Parisian mistress. Living in daily contact with paroled criminals, informers, double agents, and impecunious aristocrats—all of them devoted to self-advancement by devious means—the rough and ready Colonel Sandherr not only perfected their techniques, he began to adopt their amorality.

Colonel Sandherr's spy system had worked amazingly well. In February 1889 one Blondeau, a former noncommissioned officer in the Ministry of Public Works, was arrested and sentenced for selling the plans of Fort Lionville to the Germans. While Blondeau was being tried, a lieutenant in the reserves, Jean Bonnet, was apprehended in a similar transaction. Then in August 1890 an obscure clerk in the War Ministry, one Boutonnet, was caught delivering secrets to the German Embassy. He had been interrupted before much damage was done, and he received the penalty generally imposed in such cases—five years in prison.

Next came the complicated affair of the inventor Turpin. For the invention of melinite, a high-explosive agent, Turpin had been awarded the lavish sum of two hundred and fifty thousand francs and a high decoration. But Turpin's temperament matched the volatility of his invention. He thought his subsequent discoveries were undervalued so that the government could acquire them cheaply. He warned the Minister of War that he would take his case to the public, and when he failed to receive satisfaction, he published an essay that revealed both the secret of melinite and the details of his most recent researches. The Minister ordered his prosecution and, in a trial marked by fierce countercharges, Turpin was found guilty of divulging secrets and sentenced to five years in prison.

Hardly had Turpin been sentenced before another case of

espionage surfaced, this one diplomatically embarrassing. Again the traitor was a trusted clerk, Joseph Greiner, who was employed in the Naval Ministry. He had been selling secrets to an intermediary who passed them to the Germans. The intermediary, whose shredded messages Madame Bastian had fished from the wastebasket of Schwartzkoppen's predecessor, was none other than the military attaché of the United States, Captain Borup. Born in Germany, Borup had remained faithful to the Kaiser even after his naturalization as an American. He was recalled and dismissed from the Army while the United States gave an appropriately shamefaced apology to the French government. Germany withdrew her attaché and assured the French that German emissaries would never again abuse their diplomatic privileges. The traitorous clerk received a twenty-year sentence.

Almost two years later, in January 1894, Counterintelligence had its worst jolt. The jealous mistress of one of Sandherr's key agents, Martin Brucker, went in a huff to the first secretary of the German Embassy and exposed Madame Bastian. Incredibly, the newly arrived Colonel von Schwartzkoppen insisted that the accusations were totally groundless. Meanwhile, Brucker had become suspicious of his mistress and reported her to Colonel Sandherr's organization: Mademoiselle Millescamp was arrested, badly defended, and convicted of giving information to the enemy with a speed that must have owed something to high-level intervention by the Ministry of War.

If the French were proud of the Army's Counterintelligence organization, they knew that for every discovered betrayal of the nation there must be several successful treasons. Over the years the French became far more obsessed with spying than the citizens of other European countries and, by 1894, France was vastly outspending her rivals in Intelligence.

Now Colonel Sandherr had yet another case of treason on his hands. What alarmed him about the *bordereau* was that its author appeared to possess a far broader range of knowledge than the spies of the recent past. The *bordereau* touched on classified artillery data, the new mobilization plan, the occupation of Madagascar. To the Counterintelligence chief it revealed the hand of a master spy. Colonel Sandherr appreciated that within a year or two the Germans, by patient collation and intelligent surmise, would inevitably learn as much as an informer could tell them. But he feared that the carefully controlled misinformation his agents were regularly transmitting to the Germans might now be exposed by the revelations of the man behind the *bordereau*. The *Nachrichtenbüro* might awaken to the machinery of deception so carefully lubricated by Sandherr's Counterintelligence. And there was also the possibility that yet another case of treason by an officer might enrage the public.

When Minister of War Auguste Mercier saw the *bordereau* on September 28, he was nearly frantic, and his reactions were to have an unfortunate impact on Colonel Sandherr's investigation. As recently as six months earlier, irascibility and haste would have been unthinkable in General Mercier. A protégé described him as a cold man, methodical and resolute, slow of speech, who never laughed, was never impatient, and never showed anger. In fact, Mercier was a caricature of the École Polytechnique graduate, an officer who supposed that emotions and blunders characterized cavalry officers and fools. Because of his republican politics and his reputation as a level-headed, highly professional general, he had been chosen by Prime Minister Jean Casimir-Périer for Minister of War in 1893.*

Mercier's first months in office had been almost brilliant. On December 9 he became the politicians' idol when an anarchist's bomb racked the Chamber of Deputies. While the members were still crawling out from under their benches, the seated Minister calmly removed a splinter from his coat and disingenuously asked one of them, "Does this belong to you?"

---

* Prime Minister is used throughout in place of the correct French title, Président du Conseil des Ministres.

Six months later, when the Republic's fourth President, Sadi Carnot, was assassinated by a young Italian anarchist, Prime Minister Casimir-Périer stepped into the Presidency. The new Prime Minister, Charles Dupuy, regarded Mercier as the vedette of his cabinet.

But then Mercier seriously faltered. First, there was his mismanagement of the Turpin case. Pardoned near the end of 1893, the irrepressible inventor had offered the Army yet another invention, a self-propelling, gyroscopic bullet. Mercier rejected it perfunctorily. Turpin took his case to the parliamentary opposition and to the newspapers, announcing his intention to expatriate to Germany taking his invention with him. When the matter came up in the Chamber, Mercier, in lean, precise phrases, ably acquitted himself. Unfortunately, though, he botched his conclusion by an arrogant blunder in rhetoric. He declared that from the outset his *"flair d'artilleur"* had told him Turpin's scheme was harebrained. Time and again, in the years to come, he would be taxed with the barb, "What, his artilleryman's intuition has deceived him again?"

Then things went from bad to worse for Mercier. During the summer of 1894 he advanced the release of some sixty thousand Army conscripts on the mistaken assumption that President Casimir-Périer had been informed. Learning of the decree from the press, the high-strung bachelor President convened a special session of the Cabinet to rescind Mercier's decree. The Nationalist press was overjoyed by the ensuing confusion. From then on the newspapers lay in wait for another blunder by the new government. Prime Minister Dupuy was a cynical politician who knew how quickly honest mistakes could lead to votes of no confidence. Rumor spread that Mercier would be dropped as soon as possible.

General Mercier, who had not wished to become a politician, was a different man after nearly two years in power. With an imperturbable sense of personal destiny, he reconnoitered the political terrain with the same dispassionate eye that had scanned the battlefields of Mexico and concluded that he could become that rarest of parliamentary creatures, a permanent minister. His early successes in the Chamber of Deputies had suggested that he might even become President of the Republic if he maneuvered deftly. Another mistake would be fatal, however. What Mercier really needed was a notable triumph— any sort of newsworthy coup—and it was in this frame of mind that he learned of the *bordereau*. This development, he knew, could either ruin or save him. The War Minister's command to "get to the bottom" of the case immediately was probably transmitted with threatening urgency to Counterintelligence by the timorous Vice Chief of Staff in the Chief's absence on summer leave.

Sandherr's staff was doing its best, but nothing in the voluminous archives of the Counterintelligence Section shed any light on the *bordereau*. In a last throw of the dice Sandherr had the document photographed and copies distributed to the General Staff's departments. By the end of the first week in October Counterintelligence was ready to report that it had failed. That same week Lieutenant Colonel the Marquis Albert d'Aboville of the Bureau of Communications and Transport returned from furlough.

When he asked for news of events during his absence, his chief, Colonel Fabre, handed him a copy of the mysterious *bordereau*. But the solution is evident, a matter of logic, d'Aboville told the colonel. The officer who wrote the *bordereau* must be a Staff trainee, because of his encyclopedic military knowledge. Who else could give the Germans reliable information about such a variety of classified items? They hurried to examine the list of trainees; eliminating first one name, then another, d'Aboville and Fabre arrived at Alfred Dreyfus, Captain. Fabre had always believed that Dreyfus was out of place on the General Staff; he would be pleased to verify his judgment. They found one of Dreyfus' written reports and compared it with the *bordereau*—the two handwritings appeared to them to be identical. The officers fairly ran down the hall to the office of the chief of the Counterintelligence Section;

Colonel Sandherr listened to d'Aboville's argument, studied the handwritings before him, and decided, "There's no doubt about it."

Colonel Sandherr took the new evidence to General de Boisdeffre, who had recently returned to Staff headquarters. The Chief of Staff immediately made an appointment with General Mercier. Both concurred with Sandherr's and Fabre's opinion on the matching handwriting. It seemed clear to the Minister of War that Dreyfus was guilty of treason. He ordered Counterintelligence to conduct a thorough but expeditious inquiry. General de Boisdeffre asked his cousin Major Armand Du Paty de Clam to be preliminary investigator. Du Paty's reputation for intelligence and discretion and his dabbling in graphology made him ideal. He was urged to have his conclusions ready the following Monday, October 8. Throughout the weekend Major Du Paty pored over the *bordereau* and the specimens of Dreyfus' handwriting. Monday morning he delivered his report to Sandherr, who saw Mercier immediately. Major Du Paty had been cautious, sensibly restrained by the inconclusive nature of the evidence and his own amateurishness as a graphologist. Although there were significant dissimilarities, he found that the handwriting of Dreyfus and that of the *bordereau* clearly belonged "to the same family." In his opinion, there was adequate ground for a formal investigation. The Minister of War seized upon Major Du Paty's tentative finding as conclusive. The following morning the Minister obtained the name of an official handwriting expert, a Monsieur Alfred Gobert of the Bank of France. On Wednesday Mercier informed the Prime Minister and the Minister of Foreign Affairs of the suspicions against Captain Dreyfus. On Thursday Mercier asked Gobert for his expertise.

Meanwhile, the Minister of Foreign Affairs, Gabriel Hanotaux, began to worry. Hanotaux was that rarity among the Third Republic's notables, a statesman who was willing to experiment with diplomacy to bring about a Franco-German entente. The more he thought about it, the more he dreaded the prospect of an exposé involving a Staff officer and Germany's military attaché. On Thursday he called on General Mercier to plead that the Army not arrest the suspect until further evidence from police surveillance could be gathered. Hanotaux argued that similarity of handwriting by itself was much too indefinite, but to no avail. "I found General Mercier unshakable," he recalled; in fact, the visit accelerated the very development he wished to prevent. Mercier suspected that Prime Minister Dupuy was waiting to use the *bordereau* against him, to accuse him of procrastinating in a matter of national security. Therefore, a traitor had to be found: if not Dreyfus, then someone else. When Hanotaux left Mercier's office, the General summoned the Chief of Staff, the chief of Counterintelligence, and Vice Chief, Brigadier General Charles Gonse. He ordered them to come up with an immediate solution.

On Friday, October 12, Vice Chief Gonse paid two visits to the graphologist Gobert. The Bank of France expert had had the documents less than one day; he required more time. He also sensed that something was amiss. The Army's haste bothered him. Gobert asked the Vice Chief of Staff for the name of the probable author of the *bordereau*. General Gonse refused but Gobert was able to identify Dreyfus by comparing the limited information in his possession with the biographical sketches in the Army's directory. The fact that Dreyfus was a Jew made the graphologist even more cautious. When Gonse returned the second time, Gobert said he needed at least another day before making a final decision.

Dreyfus' religion was also a matter of concern to War Minister Mercier. Just a few days before the arrival of the *bordereau*, he had quashed the conviction of an Army physician without waiting for the decision of the Court of Military Review. The physician's conviction had been highly questionable, but Mercier's intercession had been a high-handed violation of the statutes. The physician was a Jew. The awful realization dawned

on Mercier that he could be accused of acting in behalf of the
Jews. It was an impossible situation, a story tailored for
Drumont's *Libre Parole*.

On the same Friday afternoon Mercier took the fatal plunge.
Summoning General Gonse, Colonel Sandherr, and Major Du
Paty, he told the trio that he wanted conclusive evidence of
Dreyfus' guilt by the next evening. Furthermore, and Du Paty
was stupefied by the order, he commanded the Major to arrest
Dreyfus on Monday morning. Apparently, Mercier was afraid
the suspect might escape to Switzerland or Spain.

Vice Chief Gonse was frantic. If Dreyfus was to be arrested,
the question of the *bordereau* handwriting had to be settled
rapidly. Gonse sensed Gobert's doubts and anticipated that the
handwriting expert's report would be unsatisfactory. From Sandherr the Vice Chief acquired the names of four other graphologists. Photocopies of the *bordereau* and specimens of Dreyfus'
handwriting were rushed to these specialists. They were told, in
strictest confidence, that the Army had other evidence against
the suspect, that he was a Jew, and that time was running out.
The General Staff had to have their reports the following day,
Saturday, or by Monday morning at the latest. The experts were
Alphonse Bertillon, of the Prefecture of Police, and Messrs.
Charavay, Pelletier, and Teysonnières. Bertillon was not a
graphologist but he was known to be an anti-Semite and a
reverent Nationalist. Monsieur Teysonnières, a bona fide graphologist, was currently under investigation by his colleagues for
flagrant misconduct.

Later that Friday Chief of Staff de Boisdeffre summoned
Major Du Paty de Clam. "You are the only Staff officer filling
the requisite conditions to be charged with this mission," he
confided. "You aren't a pupil of the Jesuits, you've got no
Jewish attachments, you know our affairs here . . . and then
there's a bit of a risk." Major Du Paty left the Chief of Staff
with a gnawing suspicion that the honor of this mission was
dubious. When the verdicts of the handwriting experts arrived
early Saturday, he became alarmed. Gobert of the Bank of

France strongly doubted that Dreyfus had written the *bordereau*; so did Pelletier. Charavay gave a qualified yes and Teysonnières absolutely affirmed Dreyfus' authorship. Bertillon found that the *bordereau* handwriting, although disguised, was definitely attributable to the captain. Du Paty did not know at the time that Bertillon was a lunatic, but it was clear, nevertheless, that a three-to-two decision in favor of Dreyfus' guilt was insufficient to justify an arrest.

When Major Du Paty prepared the telegram that would summon Dreyfus to Staff headquarters, a sense of fair play made him bridle momentarily at the prospect of arresting a fellow Staff officer against whom evidence was tenuous if not entirely flimsy. Vain to the point of silliness, Du Paty was not altogether blind to the risks of being the preliminary investigating officer. Like Major Picquart and Captain Dreyfus, the major had a service record of such brilliance that he figured among the Army's handful of top young officers. But if the Monday morning inquisition of Dreyfus backfired, or if the suspect managed to contact the powerful supporters he was presumed to have in the Chamber of Deputies, Du Paty could be the chief victim of Mercier's unreasonable order.

According to his diary, at five on Saturday afternoon, October 13, Du Paty went to Mercier's office to argue for an annulment of the arrest order. The Minister of War assured Du Paty that both the President and the Prime Minister had approved his decision to incarcerate Dreyfus. There could be no appeal from such a consensus. Meekly, Du Paty retired to spend the night and the following Sunday preparing his interrogation.

The lack of hard evidence also bothered Colonel Sandherr. As the archivist Gribelin ransacked the section's files for any documentary shred that might help, Sandherr remembered a note that Madame Bastian had delivered that spring. It was found, and the colonel studied it carefully. It read, in part,

> I'm very sorry not to have seen you before leaving. In any case, I'll have returned in eight days. I'm including the

twelve master plans for Nice which that scoundrel
D [*ce canaille de D*] gave me for you.

The intriguing closing, "Don't do too much ramming" [*Ne
bourrez pas trop*] and the odd practice of feminizing the signature—"Alexandrine"—had been construed long ago as a per-
verse endearment between Colonel Alessandro Panizzardi, the
Italian military attaché in Paris, and Colonel von Schwartzkoppen, the German military attaché. Nor was the identity of
the person referred to as D unknown. D was Dubois, another
civilian clerk whose career as a spy Sandherr had terminated
more than a year before. But there was the initial. It could be
used. Sandherr thought, then added the note to his almost
empty tray of Dreyfus documents.

The search continued for all possible evidence. Sometime in
February Madame Bastian's wastebasket forays had provided
another "Alexandrine" letter, this one bearing the salutation,
"Dear Rammer." There was no mystery about the contents of
this one either. Panizzardi wrote that "*un ami*" had been helpful
in securing information about French military policy, and
Sandherr knew the reference was to the General Staff's own
man in charge of disseminating approved information to foreign
officers. But he decided to forward the note to his superiors
with the comment that the "*ami*" could refer to Dreyfus.

The absence of motive, the skimpy evidence, and total misfire
of Major Du Paty's Monday morning interrogation of Dreyfus
alarmed the General Staff. The jailing of a brilliant, wealthy
Staff officer would destroy a few careers unless an airtight case
was put together. For this reason, the chief of Army Counterintelligence decided to enlist the support of the intelligence
service run by Maurice Paléologue in the Ministry of Foreign
Affairs. During one of their regular weekly conferences, several
days after the arrest of Dreyfus, Colonel Sandherr confided:
"We're engaged in a very delicate business, a bad business,
and Schwartzkoppen's in it again, caught red-handed. So if you
find anything whatever about what he's been up to, don't fail

to let me know." And Sandherr dashed back to Staff headquarters.

It was not until the newspapers broke the story of Dreyfus'
arrest at the beginning of November that Paléologue's staff was
able to come up with something. When the Quai d'Orsay's de-
coders alerted Counterintelligence, they cautioned that the final,
accurate deciphering of a telegram to General Marselli, the
Italian Chief of Staff, from Colonel Panizzardi might require
several more days as the Italians were using a new, quite difficult cipher. Studying the decoding sheet, Sandherr copied parts
of the tentative texts and raced back to Staff headquarters. This
admittedly provisional translation offered an irresistible opportunity to editorialize.

Panizzardi had wired Rome:

> If Captain Dreyfus has never been in contact with you, it
> would be convenient to instruct the ambassador to publish
> an official denial in order to avoid the commentary of the
> press.

With Sandherr's permission Major Henry changed this to read:

> Dreyfus arrested, precautions taken, our emissary warned.
> It would be convenient to instruct the ambassador to
> publish an official denial in order to avoid the commentary
> of the press.

This new version was then sent to the Chief of Staff and the
Minister of War. A few days later, when Paléologue's intelligence service passed along a corrected copy of Colonel Panizzardi's telegram, as well as the Italian Chief of Staff's reply
denying any knowledge of an Alfred Dreyfus, it was clear that
this latest bit of evidence could not be used. Nevertheless, it
would surface again.

By the end of October 1894 the Minister of War was ready
to concede that the Army had failed to establish a case against
Dreyfus, but his shaky political position prevented him from

ordering a dismissal of charges. On the day Dreyfus was arrested, *La Libre Parole* had broken the dreaded story of Mercier's irregular role in the case of the Jewish Army physician whose conviction he had set aside. "*Monsieur le Général* Mercier has just committed an infamous act," the paper announced. "He has forgotten that he is in the Army—that he is its leader." Drumont's paper claimed that the physician's powerful friends in the Chamber of Deputies were behind Mercier's intervention. Although the Minister pretended not to care about the press, even a fairer and less ambitious man could scarcely have been unaffected by the vicious editorials that followed the announcement of Dreyfus' arrest.

On November 4 *La Libre Parole* charged that the Jews were mobilizing their friends in the Chamber ("and God knows they are numerous"). The Jews' supposed tactic was to threaten politicians with terrible revelations of misconduct and corruption. "If Mercier doesn't keep quiet, Reinach [a prominent Jewish politician] will talk. That," said Drumont, "is the code word that is making the rounds of the [Chamber] as well as the Senate." On the same day the Nationalist newspaper *L'Intransigeant* dismissed the Minister's judiciary caution as an attempt to suppress the Dreyfus case. If, as the newspaper suspected, Dreyfus was a German spy planted on the General Staff, then the War Minister was even "more guilty and more of an ignoramus than one supposes." *L'Intransigeant* also predicted that Mercier would minimize the importance of the secrets compromised by Dreyfus.

The Minister of War tried desperately to salvage something of the public confidence he had recently enjoyed. In an interview with a reporter from *Le Journal*, he promised that the preliminary investigation would be concluded within ten days. Furthermore, he insisted, the betrayed secrets were of "a secondary nature." Mercier had urgent reasons for giving such positive assurances. Less than twenty-four hours earlier two German junior officers had been arrested by French police for spying, a development encouraging further adverse rumor and comment by Nationalists on the Minister's vigilance. Eleven days later, November 28, he flagrantly exceeded his authority by telling *Le Figaro*'s reporter that "the guilt of [Dreyfus] is absolute, certain." This was too much even for the phlegmatic Prime Minister; he ordered the War Minister to issue an official denial of the *Figaro* article. But the damage was done. Finally, the ultrapatriotic *L'Autorité* warned that if Dreyfus were allowed to escape, "Mercier ought to be ignominiously chased not only from the Ministry but from the ranks of the Army."

By the end of the first week in November what had begun as a clumsily handled case of espionage had become a crisis threatening the government of Prime Minister Dupuy, the careers of the War Minister and the Chief of Staff, and even the reputation of French Counterintelligence. The Minister of War had begun to act like a fugitive, refusing to discuss the details of the case with his colleagues, declining to answer the worrisome communications from the Ministers of Foreign Affairs and Finance. Not even Dupuy could get Mercier into a discussion of the investigation. Mercier knew that he had more to fear from his own colleagues than from the noisy Paris press. He knew that the Prime Minister still intended to drop him at the first convenient moment and that the Foreign Minister was lobbying in the Cabinet for votes against the prosecution of Dreyfus. When Raymond Poincaré, the Finance Minister, exercised his prerogative to request a special session of the Cabinet on Saturday, November 3, General Mercier showed up determined to rout his opponents by sheer force of personality. For reasons which even he probably did not understand, his bluff succeeded. The unrelated struggle between the Minister of Foreign Affairs and the Minister of Colonies influenced the outcome. At the center of their dispute was the wisdom of sending a French expedition across Central Africa to stymie British expansion from the Cape to Cairo. The Minister of Colonies favored the scheme and had won the support of the Cabinet.

Because the Foreign Minister opposed Mercier on the Dreyfus case, the ministers supporting the Colonial Minister resisted Hanotaux's arguments.* Mercier was allowed to pursue the Dreyfus affair as he saw fit, but he soon discovered that his ministerial *carte blanche* accomplished very little.

For the next six weeks Mercier's subordinates floundered. They could produce not one shred of supporting evidence. Finally, even *France Militaire*, the prestigious daily paper of military affairs, attacked the investigation: "What is at the bottom of this scandal? . . . A document of such controversial value that the handwriting experts have failed to agree upon it, that the prosecution is compelled to accept a mass of presumptions of moral proofs in the absence of better evidence. All this is sufficient to make one knock on wood because this case has been so awkwardly, so foolishly undertaken." This editorial was suspiciously similar to statements being made privately by General Saussier, the Military Governor. Mercier undoubtedly heard that, at a weekend hunt at Marly, Saussier told the President of France that the General Staff was over its head. "That fool Mercier has put his finger in his own eye again," his rival boasted.

President Casimir-Périer was deeply worried. On December 18, the eve of the court-martial, Paléologue, head of intelligence for the Foreign Ministry, called on this neuralgic bachelor who shared the Élysée Palace with his domineering mother. Paléologue was astounded by the President's attitude. Pausing to make certain the servants were out of hearing, Casimir-Périer asked Paléologue for his impression of Bertillon, the handwriting expert. "He's very highly thought of at the Prefecture, he's said to be ingenious but rather odd."

"Odd, odd," the President interrupted, "he's not odd; he is mad, and in such a cabalistic way that I'm completely overwhelmed by him!" The President also confided that the War Minister had sworn the documents listed in the *bordereau* were

---

* Roger G. Brown, *Fashoda Reconsidered* (Baltimore, 1969), Ch. 6.

of "no great importance." The President of France was inclined
to believe that Dreyfus would be acquitted.

Years after the conviction of Captain Dreyfus, General
Mercier admitted that he "would have preferred to have taken
more time [with the investigation] but the newspaper dis-
closures made this impossible." His refusal to question Dreyfus'
guilt made it easier—even reasonable—for him to expedite
punishment of the traitor. And since Dreyfus was guilty *a priori*,
Mercier saw no harm in exaggerating the defendant's crime.
Mercier knew that the items listed on the *bordereau* had no
great importance to German military intelligence. Eleven days
after the degradation he reassured the commanding general of
the Seventh Corps that the plans for the covering troops "have
not been the object of any revelation whatsoever and that,
consequently, the allegations published by the press are without foundation." Nor would the Army be compelled to revise
its mobilization plans. But Mercier confided such assurances to
a small circle of senior generals while the most alarmist supposi-
tions by the public grew apace.

Qualities which would have recommended Mercier in war-
fare—supreme self-confidence, careful planning, and vigorous
initiative—were disastrous to Dreyfus. While the Military Governor smirked and Staff officers fretted, the Minister of War
knew precisely what tactics were necessary to convict an
accused traitor. Shortly after the arrest he wrote the Military
Governor insisting that the court-martial take place *in camera*.
Then came his statements to the press. Next there was the
matter of evidence. Mercier ordered Major Du Paty to prepare
a "commentary," an adverse summary of Dreyfus' character
based on the gleanings from Sandherr's files and the gossip
assembled by agent Guénée. He also ordered Sandherr to bring
everything from his files which might bear on the case. When
Du Paty's commentary proved too mild, Mercier substituted
his own composition. At that moment he knew that henceforth
he could never abandon the role of Dreyfus' persecutor.

Mercier's several-page commentary claimed that information from the Russian military attaché and research by Counterintelligence revealed a history of suspicious behavior dating from the years before the War College. Dreyfus had praised the German administration of Alsace, had made secret trips to Mulhouse and to Germany, and had been conspicuous in learning about matters unrelated to his assignments. Specifically, Mercier's commentary charged that while assigned to Bourges Dreyfus had sold the Germans details of Turpin's melinite explosive and that at the War College he sent them his lecture notes on troop mobilization.

The so-called Secret Dossier which Mercier entrusted to Major Du Paty for the court-martial judges contained five documents in addition to the commentary:

1. The "Scoundrel D" (Alexandrine) letter written by Panizzardi, the Italian military attaché, and taken from Schwartzkoppen's wastebasket.

2. The letter about securing information from *"un ami"* written by Panizzardi, also taken from the military attaché's wastebasket.

3. A collection of torn pieces of paper delivered by Madame Bastian whose unintelligibility gave them an aura of malign significance.

4. A summary of the warnings of former Spanish military attaché Val Carlos to Counterintelligence—notably his statement, "There is a wolf or two in your sheepfold."

5. The original, erroneous version of the Panizzardi telegram with Major Henry's contribution, "Dreyfus arrested, precautions taken, our emissary warned."

By communicating these documents secretly, Mercier flagrantly violated the rights of the defendant. Therefore, when Major Du Paty returned the Secret Dossier, the Minister of War was compelled to commit another crime: in the presence of Colonel Sandherr and Du Paty he burnt his commentary and ordered the chief of Counterintelligence to scatter the other documents throughout his archives. But Sandherr disobeyed.

Inserting a copy of Du Paty's commentary in the Secret Dossier, he sealed it and filed it in a special cabinet. After all, the day might come when questions about Dreyfus would be raised, and Sandherr knew that General Mercier would then no longer be the Minister of War.

Sandherr was already concerned about the German reaction. At first Ambassador Count Münster had forbearingly dismissed newspaper attempts to "gather dirt to throw at the embassy and at me." As a formality he protested to the French government, on December 12, when the press openly accused Germany of dealings with Dreyfus. The truth was that, for the German Ambassador, the case was unintelligible. "The secret has been well-kept and nobody knows what really happened," he wrote Berlin. Dining in Berlin at the end of December with the Kaiser, the Chancellor, and the Army Chief of Staff, Colonel von Schwartzkoppen was equally perplexed—"I was only able to say that the whole affair was incomprehensible to me." The Kaiser remarked that the French appeared to be going to extremes to insult Germany. On the evening of the degradation, with the Paris press damning Germany and publishing Captain Lebrun-Renault's mangled conversation with Dreyfus, William II exploded. His Chancellor cabled Ambassador Münster an insulting message for the French President:

> If it is proved that the German Embassy has never been involved in the Dreyfus Affair, His Majesty hopes that the government of the Republic will not hesitate to declare the fact. Failing a formal declaration, [this] would compromise the situation of the Kaiser's representative.

Although the Ambassador softened the prose before delivery on the evening of January 6, he demanded the French government issue a communiqué exonerating "the embassies and legations in Paris" of espionage. Foreign Minister Hanotaux's fear of serious Franco-German diplomatic rupture had not been alarmist. The French government immediately used its considerable influence with the press to end comment on the Dreyfus case.

If Dreyfus had been a vindictive man, he might have been consoled by the calamities which shortly overtook both Mercier and Sandherr. President Casimir-Périer, who had never wanted to be President, unexpectedly resigned eleven days after the degradation ceremony. Keen political observers believed the resignation to be partially motivated by Casimir-Périer's session with Münster, during which he had felt humiliated by his Cabinet's failure (especially that of the Foreign and War Ministers) to keep him fully informed of developments in the case. On January 17, in accordance with the Constitution, the Chamber and Senate convened at Versailles to elect his successor. Mercier allowed his name to be placed in nomination. He received three votes for his pains, and on the second ballot Félix Faure, the Minister of the Navy, became the sixth President of the Third Republic. The new Prime Minister, Alexandre Ribot, selected another general, Émile Zurlinden, to hold the portfolio of Minister of War. General Zurlinden took Mercier's advice about sending Dreyfus to Devil's Island, a comfort of sorts to the erstwhile War Minister now reassigned to command an Army corps away from Paris.

Colonel Sandherr was fatally ill, for several years the victim of a progressive paralysis. Within a few weeks his incurable malady worsened. The fifty-year-old chief of Counterintelligence forced himself to remain at his post for another four months, increasingly paralyzed and stuporous. When a zealous editor wanted to publish an account of Dreyfus' alleged confession to the captain commanding the military escort at the degradation, Sandherr wrote a letter to the editor begging him to abandon the article. He ended on a note of such complete spiritual fatigue that it had the resonance of an epitaph:

> No, don't publish the article! Dreyfus did not confess to the captain of the Garde Républicaine. The less we speak of this sad affair the better.*

---

* "Les Aveux de Dreyfus," *Figaro*, July 31, 1899.

chapter six:
EXILE AT WORLD'S END

SOUTHEAST OF VENEZUELA, ABOUT FOUR DE-
grees above the equator, lies the overseas department of French
Guiana or Cayenne. Columbus had been disappointed by the
region, dismissing it as a deadly spot of impenetrable jungle
and treacherous swamp populated by inhospitable natives. By
the late sixteenth century, however, when Europeans were
searching desperately to find the pre-Columbian Eden, Guiana
came to be included within the vast, vague borders of the land
of El Dorado. By the dawn of the eighteenth century the territory, now a possession of the King of France, was known with
certainty not to be the land of wealth and eternal life. It was
forgotten.

In the year of the Treaty of Paris, 1763, when England
stripped France of most of her colonial empire, Louis XV
commanded that Guiana be peopled. Royal whim was enforced,
and some twelve thousand Frenchmen (mostly Alsatians) were
beguiled and compelled to South America. Hostile Indians,
warring mosquitoes, and an intractable jungle decimated this

ill-provisioned expedition. A year later only a few demoralized hundreds still huddled together on the three offshore islands, Royale, Saint Joseph's, and Devil's—the last, the smallest and least accessible because of the swift current around it. The survivors understandably named the three, *Les Îles du Salut*— the Salvation Islands.

The government soon learned the secret of economic success in large sugar, pepper, and hardwood plantations tended by African slaves. Under the overseer's whip the slaves constructed an ingenious irrigation network and turned the jungle's edge back upon itself. By the middle of the nineteenth century Guiana promised to become as prosperous as Haiti had once been under French rule. Then in 1848, after deposing the uninspiring Louis Philippe, the French proclaimed the Second Republic and, as the First had done, the Second Republic abolished slavery.

When Napoleon III abolished the Republic four years later, the jungle had advanced across the rich plantation fields and through the open irrigation veins to the banks of the Atlantic. The new emperor believed he had a solution combining colonial prosperity and humanitarianism: he declared the area a penal colony. This scheme also failed. The climate, the jungle, the Indians, and the ex-slaves were too much for the criminal dregs of France. In 1867 Napoleon III decreed that convicts were no longer to be deported to the South American possession and its islands.

Alfred Dreyfus was as yet unaware of the unique perdition reserved for him by the Minister of War. While he waited for Lucie to visit him in Saint-Martin on the Île de Ré, Devil's Island was being readied. Its small leper colony had already been evacuated and a stone dwelling was rising tier by tier to the tropically slow rhythm of convict labor. In 1884 righteous politicians of the Third Republic had reestablished a penal colony for hardened criminals on the Guiana mainland, a short distance from Cayenne, the capital city. On February 9, 1895, President Félix Faure signed legislation allowing the Salvation Islands to be used again for criminal confinement, and General Zurlinden, the new Minister of War, immediately obliged Mercier by applying the law retroactively to Dreyfus.

The climate of Devil's Island, less than a mile long, is healthier than on the mainland. In July and August the temperature in the shade spurts to near ninety but there is the steady relief of ocean winds, and during the good months of February and March there is an invigorating breeze over the island. The heat, even at its stabbing, sudorific worst, is almost humane when compared to the rainy season. The rains begin in April and last three months, then begin again in November, falling on and on until the end of January. It is a time of insect-breeding clamminess that seems endless, a time of madness.

Escape from Devil's Island is all but impossible. The current around the island is so powerful that only a sturdy vessel can slice through it. To swim it is certain death because of the sharks. Even should the escapee survive these perils, he must still reach the mainland ten miles away without being observed from the neighboring islands of Royale and Saint Joseph's. Napoleon's rival, General Charles Pichegru, managed the impossible and returned to France; so did the twentieth-century spiritual disciple of Alexandre Dumas, Papillon. They and one other escaped from Devil's Island. But for the other political prisoners marooned there, the only consolations have been the sea, the breezes, and a desperate hope of pardon.

Had Dreyfus known his fate, he might not have cared much at the time. At Saint-Martin he was totally involved in his correspondence with Lucie. He was forbidden to receive letters from others, even Mathieu, and he could write to no one but Lucie. Until the end of January Lucie's letters arrived regularly. Then, abruptly and without explanation, they were withheld. "I've not had your news for ten days," he wrote. "It would be impossible to tell you about my sufferings." In her last letter, written on January 27, three weeks after the degradation, there had been news of the children. His son, Pierrot, now almost four years old, had spent Sunday morning showing his two-year-old sister photographs of their father. There was the especially impressive one of Dreyfus in uniform on horseback and another when he was a first lieutenant at the Bourges artillery school. Lucie described for him the charm of the scene: Pierrot gravely lecturing little Jeanne on details of the uniform, the pedigree of the horse, the skills taught at Bourges—all of which "was over her head, [but] Jeanne was listening respectfully." Until February 7 there were no more letters.

On February 13 Dreyfus saw his wife for the first time since leaving Paris, a month earlier. The terms were harsh: two visits of one hour each, weekly; the prison director was to be present, standing between them in his office; physical contact and discussion of the case were forbidden. When Lucie returned for her second visit, she pleaded with the director for permission to embrace her husband; his hands could be tied behind his back if only she could simply touch him. This request was refused. The next week she visited for the last time. Immediately after their meeting the prisoner was stripped, searched, and ordered to gather his toilet articles. Late that afternoon he was returned to the port of La Rochelle and put aboard the transport ship *Saint-Nazaire*, anchored in the harbor of Rochefort. His iron cell was like a refrigerator, the temperature outside seven degrees above zero. The evening of February 22, nearly twenty-four hours later, the *Saint-Nazaire* weighed anchor.

When Dreyfus was at last able to write about the voyage to Guiana, he said very little to Lucie about its rigors, sparing her any mention of the freezing temperatures of the first seven days at sea. He said nothing about the near inedible stuff dished up in rusting food tins; nothing about the silent, armed sentinels standing day and night at his door. He did mention that on the fifth day he was allowed an hour's walk on the deck. He told her how glad he had been for the warming weather. But he found the heat of the final week of the journey increasingly uncomfortable.

Alfred confessed to Lucie that the physical hardship was severe but far less punishing than the spiritual anguish he suffered. The Army, the nation, the world believed he was a traitor; a lifetime of humane confinement with his wife and children in scenic New Caledonia would have been no antidote to his pain. He remained the tortured but objective Staff officer. He wrote: "One can accord no pity to a traitor; he is the lowest of scoundrels. So long as I represent this wretch I can only approve these measures. But your heart will tell you all that I have suffered."

The worst part of Dreyfus' crossing occurred at the end. For three days, March 12–15, the *Saint-Nazaire* anchored offshore. The house on Devil's Island was still under construction. While messages were cabled back and forth between Cayenne and Paris, Dreyfus sweltered below deck in his iron cell until final instructions arrived from the Ministry of Colonies.

Finally, Paris ordered him placed temporarily in a cell on the offshore island of Royale. For a month, while the convicts on Devil's Island languidly toiled, Dreyfus was shut away in an incubator on Royale, denied even a few minutes' exercise, spoken to by no one, and aware of the progress of night into day only because of the sunlight wedging between the slats of his shutters. The house on Devil's was ready just in time to save him from going mad, but not before he suffered his first apoplectic seizure. There would be many more.

After the bitter experience of the *Saint-Nazaire* brig and the stifling cell on Royale, the transfer to Devil's Island seemed a blessing. It would have been more agreeable if the stone hut had been erected at the opposite end of the island which rose fifty feet above sea level in a crown of palms and waxy green vegetation. But even the lower, unshaded location afforded a remarkable view of the sea and of the sister islands. Behind the hut was a bench. There, after the baking sun had wound around the hut, he could gaze upon the endless expanse of water. The little prison house measured four yards square; its two windows unobstructed except for thin iron bars. Built onto the front was a smaller dwelling, two yards by three, in which Dreyfus' guards sat for two-hour stints observing his slightest movements through an open steel door. The guards were not supposed to talk to their prisoner. But they were an independent lot and Dreyfus' passion for chess seduced them. Very shortly most of them became chatty adversaries and one became a fanatic chess partner.

While Dreyfus won at chess, Lucie and Mathieu took steps to provide him with the special amenities customarily permitted a political prisoner. In Cayenne, the capital of the colony, was a prosperous mulatto merchant whom they asked to serve as their agent to deliver food, clothing, and medicines to the island. The request was in no way unusual. Even among ordinary prisoners, the *bagnards* convicted of theft and murder, there was a flourishing trade in such commodities. But Dreyfus' case was destined for special handling. That honor among thieves which embraces every offense known to man excluded the unnatural crime of treason. When Monsieur Dufourg's clients (nearly all ex-convicts) heard the news of the merchant's new commission, they were scandalized; they began to boycott his store. That was not the worst of it. Monsieur Dufourg received an admonitory visit from the commissioner of police. Within the month the merchant regretfully informed Lucie and Mathieu that he was compelled to renounce his commission.

Alfred Dreyfus was a quietly resilient man, a man who behaved, at least in the beginning, as if it were improper even to complain of the compounding severities of his punishment. Because of his family, his honor, and his stubborn faith in the Army and the nation, he met each outrage with admirable dignity. He had the satisfaction of knowing that in dishonor he had behaved with a nobility that troubled, embarrassed, and impressed France. "Your dignity, your splendid behavior struck the hearts of many people," Lucie had written. It was true. She also felt that when his day of exoneration came, "the remembrance of the suffering you endured . . . will be engraved upon men's memories." He believed this also—had to believe it. And yet, three months and eight days had elapsed since then, and he was nearly six thousand miles from France.

The Gehenna of the passage and the weeks on Royale had

already made a profound difference. His perdition was assuming a timelessness, taking on a pedestrian character. For the first time Dreyfus began to face up to the possibility that he might die on Devil's Island and that his innocence might become a matter for conjecture by lawyers and historians. On a Sunday evening, April 14, 1895, the second day after his transfer to Devil's Island, he began his diary. On the covering page was the ominous instruction, "To be handed over to my wife." A man of ideals and of logic, he was becoming bewildered to the point of despair. The second paragraph of the diary was an eloquent testimony of his mood:

> Until now I made a cult of reason. I used to believe in the logic of things and events. Finally, I used to believe in human justice! Whatever was bizarre, out of the ordinary, penetrated my brain only with the greatest difficulty. Alas, what a total collapse of all my beliefs, of all my sound faculties of reason!

Honor was life for Alfred Dreyfus and family dishonor was infinitely worse than death.

> Who steals my purse steals trash; 'tis something, nothing;
> 'Twas mine, 'tis his, and has been slave to thousands;
> But he that filches from me my good name
> Robs me of that which not enriches him
> And makes me poor indeed.

These lines from *Othello* he recited to himself over and over and they found their way into letters to Lucie. So long as the stigma of treason existed, he had to survive. "When I promised you to go on living," he had written his wife a few hours after the degradation, "when I promised to bear up until my name has been vindicated, I made the greatest sacrifice possible for a man of feeling and integrity." He had entered into a covenant whose terms were irrevocable.

The ex-captain still had the reflexes of a soldier. In captivity the important thing was to keep busy, to have a routine. He created a regimen for himself; up at five-thirty for his toilet, fol-

lowed by the lighting of the kindling to heat water for tea or
coffee and to boil the dried vegetables. At eight o'clock a guard
brought the daily ration. If there was meat, he put it on the stove
immediately to slow the rot (meat became rancid very quickly in
the tropical heat). At nine o'clock he had breakfast. After that,
he cleaned up, did the laundry, and chopped wood for the next
day. He could then add to the diary and write to Lucie. After
that, "I read, I work, I dream, and I suffer until three o'clock."
Then he strolled around the island, paced around the stone
house, and sat on the bench behind it to stare at the sea. In
the evenings, after dinner, he wrote another letter to Lucie,
spoke to the diary, and read.

There was no physical cruelty yet. His Corsican guards were
sometimes surly, but they were still an easygoing lot. It was
the unaccustomed climate that tortured him. The infernal heat
made tremendous demands upon a constitution formed in Alsace and northern France. The dearth of green vegetables and
eggs and the few proteins derived from the tiny ration of rancid
meat were more debilitating than the heat. Dreyfus was lucky
to discover a small patch of tomatoes at the far end of the island
left by one of the evacuated lepers. There was also the sporadic
kindness of the colony's governor who sent boxes of concentrated milk. But it was impossible to make up for the deficiencies
of the diet. Dreyfus' body compensated by shriveling in upon
itself, the hair thinned, the teeth loosened, and the flesh pared
down until it was little more than yellowed membrane stretched
over weakening bone. Physical debilitation progressed slowly
and even with deceptive reprieves, but it came as certainly as
the weeks of rains and the months of blinding, stupefying heat.

Dreyfus was allowed a small library of French and English
classics, an English dictionary, and a grammar. In addition, he
received a few anodyne magazines posted by Lucie. But none
of this was proof against madness. Horizons of shoreless waters,
the canopy of luminous sky stretching endlessly over a steamy
islet forgotten by France, the circuit of footsteps round and
round the stone hut—neither Lucie's letters nor the balm of

his own innocence could relieve the mental agony. "This tyranny of the sea over me is violent," he protested. "This roaring sea endlessly growling and shouting at my feet, how it echoes my soul! The froth of the wave breaking on the rocks has such a milky whiteness that I want to roll myself up in it and lose myself there."

Fantasies of escape into the sea were unusual for Dreyfus. He was neither a mystic nor a fatalist; the occasional visions of suicide served only as a release for his rage. His moods rotated: black despair, then anger; torpor, then alert mental activity. Yet, despite all that had happened which was irrational and obscure, Dreyfus was emotionally incapable of disbelieving in the primacy and ultimate victory of reason.

That same trust in justice and reason must also have kept him from cynicism. To Dreyfus the whole thing was simply too preposterous, too unintelligible: "Where are my fine dreams of youth?" he asked his diary. "Where are the aspirations of my adult life? . . . What is the mystery of this drama? Even today I don't understand it." A few days later he returned to the theme: "How can it be said that in our century and in a country like France, imbued with ideas of justice and truth, something as fundamentally unjust as this can happen?" The prisoner on his island believed that in France they must already suspect a terrible mistake had been committed; Du Paty de Clam was likely to be on the trail of the real spy. A week after he opened his diary he wrote to Félix Faure, the new President of France. He also wrote Major Du Paty about his promise to continue the investigation. General de Boisdeffre, the Chief of Staff, received a letter at the same time. Dreyfus' faith in the Army was as strong as ever.

Throughout April, he suffered from attacks of colic and fever. "I have just tried to sleep but after a few minutes of drowsiness I wake up with a burning fever." The nights without sleep left him stuporous and weak. When occasionally he did sleep, it was only because of immense exhaustion, and when he awakened, the dreams of the night—of Lucie and the professional triumphs of the past—pursued him cruelly. The rains had not reached their full force yet, but as they fell with greater intensity several times each week, he was forced to remain indoors. When it was not raining, the heat was still too intense for him to leave the hut between ten and three o'clock. "I can't study English during the entire day," he complained to the diary. "But the moment I turn in, no matter how exhausted I am, my nerves take over, my brain starts to work." It was the last week of April and the winds had begun to rake the island. In a few days the monsoons would begin in earnest.

The therapy he needed was news from Lucie. He knew that the mail came twice monthly. From his hut he could see the steamer heading for the mainland. A day or so later the mailboat would dock at Royale, less than a quarter of a mile away. If there was mail for him, a small boat would be sent over from Royale. More than six weeks had elapsed since the *Saint-Nazaire* had brought him to Guiana, six weeks of censored silence from his family. On the morning of May 2, Dreyfus watched anxiously from his window as the rowboat navigated the fast current between Royale and Devil's. "My heart is beating until it's about to break. Is it at long last bringing me the letters from my wife that have been at Cayenne for more than a month? Am I going to be able to read her sweet thoughts finally, to get an echo of her affection?" The guard brought a thin packet containing Lucie's letters. His joy was hysterical. He fell upon them like a nomad at an oasis. But the packet contained only the letters Lucie had written while he was at the prison of Saint-Martin-de-Ré. Lucie's letters to Devil's Island had been returned to France, because the Colonial Ministry had failed to inform the family that correspondence would not be delivered unless first deposited at Paris headquarters. "In spite of that," Dreyfus told the diary, "I cried a long while over these two-and-a-half-month-old letters." That night he slept and dreamt of Lucie and the children.

Eight days later, on May 10, his fever increased. "I have to fight against my body. It mustn't be allowed to collapse before

I'm vindicated." Nevertheless, he and his diary were powerless
to stop the rot; he was beginning to sink. In the next sentence
he spoke of the "frightful day—fits of crying, crises of nerves."
By May 16 there were "continual fevers, a stronger outburst
than yesterday, followed by a stroke." His guards became increasingly concerned. At first, they gave him coffee and extra
rations of bread. They had a vested interest in his survival;
watching over a solitary political prisoner on Devil's Island was
much more pleasant than custodial duty on Royale or the mainland. When the situation called for the ultimate remedy, they
prepared a broth made from dried snakes. Dreyfus found the
brew only slightly worse than his normal diet of rancid lard,
grounds of green coffee, granules of brown sugar, and "a few
grains of rice." "I threw all this into the sea." The next day
the commandant of the islands was alarmed enough to send
Doctor Delrieu, the resident physician on Royale, to examine
the prisoner. Delrieu prescribed forty grams of quinine daily
and authorized the delivery of twelve boxes of condensed milk
along with a supply of bicarbonate of soda.

Quinine and milk checked Dreyfus' fever somewhat—enough,
at least, so he could write several pages to Lucie on May 18.
It is the only surviving letter that contains a long message to
his son. Why Dreyfus wrote so few letters to Pierrot during these
years of exile is a mystery. Certainly it was not any lack of
deep affection. Perhaps it was from a desire to shield the boy
and his sister from their own natural curiosity. By not writing
to his children directly, Dreyfus let Lucie fit "Papa's" messages
to their moods and to the explanations she gave them of his
mysterious "voyage," the special mission which kept him away
from home. Dreyfus wrote his son:

> *Cher petit* Pierre,
> Papa sends you and little Jeanne great big kisses. Papa
> often thinks of both of you. You must show little Jeanne
> how to make pretty little towers with the wood blocks, tall
> ones like I used to make for you which toppled over so
> nicely. Be very well-behaved. When your mother is sad give

her fond and good caresses. . . . When Papa comes back
from his travels you will come and find him at the
station. . . . More big kisses for you and Jeanne.

Ton Papa

"Continual rains," the diary complained, as nearly six weeks
of primeval rains beat down furiously. "Heavy weather, suffo-
cating, sapping. Ah, my nerves, what they make me suffer!"
Inside the clammy hut the insects materialized as if by spontaneous combustion. During the day the hut was a miasma of
smoke from the primitive stove, of decomposing insect carcasses,
and of human excrescence. During the night the endless drub-
bing on the roof, the clamminess, and the bugs made sleep impossible. "I'm covered with pimples caused by the bites of flies
and other insects." The legions of ants were the worst; the tins
filled with kerosene which the prisoner placed under the table
legs and supports of the stove and bed were not effective. The
ants still swarmed everywhere.

The guards were still determined to help with snake broth,
extra rations of salt, and advice. The commandant released two
boxes of preserves from the prison stores. The medicines, the
lepers' tomatoes, the milk, and occasionally the tough meat made
Dreyfus feel better. By the end of May he was limiting himself
to milk, tea, bread, and water, "no longer eating that food which
repels me so much."

On June 9, nearly a month after the last letters from Lucie,
Dreyfus despaired: "My heart bleeds so that everything is a
wound for me. Death would be a deliverance." Then three days
later the commandant of the islands himself brought letters from
Lucie. "They want to know at Paris whether or not you have
a code dictionary," he told Dreyfus. "Look for it," the prisoner
challenged. The bureaucrats in the Ministry of Colonies suspected that Dreyfus' letters might be in code. Violating regulations, Dreyfus tried to grill the officer about the disposition of
his case. "Well, they certainly don't seem to believe you're
innocent," was the extent of the commandant's reply. The de-

livery of the letters was merely fortuitous, for the commandant was charged with another mission. Dreyfus learned that he would have to remain in his hut whenever convict laborers came from Royale to work on the island. The order went into effect that same day.

"They've locked me up in my hut—ah, the ugliness of humanity!" At first, the restriction did not seem too burdensome. Lucie wrote that the children were well, that she believed in him, that he should not worry. She was forbidden to discuss his case or to talk about politics. He read the letters over and over. He heard the convicts outside, hammering and cursing. He tried to console himself with the letters and the family photographs. He had nothing to say to the Royale convicts and certainly nothing could have been learned from them. Ordinary criminals felt no solidarity with a Staff officer convicted of treason. They knew that France was spending more than ten thousand gold francs annually for the maintenance of this special prisoner. They resented him and thought he should have been shot.

During the second week of June, two months after his transfer to Devil's Island, there were a few minutes of sunlight during the convicts' absence when Dreyfus was able to stroll about the island barefoot. When the torrent resumed, marooning him indoors, he fixed his restless attention on the photographs of Lucie, Jeanne, and Pierrot which he kept on his small table. Sometimes he sat staring at them for hours until he could almost hear Lucie's low voice and the children's noises. Sometimes he talked to them in the diary, usually with patience and great tenderness. But there were times when anxiety and rage broke through and spilled over into his letters. "I ask you to forgive me," he begged Lucie two months after reaching Guiana, "if I have added to your grief at times by my complainings, by showing a feverish impatience to see the light . . . shining in upon this mystery against which my reason is battling in vain. But you know my nervous temperament, my hasty, passionate disposition."

The bitterness of his monologues was as understandable as

the rebellion of his digestive system before its grisly diet. Someone, somewhere in France, had to uncover new evidence. The
traitor might still be operating. Lucie, Mathieu, the family,
General de Boisdeffre, Major Du Paty must not waste too much
more time finding the man: "I want absolute and total light shed
on this dark affair—it must happen." Looking at Lucie and the
children, brooding over his brilliant past, Dreyfus would savagely assault the diary when he thought about the traitor:

> The wretch who committed this infamous crime will be
> exposed. If only I had him for just five minutes I'd make
> him go through all the tortures he's made me endure. I'd
> tear out his heart and his guts without pity!

Righteous anger nourished sanity; it was the surrogate of
hope. The rains ended, the season of blistering dry heat began.
Restriction to his hut was now a brutal sentence. Colic and
fever returned; he was plagued by insomnia. "But all this is
nothing," the diary recorded. "It's my brain, my heart, which
suffers and achingly howls. When will the traitor be discovered,
when will I understand the truth about this tragic case? Will
I live that long?" Outside the stone cabin the convicts slowly
finished their job, and on July 7 they left the island. Few days
excepted, Dreyfus had been confined to quarters for twenty-
five days. Now that he was allowed greater freedom to move
about, he was unable to do so.

> The heat is terrible. The portion of the island open to me
> is completely exposed. Even the palm trees manage to live
> only on the other part.
> I spend the greater part of my days in my cabin. And
> nothing to read! Last month's magazines have not yet
> reached me.
> And during this time, what is happening to my wife,
> my children?
> And always this tomb-like silence surrounds me.

By July 21 he was again seriously ill: "fever all night, an
urge throughout the night to vomit." Two nights later he was

suffering rheumatic spasms "mostly in the region between the shoulders." Again, milk, tea, quinine, and willpower brought him around, but the heat had become deadly. And while he waited for better weather, Paris ordered his ration of meat reduced to half a pound twice a week.

Nine days later his favorite guard was relieved of duty because of fever. This was the second guard to succumb to fever in the three and a half months Dreyfus had been on Devil's Island. Two days later he saw the mail ship sailing past to Cayenne. There was nothing on it for him—"*toujours rien.*" His insomnia returned and the heat was unbearable. He neglected the diary; the entry for August 10 reads: "It's been a long time since I added anything. . . . What's the use?" A few days later he managed the despondent comment, "How happy are the dead." At last, on September 7, the rowboat lurched through the current with mail.

"My dear Fred," Lucie wrote:

> Today it is raining and I can't take the children for their walk. And so I have spent the entire afternoon reading the letters you have written since our frightful disaster. I have been terribly shaken. I have relived hour by hour those painful crises through which we have passed. But all that is over now; let us say no more about it. I am calm now and full of confidence. I feel that happiness is coming.

"Full of confidence," Lucie soothed, but this was not enough. "The guilty party still hasn't been discovered," the diary protested.

The heat was subsiding now, but the island was buffetted by winds so strong that his guards had difficulty reaching the hut and the small meat ration could not be brought over from Royale. At the end of September Dreyfus' depression was so severe that he was almost ready to welcome death: "Sometimes I am so utterly disheartened, so utterly tired, that I want to stretch myself out, to let myself go and be through with living, but without killing myself, for, alas, I don't have the right—I don't have this right and I shall never have it." Again he wrote to the President of the Republic:

> If I have survived, *Monsieur le President*, if I am still alive, it is because the sacred duty that I must fulfill vis-à-vis my family fills my soul and governs it. Otherwise, I would already have succumbed under a burden too heavy for human shoulders.

President Faure forwarded the letter to a bureaucrat who would draft the brief negative reply. Meanwhile, Lucie's letters piled up in the drawers of Colonial Ministry censors or on the desk of the official in Cayenne assigned to read her letters a second time. Another month went by and the diary became anemic and fitful. "I no longer know how I manage to live," it confessed. "My brain is pulverized."

chapter seven

A SENSATION OF IMPOTENCE

In FRANCE THE DREYFUSES AND THE HADA-mards, Lucie's family, were nearing the end of their tether and were beginning to fear the riddle might never be solved. Immediately after the degradation, Mathieu had written to the Kaiser and had canvassed the politicians and journalists who might be willing to aid the family. The results had been disappointing. Senator Auguste Scheurer-Kestner, a fellow Alsatian, was polite but uninterested. Jules Siegfried, a former Minister and prominent Protestant Deputy, promised to use his influence to make sure that Dreyfus was treated humanely, but more than that he could not do for a traitor. The Minister of War, General Zurlinden, another Alsatian, informed a cousin of his from Mulhouse (the cousin was a friend of Mathieu's) that the evidence against Dreyfus was conclusive. Maître Demange was given the same assurance when he spoke to the Attorney General, another outstanding public servant.

Among the politicians only two offered to help the Dreyfuses. One was an Alsatian, Auguste Lalance, and the other a

retired Army officer, General Théodore Jung, who had been
private secretary to the music-hall Napoleon, General Boulanger.
Jung told Mathieu that he was certain his brother was innocent
and that the verdict "was the work of the Jesuits." The Paris
press, which customarily swarmed at the slightest hint of political scandal, drew back from Mathieu with uncharacteristic
integrity. Neither *Le Figaro* nor *Le Journal*, enlightened and
influential newspapers, would touch the case. The respected
editor of *Le Siècle*, Yves Guyot, was renowned for defending
unpopular causes but he sympathetically counseled Mathieu to
abandon any ideas of a press campaign. "The current against
your brother is so strong, so powerful," Guyot warned, "that
only the discovery of the guilty party could lead to a change
of course." As Mathieu said, "After the degradation, a void
grew around us."

Even Bernard Lazare, the brilliant and pugnacious Jewish
littérateur, wanted nothing to do with the family at first. "Why
should I?" he replied to a well-meaning friend. "Of course, if
he were some poor devil, I would be worried about him soon
enough. But Dreyfus and his people are very rich, they say;
they will know how to get along very well without me, especially if he is innocent." When it became obvious to him that
the Dreyfuses could not get along very well, Lazare did vol-
unteer his services. Expose the flimsiness of the evidence,
Lazare urged, denounce anti-Semitism, attack the good faith
of the officers. But neither the Dreyfuses nor the Hadamards
had wanted to declare war on the Army in the newspapers.
Before the court-martial and afterward, they were restrained
by a prudence typical of assimilated, upper-class Jews.

There were some who were only too willing to help. A
Madame Bernard volunteered her knowledge of the treasonous
activities of a particular officer. Without payment she offered
to give Mathieu certain documents that this officer was about
to pass to the Germans. Madame Bernard was convincing, but
Mathieu divined that she was a police agent assigned to entrap
the family. Then there was the distinguished, retired major of

martial bearing, mustaches and beard à *l'Empire*, who played his part superbly and was discovered just in time to be another police plant.

The families also received letters containing spurious information and requests for money in exchange for important revelations. Packets were deposited at the Hadamards' or Mathieu's door with notes announcing that their contents would clear Alfred Dreyfus. More often than not they contained documents prepared by vigilant police who still hoped to entrap the family. Sometimes the well-intentioned and the opportunists, as well as the masquerading police, had to be forcibly ejected from the Hadamard household by Henri and Reine Lacour, the faithful couple who spent thirty-five years in the service of Lucie's parents.

Then there was Doctor Gibert from Le Havre and his friend, Léonie, a professional medium. The President of the Republic himself had confided to Doctor Gibert that certain documents were presented secretly to the judges in order to assure Alfred Dreyfus' conviction. Astounded, the physician begged President Faure to intervene before the prisoner was transported to Devil's Island. The President conceded that the judicial proceedings had certainly been irregular and perhaps regrettable, but he frankly admitted that the legal quibble could rout him from the Élysée Palace. Besides, how much justice was owed a traitor in uniform?

When the doctor returned to Le Havre, he sought the advice of his medium friend, Léonie. Soon Mathieu went to Le Havre at Gibert's invitation but without revealing his identity to the seer.

At the séance Léonie identified Mathieu, cited personal details of his life, and, sinking deeper into her trance, transported herself aboard the *Saint-Nazaire*. "Why are you wearing spectacles? Who gave you these spectacles?" Léonie intoned.

But his brother never wore spectacles, only a pince-nez, Mathieu interrupted.

"No, no," Léonie cried out angrily, "I know what I'm say-ing. I say they are spectacles."

Her trance continued as she addressed Alfred Dreyfus: "You will go farther, much farther, but you will return, that is certain. I do not know when. I do not know the time, but for certain, for certain, you will return."

Clairvoyance was very much in vogue among wealthy Euro-peans during the 1890s and Mathieu did not doubt its validity. But, after several sessions, Léonie's visions remained vague and Mathieu turned his attention to more practical investiga-tions. Later, when Lucie received her first letter from Alfred, she and Mathieu learned that he had, in fact, broken his pince-nez and now wore the spectacles given him by the ship's captain.*

Each day was a nightmare for the Dreyfuses. The respect for privacy which the French have perfected to an almost anti-social degree did not apply to the Dreyfus family. Strange, sinister people hovered around, pestered the concierge, wrote terrifying letters. Occasionally Lucie took her children for a stroll. More often she entrusted them to Virginie, their strong, silent nurse. With Virginie there was less risk that Pierrot and Jeanne would be molested by some crude anti-Semite or drunken patriot. There were few visits from old friends, and the children had no playmates except Mathieu's two children, five-year-old Marguerite and Émile, one year younger. ("We were pariahs," Jeanne remarked many years later.)

Worse than that, they were completely helpless. With his peculiar courage, Dreyfus wrote encouragingly to his father-in-law, "Console yourself, dear father, we must look to a future before which we haven't the right to give way." The advice was splendid but the whole family still felt what Mathieu described as "this sensation of impotence, of the nullity of our efforts." None of them could forget those other letters in which the despair between the lines was in larger script than

* Mathieu Dreyfus, "Souvenirs."

the heroic formulas. Mathieu knew that "each hour that passed was a century of suffering for the agonizing unfortunate over there and a step more toward death."

Summer 1895 came. To escape the curious, the malevolent, and the vigilant, Mathieu rented an estate near Saint-Cloud, a few miles outside Paris, in the name of his married sister, Henriette Valabrègue. For the children it was to be an idyllic vacation. Every day two-year-old Jeanne gathered flowers for Uncle Mathieu to send to Papa. Pierrot, now four, supplied accompanying letters asking his father why he was staying away so long. Although Lucie continued to wear black, as she had since the degradation, she seemed almost gay. It helped a little just to be together that summer without the dread of unknown callers and unwanted parcels. The assurances of the Grand Rabbi, Zadoc Kahn, that he believed in Dreyfus' innocence consoled the families, as did the visits of Major Forzinetti and his son. At least a few people in positions of authority would stick by them.

Forzinetti's loyalty was remarkable. At great risk to his career, the lame prison commandant had done what even the defendant's lawyer, Maître Demange, would not. A few days after the degradation, when Mathieu went to Cherche-Midi prison to express appreciation, Forzinetti gave him a copy of d'Ormescheville's indictment along with Dreyfus' rebuttal to the charges. "I insisted upon your brother's making this copy," Forzinetti told Mathieu at the time. "It will be very useful to you when the day comes that you believe you should start up a press campaign." Demange had dutifully surrendered his copy to the Ministry of War.

Forzinetti's visits gave the Dreyfuses pleasure for another reason. His young son was barely able to hide his infatuation for Mathieu's wife, Suzanne. Blonde, sparkling, strikingly proportioned, she complemented her husband admirably. The young Forzinetti was captivated and the ladies found his attentions a source of titillating diversion. But the Saint-Cloud idyll had to end and the two families returned to the capital at the close of September 1895, somewhat refreshed and determined to hasten the return of the prisoner on Devil's Island. It was going to be extraordinarily difficult.

Since the degradation the families had found only one promising lead—the irregularity of the court-martial evidence. Demange had heard of the secret documents given to the judges, and he consulted former Attorney General Ludovic Trarieux about it. The sincerely mistaken Trarieux replied that, although the Counterintelligence Section did have a document mentioning Dreyfus by the initial D, it had not been offered in evidence. So another lead seemed to go nowhere, and the year ended bleakly for the Dreyfuses.

Early in 1896 Mathieu learned just how far the police were prepared to go in order to stop his investigation. The Prefect of Police had assigned an agent to seduce Lucie's cook, whom Mathieu had employed when Lucie moved to her parents' home. The vigilant concierge informed Mathieu of the tryst just in time to prevent the compromise of several of Mathieu's schemes.

The first of these schemes involved a porter named Pessin who had been fired from his post at the German Embassy. Pessin's wife was English and, Mathieu's source claimed, felt still somewhat alien. On the slim chance that the Pessins knew something, Mathieu traveled to London on April 15 to hire a private detective. The ex-porter's wife was as lonely and as confiding to the lady detective as the Dreyfuses had hoped. Unfortunately, though, neither she nor her husband knew anything about German spies.

Two possibilities remained—the German military attaché, Schwartzkoppen, and the press. On the advice of his English private detectives, Mathieu hired an accomplished *femme fatale* to win the affections of the attaché. An intimate dinner was arranged. Schwartzkoppen attended and was "*très aimable*," but nothing came of it. Had Schwartzkoppen's dinner companion been a charming male, Mathieu's scheme might have had a better chance of succeeding.

The belated decision to use the newspapers was also an extremely dangerous one. No French newspaper would touch the Dreyfus case without positive evidence of judicial error. Still wary of Bernard Lazare's services, Mathieu did the next best thing. On his London trip he had arranged for a British newspaper to stand by to publish a fabricated report of Alfred Dreyfus' escape from Devil's Island. On September 3, 1896, obedient to Mathieu's instructions, the *Daily Chronicle* printed a brief article allegedly reprinted from the *South Wales Argus* which reported that Captain Dreyfus, almost a year and a half after confinement on Devil's Island, had escaped aboard the ship of a Captain Hunter. The French press took note of the story immediately. The next day the disreputable *Libre Parole* even provided its half million readers with a verbatim text of an interview with Captain Hunter. That the captain and his ship were shortly proven to be nonexistent was airily dismissed by Drumont's subscribers as another proof of *La Libre Parole's* creative passion to amuse and to satisfy. The French government issued a denial of the escape almost immediately. Nevertheless, Mathieu's intended result was achieved: for a few days Alfred Dreyfus lived again in the minds of his countrymen. There was even an encouraging notice of a forthcoming series on Dreyfus in the newspaper *Le Jour*. (Unfortunately, the journalist, Adolphe Possien, accepted a bribe from the General Staff to remain silent.) It was not too much to hope, the family believed, that the gossip and interest stirred up might somehow yield the first clue.

On the eleventh day after the *Daily Chronicle* ruse Mathieu had his clue. An anonymous article entitled "The Traitor" appeared in the sensationalist *Éclair*. After a résumé of the facts of the case, the author revealed for the first time in public that Dreyfus' guilt had been established by a secret document intercepted by Counterintelligence and which, unknown to the defense, had been presented to the seven officers of the court in closed session. The article explained that this document had been prepared in the most complex cipher used by a certain foreign power. Dreyfus' judges had received it with an attached translation. In the interests of national security, it was unthinkable that a traitor and his attorney should see the original document, lest the foreign power in question learn that its code had been broken.

Mathieu had no way of knowing then that the pen behind the anonymous article belonged to Major Du Paty de Clam, but it was obvious that the *Éclair* piece had been written with semiofficial sanction. Someone, probably in one of the ministries or in the Army High Command, was worried enough to inspire a spirited counterattack intended to sweep Dreyfus sympathizers from the field. The same strategy that had been used on the seven court-martial judges was now being tried on the public —but with a serious miscalculation. Mathieu now knew that his brother's conviction had been in violation of the rights of the accused. It was a revelation that outraged Ludovic Trarieux, the former Attorney General. Professor Albert Réville's reaction was typical of those who were capable of objectivity. "One can breathe again," Réville had the quasi-fictional hero of his contemporary novel declare:

> Ah, but hold on there. What's this? This document has been presented to the military judges in order to finish convincing them without either the accused or his lawyer having any knowledge of it? That's what spoils my peace of mind.

At the Élysée Palace President Faure must have recalled the advice of his friend Doctor Gibert—not to imprison Dreyfus on Devil's Island without fully investigating his conviction. The politicians in the Chamber were also in an awkward position. With Maître Demange's assistance Lucie prepared a request for her husband's retrial. This request was delivered to the President of the Chamber of Deputies on September 19, 1896, exactly one year and nine months after the original court-martial had convened.

Another consequence of Mathieu's contrived *Daily Chronicle* article was unfolding; this one entirely unforeseen. At the end of April 1896 a new government had been installed under the leadership of Jules Méline. André Lebon, the new Minister of Colonies, the man ultimately responsible for the conditions of Dreyfus' imprisonment, had the impressive bearing of a well-born squire and the literary culture which distinguished the cream of the French bourgeoisie. It was not generally known, even in government circles, that the new Minister of Colonies belonged to a close-knit group of patrician republicans who were convinced that republican democracy was much too serious a business to be left to the people, to a "rule from the streets." "Today, anti-Semitism is in," Colonel Hubert Lyautey, the future conqueror of Morocco, had written to the group after the degradation, just as the masses "were shouting a hundred years ago—'Hang the aristocrats from the lampposts!' and in 1870, 'On to Berlin!' "

Sensing that the Dreyfus Case had great potential to excite popular unrest, the new Colonial Minister suppressed his natural compassion in everything relating to it. His duty was to treat Dreyfus sternly, without any concern whatsoever for the opinions of the prisoner's few sympathizers or his innumerable enemies. Lebon was much disturbed by the *Daily Chronicle* bombshell; the cable from Cayenne stating that Dreyfus was still on the island came as an immense relief. But no sooner had it arrived than the Colonial Minister's private secretary handed him an intercepted letter mailed to Dreyfus from Paris and dated September 4. Lebon was staggered. It was hurriedly arranged for the General Staff's archivist, Gribelin, representing the Minister of War, to meet with Lebon. Together they examined the letter. Written in invisible ink, between innocuous lines relating a marriage in Basel, was a message "Impossible to decipher last communication. Give me precise information as to where the documents of interest are—also the combination to the strongbox." The signature—Weil, Weiss or, probably, Weyler—was illegible. Was it possible that Dreyfus had an accomplice, that there was a cache of undiscovered secrets vital to France's security somewhere, and that Dreyfus had some secret means of communicating with the outside world?

Lebon's and Gribelin's panic would have been even greater had they known that in October 1895 another letter containing an invisible message actually reached Dreyfus. "Wire broken," the fictitious writer, "Cousin Blenheim," said. "Try to repair it. Our two attempts have failed. We must be careful. They nearly discovered all. Let me know where 2249 was hidden. They know about Jura 34." For some reason the special ink in the Cousin Blenheim letter failed to become visible and the puzzled Dreyfus filed it away in a drawer. The author of these mysterious letters remains unknown to this day, although the technique is similar to that of Du Paty's *bordereau* dictation.

After conferring with Prime Minister Méline's new Minister of War, General Jean-Baptiste Billot, Colonial Minister Lebon decided to have the intercepted letter copied—including the secret message—and forwarded to Cayenne with instructions that Dreyfus should be spied on while he read it. After several weeks the report of Guiana's governor arrived: the prisoner had appeared puzzled and had put the letter in a drawer. Lebon did not wait for this news before dispatching instructions so severe that the only man Dreyfus came to hate was the Minister of Colonies. On September 4 Lebon commanded that Dreyfus was to be confined to his hut during the day and manacled to his bed at night until further orders. The commandant of the islands was also told to construct two wooden palisades around the hut and to double the guards.

On Devil's Island the neglected diary began to speak again: "I was placed in irons yesterday evening! Why?" Dreyfus had experienced nothing like this during the seventeen months he had been on the island. His limbs immobilized by four U-shaped iron bars inverted and fitted into wooden blocks at the head and foot of his bed, Dreyfus lay like a mounted insect from sunset till daybreak. This torture was the final, physical

version of a crucifixion that until then had been largely mental
and spiritual. And it was consummately horrible. "How much
more time will I spend like this?" There was nothing his guards
could tell him. If his jailers thought he could endure such treat-
ment, they misjudged the capacity of a man to will his survival.
"I hope that this horrible torture ends soon—if not, I leave
my children to France, to the motherland that I have always
served with devotion and loyalty." On the second day, September 7, he still refused to rage against the authorities. He
felt "only a great compassion."

Two days later the commandant of the islands crossed from
Royale to explain what was happening. He did so on his own
authority and with a sense of shame he made only a half-
hearted effort to hide. He told the prisoner that the shackled
confinement "was not a punishment but a security measure."
That was too much. Fury which had been mastered only by
Dreyfus' tremendous self-control, which had spurted through
in only a few letters to Lucie, now overflowed onto the commandant:

> No, things have to be told as they are! This is a measure of
> hatred, of torture, ordered from Paris by people who,
> because they can't strike down a family, smash an innocent
> man because neither he nor his family can nor should give
> up before the most shameful miscarriage of justice
> that has ever been committed!

The commandant was moved. In an act rare for a civil servant
anywhere, he wrote an official protest to Paris. The result was
that he was immediately recalled and the stupidly brutal Deniel
was appointed commandant. Deniel would exceed even Minister
Lebon's cold-blooded desire for relentless vigilance.

Less than twelve hours after the commandant's visit Dreyfus
wrote: "I am so terribly tired, so utterly broken in body and
soul, that I am stopping this diary as of today." His next letter
was alarming. The original has been lost and Lucie's censored
copy bears the month but not the day Dreyfus wrote it. Its

tone suggests that the letter was composed around September 10, the day the diary was silenced: "I have endured so many things that I am indifferent to life and I speak to you as though from the grave, from the eternal silence which lifts one above all things."

For more than two months Dreyfus was subjected to the Minister of Colonies' regimen. During the day he swooned in his incubator of a hut and fought the ants, spider crabs, and anopheles mosquitoes. At night the iron loops rubbed the flesh of his wrists and ankles until they bled. Outside, the convicts from Royale constructed the two palisades as ordered by Lebon. The first, made of thick wood, was eight feet high and precisely five feet away from the walls of the hut: it totally blocked Dreyfus' window view of the sea and cut off the slight circulation of air which had once cooled and freshened the infernal dwelling. The second wooden palisade was one hundred and thirty feet long and fifty-five feet wide. Encased in his double *cordon sanitaire*, Dreyfus had the sensation of dying slowly on an unknown planet. The edict against conversation with his guards, which had never been enforced before, was now rigorously applied. The ration of wine was reduced and the supply of magazines from France was cut off.

Lucie knew that now more than ever her husband needed the love and admiration of his family, so she had Pierrot and Jeanne write to their father. On October 10 three-year-old Jeanne printed: "Papa darling, I want you to come back soon. You must ask God. I ask him every day. With much love. *Ta petite* Jeanne."

"Dear Papa," Pierrot wrote; "I cried this morning because you do not come back and that makes me very sad. I want to say something which will please you: I am very good and Mama told me that she was pleased. With much love. Pierre." Dreyfus was fortunate to receive these letters. Lebon did not allow any of the other letters written in October to pass. Even so, these letters from the children were not delivered until December. During the same period, from early October until

December 15, 1896, the family heard nothing from Devil's Island. At Lebon's Ministry of Colonies clerks were reading and rereading the prisoner's mail for the slightest hint of coded message.

Cut off from the world, Dreyfus consoled himself with his small library. Fortunately, it was varied. There were several works by Balzac, the complete works of Shakespeare in French, Montaigne's *Essays*, Gustave Lanson's *Histoire de la Littérature Française*; *Études sur la Littérature Contemporaine* by Edmond Schérer, Augustin Thierry's *Récits des Temps Merovingiens*, the *Mémoires* of the Revolutionist Vicomte de Barras, and volumes seven and eight of the *Histoire Générale* of Lavisse and Rambaud. What he read most, committing passages to memory and peppering his letters with quotations from them, were the works of Shakespeare. He read *Hamlet, King Lear,* and *Othello* over and over. "I never understood the great writer so well," his autobiography says, "as during this tragic epoch." He also would ponder the words of Schopenhauer: "If God created the world, I should not wish to be God."

Colonial Minister Lebon continued to worry about his prisoner during 1897. It occurred to him that even Dreyfus' death could embarrass the government. Therefore the next ship to Cayenne carried a quantity of embalming fluid with special instructions to be followed should Dreyfus die. Standard procedure for inhabitants of the Safety Islands was burial at sea. The sharks usually devoured the corpse as it touched the water. But Lebon wanted Dreyfus preserved: "There would always be doubters who would refuse to admit his death and would accuse you of having allowed him to escape. If he dies, embalm him immediately and send his cadaver to France so that it can be seen."

There was another reason for the Colonial Minister's precautions. In a set of instructions to Cayenne, he had improved upon the government's chances of being rid of Dreyfus by commanding that the prisoner be shot if he acted suspiciously or if any attempt was made to rescue him. Lebon had heard that "international Jewry" was offering half a million dollars for Dreyfus' rescue. On June 6, 1897, therefore, the islands had their first mock alert. Dreyfus was wise enough to remain motionless on his bed during the excitement while his new guard nervously fingered a revolver.

Shortly after this alert the medical officer of the islands, Doctor Delrieu, recommended that the prisoner be housed in a larger building erected at the other end of Devil's Island, on the cooler, small promontory of palms and foliage. The doctor reported the prisoner's health and morale had deteriorated markedly. But Lebon took another pound of flesh first.

While the building went up, Dreyfus was kept in the hut. When he finally moved to the new house on August 25, 1897, he found that even the minimal privacy he had once enjoyed became impossible because of a metal grill dividing his quarters in half: on one side, he would endure his existence; on the other, an armed guard would observe his every move. The windows were too high to see from but they gave better light and ventilation than had those in the old dwelling. Eventually the iron bars on these windows were covered with wire mesh and, afterward, with triangular pieces of sheet metal. The single palisade around this house was a good distance from the walls and allowed some air to circulate. "All said and done," Dreyfus was somewhat relieved to find that this larger prison "was preferable to the first."

What became worse from then on—much worse—was the harassment and the custodial measures enforced by the paranoid Commandant Deniel. An observation tower was built supporting a Hotchkiss machine gun, there were more alerts, and guards were ordered to talk at the tops of their voices and to march about noisily at night. It was a nightmarish time:

> More than ever I had to maintain a haughty attitude in order to keep them from getting a hold on me. Traps were set for me, insidious questions were asked me. . . . In my restless nights, when I was a prey to nightmares, the

guard came near my bed in order to catch words escaping
from my lips.

On October 1, after Dreyfus had suffered a severe fainting
spell probably brought on by a weakened heart, the governor of
the colony accompanied Deniel to the island to investigate.
On his previous visits the Governor had always found that the
prisoner "maintained the greatest reserve and often even a
complete silence." Once or twice he had complained but "without any acrimony or violence." But just before his collapse
Dreyfus had demanded special medication from the pharmacy,
which Deniel had refused. The prisoner's mood now was fierce.
It was inhuman to make him suffer this way, he shouted.
Deniel warned him to be quiet, but the prisoner continued to
shout as the two officials began to walk to the boat. Dreyfus
asked his guard to catch up with them and beg them to return;
he would be calm if they did. He made a stupendous effort at
self-control but the strain had been too great for too long:

> They want to terrorize my wife; they want to terrorize my
> whole family but patience has limits to it and one of
> these days, finding herself at the end of her strength, my
> wife will go to see the Kaiser, holding each of our children
> by the hand, and throwing herself on her knees she will
> say to him: "Sire, you who know the truth, put an end to
> my husband's martyrdom, restore a rehabilitated father to
> his children."

Glaring at the commandant and the governor through thick
glasses, Dreyfus the patriot and the correct officer warned,
"Somebody wants a scandal; he'll have it."

It is clear from his report that the governor was shaken.
However, he did not want to lose the Colonial Minister's confidence. In his report to Paris he hinted that Dreyfus may
have been shamming, citing Dreyfus' pause to retrieve his hat
from the house before continuing his show of anger. "For a
man who wished for death more than anything else, he did

not forget to take precautions to stay alive," the governor wrote, adding that, "while busy appearing to be mad, he did not lose control of himself easily." This sort of evasion was characteristic of the Guiana authorities. In early July, with the governor's endorsement, they had forwarded to the Ministry of Colonies their opinion of the letters Dreyfus had received since his arrival. The evaluation of Lucie's letters was cruelly disingenuous. "One senses," the writer declared, "that the author of these letters does not have a well-founded conviction of the innocence of her husband." This, of course, was just what Paris wanted to hear.*

After more than two and a half years of agony Captain Alfred Dreyfus finally believed that he could no longer sustain either mind or flesh and that the act he had sworn he would never commit was, after all, inevitable. Obliquely he made his intention known to Doctor Delrieu in mid-December 1897. "I am sick, Doctor, that explains the state of my morale. I am feverish; I can no longer stand up. I have given up. I'm at the end of my forces, Doctor, but what I dread most is losing my mind." He asked Delrieu to give him something to keep going for just one more month. Then, if there was no news from France about the traitor, he was going to end the suffering.

---

* Rapport de M. le Gouverneur [Guyane Française–Cayenne, 7 Octobre, 1897], *Secret Dossier*, No. 115.

chapter eight:

AN HONEST MAN

MAJOR GEORGES PICQUART WAS NOT A VIRU-
lent anti-Semite who contended that the Jew, because of his
retarded religious precepts and mean political convictions, was
an everlasting enemy of morality and the social order. Picquart's aversion to Jews was more casual–and more complex.
Like the Marquis Du Paty de Clam, whose intellectual arrogance and elevated tastes he shared, Picquart was politely
indifferent to Jews, sometimes even convivial in his social and
professional dealings with them. For a sensitive, cosmopolitan
man, frank bigotry would have been out of character.

On the other hand, Picquart's refinement made him dislike
Jewry in general because of its supposed lack of the finer
graces. Observing Dreyfus' red-eyed glance at the heap of braid,
epaulettes, and stripes torn from his uniform during the degradation, Picquart had superciliously remarked to another
officer, "He looks like a Jewish tailor estimating the value
of the cloth." Later, after the fate of Alfred Dreyfus became
enmeshed with his own, he would be testy with those who

misspelled his name: "P-I-C-Q-U-A-R-T—not Picard!" he would admonish, the latter being a name borne by many French Jews.

The major's views about Jews in general and Alfred Dreyfus in particular would probably never have changed, and would certainly have remained unimportant, but for the death of the chief of the Counterintelligence Section, Colonel Jean Sandherr. When Dreyfus was shipped off to Devil's Island, Picquart, like Du Paty de Clam, was relieved to be rid of the whole affair. It had bothered him because he knew his former student well enough to doubt the accusation and because he felt that the Army's evidence had been exceedingly circumstantial, if not shabby. He had expected an acquittal; when Dreyfus was found guilty, Picquart easily persuaded himself that the secret evidence submitted to the court must have contained definitive proofs. Though he had no liking for Sandherr, he was impressed by his extraordinary dedication. Picquart knew that Sandherr was dying, that the Dreyfus conviction would be his last triumph. Picquart marveled that Sandherr held himself erect until the end, reporting for duty like a zombie, racked by pain, the focus gone from his once alert, skeptical eyes, his single-track mind no longer able to concentrate. By the end of June 1895 Sandherr was dead. Immediately General de Boisdeffre asked Picquart to replace him.

For Picquart there was no honor in the offer. He shared the prejudices of the Army's elite officers about counterintelligence. Although a Saint-Cyrien, Sandherr had been an intelligent and pleasant vulgarian. Picquart was the soigné bachelor who enlivened evenings at the Comtesse Blanche de Comminges' and did his best to avoid the rough and unread equestrians of the officer corps. To be chief of Counterintelligence was to hold a position appropriate for some officer whose breeding permitted him to read other people's mail or to bend a knee before a keyhole. Picquart wanted to decline. The Chief of Staff insisted; the Minister of War, General Billot, tried flattery. What Billot said was true; there was probably not an officer of equal rank in London, Berlin, Saint Petersburg, or Rome who was

superior to Picquart in languages or general military knowledge.
He spoke and wrote Italian, German, English, and Russian
fluently. His familiarity with the materiel and organization of
foreign armies was dazzling. Given the lavish funds provided
by the French government for intelligence work, his appointment would produce an ideal union of talent and resources.
General the Marquis Gaston de Galliffet, a permanent member
of the Army's Superior War Council and Picquart's most important patron, was of the same mind as the Chief of Staff and
the Minister of War. Reluctantly Picquart agreed; on July 1,
1895, six months after Dreyfus' degradation, the forty-two-
year-old Staff officer assumed command of Counterintelligence.

The Counterintelligence Section was in a deplorable mess.
During Sandherr's last months Major Joseph Henry and Captain
Jules Lauth had been in charge. They had not been efficient.
Entry to the Statistical Section had been uncontrolled.
Picquart had passes printed and insisted that the guards deny
admission to any caller without one. Sandherr had allowed his
subordinates complete discretion in handling incoming documents. Picquart ordered that henceforth information was to
be submitted directly to the Section chief, who would judge
its value before final deciphering and reconstruction. But not
even he thought of having the Section's documents dated upon
receipt, and this oversight was to prove troublesome later.
Picquart also broke contact with Sandherr's agents. It was
a healthy decision, as some of them, like Guénée, were both
corrupt and stupid. However, it had not occurred to Picquart's
predecessor to prepare a list of reliable agents, and as a result
Counterintelligence temporarily lost contact with one of its most
useful agents in Berlin.

It is also unfortunate and even strange that Major Henry
said nothing to his new superior about the Dreyfus Case. Just
before dying, Sandherr had told Henry to "nourish" the Dreyfus Secret Dossier, a recommendation reiterated by the Chief
of Staff. Picquart would have been interested in what Henry

knew. He was ignorant of the telegram sent by the Italian Chief of Staff to his military attaché in Paris, Colonel Panizzardi, immediately after the public revelation of Dreyfus' arrest, which stated that Italy had no knowledge of a Captain Dreyfus. At the time, what was known in Berlin about French espionage was known in Rome as well. Picquart was also unaware that only a few weeks after the degradation Counterintelligence had received a message from Berlin which should have triggered a careful investigation. "In Paris there is someone who is admirably well informed and in the pay of Lieutenant Colonel von Schwartzkoppen," it revealed. The source of the message was an employee in the *Nachrichtenbüro*, Richard Cuers, one of Sandherr's most valuable agents. Cuers had described the author of the *bordereau* with uncanny accuracy:

> The person in question is about forty-five and decorated with the Legion of Honor but it is not known whether he is a civilian or an officer. He goes to the embassy in the Rue de Lille frequently and even wears his Legion of Honor ribbon in his lapel. He passes numerous reports to Schwartzkoppen. The last report relates to the manufacture in France of a new artillery piece.*

Cuers promised to obtain the name of the spy shortly. In a later message, he confirmed that the subject was an officer. The name, however, continued to elude him.

Why nothing came of Cuers' revelation is one of the major mysteries of Dreyfus' fight for exoneration. Nothing in Sandherr's career suggests that he would have tolerated treason. Sandherr's death within a few months of the Cuers report may have aborted a plan to bring the spy to justice. But there is another, more plausible explanation of Esterhazy's continuing immunity. Rather than outrage the public with another scandal involving a traitorous officer, rather than ruin the careers of high-ranking officers and politicians, Sandherr may have intended to trap Cuers' spy and force him to act as a double

---

* Note of April 1895. *Révision du Procès de Rennes*, March 1904, p. 19.

agent. This is certainly the best explanation why Cuers' startling information was filed without comment.

Picquart had been in charge of Counterintelligence about eight months when his predecessor's unfinished business began to surface. Once again, it was the cleaning woman, Madame Bastian, who was the bearer of alarming news. Sometime in mid-March 1896 Captain Lauth handed Picquart a small, folded note reconstructed from thirty-seven scraps of paper retrieved from Schwartzkoppen's wastebasket. The document, a blue express letter (or *petit bleu*) issued by the Paris postal department, had never been transmitted through the underground pneumatic tube system. This particular letter was addressed to Major Esterhazy, 27 Rue de la Bienfaisance. At this point the chief of Counterintelligence knew nothing about Major Esterhazy, but after reading the message in the *petit bleu*, Picquart decided to learn as much as possible as soon as possible.

Despite his devotion to espionage, Ferdinand Esterhazy's affairs continued to deteriorate after delivery of the *bordereau*. Schwartzkoppen was a tightfisted benefactor, paying a thousand francs for this and seven hundred francs for that piece of information rather than a fixed annuity. It was barely enough to placate creditors. Meanwhile, Esterhazy's fixed expenses were rapidly mounting. His property, what was left of it, was heavily mortgaged. And despite his energetic tutelage, Madame Esterhazy refused to improve her mind. She still read trashy novels, and Saint-Simon for the genealogy. In the early years she had been an avid if maladroit sexual partner; now even this bond had snapped because of her illness, the neurasthenia inherited from her father. There was nothing Esterhazy could do but take a mistress, a strong-backed peasant girl named Marguerite Pays, for whom, of course, he had to lease a Paris apartment. His two sickly daughters also required regular and expensive medical supervision. Esterhazy tried diligently to gamble himself into solvency but was consistently unsuccessful.

In early 1895 he engineered an assignment with the Seventy-fourth Infantry Regiment in Paris where he hoped to push his career through his old friend Maurice Weil and his powerful patron in the Chamber, Jules Roche. Nothing happened fast enough, however, and his mistress, his daughters, and his creditors were suffering greatly.

Ironically, the anti-Semitism which Esterhazy had done much to foster benefited him through Jewish largesse. Just as Dreyfus was being transported to Devil's Island, Esterhazy with Weil's help was exploiting the gratitude of prominent Jews who remembered Esterhazy's support during the *Libre Parole* duels. In advising his friend, Weil was highly effective. "Leave this to me. I was born among these people. I know the approach to take." Even the Grand Rabbi, Zadoc Kahn, agreed to liquidate six thousand francs of Esterhazy's debts. Baron Edmond de Rothschild sent Esterhazy a check for two thousand francs. If the sum was modest, a philanthropic gesture by a Rothschild possessed an almost sacramental importance. Obviously, certain Jews did not intend that an aristocratic officer should suffer on their account without offering their help. Delighted, Esterhazy tried to inveigle the baron into making a further donation. He wrote a ridiculously familiar letter promising to hand over some highly useful information if his old high school friend would pay a visit "around ten some morning" to the military barracks. It appears that Baron Edmond never bothered to reply. There were also several liberal Catholic prelates who contributed to Esterhazy's favorite charity at this time. Weil, whose uncle was a bishop, had represented his friend as a reckless, high-minded aristocrat who could be of inestimable value to the cause of religious tolerance in the Army if his brilliant career were not jeopardized by mean-spirited superiors.

The few thousand francs Esterhazy shared with Weil were far from sufficient to save him from his creditors. Schwartzkoppen was still his last best hope. If he could deliver more valuable material to the Germans, if he could really betray his country instead of conjuring facts out of gossip and thin air,

Berlin would have to meet his price. He decided the only position worth his talents was one on the General Staff. Throughout most of 1896 and into the following year Esterhazy used and abused every possible contact, sending a stream of letters to politicians and generals as he tried to maneuver himself behind a desk at Staff headquarters. His political patron, Deputy Roche, gave him flattering references; General Saussier gave Weil promises. A three-star general who had been a friend of Esterhazy's father wrote a letter on Esterhazy's behalf and even went to see the Minister of War to hasten the transfer.

All this august patronage resulted only in vague promises for Esterhazy and his supporters. Tugging at his otter-like mustache and muttering ambiguously, General Billot, the Minister of War, refused to hurry, almost as though he suspected that there was something not quite right about the applicant.

Maurice Weil resented these delays as much as Esterhazy did. Unprincipled, but as loyal to his friends as his wife was generous to them, Weil told Esterhazy, "As I do not want to neglect anything that could assure your success and as I am determined that you will not be able to reproach me for anything, not only will I write the boss [Saussier] . . . but even my wife, who has never asked him for anything, will make an exception in her habits and join the warmest of letters to the one I am writing to him."

While Madame Weil wrote "the warmest of letters" and Esterhazy's other protectors pressed his case, the *Nachrichtenbüro* was having grave doubts about the quality of the information it had been receiving through Schwartzkoppen. So far, nothing new had come in about the 75-mm. field gun or the French Army's new mobilization plan, matters about which Berlin was impatient to learn more and about which Esterhazy had promised to provide valuable details. He had done the best he could but with notable lack of success. Sometime before July 1895 Esterhazy had been reprimanded by Schwartzkoppen for a garbled report on the loading and firing speeds of an artillery weapon. At the beginning of 1896, when

Esterhazy was busy trying to arrange his Staff appointment, the Germans were becoming thoroughly exasperated. Exasperation turned to disgust when the chief of the *Nachrichtenbüro* learned that Esterhazy was demanding more money from the embassy. At the end of February Schwartzkoppen was ordered to break the contact.

Maximilian von Schwartzkoppen was the ultimate Prussian officer. Long-necked and tall with a slender but athletic figure that was a military tailor's delight, he was all steely elegance and composure. The public Schwartzkoppen was a charming, impeccably correct servant of his sovereign. The private man was more interesting, more suited to the sensual mouth nearly concealed by a handlebar mustache and to the doelike eyes accentuated by pencil-thin eyebrows. This Schwartzkoppen—"Maximilienne" to his intimates—was a lover of music, literature, and of those who shared with him what the French roguishly called *"le vice anglais."*

It was while spending an evening with a male friend in his apartment next to the embassy—it must have been a few days before the end of February—that Schwartzkoppen decided to inform Esterhazy that Germany was terminating his services. Although the identity of the person who served as scribe that evening will never be known, it was probably a young employee of the embassy. In any case, the hour must have been growing late; before enjoying a good cognac and soulful conversation, Schwartzkoppen had to take care of the irritating business of the letter to Major Esterhazy. He dictated a long message:

> Monsieur, I regret not speaking to you personally of a matter which is going to upset you considerably. My father has just refused the necessary funds in order to continue the voyage under the stipulated conditions. I will explain his reasons. However, I begin by informing you that, as of today, he considers your conditions too harsh for me and fears the results that may come from prolonging this journey. He proposes another round to me about which we can come to an understanding. In his judgment, the

relations that I have contracted for him to this point are not
in proportion to the expenses of these journeys. Finally, it
is essential that I talk to you as soon as possible. I am
sending you the sketches that you gave me the other day.
They are not the only ones I shall be returning.

Schwartzkoppen asked his friend to read him the text. It
was too long, too strong, too transparent in its meaning if
intercepted by French Counterintelligence. He tore up the letter
and threw it into the wastebasket. A short note sent by the postal
tubes would be better. Schwartzkoppen handed his friend a
small sheet of blue paper, the regulation paper on which such
messages were sent. It was addressed to Monsieur le Commandant Esterhazy, 27 Rue de la Bienfaisance, Paris.

Monsieur, I am above all awaiting a more detailed
explanation than that which you gave me the other day
concerning the question which is in abeyance. Hence, I beg
you to give it to me in writing so that I may be able to
decide whether or not I can continue my relations with
the House of R.

C.

That was better, more diplomatic and more cryptic. Tomorrow
he would think about sending it—it was still not quite right.
Schwartzkoppen apologized to his companion for attending to
business; then he threw the second message into the wastebasket.

On March 1 Major Picquart granted Major Henry leave to
be with his dying mother. Henry was absent, therefore, when
Captain Lauth handed the chief of Counterintelligence the
latest gleanings from Madame Bastian's wastebaskets. Picquart
was staggered. Here was another Dreyfus Case. Checking the
Army's directory, he found that Major Esterhazy belonged to
the Seventy-fourth Infantry Regiment in Paris. Picquart had
a friend in the regiment, a Major Curé. Immediately, he asked
Curé to find out what he could about Esterhazy. When Henry

returned to duty in late March, Picquart asked him to recommend an agent to shadow the suspect. Esterhazy's dossier rapidly thickened. Major Curé reported that his colleague was considered to be a sleazy officer, what Curé called a *"rastaquouère,"* an unsavory adventurer. Henry's agent confirmed the report. Picquart was convinced that Esterhazy's was the profile of a traitor. But gambling debts, a mistress, and an uneven service record would not support a charge of treason. Picquart gave orders to have Esterhazy watched day and night.

Picquart was absent from Staff headquarters during most of May because his own mother was fatally ill. Shortly after his return, recently promoted to lieutenant colonel, he was told that Richard Cuers, Sandherr's ex-double agent formerly employed by the German *Nachrichtenbüro*, knew of a French officer closely connected to the General Staff who was providing Berlin with secrets about France's defenses. Cuers, now living in Geneva, offered to identify the officer for a reasonable sum of money. Picquart would have gone to Geneva himself, but he was busy with preparations for the October visit to France of Czar Nicholas II. Instead he sent Major Henry, Captain Lauth, and Monsieur Tomps of the judiciary police to Switzerland. In Geneva, unemployed and alcoholic, Cuers hazily recounted what he knew about the French Army spy who regularly sauntered to and from the German embassy with the Legion of Honor in his lapel; but for the second time he failed to provide the name. Supporters of Dreyfus would later allege that Cuers was intimidated by the delegation from Paris, that Major Henry, especially, bullied the ex-agent each time he verged on revealing the spy's identity. In reality Cuers had simply never uncovered Esterhazy's identity, and, down on his luck, he tried to finance his recovery with professional gossip. Henry and his associates returned to Paris disgusted and informed Picquart that Cuers was an unreliable and Homeric drunkard. Henry said nothing about Cuers' first reports to Sandherr more than a year before.

Picquart was becoming obsessed by Esterhazy. He was wait-

ing for a handwriting specimen before he set his staff to thumb-
ing the section's voluminous files of unsolved cases. On
August 26 or 27, 1896, Major Curé sent Picquart a note
written by Esterhazy. Simultaneously Picquart discovered a
letter from Esterhazy applying for a position on the General
Staff. He examined the documents with an ineffable malaise.
Where had he seen this handwriting before? He was reminded
of something, a document he had looked at when Alfred Dreyfus was being tried. Of course, it was quite impossible that
. . . nevertheless, the similarity was too striking to be ignored.
Picquart summoned the archivist, Gribelin. Hadn't Colonel
Sandherr kept a special file on Dreyfus? Gribelin nodded.
Picquart wanted the Secret Dossier brought to his office im-
mediately.

A few minutes later Picquart began to tremble. For the first
time he read the documents that had damned Alfred Dreyfus
in the eyes of his military judges: the worthless scraps from
the files of Counterintelligence, the Scoundrel D letter, the one
referring to "*un ami,*" the warning from the Spanish military
attaché, and Du Paty de Clam's original essay in character
assassination which General Mercier had freely expanded. But
what unnerved Picquart was the handwriting of the *bordereau.*
The best graphologists would have to be consulted, of course,
but his knowing eyes moved back and forth from the handwriting of the *bordereau* to the letters of Esterhazy before him:
they appeared to be identical.

Like most Lorrainers, Georges Picquart was seldom im-
petuous. For two days he pored over Sandherr's file on Dreyfus,
carefully absorbing its meaning and presciently calculating the
consequences of taking action. Before making up his mind, he
spoke to Major Du Paty, who had already heard something of
the amazing discovery, probably from Gribelin. "It's the writing
of Mathieu Dreyfus!" Du Paty exclaimed upon seeing Picquart's
photocopy of Esterhazy's letter applying for a position on the
General Staff. Although the two hands were not radically dissimilar (Mathieu's was the more legible), Du Paty's reaction

was probably intended to cast more suspicion upon the Dreyfuses, to protect the verdict of the 1894 court-martial. By dragging Mathieu into the picture, the officers who had assisted in convicting Dreyfus tried to suggest that, to save Dreyfus, the Jews were inventing evidence against an innocent officer.

Because of his uncommon honesty and courage, Picquart was to become a legend in his own time. For the present, however, Lieutenant Colonel Picquart was more concerned about General de Boisdeffre's reaction to the contention that Alfred Dreyfus was expiating the treason of Ferdinand Esterhazy. Generals were not known to suffer embarrassment readily. The hint of a mistaken indictment and an irregular conviction de Boisdeffre would recognize as an intolerable arraignment of his Army stewardship. Picquart's report at the end of the month to the Chief of Staff confined itself to the gravity of the circumstantial evidence against Esterhazy and the desirability of "demanding explanations from Major Esterhazy about his relations with the German Embassy." There was no mention of the prisoner who had already spent nearly seventeen months on Devil's Island. Picquart knew that his investigation, guarded as it was, would impel the Army to review the judgment of the 1894 court-martial. Few officers would have risked as much. But then, few officers had the power and prestige of Lieutenant Colonel Picquart.

Born in Strasbourg (one of the cities wrenched away from France by the Germans in 1870), Georges Picquart had amassed one of the most remarkable records at Saint-Cyr and the War College and had sustained several injuries in colonial wars. The descendant of outstanding soldiers, lawyers, and civil servants, a *grand seigneur* without title, a Catholic republican, a favorite of the mighty General the Marquis de Galliffet, Picquart seemed assured of a brilliant future. He so enjoyed the confidence of the Chief of Staff that he scarcely bothered to observe the protocol of first consulting Brigadier General Gonse, the Vice Chief. On September 1, 1896, Picquart was invited to de Boisdeffre's office to discuss his day-old written report. He told the General more than he had included in the report; he suggested that Esterhazy's crimes might have been attributed to Dreyfus.

The Chief of Staff, whom Picquart had told about the *petit bleu* in mid-August, was stunned by the development of Picquart's investigation. "Can you imagine that I was able to sleep after what you told me?" he wrote Picquart the next day. The Chief of Staff agreed that the Minister of War should be informed. He might have hesitated had he known that the Counterintelligence chief had examined the Secret Dossier used to convict Dreyfus—the dossier that should have been destroyed by Sandherr. General de Boisdeffre did retain sufficient presence of mind to advise Lieutenant Colonel Picquart that it was more important to prove the guilt of Esterhazy than the innocence of Dreyfus.

The following morning, September 3, Picquart conferred with the Minister of War, General Billot, who possessed something of the younger officer's sense of fairness. When uninfluenced by politics, the Minister of War was known to approach a matter honorably. He shared Picquart's consternation. He was astounded when he learned of a secret Dreyfus file that proved the 1894 court-martial judges had been influenced by documents submitted illegally. And as Picquart described the file's flimsy contents, Billot expressed impatient disgust. However, one lobe of the Minister's brain was simultaneously pursuing another train of thought. He already knew a good deal about Esterhazy. On his desk were importunate letters from the so-called Count demanding assignment to the General Staff. He had also received several letters from Esterhazy's powerful supporters, including one from Deputy Jules Roche. While the military budget was being studied by Roche's commission, Billot reflected that it might be unwise to arrest the Deputy's client as a suspected spy. Heartily approving Picquart's initiative, the Minister of War invited him to return in a few days for a final decision.

Picquart left General Billot believing that he would soon be

empowered to arrest a traitor and reprieve an innocent. Buoy-
antly, he told the Chief of Staff that same day of his audience
with the Minister of War. While Picquart was relating the
outrage of General Billot over the flimsiness of the secret
dossier, General de Boisdeffre suddenly lost his composure: the
purplish veins of his cheeks, which Marcel Proust described
as Virginia creeper manured in the finest brandies, turned
white. "But why wasn't it destroyed?" he blurted. It was incredible, he continued, that Picquart had revealed a Staff secret
of such sensitivity to the Minister of War. Ministers of War
came and went almost too rapidly to be counted. The General
Staff alone had continuity, and to safeguard its mission it
adhered to an unwritten code which ordained that certain
secrets could be shared only among Staff officers. His three
stars and portfolio notwithstanding, Billot had never been "Staff"
despite his distinguished service in the Crimea and the Franco-
Prussian War.

Regaining his composure, the Chief of Staff told Picquart to
take up this business with General Gonse immediately. This
order was an unmistakable signal of the Chief's displeasure,
since it placed the commander of Counterintelligence in the
hands of a superior whose character he despised, whose intelligence he disdained, and whose authority he had consistently
ignored—so much so that he had never bothered to inform the
Vice Chief of the existence of the *petit bleu*. It may not have
been true that General Gonse owed his rank to a physical
resemblance to Napoleon III (many of the Army's senior
officers had begun their careers during the Second Empire),
nor was it quite accurate to call him, as one general did, a
"nullity become man," but certainly the rough and ready
officer was neither very bright nor notably ethical.

The Chief of Staff, General de Boisdeffre, was well aware of
Picquart's distaste for General Gonse, and the latter's bluntly
expressed disapproval of Picquart was no secret. The sole
blemish on Picquart's record was an efficiency report prepared
by the Vice Chief which stated: "In spite of [Picquart's] zeal,

he has lost ground during these last months. He has not always demonstrated a sure and correct judgment. . . . It might be beneficial to assign him to field duty where he would undoubtedly lose his fidgetiness."

Whatever ill-will the men bore one another was concealed under a mask of affability when Picquart arrived at General Gonse's summer retreat on September 3. The two of them achieved a candor and amity that promised to repair the tense mistrust of the past. De Boisdeffre had probably wired his Vice Chief to handle this prodigy gently.

All understanding and avuncular compassion, Gonse begged his subordinate to divorce the two cases; to undertake, solely for the moment, the investigation of Esterhazy's behavior. The Vice Chief argued that a conviction against Esterhazy might provide grounds for a subsequent review of the Dreyfus verdict but that each case must be treated separately. Finally, Gonse warned of the terrible Pandora's box Picquart's investigation could open. Picquart conceded much of this. However, he told Gonse that Mathieu Dreyfus had gone to London and that the family was planning somehow to agitate for Dreyfus' release. Picquart added that if, as he strongly suspected, there was a connection between the two cases, Mathieu's relentless probing could be much more damaging to the Army than the consequences of Picquart's own investigation. Gonse waved such fears aside. Unpersuaded but shaken in his confidence, Picquart returned to Paris sworn to separate Esterhazy and Dreyfus.

Returning to the capital that evening, Picquart found the newspapers carrying accounts of the apocryphal escape from Devil's Island. Before he knew what to make of this news, the Minister of Colonies, Lebon, was on the telephone about the interception of the Weyler letter, that mysterious communication inviting Dreyfus to "repair the broken wire." Picquart's first reaction—illogical but comprehensible under the circumstances—was to ascribe the letter to Mathieu. It was probably on September 6 that he decided to see the Minister of War again. Billot, whose name literally means "executioner's block," did not at all like the recent complications. "I found the Minister completely changed," Picquart said. The Minister of War snorted that Dreyfus was as guilty as sin; the matter could not be reopened. The Chief of Staff had done his work well, for he had spelled out to the Minister in Picquart's absence that Saussier, the Military Governor, who had authorized the investigation of Dreyfus and approved the court-martial would be humiliated by a full-scale review. And to investigate Esterhazy was to reinvestigate Dreyfus as well. Ruffling Deputy Roche was bad enough; smearing the reputations of the Chief of Staff and the Generalissimo, the two most important officers (after himself) in France, was out of the question. The Generalissimo was one of the untouchables of the regime. General Billot had probably heard the rumor that certain officers loyal to the memory of General Boulanger wanted to use the Dreyfus Case to avenge their lost leader whom Saussier had helped to destroy. The Minister of War decided that this fellow Picquart was not so bright after all.

For Picquart it was a difficult moment. Rebuffed by his superiors and by his own staff, he might have adopted a course of cautious subservience. Instead, he forgot the promises to General Gonse. He decided that his higher allegiance to the Army and the national welfare commanded that he get to the bottom of the two treasons before the Dreyfus family forced the truth into the open through newspapers and parliamentary allies. On September 8, nearly two weeks after connecting Esterhazy and Dreyfus, Picquart wrote to Gonse:

> A number of indications of which I will speak to you on your return show me that the moment is near when persons who are convinced that a mistake has been made regarding them are going to do their utmost [to prove it] and to cause a huge scandal.
>
> I believe that I have taken the necessary steps to allow the initiative to come from us. . . . I should add that these persons do not appear to have the same information we do and that it appears to me that their undertaking must end

in an awful mess, a huge noise which, nevertheless, will
not end by clarifying things. This will be an annoying and
useless crisis, one that it is possible to avoid by rendering
justice *in time.*

Gonse was beginning to regret his role of paterfamilias. By
return mail he cautioned again:

At the point where you are in your investigation, it is
assuredly not a matter of avoiding the light, but it must be
understood how one ought to proceed in order to arrive
at the truth. False and fatal steps have to be avoided. . . .
Prudence! Prudence! That's the word that you ought to
have before your eyes always.*

But it was not prudent of Gonse and de Boisdeffre to have inspired the article in *L'Éclair* by Major Du Paty which revealed
that a secret document, shown only to the court-martial judges,
had been used to convict Dreyfus.

Picquart's life, his career, his noble conception of his country
now weighed in the scales of forthcoming events. From this
point onward, Georges Picquart began to resemble the man
he feared most, Mathieu Dreyfus. It was one of the innumerable
ironies arising out of the *bordereau* and the *petit bleu* that
France's chief Counterintelligence sleuth and the brother of
the nation's supreme traitor, who looked so much alike physically, became devoted friends and political allies.

At the beginning of October, after Vice Chief Gonse's return
to Paris, Picquart proposed a way to determine conclusively
the guilt or innocence of Esterhazy. Gonse was asked to authorize the dispatch of a fake *petit bleu* to Esterhazy's address.
If Esterhazy came to the bogus rendezvous, he was to be arrested and questioned. Not a bad idea, Gonse thought. Picquart
was told to put his suggestion in writing. He did so, but then
was told that the Minister of War must give his approval. The
War Minister demurred: "A chief of Counterintelligence has

---

* Marcel Thomas, *L'Affaire sans Dreyfus,* pp. 217–221.

better means at his command than that." Moreover, it was too
extreme a step to take without more positive proof. General
Billot took a stand firmly in the middle. He declined to authorize
Picquart's plan in writing but left Picquart free to lay the trap
on his own authority.

Picquart faltered. The pains he had taken to secure official
sanction to trap Esterhazy were really not necessary. The
Counterintelligence Section was usually permitted a wide lati-
tude in its operations, but it had become apparent to Picquart
that even he was subject to the political and corporate rules
governing ordinary officers. The message became amply clear
in the following weeks. Monsieur Tomps of the judiciary police
had a confidential chat with Picquart; he mentioned secret
evidence of Dreyfus' guilt in the possession of the Prefecture,
insinuating vaguely the bottomless implications of a case best
left alone. Picquart was irritatingly persistent, however, and
Tomps reported to Gonse that he was not sure he had convinced
the lieutenant colonel.

Then it was Major Henry's turn. It was rare for these two
officers to have a fraternal tête-à-tête. "When I was in the
Zouaves, a private, the son of a colonel, committed a theft,"
Henry recounted. "His captain wished to prosecute: the higher
officers didn't." He told the full story of this Algerian incident
before applying a sledgehammer to the moral: "The captain
was demoted and the thief got away." Henry was condescend-
ingly thanked by his superior.

Picquart continued to probe. He told General Gonse that
Esterhazy had given his former private secretary certain documents to copy. These documents, the private secretary said in
an affidavit, corresponded to some of the shredded findings gathered from Schwartzkoppen's wastebasket. The Vice Chief had
had enough. "What is it to you if that Jew stays on Devil's
Island?" he roared.

Picquart thought he had not made himself clear or that he had
misunderstood.

"But General, he is innocent."

"It is a case that we can't reopen. General Mercier and General Saussier are involved in it!"

"But since he's innocent, General—"

"If you say nothing, no one will be any the wiser," Gonse declared.

Picquart measured his words with care, fixing the stubby-legged Gonse with a stare of ineffable defiance: "General, what you have just said is an abomination! I don't know what I shall do, but in any event I will not carry this secret to my grave."

The Vice Chief decided this brazen junior officer deserved to be broken, but the Chief of Staff would not hear of it. The Russian Czar was due in a few days for an official visit. General de Boisdeffre was sure that the Czar's visit would give him the final accolade of his career, the Saint Petersburg Embassy. Throughout October 1896 Picquart's section, sharing responsibility for security precautions, was unprecedentedly busy. Picquart did more than was expected but Gonse detected an attitude of amused contempt. A report by the Vice Chief states that "the agitation and the preoccupation [Picquart] manifested recently has given way to a certain serenity. He even affects an assured and bantering manner that seems to say: 'They're all imbeciles.' "

On October 5, 1896, the yacht of Czar Nicholas II and Czarina Alexandra was duly escorted into port at Cherbourg by the entire Channel fleet of the French Navy. The Franco-Russian Alliance became an apparently indissoluble bond only from that moment. Prime Minister Méline and President Félix Faure saw to it that no expense, no obeisance, no extravagance of public acclaim was lacking. The government, some said, gave the impression of being ashamed "at the thought of France being a Republic." There were visits to the Louvre, Notre Dame, Napoleon's tomb. Nicholas II laid a building stone for the magnificent span over the Seine named for his father, Alexander III. Alexandra slept in Marie Antoinette's bedchamber at Versailles. On the last day, seventy thousand troops paraded before the Czar, who was dressed for the occasion in a Cossack uniform, and, as a martial finale, the Algerian horsemen thundered past in a cloud of dust. Nicholas was impressed, and the French, who had not been hosts of monarchs since the fall of the Second Empire—a visit from the Shah of Iran was not to be counted—broadcast to the world the end of their enforced isolation. Taking final leave of President Faure, the Czar was reported to have asked affectionately, in the moment of embrace, *"C'est pour toujours, n'est-ce pas?" "Oui, sire, pour toujours,"* the President replied with equal feeling.

If the Romanovs and Félix Faure had been the stars of the pageant, de Boisdeffre justly esteemed himself to have been its indispensable genius. The mechanics of the Franco-Russian Alliance, if not the policy behind it, were his chef d'oeuvre, and he was elated. Now that the award of the Saint Petersburg Embassy seemed a matter merely of intelligent patience, the Chief of Staff turned his attention to Picquart's smoldering investigation. De Boisdeffre fancied himself something of a connoisseur of men; unencumbered by principles, he believed that he understood all the better the mainsprings of ambition. Billot, Gonse, Henry, all had failed with Picquart. What was needed was General de Boisdeffre's own special brand of confidentiality. Toward the end of October he invited Picquart to ride with him in the Bois de Boulogne, to discuss the mysterious letter written in secret ink to Dreyfus, the Weyler letter. It's a forgery, Picquart explained; mistakenly, he believed that Mathieu was behind it.

"Yes, but if it's not a fake," de Boisdeffre casually observed, "what a splendid proof of the guilt of Dreyfus."

They ended the ride in a show of mutual respect, but Picquart was still without permission to interrogate Esterhazy. If he insisted on that tack, the Chief of Staff drawled, Picquart could very well persevere on his own authority. Whereupon the General put spurs to his mount and rode away.

While Picquart was brooding over the apparent injustices done to Alfred Dreyfus and the unexplained behavior of Major

Esterhazy, Mathieu was making new plans to publicize his brother's case. The hoax of the escape from Devil's Island had attracted attention, and Mathieu decided to prepare another journalistic stroke in collaboration with Bernard Lazare, the militant Jewish journalist who wrote for *L'Aurore*. When Lucie's appeal for a retrial was rejected by the Chamber of Deputies at the beginning of November 1896, Mathieu decided to abandon the cautious advice of the lawyer Demange, that the family avoid action through the press. Mathieu's decision also ran counter to the counsels of the leaders of the Jewish community. For these Jews the innocence of Alfred Dreyfus was less important than the anti-Semitic furor which would arise out of public dispute. Shortly after the degradation there had been a meeting of prominent Parisian Jews at the Hadamard home to determine the measures most suitable for rehabilitating the captain. The decision of the majority was to do nothing provocative. Public action would run the risk of infuriating the government and provide ammunition to Drumont and his *Libre Parole*. Now, almost two years after Alfred's humiliation, Mathieu decided that his brother's salvation was more important than the tranquility of the Jewish community.

Mathieu and Lazare decided upon a small pamphlet as the opening salvo of their campaign. Lazare's *Une Erreur Judiciaire: La Vérité sur l'Affaire Dreyfus* appeared on November 6, 1896, published in Brussels and then immediately reprinted by the sympathetic publishing house of P.-V. Stock in Paris. Before the French edition appeared Lazare sought the cooperation of one of the most widely read chauvinist newspapers, *L'Intransigeant*, edited by the vicious Henri de Rochefort, a maverick nobleman and slightly deranged patriot. The prison commandant, Forzinetti, was asked to help. Forzinetti was to remain outside the offices of *L'Intransigeant* until Lazare signaled. Rochefort listened and seemed convinced. To clinch the argument, Lazare revealed that in the street below there was someone who was uniquely qualified to judge the guilty and innocent. If Rochefort swore to keep his identity secret, he would agree to an interview. The Nationalist editor agreed and Lazare returned after a few

minutes with Forzinetti. The commandant of the military prisons
of Paris was eloquent. Shaking hands warmly, Rochefort assured
them that his paper would remain neutral when *Une Erreur
Judiciaire* appeared the next day, November 8.

There was hardly a member of the Chamber or Senate whose
mail did not bring a copy of Lazare's electrifying pamphlet on
Monday morning, the day after its appearance. A large number
of journalists, academics, and ranking officers were included on
P.-V. Stock's list of complimentary recipients. Generals de
Boisdeffre, Saussier, and Billot had their breakfasts spoiled by
it. "I am determined to establish that the guilt of Captain
Dreyfus has never been proven," Lazare began. The ensuing
twenty-four pages revealed the conflicting opinions of the handwriting experts, denied the authenticity of the *bordereau*
(Lazare believed that a traitor would never have used his own
handwriting), and proved that the court-martial judges had been
provided with secret information forbidden the defense in
violation of the Criminal Code. What Lucie and Mathieu suspected but had never said publicly, Lazare's pamphlet broadcast as an obvious fact:

> Did I not say that Captain Dreyfus belonged to a class of
> pariahs? He is a soldier, but he is a Jew, and it is as a
> Jew above all that he was prosecuted. Because he was a Jew
> he was arrested, because he was a Jew he was convicted,
> because he was a Jew the voices of justice and of truth
> could not be heard in his favor, and the responsibility for
> condemning this man falls entirely upon those who
> provoked it by their shameful excitations, by their lies, and
> by their calumny.

Lazare concluded: "Captain Dreyfus is an innocent man and
his conviction was obtained by illegal means. I demand a review
of his trial."

It was a good try but the opposition was already on the move.
Rochefort, the "prince of the gutter press," had never intended
to honor his promise. Monday's *L'Intransigeant* carried blatant
headlines: "Vain Attempt To Rehabilitate A Traitor!" The

revelation of Forzinetti's loyalty to the Dreyfuses brought him a summary dismissal from his post and compulsory retirement from the Army. Rochefort's behavior was cruel but hardly out of character. Much more distressing was the contemptuous reaction of the Socialist press, which dismissed Lazare's essay as a "new maneuver in the campaign underhandedly led by the press, high finance, and Jewry to create public doubt about the guilt of a traitor." Mathieu began to think that the warnings of the Jewish community were justified.

Then, on November 10, came a major breakthrough. Teysonnières, the discredited handwriting expert whose testimony had helped convict Dreyfus, sold his copy of the *bordereau* to *Le Matin*, one of the largest dailies. Philippe Bunau-Varilla, the owner of the newspaper, recognized Dreyfus' miniature scrawl because, years before, two of the prisoner's essays had helped him pass an examination at the *École Polytechnique*. Bunau-Varilla saw immediately that the *bordereau* script was similar yet different and decided to have *Le Matin* reproduce the document.

While *Le Matin's* readers speculated about the *bordereau* that Tuesday morning, two men in Paris studied the document with incredulity. Schwartzkoppen had not known until that moment that it was Esterhazy's memorandum that had caused suspicion to fall upon the Jewish officer. Of course, there was nothing he could do about it—officially. But he and the Italian military attaché, Panizzardi, did agree to tell select officers in Paris, Vienna, and Rome a portion of the truth and in this way fuel the rumors of Dreyfus' innocence.

Ferdinand Esterhazy was also flabbergasted by the publication of the *bordereau*. He suspected that the Germans were behind the leak because of their recent dissatisfaction with his merchandise. He rushed to see Schwartzkoppen the next day and, to his immense relief, discovered that the latter was equally surprised. He was reassured that only the two of them (and the Italian military attaché) knew the true identity of the author of the *bordereau*. The fact that Dreyfus had been unjustly convicted was of no interest to Esterhazy.

The editor of *L'Autorité*, Paul de Cassagnac, the voice of responsible Nationalism, was becoming more alarmed with each revelation in this drama. Four days after the publication of the *bordereau* de Cassagnac broadcast his doubts about the case. Beyond an unsigned note of contested authorship, he declared, Dreyfus' judges had relied upon illegal evidence for their verdict:

> Dreyfus was convicted by the court-martial on the basis of a piece of evidence of which he knew nothing, that was never produced, and that his honorable attorney, Maître Demange, never saw! Now then, the fact of being a Jew does not give anyone in a civilized country the right of execution in such a manner.

Here was another victory for the Dreyfuses.

Who else but Picquart could be leaking information to Mathieu Dreyfus and his allies? Vice Chief Gonse was sure he could read smugness on his subordinate's face whenever they met these days. Chief of Staff de Boisdeffre decided the stakes were much too high to ignore Gonse's warnings. But action against Picquart required the support of the Minister of War. On November 12 General Billot summoned the chief of Counterintelligence to his office. Affable and confidential, Billot listened while Picquart explained the latest developments in the Dreyfus Case. Abruptly the Minister changed the subject to a new artillery shell which the Germans were rumored to be supplying to their batteries. Picquart respectfully stated that the Minister's information was erroneous and that it was not possible, as Billot suggested, for him to certify it. Picquart's word could weigh heavily in securing an upward revision of the Army budget, Billot said. Gonse immediately ordered Picquart to leave Paris that weekend to inspect intelligence organizations along France's eastern border.

Ingratiating, bovine, but far from stupid, Major Henry had remained perfectly correct in his relations with his superior.

But with Picquart away on a special assignment of indefinite duration, Henry became the acting chief of Counterintelligence. More than that, because of his dominion over the dull Gonse, he saw that his influence might make him the confidant of the Chief of Staff himself. The temptation to win the approval of his superiors at any cost was enormous. Henry had always felt that he was the true heir of Sandherr, far more so than the elegant amateur, Picquart, whose queer notions of honor threatened to embarrass the Army and wreck the careers of some of its most distinguished officers.

Throughout November 1896 Henry worked diligently. General de Boisdeffre encouraged him, as he had encouraged Du Paty more than two years before, to do what he could to find documentary weapons for the Army. One of Henry's "discoveries" was a telegram sent by Schwartzkoppen to Berlin on December 31, 1894. Decoded and translated by Henry, it read: "Your Lordship would do better to abstain from entering into relations of any sort with this person." Even with the best will, Henry's text might have been imperfect because of his ignorance of German. But Henry's text was intentionally distorted. The truth was that Schwartzkoppen's telegram clearly stated that he had knowledge neither of Dreyfus' crime nor of the full circumstances of the conviction.

Next, Henry doctored one of the intercepted "Alexandrine" notes to Schwartzkoppen pertaining to railroad timetables of the French Army. Falsifying its age by more than a year, he dated the note April 1894, because Dreyfus had served until that April in the Fourth Bureau which organized railroad timetables. One of Henry's most heinous revisions involved a wastebasket note in which the phrase, "for P . . . has brought me a lot of very interesting things," was altered to, "for D has brought me a lot of very interesting things." This note had been found in 1892 or 1893.

In order to assure the quality of his documents, Henry hired the services of a professional forger named Moise Leeman who used the alias Lemercier-Picard. Leeman edited one of the Italian military attaché's innocuous dinner invitations to his German confrere to read: "Here is the manual. I paid for you according to agreement. . . . I have invited three people from my embassy, including a Jew. Don't fail to show up." In the original, Panizzardi had said nothing about a manual, and there were no Jews in the Italian Embassy in June 1894, the spurious date assigned to the note by Henry and Leeman.

Henry's chef d'oeuvre was a remarkable fabrication, as crude as it was audacious. He had prepared it without Leeman's assistance a few days before Picquart left Paris. On November 1, 1896, Counterintelligence had received from Madame Bastian an intact envelope containing a banal message from the Italian military attaché with the salutation, "*Mon cher ami*," and the usual signature, "Alexandrine." The message was written in blue pencil on cross-ruled blue paper. That night in his apartment Henry took a blank sheet of cross-ruled paper, identical in size and texture to that used by Panizzardi, and placed it back to back with the intercepted note. He then tore them carefully so that the body of Panizzardi's message was separated from its salutation and signature. Henry discarded the message and on the center portion of the twin blank sheet he carefully forged a message in Panizzardi's handwriting. Henry knew that on November 18 a Royalist deputy had notified the President of the Chamber that he intended to question the government about a recent Dreyfus debate in the press. Henry also knew that Panizzardi's French was imperfect. His forgery took both factors into account:

> *Mon cher ami,*
> I have read that a deputy is going to ask a question about Dreyfus. If they ask for any new explanations in Rome, I will say that I never had relations with this Jew. That's understood. If anybody asks you, say just that for nobody must never know what happened with him.
>
>   Alexandrine

Taping the authentic salutation and signature to the forged body, Henry placed them in the original, postmarked envelope. He gave the letter to Gonse sometime between November 10 and 14. Eventually it became known as the "False Henry."

It seems certain that Henry went even further in his forgeries, that he and Leeman fabricated letters from Dreyfus to the Kaiser and one from William II to Ambassador Münster mentioning Dreyfus by name and implicitly establishing the captain's collusion. General de Boisdeffre and former Minister of War General Mercier were soon to whisper that Counterintelligence possessed evidence of Dreyfus' guilt from the pen of the German sovereign. In any case, although the current War Minister, Billot, may have wondered about the Army's extraordinary good fortune in obtaining this treasury of evidence so suddenly and so conveniently, the General Staff was ecstatic. One officer was not. When Vice Chief Gonse delightedly showed Major Du Paty a portion of Henry's evidence, Du Paty observed, "Some of them strike me as suspicious." When the Vice Chief of Staff deplored his wariness, Du Paty mournfully admitted, "General, I am not enthusiastic."

To Henry, he was bluntly skeptical about these "discoveries." "Henry," Du Paty warned, "take care. Your papers have a bad smell about them." * He could not have realized how fateful his warning was.

---

* *Révision du Procès de Rennes*, March 1904, pp. 252–253.

chapter nine:
THE ELUSIVE FACTS

THE TRAIN SPEEDING EASTWARD TOWARD THE
Vosges on Monday morning, November 16, 1896, carried a
deeply troubled Lieutenant Colonel Picquart. It was not easy for
him to admit that he had been outmaneuvered by a mediocrity
like Vice Chief of Staff Gonse, or that by his own miscalculation
he had forfeited, at least temporarily, the confidence of General
de Boisdeffre. Not once but several times during the past ten
weeks General Gonse had reminded Picquart that the Chief
of Staff wanted the Dreyfus Case separated from Esterhazy's.
It was clear now that when General de Boisdeffre counseled
the lieutenant colonel to watch for new facts, the only facts
were those that would keep Dreyfus on Devil's Island forever.

Gazing from his compartment window at the gray landscape,
Picquart pondered the real motives for his own actions: integrity, certainly; it was important to him that no one should
ever reproach him for moral cowardice. But Picquart knew that
his own professional ambition had weighed as heavily as his
obligation to an innocent man. That ambition still stirred within

him as he thought about what was at stake. It would be the achievement of a career as well as the counterintelligence coup of the decade to break Esterhazy and free Dreyfus. More than that, such an accomplishment would snatch the rug from under the doggedly resourceful Mathieu Dreyfus and spare Frenchmen the demoralizing revelations that Mathieu sooner or later was bound to make—revelations that might cost the Army its image of incorruptibility. Picquart would have been outraged by the suggestion that General Gonse and Major Henry were acting from similar motives of careerism, horror of scandal, and love of the Army and France.

Picquart knew that he was right, that the trial of Esterhazy and the saving of Dreyfus would finally be more important than even the careers of generals or the security of a Minister of War's portfolio. He remembered the advice of his close friend and lawyer, Louis Leblois, who urged him to take his evidence to certain politicians. He had thought then that he could never stoop to that, but now he was determined to make his superiors see where the Army's true interests lay. It was not too late, he thought, to save his career or the situation.

Picquart was in for a rude jolt. Two days after arriving at Sixth Corps headquarters in Châlons, he wrote Gonse that he intended to return to Paris over the weekend to collect some personal belongings. Immediately, a telegram ordered him to stay where he was. Two days later, on November 21, Gonse dispatched written instructions that Picquart was to expand his mission to the Alps, Grenoble, and Briançon, an undertaking which the Vice Chief estimated would keep Picquart away for another six weeks. Reading the local newspaper, Picquart found that the Dreyfus Case had been discussed in the Chamber of Deputies for the first time. Three days earlier General Billot replied to the interpellation of Royalist Deputy André Castelin that Dreyfus was securely imprisoned on his island and that the evidence of his treason was more certain than ever. Picquart assumed that the Vice Chief's orders were meant to keep him away from Paris at a time when the press and public were discussing Dreyfus. He could not have suspected that his own organization was preparing evidence against him far more efficiently than it had against Esterhazy. Agent Guénée, who was always more adept at collecting gossip than at unearthing facts, was back on the job and on the morning of the twenty-first had submitted a report to Gonse stating that Picquart's lawyer knew all the details of the Dreyfus-Esterhazy investigation. Nor could Picquart imagine that the weak and gullible Minister of War had been shown the False Henry which dispelled the last doubt of Dreyfus' guilt.

No one really wanted to destroy Picquart. Gonse disliked his impertinent superiority and independence, but the Vice Chief was not stupidly vindictive. He probably thought that after a stint of garrison duty in the hinterlands, Picquart would be more more than willing to fall into line. The Chief of Staff agreed. The essential thing, for the moment, was to keep the lieutenant colonel out of Paris without alarming him. Gonse wrote several friendly letters, each alluding to the "affair" they would carefully review upon Picquart's return to Staff headquarters. Henry was even more reassuring in an early December letter to his exiled chief, when he wrote that he agreed fully with Picquart's position but was compelled to keep his views secret until the Vice Chief changed his mind. Then, just before Picquart was about to return to Paris, the Vice Chief wrote again ordering him to Marseille, where he would be contacted by the Minister of War himself. This was a highly unusual order. The day after Christmas, Picquart knew that Gonse had won. From Marseille he was ordered to continue his inspection tour in Algeria and Tunisia without returning to Paris. It was the kind of solution that the War Minister was known to prefer for worrisome or compromised officers.

At the beginning of March 1897, nearly four months after quitting Staff headquarters, Picquart obtained a leave of absence from the Tunisian regiment to which he had been temporarily assigned to return to Paris. As he had feared, the Minister of War was too busy to see him. The only general with whom he did confer, revealing everything about the Esterhazy affair except the name, told him that his conclusions were exaggerated. There was one friend, though, whose confidence Picquart retained, Lieutenant Colonel Mercier-Millon of the General Staff's Third Bureau. If anything happened to him, Picquart confided, Majors Henry and Du Paty would know the reason why. Picquart's attorney, Maître Louis Leblois, begged him to take his case to the Vice President of the Senate, Auguste Scheurer-Kestner, or to authorize Leblois, to canvass a few reliable politicians. Picquart was contemptuous of such a course. He was an officer and still the chief of French Counterintelligence (Gonse continued to assure him that his "mission" was temporary), not an agitator. At the end of the week he dutifully returned to his regiment of *tirailleurs*. By now, though, his subordinates in the section were certain that Picquart would not confine the fight for his own and Dreyfus' rehabilitation to the offices of generals. His movements in Paris had been carefully observed; it had been concluded that he must be compromised or, if necessary, liquidated.

Shortly after he returned to Tunisia, Picquart was thrown from his horse. He was only slightly injured but found himself thinking of Dreyfus and Esterhazy as he was carried to the infirmary. What if the accident had been fatal? He had promised Gonse that he would not carry his secret to the grave. Now he suddenly realized that he had done almost nothing to prevent it from expiring with him. For the first time he wrote a detailed account of all that he knew; on the covering envelope which he placed among his papers he wrote that in the event of his death the document was to be delivered to the President of the Republic. The riding accident was a turning point, the first tentative stage in his reluctant transition from soldier to advocate.

The next stage followed hard upon this one. Picquart was disturbed by signs that his mail from France was being opened. By now it was clear to him that the duplicity of which he was a victim involved his subordinates in Counterintelligence as well as Gonse and, perhaps, included the Chief of Staff and the Minister of War. He wrote Major Henry protesting the surveillance of his correspondence as well as the "lies and mysteries" surrounding his situation. About June 6 he received Major Henry's insolent reply. To be accused of prejudice against Esterhazy and lectured on his disloyalty to Counterintelligence by a crude officer who had risen through the ranks was an intolerable insult; Picquart knew his fate on the General Staff had been sealed. He was right. Within six weeks he would receive orders posting him to duty along the restive Libyan border—an assignment carrying a high risk of mortality.

Had Georges Picquart been left alone in his Tunisian exile to mull over the destinies of Dreyfus and Esterhazy, he might not have risked what was left of his career to force the Army's hand. Courageous and high-principled, Picquart had thus far been motivated largely by his pugnacity, intellectual hauteur, and a pragmatic appreciation of the pros and cons of letting Dreyfus rot and Esterhazy escape punishment. After all, his duty was to obey the Army—all the more so in this instance since disobedience entailed humiliating the institution which had favored him with a position of highest trust.

But Henry's letter stitched Picquart's fate to that of Alfred Dreyfus. "Instructed by the example of the Dreyfus Case," Picquart said later, "I knew how a suspect officer could be rapidly indicted and convicted on false evidence." To protect himself he had to do what he could to save Dreyfus.

Two weeks after Major Henry's letter lecturing him on loyalty, Picquart was briefly in Paris again. That night he made a copy of the statement he had prepared shortly after his riding accident. This he gave to his attorney, Leblois, on June 21, with instructions that the information was to be divulged only if he, Picquart, died mysteriously or if he specifically instructed Leblois to do so. Picquart must have bridled at this breach of trust and law; for an officer to communicate classified information to his civilian attorney was a flagrant violation of his oath.

Three weeks later, Leblois entrusted Picquart's secret to the Vice President of the Senate, Auguste Scheurer-Kestner. Leblois knew that the Alsatian politician had been puzzled by Dreyfus' crime and was still interested in the case. He also knew that the only way to help his client as well as the prisoner on Devil's Island was to break his agreement with Picquart.

The next day, July 14, at the traditional Bastille Day military parade down the Champs Elysées, Senator Scheurer-Kestner found himself concentrating more on the generals' box where the Chief and Vice Chief of Staff sat than on the seemingly endless march-past of the troops. As he watched these two men, his thoughts ran to the missing officer, Alfred Dreyfus, who but for their callous machinations would have marched with the Fourteenth Artillery Regiment as it descended toward the Place de la Concorde. A few days later the Senator met with the eminent writer and Deputy, Joseph Reinach (the nephew of the Baron de Reinach of Panama infamy). Without explaining his reasons, Scheurer-Kestner asked Reinach to inform Lucie Dreyfus that he "has become convinced of Captain Dreyfus' innocence." At the same time, he wrote to Leblois of the dangers of a Jewish monopoly of the case. "As I've already told you, we must take great care to ensure that the Dreyfus question does not remain within the Jewish domain. It is too much there already. The question is one of justice."

Senator Scheurer-Kestner spent the rest of the summer at his residence a few miles from Mulhouse, considering Leblois' revelation. The attorney had sworn him to secrecy about Picquart and Esterhazy, and the Senator had been schooled in the tradition of the hallowed word. As summer wore on, he became more and more oppressed by this vow. "It seems to me that there is someone [i.e., Picquart] who ought to sense more forcefully the immense moral responsibility that he is wedded to," he wrote Maître Leblois. "It is impossible to admit that an honest man keeps in his possession so terrible a secret and leaves an unfortunate to the undeserved torture of Devil's Island."

When he returned to Paris in early September, the Vice President of the Senate, whose probity was often a weakness, asked Deputy Reinach to see Lebon, the Minister of Colonies, to announce officially the Senator's interest in Dreyfus and to obtain permission to send an encouraging letter to Devil's Island. Lebon politely refused. Reinach was astounded: the Vice President of the Senate of France wished his concern to be communicated to the prisoner and had collaborated in drafting the text of the letter. Becoming annoyed, the Minister of Colonies replied, "I would submit your letter to the Cabinet which would decide the question of its own responsibility" if it were appended to a letter from the Senator, who was not a Jew. It was Scheurer-Kestner's and Reinach's first example of the formidable hurdles ahead.

Shortly thereafter, the Senator hired a private detective in an effort to duplicate Picquart's evidence against Esterhazy. A specimen of the traitor's handwriting was secured. Unfortunately Esterhazy's hand was as unreliable as his character; Scheurer-Kestner's example did not correspond closely enough to that in the photocopy of the *bordereau*. Even so, the Senator learned enough about the subject to feel certain that Esterhazy was guilty. He could wait no longer while Picquart grappled with conflicting urges; his word to Leblois weighed less than the national interest. Reluctantly, he told Emmanuel Arène, a steadfast colleague in the Chamber, what he knew, swearing Arène to secrecy. He also confided the full story to Joseph Reinach.

It was the moment of truth for members of the General Staff. They knew of Scheurer-Kestner's involvement and of the sieve-like dissemination of the Picquart story. In the closing months of 1897 the key men at Staff headquarters should have seen that it was time to invite Picquart to return from Tunisia so they could nail Esterhazy and foist onto the government the problematic review of the Dreyfus Case. It would have been an ideal solution. Colonel Sandherr was dead, General Saussier was preparing to retire, and former War Minister Mercier was finishing his days of active duty in a provincial command. General de

Boisdeffre was still Chief of Staff, however, and still aspiring to be Ambassador to Russia; a scandal arising from the *bordereau* could very well deny him this. A faulty conscience also hampered de Boisdeffre. Having pressed Counterintelligence for additional evidence against Dreyfus, he had placidly endorsed Henry's documents before they were passed on to the Minister of War. Pretending to be above the Dreyfus hurly-burly, yet tainted by his involvement, General de Boisdeffre became entangled in the chain of events caused by his own decisions.

Major Henry, the acting chief of Counterintelligence, knew that his ingenuity had become so monstrous that its discovery would be as fatal to himself as to the Army. Fortunately for him, his second-in-command, Captain Lauth, another Alsatian, was a pliable, unscrupulous anti-Semite. Henry's mastery of Vice Chief Gonse was greater than ever. Prodded by Henry, Gonse summoned Captain Lebrun-Renault of the Garde Républicaine in early October and ordered this frightened officer to repeat his account of Dreyfus' confession. Captain Lebrun-Renault's thirty-two-month-old story that Dreyfus had admitted his guilt the hour before the degradation was widely believed to be the sheerest fantasy. Picquart had checked the story at the time and found no mention of a confession in the captain's log book. The President and the Prime Minister had summoned the captain to the Élysée and were unable to obtain confirmation of the story. But neither the government nor the Army had issued a public denial at the time, and for Major Henry an opportune falsehood, officially undenied, became a truth.

It was not always so easy for Henry to manipulate evidence. The chief of the Foreign Ministry's intelligence service, Maurice Paléologue, called at Staff headquarters on November 17 to inform the Vice Chief of a statement made to the Austrian military attaché by Schwartzkoppen that he had never had dealings with Dreyfus. While imparting this information, Paléologue also wondered what Counterintelligence made of Ambassador Count Münster's recent declaration reiterating that Dreyfus was unknown to Germany. Major Henry was present, and the confused

Gonse turned to him to stammer, "Dreyfus' guilt is beyond doubt. We find new evidence every day—is that not so, Henry?" "You certainly know that Panizzardi was the intermediary," Henry stated forcefully. "We never said that Dreyfus dealt with Germany directly." Paléologue found this explanation puzzling because the Quai d'Orsay had deciphered the Italian military attaché's telegram to Rome and concluded that Panizzardi had never heard of Dreyfus. Gonse was overwhelmed; he turned to Henry with a frantic expression. After a long pause Henry queried, "But do you have the document? I saw it only once, in the hands of Colonel Sandherr." Paléologue found it inexplicable that Counterintelligence had no copy of a document that he himself had dispatched to Staff headquarters.

The officers of the General Staff made a swift descent into rank treachery during the final days of October 1897. They were racing against revelations that Senator Scheurer-Kestner was known to be on the verge of making. Attention drawn to Esterhazy's past could unleash a public cry for a thorough investigation. If Esterhazy committed suicide, which was unlikely, or fled the country, Dreyfus' retrial was as good as decreed. On the other hand, it was impossible to place Esterhazy in protective custody for the same reason. Henry hit upon a solution for the troublesome officer. In return for his immunity from prosecution, Esterhazy would place himself under the guidance of Counterintelligence.

Whatever moral delicacy Vice Chief Gonse still possessed was overcome by Henry's and Lauth's arguments that Esterhazy's Jewish connections and debt-ridden misfortunes were being exploited by the Dreyfus family and its allies. He was being ruined by the "Syndicate" which would stop at nothing to save the prisoner on Devil's Island. Gonse then explained to Du Paty how desperate things were for the Army at that moment. The mobilization plan was being revised again and the new heavy field gun was still in the prototype stage. With the Jews and other subversives seeking to embroil France with Germany over this Dreyfus-Esterhazy farrago, something must be done to buy time. "You see, Du Paty, no plan, no cannon," Gonse sighed. "*Voilà*," Gonse sighed again, "that's where we are." They had a plan but needed Du Paty's cooperation.

On October 17, 1897, Du Paty took the first step to put the plan into operation. The next day, at his chateau east of Paris, Count Esterhazy received a letter signed "Espérance," alerting him that he was about to be publicly accused of writing the *bordereau*. This time Esterhazy was worried. He had never trusted the haughty Schwartzkoppen and had suspected that the Prussian was about to betray him. The Count took the first train to Paris. There he found another "Espérance" note at his town house, inviting him to a rendezvous in the Montsouris Park on Saturday, October 23.

In the early afternoon of that Saturday Esterhazy stopped at the German Embassy to see Schwartzkoppen. His mood was bombastic. The Dreyfus family was after him, he ranted. They had even convinced the Vice President of the Senate that he should espouse the Dreyfus cause. He demanded that Schwartzkoppen tell Lucie Dreyfus that he had been her husband's contact with Germany. When the German military attaché disdained this suggestion as absurd and impossible, Esterhazy turned violent. Waving his revolver wildly, he threatened to commit suicide on the spot. Icily, Schwartzkoppen waited for the fit to spend itself; he then invited Esterhazy to leave the embassy.

If he hoped that the histrionic Count might actually blow out his brains, Schwartzkoppen was disappointed. A few hours later Esterhazy again barged into Schwartzkoppen's apartment. In the Montsouris Park he had met with Major Du Paty, disguised by dark glasses and heavy civilian overcoat, along with the archivist Gribelin. He was told the Army would protect him from the Dreyfuses if he cooperated fully. Exultant, Esterhazy rushed back to the German Embassy to put Schwartzkoppen in his place. He made it known that henceforth he embodied the

honor of the French Army, that he could no longer be thrown
to the wolves by Germany. Schwartzkoppen was glad to be leaving France soon.

On October 29, a day after Du Paty and Esterhazy held another meeting, Scheurer-Kestner went to the Élysée to see President Faure. The venerable Senator had used his influence to
elect Félix Faure and he believed deeply in the good sense and
decency of the leaders of the Republic. But Scheurer-Kestner
was greatly disappointed. As President Faure pointed out, all
the Senator had was a story repeated to him by the attorney
of a man who refused to testify in public. Furthermore, the
President shrugged, even if it were true that Dreyfus had been
convicted on evidence withheld from the defense, any ministry
authorizing a retrial on those grounds would sentence itself to
death. In any event, Faure concluded, the matter was in the
hands of the Minister of War.

As the dejected Scheurer-Kestner left the Élysée, Esterhazy
was addressing a letter to the President which arrived the next
morning. Obeying Du Paty's instructions, Esterhazy wrote that
he had a "liberating document" which proved that he was innocent of certain calumnies being circulated by the Dreyfus family but that this document was of such an explosive character
as to threaten France's relations with a certain foreign power.
A "veiled lady" had given him this terrible instrument for his
own protection, but he was ready to surrender it as soon as
the government signaled its willingness to defend an honorable
officer. If he were not defended, Esterhazy said, he would appeal to the "chief of my house, the suzerain of the family of
Esterhazy, to the German Emperor." This was an incredible
letter for a major to send to the head of the nation. There were
countries in Europe where Esterhazy's reply would have been
an arrest warrant; that was what even Esterhazy expected. But
the politicians of the Third Republic were cautious men. Félix
Faure sensed that there was much more behind this major's
audacious letter than insolent courage, and Esterhazy's second

letter, which arrived almost immediately afterward, confirmed the President's suspicions:

> Let me be defended and I will send the document back to the Minister of War without anyone having laid eyes on it. But I had better be defended quickly because I can't wait any longer and I won't stop for anything whatsoever in the defense or in the avenging of my unjustly sacrificed honor.

The third and last of the letters, November 5, repeated the warnings of the second. The President had each letter copied and forwarded to the Minister of War.

From the Élysée Scheurer-Kestner had gone that same evening, October 29, to the home of General Billot. Billot's family was also Alsatian and he and the Senator had been good friends for decades. After an excellent dinner they took their brandies to the study. Instead of a sympathetic listener, the Senator found the Minister of War to be an antagonist ready with an exception for every point. What Scheurer-Kestner said about this Esterhazy scoundrel was altogether correct. The man was a disgrace to the uniform and would be forced to resign his commission shortly. But, Billot insisted, he was not a traitor. Because of Esterhazy's disgraceful conduct, the Jews were trying to convince certain journalists and politicians that he should be sent to trade places with Dreyfus. Dreyfus, Billot stated as firmly as possible, was guilty.

"Are you quite sure that nothing has been hidden from you by a certain office?" Scheurer-Kestner pressed.

"All the information that I have has been given me by a worthy man, General Gonse. He is the brother of the former State Counselor who was the Attorney General." Billot added for good measure that Vice Chief Gonse had Jewish relatives.

"Are you sure that Gonse himself hasn't been deceived?"

"As I've told you, I've occupied myself with this affair since becoming Minister and I've searched for the truth. I have only confirmed my opinion that Dreyfus is guilty. Now I don't say that he didn't have accomplices—one always does in affairs of this kind. But we have additional proof since the trial. Dreyfus is guilty, that's certain. Furthermore, he admitted having relations with foreign military attachés."

"I don't believe that," Scheurer-Kestner replied solemnly.

"But yes, it's true—he confessed."

It went on like this, two old friends beginning to distrust one another, as so many others would, over an affair that was rapidly becoming an obsession. In a final throw of the dice the Minister of War recited from memory the Lebrun-Renault confession and the False Henry letter. "You don't know a quarter of this case, old friend," he concluded. The Senator still didn't believe the Minister, but he was sufficiently shaken to agree to remain silent for two weeks while the Army conducted a final, rigorous investigation.

Two days later *Le Matin* announced another Dreyfus scoop. The newspaper reproduced almost verbatim Scheurer-Kestner's discussion with Billot in the latter's locked study—but still without identifying Esterhazy. "Nothing was disclosed by me," Billot replied to the Senator's wounded letter. "I am ordering a personal and severe inquiry." Now Scheurer-Kestner began to glimpse what he was up against. Old friendships counted for nothing when an institution was fighting for its life. Possibly Billot told the truth when he denied any part in the newspaper revelation. Having discussed the incident with General de Boisdeffre, the General's aide-de-camp might have informed *Le Matin* of the tête-à-tête. All this, however, was mere quibbling from Scheurer-Kestner's point of view. Billot, after all, was the Minister of War.

What shock effect Scheurer-Kestner's information might have possessed for fellow parliamentarians was dissipated now. Also, the vagueness of his news—no name, no sources—would have little impact on an already skeptical public. And the one man who could corroborate his statements, Picquart, had been ordered to the deadly Tunisian-Libyan border. Picquart's anticipated death would be a boon to the General Staff. Before that happened, Henry wanted his chief fully compromised. Henry inspired Du Paty to have Esterhazy send two telegrams to Picquart. Esterhazy signed the first "Speranza": "To be feared that the whole works is discovered. Take the document back; don't write anything." His second wire sent a few hours later on November 10, signed "Blanche," was more explicit. "They have proof that the *bleu* was fabricated by Georges." If Georges Picquart survived his African penance to face a court-martial, it was certain the prosecution would stress that Picquart had frequented the salon of the Comtesse Blanche de Comminges. Copies of both telegrams were delivered to Billot as having been intercepted.

The Minister and the General Staff knew that time was running out. Stories were circulating in the salons and the diplomatic circles about Dreyfus' innocence. On November 4 Panizzardi was visited by a young French officer who had been recently decorated with the Order of the Crown by the Italian King. As the conversation wound around to a mention of Dreyfus, Panizzardi told the young officer that "Schwartzkoppen gave me his word of honor that Dreyfus was innocent." Major de Fontellinat left the Italian Embassy distressed, not yet convinced, but anxious to share the news with trusted friends. Such revelations, Henry's agents reported, were becoming increasingly frequent. Indeed, on November 11 Schwartzkoppen called on President Faure before leaving Paris for his new assignment in Berlin and gave his word of honor that he had never known Dreyfus. The government was becoming annoyed by the case while an increasing number of politicians wondered about the credibility of certain officers.

While Scheurer-Kestner and his allies lost valuable time, the anonymous traitor, guided by Henry and Gonse, exploited their honorable silence. Not the least remarkable of Esterhazy's performances as innocent victim was his appearance before General Billot toward the middle of November. Esterhazy was at his histrionic best, swearing that his friendship with Jews had led to this campaign against him; that if the Jews and the others dared to name him publicly, he would demand a formal inquest;

and that, as proof of his fidelity to the Army, he was returning the "liberating document" mentioned in his letters to President Faure. Billot reassured Esterhazy, thanked him for his cooperation, and on November 16 sent him a signed receipt for the "liberating document." Incredibly, Esterhazy had never possessed the document which the receipt officially certified he had surrendered; it had been pure fabrication. Billot, by his cold-blooded resolve to save the reputation of the Army, now joined Henry, Gonse, and Du Paty in willfully hiding the truth.

Finally, when the Billot truce expired, Scheurer-Kestner tried to frighten Esterhazy while still declining (in deference to Picquart) to identify him by name. On November 14, under the pseudonym Vidi, the Senator's colleague Emmanuel Arène declared in *Le Figaro* that the *bordereau* was not in Dreyfus' handwriting, that the nature of the text itself disproved Dreyfus' authorship, and that another document intercepted from a foreign diplomatic source and used to convict Dreyfus was a forgery. The real traitor, Arène announced, "still has his home at this moment in one of the rich neighborhoods of the capital. He is titled, married, and very much in evidence."

Too many officers fitted this description, however, and the newspaper *La Liberté* impetuously accused an innocent captain. To compound the confusion Du Paty, masquerading as a female at their rendezvous, prepared Esterhazy for an immediate reply. Writing under the pseudonym Dixi in *La Libre Parole* on November 15, Esterhazy stated that a superior officer unconnected with the Dreyfus Case was soon to be falsely accused of treason. This victimized officer's handwriting had been imitated by Dreyfus when he wrote the *bordereau*, Dixi explained, and the Jews, aided by the chief of Counterintelligence, Lieutenant Colonel Picquart, were now about to attempt to substitute an innocent man for their traitorous coreligionist.

Lucie had received news of Senator Scheurer-Kestner's interest in her husband on September 17. A few weeks later there

LEFT 1. Alfred Dreyfus as a young student, circa 1874.

BELOW 2. Dutch postcard featuring Captain Dreyfus, with photo of Devil's Island (foreground) and comparisons of Dreyfus' handwriting (top and bottom) with that of *bordereau*.

3. The *bordereau* (front and back). Top right, letter written by Ester-hazy on paper identical to that of *bordereau*. Bottom right, the letter dictated to Captain Dreyfus by Major Du Paty de Clam on the morning of October 15, 1894.

PAUL·DÉROULÈDE

ABOVE LEFT 4. Rare photograph of Major "Count" Ferdinand Esterhazy, the traitor.

ABOVE RIGHT 5. The father of modern anti-Semitism, Edouard Drumont, the editor of *La Libre Parole.*

LEFT 6. Paul Déroulède, founder of the Ligue des Patriotes. Anti-Dreyfusard and specialist in abortive coups d'etat.

7. Document proving the innocence of Dreyfus—the *petit bleu*.

8. Colonel Jean Sandherr, Chief of Military Counterintelligence.

9. Lieutenant Colonel Armand Du Paty de Clam of the General Staff.

ABOVE LEFT 10. Lieutenant Colonel Hubert Joseph Henry of the General Staff.

ABOVE RIGHT 11. Félix Gribelin, archivist of the General Staff.

LEFT 12. Vice Chief of Staff General Charles Gonse at Rennes.

13. General Auguste Mercier, the infallible Minister of War and Senator.

14. Army Chief of Staff General the Marquis Raoul Le Mouton de Boisdeffre.

16. Lieutenant Colonel Marie-Georges Picquart, Chief of Military Counterintelligence.

15. General Félix-Gaston Saussier, Military Governor of Paris and wartime Generalissimo.

17. Colonel Maximilian von Schwartzkoppen and Major Esterhazy, a rare composite photo.

18. Senator Auguste Scheurer-Kestner, Vice President of the Senate.

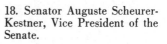

19. A mild photograph of the ferocious Georges Clemenceau.

20. Deputy Joseph Reinach.

21. Jean Jaurès, the Social-ist leader.

ABOVE 22. Émile Zola with his mistress and their children after the escape to England.

LEFT 23. The degradation [of justice], a Dutch design.

UN DINER EN FAMILLE

(PARIS, CE 13 FEVRIER 1898)

PAR CARAN D'ACHE

— Surtout ! ne parlons pas de l'affaire Dreyfus !

— Ils en **ont** parlé...

24. The most famous cartoon of the Affair, by Caran d'Ache. Captions: "Absolutely, no talk of the Affair!" "They talked about it!"

25. German postcard representing Esterhazy and "Die verschleierte Dame" (the Veiled Lady) or Du Paty de Clam in drag.

Affaire Zola-Esterhazy
Die verschleierte Dame!
No 2.

Zu Befehl, Herr General!
Bien, mon général!

La dame voilée!

La dernière quille

26. Cartoon from anti-Dreyfusard review, *Le Psst*, "The Last Pin." German officer encourages Jewish baron—"One more to go, baron, and we've won."

— Allons, cher baron, encore celle-là... et la partie est à nous.

27. "Rules of the game." A form of Dreyfus parcheesi enormously popular in Europe after the Zola trial.

28. Presidents of the Republic: Messrs. Jean Casimir-Périer, Émile Loubet, and Félix Faure.

Casimir Périer.

Emile Loubet.

Felix Faure.

Präsidenten der Französischen Republik 1894–1899.

E. Baumann, Berlin C., Neue Promenade 8.

Brisson.

Charles Dupuy.

Minister-Präsidenten 1894 — 1899.

Méline.

Waldeck-Rousseau.

E. Baumann, Berlin C., Neue Promenade 8.

ABOVE 29. Prime Ministers of the Affair: Messrs. Jules Méline, Henri Brisson, Charles Dupuy, and René Waldeck-Rousseau.

LEFT 30. General Gabriel de Pellieux whose investigation cleared Esterhazy.

BELOW 31. Three Ministers of War who gave categorical assurances of Dreyfus' guilt: Generals Jean-Baptiste Billot and Émile Zurlinden, and Monsieur Godefroy Cavaignac.

32. Minister of War General Charles Chanoine, whose sudden resignation appeared to be the prelude to a coup d'etat.

33. General the Marquis Gaston de Galliffet, the objective Minister of War.

34. Dreyfus enters the Rennes courtroom passing his guard which stands with back turned.

35. Alfred Dreyfus giving name and rank before the court-martial at Rennes. Maître Demange (second from right) watches.

ABOVE 36. Troops carting a portion of the documents in the Affair to Rennes Lycée.

RIGHT 37. Maître Fernand Labori leaving the Rennes Lycée with Madame Labori.

ABOVE 38. The judges during recess at Rennes. Colonel Jouaust, president of the court-martial, stands with back to camera at left.

LEFT 39. Captain Dreyfus returning to prison from Rennes Lycée.

40. The last trial. The second United Court of Cassation (1906) prepares to annul the Rennes verdict.

41. Rare photo of Major Dreyfus a few minutes after his ceremonial reintegration into the French Army. Scene, the War College.

LA RÉHABILITATION DREYFUS

4. Après la remise des décorations
le Commandant Dreyfus s'entretient avec le
Général Gillain et le Commandant Targe

Æ. L. D.

HÉLIOTYPIE. E. LE DELEY, PARIS

LEFT 42. Sketch of Mathieu Dreyfus toward the end of his life.

BELOW 43. Lucie and the children.

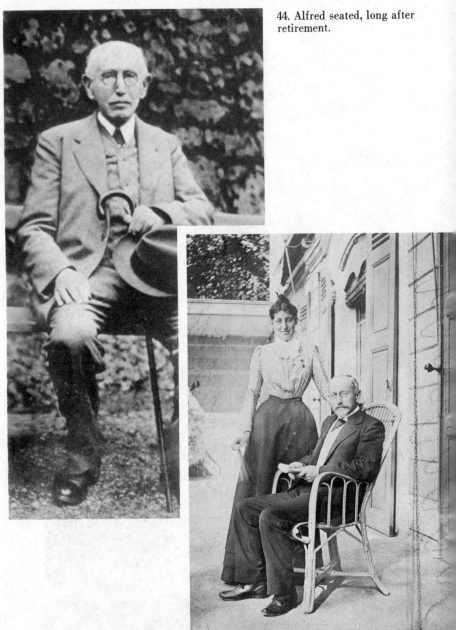

44. Alfred seated, long after retirement.

45. Lucie and Alfred in 1901.

was reliable information that the Senator knew the traitor's identity but was temporarily constrained from revealing it. Lucie's and Mathieu's impatience became almost unendurable. They faced each day expecting the traitor's name to be headlined across the newspapers of Paris. Their daily anxiety was increased because of Dreyfus' condition. Although he had been transferred to the larger, more comfortable dwelling in August, the new regime ordained for him by Colonial Minister Lebon was psychologically fiendish. In his letters the prisoner spoke increasingly not of his own rehabilitation but of Lucie's and the children's as though he believed his vindication must be posthumous. In a November letter, not to be received for many weeks, Dreyfus prophesied fatalistically:

> How could it be possible to tell you of my confidence so long as I remain under the limitations imposed on me? It is difficult, and I can only give you a formal guarantee that in the very, very near future *you* shall be rehabilitated.

Sentiments such as this Lucie read as medical bulletins on the chronic decline of her defiant husband.

While Lucie and Mathieu were waiting for more news from Scheurer-Kestner, Mathieu received a visit from a Jewish banker, Monsieur De Castro. After the newspaper *Le Matin* published a photocopy of the *bordereau*, Mathieu had paid for thousands of *bordereau* reprints to be placarded throughout Paris. Seeing one of these copies, De Castro thought he recognized the handwriting as that of one of his bank's consistently overdrawn depositors. Removing the sample, De Castro carefully compared it with the calligraphy of his problem depositor, Esterhazy. Shortly before the end of October, he contacted Mathieu. Then, when Deputy Emmanuel Arène's *Figaro* article appeared, Mathieu called on Scheurer-Kestner to verify his own suspicions of Esterhazy. Distressed by the allegation against the wrong officer in *La Liberté*, Scheurer-Kestner finally divulged the secret entrusted to him by Leblois.

The Dreyfuses had at long last got to the bottom of the mystery. On November 15 Mathieu wrote a letter to the Minister of War exposing Esterhazy:

> The unique basis of the accusation of 1894 against my unfortunate brother was an unsigned, undated letter [i.e., the *bordereau*]. . . . I have the honor to inform you that the author of that document was Count Walsin-Esterhazy, major of infantry, retired last spring by reason of infirmities of a temporary character. Major Esterhazy's handwriting is identical with that of the document in question. It will be a very simple matter to secure specimens of this officer's handwriting. . . . I entertain no doubt, *Monsieur le Ministre*, that, now that you have definite knowledge of the author of the treason for which my brother was condemned, you will execute immediate justice.

As an extra precaution Mathieu gave the text of his letter to *Le Figaro*; the newspaper published it the following day. This time the government and the Army would be compelled to conduct an inquiry.

The General Staff had prepared for this contingency. Twenty-four hours after Mathieu's letter appeared in *Le Figaro*, *Le Matin* published an exclusive interview with Esterhazy explaining that his "infrequent but very open" relations with Colonel von Schwartzkoppen arose from close family ties. From time to time, the Count stated, the German vacationed at Carlsbad where the Hungarian Esterhazys went for the mineral baths. Yes, he had socialized with Schwartzkoppen on occasion, gossiped with him about the goings-on of their titled friends and relatives in Budapest, Berlin, and Vienna. As for the alleged similarity of his handwriting to that of the *bordereau*, Esterhazy was flippant. "The general aspect of the writing is not mine," he was quoted as saying, "but there are some words which seem absolutely to be written by my pen." The way in which the infinitive "to obtain" was written, for example, was uncannily like his own script. He was totally at a loss to explain these coincidences. The General Staff hoped that the public would be befuddled by all this. On November 15 Dixi had predicted the victimizing of an innocent officer. The prediction had come true on the sixteenth. Now, on November 17, that courageous, liberal-spirited officer had done his best to respond candidly to these vicious charges.

Hoping the truth had been sufficiently clouded, the Army prepared to investigate Mathieu's charge. Before the Chamber General Billot solemnly swore that, although Dreyfus was certainly guilty, Esterhazy's conduct would be scrupulously examined. In the Senate Scheurer-Kestner delivered his long-awaited speech. He won no converts that day, but public interest in the speech was high. The porcine Saussier selected and authorized General Georges de Pellieux, the chief of the Paris Military Police, to whitewash Esterhazy. Once again there were several motives at play. Had the Army not stepped in immediately, Esterhazy might have been compelled to act on his own. After his bravado in the *Matin* interview, the public would have expected a duel, or at the very least a libel suit. But duels and suits for libel involved the civil authorities who might not be satisfactorily responsive to the interests of the Army.

De Pellieux was a poster general, gruff, tall, handsome, endowed with an intelligent face and an orator's voice. Unfortunately, whatever assets the chief of the Paris Military Police might have brought to the Esterhazy investigation were rinsed from his mind by Generals Gonse and de Boisdeffre. He was encouraged to regard Picquart as a disloyal, ambitious *raffiné*. Esterhazy was an extravagantly bad officer, de Pellieux learned, but he was not a traitor. Even so, the border police were alerted to stop Esterhazy if the Count decided to cross one of the frontiers.

In rapid succession General de Pellieux interviewed the interested parties. Esterhazy reminded him of comrades of his youth when he had fought for Napoleon III—reckless, flamboyant, unconventional, and a trifle mad. De Pellieux interviewed Senator Scheurer-Kestner with the greatest respect and the greatest lack of interest. Mathieu and Maître Leblois were such distasteful types that de Pellieux was hard pressed to behave correctly when he received them. Nevertheless he listened to them civilly—and then he flushed what they had said from his mind. Thanks to Esterhazy's erratic testimony, de Pellieux knew that he had once written an essay for a certain Captain Brault who currently resided in the Rue de Chateaudun where the Hadamards had lived for decades. Dreyfus himself had suggested to Du Paty that the script of the *bordereau* resembled that of a Captain Brô or Brault. Obviously, de Pellieux reasoned, that essay had served as the model for Dreyfus' *bordereau* handwriting. As for the kinship of the *bordereau* and the *petit bleu*, de Pellieux had been expressly ordered not to attempt to connect the two documents. On November 20 General de Pellieux officially concluded that there were no grounds to justify prosecution of Esterhazy. The Minister of War must have been immensely pleased by the report, for he had been excoriated in the Nationalist press for even allowing an investigation.

On November 19 War Minister Billot decided to have Picquart returned from Tunisia for formal proceedings. Precise charges were not yet formulated, but Picquart's dealings with Maître Leblois were believed to be grounds enough for the preparation of an *instruction*. It was distressing that Picquart was still alive and well, and Billot further resented that General Leclerc, Picquart's superior, had dared to countermand orders from Paris. Puzzled by Picquart's extended presence in his command, General Leclerc had asked the reason for his Libyan frontier assignment. Picquart had given him the whole story. Appalled, the General told Picquart to disregard the Libyan instructions. When Picquart returned to Paris, as Billot ordered, on November 26, he found that his every step was dogged by police agents.

With Picquart back, General de Pellieux reopened his preliminary investigation. The former chief of Counterintelligence (Henry, now promoted to lieutenant colonel, officially replaced him) was relieved to tell his story to a superior officer charged with finding out the truth. He was dismayed to find it was a story the chief of Military Police did not want to hear. How long had he been given to hallucinations, to seeing tables turning in the air? de Pellieux asked.

"General," Picquart replied forbearingly, "I have never in my life seen a table turning in the air."

Well then, what did he have against Esterhazy—some professional grudge, a woman? No, no, de Pellieux said, there would be no talk of the *bordereau*; that had to do with Dreyfus and Dreyfus had nothing to do with Esterhazy. When Picquart brought up the *petit bleu* which implicated Esterhazy, he was further disconcerted by the General's suggestion that it was a forgery. When Picquart left the interview, he wondered whether a warrant for his arrest might not follow him to his hotel.

The public was distracted by yet another scandal involving Esterhazy. De Pellieux received an anonymous letter informing him that a certain Madame de Boulancy, Esterhazy's cousin, possessed compromising correspondence. Probably Madame de Boulancy herself had apprised de Pellieux of the existence of such letters. Since Esterhazy had taken up with a new mistress, he had cruelly spurned his amorous cousin whom he still owed several thousand francs. Somehow Madame de Boulancy's packet of letters began appearing in *Le Figaro* on November 28. As the High Command and the members of the Cabinet read the Sunday edition of the newspaper, they experienced astonishment and then panic. Only a lunatic could have written such letters! In one of them (to be known as the "Uhlan" letter) Esterhazy's extravagantly acrid pen had confessed

> that these people [i.e., the French] are not worth the bullets
> to kill them, and all the little despicableness of drunken
> women which the men give themselves up to confirms me
> deep down in my opinion. . . . If someone came to me
> this evening to tell me that I am going to be killed as a
> captain in the Uhlans tomorrow while sabering the French,
> I should be perfectly happy.

More epistolary extravagances were leaked to the newspapers:

> The Germans will put all these people in their rightful
> places before long. Our ignorant and cowardly leaders are
> going to populate the German war camps once again.

Esterhazy's opinion of Generalissimo Saussier, written as early
as 1881, was grounds for prosecution under the Military Code.
The Military Governor was a "clown whom the Germans would
put in a circus."

The plotters at Army headquarters were staggered. Until
the de Boulancy letters Esterhazy had been subservient to their
instructions, dependent upon them for his survival. Abruptly
the relationship had been turned on its head. Having closed the
frontiers to him and having exposed itself to blackmail, the
General Staff was trapped henceforth into protecting the picaresque Count who would now neither flee nor kill himself.
Apprehension turned to desperation. Henry advised Esterhazy,
who was truly frightened himself, to discredit the letters. But
even Esterhazy's uncanny aplomb before the press could not
indefinitely deceive the public in a matter touching upon the
national honor.

In *L'Autorité* Paul de Cassagnac was nearly strangled by
his own indignation. No Frenchman—certainly no Army officer
—could be allowed to voice such unnatural opinions. In spite of
their past collusion, *La Libre Parole*'s Drumont demanded
Esterhazy's expulsion from the Army if the letters were proven
to be authentic. The outstanding Nationalist writer Maurice
Barrès had never quite made up his mind about the Dreyfus
Case. Now, almost three years after the degradation and as
much for his own conscience as for the health of the nation,
Barrès decided to intervene with an admonitory newspaper
piece. "Either it is going to be established that military justice
in so serious a matter has condemned an innocent man and
spared a traitor," he lectured, "or it is going to become evident
that an attempt to save a traitor has been able to assure itself
of widespread cooperation *without encountering a single word*

or deed of straightforward protest by the government of the country." A half-dozen Paris newspapers reiterated Barrès' views.

Prime Minister Jules Méline had shown in his conversations with Scheurer-Kestner that he was unwilling to be burdened with the nuisance of the Dreyfus Case and that he fully shared the views of Billot and Lebon. Méline could not afford to be wholly closeminded, however. Prime Ministers under the Third Republic (whose governments lasted an average of less than nine months) had learned that unequivocal positions—whatever their merits—were usually fatal. Méline also knew that at least one of his colleagues, Minister of Foreign Affairs Hanotaux, privately still questioned Dreyfus' guilt. If the circumstantial evidence against Esterhazy became more persuasive, the government would have to pay the high premium of an exhaustive, honest investigation.

It seemed that, after Madame de Boulancy, the Italians were most determined to force the issue by providing Méline's government with the proof which the latter had absolutely no desire to obtain. After the Uhlan letter, the Italian Ambassador made the unusual offer of suspending Colonel Panizzardi's diplomatic immunity so that the military attaché could give sworn testimony about Dreyfus' alleged relations with members of the Italian Embassy. If Panizzardi's deposition were allowed, the original 1894 telegrams between Rome and Paris would surface, and their odd disregard by Counterintelligence would raise awkward questions. It was one thing for the German military attaché to inform President Faure orally and in the privacy of the Élysée study that Dreyfus was unknown to German Counterintelligence; that confidence could be ignored. But an official request by the Italian Ambassador and the prospect of recorded statements by his attaché called for high-level treachery.

The Chief of Staff came to the War Minister's assistance. In a letter marked "secret," which was to be shown to the Prime Minister, General de Boisdeffre vigorously protested the Italian

Ambassador's proposal, stating that the Ambassador was a "*partie trop interessée*," and thereby impugning the Italian's good faith. The General Staff had intercepted three letters from the Italian military attaché to his German counterpart "in which the subject of Dreyfus is raised," the letter explained. The implication that the Italian Ambassador would lie to protect his country's reputation and to undermine public confidence was patent. Leaving nothing to conjecture, the Chief of Staff took a giant step in binding the Army to Henry's forgeries by alluding to them in writing. "The first two letters speak only of 'D'. . . . The third spells out Dreyfus completely." Until this November 29 letter General de Boisdeffre had been extremely careful to maintain the posture of an interested spectator in the Dreyfus Case. But to sabotage the Italian Ambassador's unwelcome gesture, the elegant, disingenuous aristocrat stooped to the machinations of Major Henry.* For the moment the stratagem worked well enough; the French Prime Minister rejected Ambassador Tornielli's offer.

In the meantime General de Pellieux, loyal and ostrichlike, did his utmost to save Esterhazy. On December 3 he submitted his second report to Saussier and Billot absolving Esterhazy of any fault graver than rascality. However, a few days earlier, the nervous government had ordered a formal military investigation into the evidence against Dreyfus and Esterhazy which had the effect of making de Pellieux's second report purely provisional. De Pellieux's conclusions were nevertheless enormously welcome to Prime Minister Méline. The General concluded that the *bordereau* and the *petit bleu* could not possibly implicate Esterhazy (by innuendo, Picquart was made responsible for the latter) and that the de Boulancy letters had been written by someone other than Esterhazy.

Frenchmen had not yet taken leave of their critical faculties; each day the newspapers became less reverent about the Army's conduct. The High Command worried that Mathieu's accusation

---

* BB 19 105 38 7.

and the de Boulancy fiasco would survive General de Pellieux's whitewash. At the beginning of December 1897, therefore, the normally aloof General de Boisdeffre went to the
Chamber of Deputies to pin a brief note to the door. For the
honor of France, the calumnies of the Dreyfus clique must be
terminated, the protest demanded. The government must defend
the Army. The Chief of Staff may have been an incongruous
Martin Luther, but his thesis was avidly championed by the
Chamber's patriotic purists.

On December 4 the Chamber of Deputies was packed. In
the balcony the diplomatic community and the members of the
press sat expectantly, while below, in the hemicycle, France's
popularly elected representatives shushed each other into anxious
silence. Armed with de Pellieux's two reports, Prime Minister
Méline appeared confident, even belligerent. A sober, moderate
man, Méline was not an anti-Semite or an intemperate Nationalist; but the Prime Minister was not his own master. His *Esprit
Nouveau* program—a program appeasing the Right and favoring the rich—was succeeding because of the support of the
Catholics, Nationalists, and powerful agriculturists and industrialists in the Chamber, none of whom cared anything
about one Jew stubbornly clinging to life on a tropical island
—especially when his case imperiled the Army. What he had
to do was unpleasant, the Prime Minister reflected. His own
Minister of Foreign Affairs, Hanotaux, seated nearby, believed
a mistake had been made. Méline could not really believe that
gentlemen such as Colonel von Schwartzkoppen, the Italian
Ambassador, and Senator Scheurer-Kestner would willingly
make false statements on their honor. But the time to pursue
any such doubts had passed. The Prime Minister was convinced
that he had to defend the hope and glory of France—the Army
—or risk being driven from power. Nor did he have trouble
persuading himself that much more than parliamentary censure
was at stake.
Since the 1870 debacle the French had sulked under a form

of government that had resulted largely from a statemate between Royalists, Bonapartists, and conservative republicans.
Coming into existence by a majority of one vote, the Third
Republic, according to its chief architect, Adolphe Thiers, had
"divided Frenchmen least." It was unglamorous, unstable, unloved, crisis-ridden, and scandal-rocked. The Third Republic
was a monument to the impotence of France in a Europe dominated by Chancellor Bismarck. One institution alone guarded
its ideals, its discipline, and inspired a fanaticism in all Frenchmen—the blue-coated, red-pantalooned Army. Not to defend
the Army from scandal would be an act of treason graver than
that alleged against Esterhazy. Fourteen months had elapsed
since the spectacular performance of the Republic's soldiers and
sailors had dazzled Europe during the Czar's visit. In France,
love of the Army had never been greater, and Europe was still
watching in admiration and fear. Nothing must be allowed to
blemish the institution upon which the Franco-Russian Alliance
rested, Méline told himself.

Much more was at stake than the honor of the Army's leaders. Meline's Opportunist Party and the interests supporting it
believed they were in a mortal race against the forces of social
chaos—Anarchism and Socialism. Five years after his infamy,
mention of the name Ravachol still caused them faint nausea.
Ravachol had been a solitary avenger, dynamiting the houses
of the judge and prosecuting attorney responsible for severe
sentences against his Anarchist comrades. After Ravachol the
feats of Anarchists become prodigious. Émile Henry's bomb
dismembered policemen, August Vaillant's flattened the solons
in the Chamber of Deputies, Jean Pauwel's maimed and killed
café diners; and in June 1894, Santo Caserio's knife dispatched
the President of the Republic, Sadi Carnot. The Socialists did
not take the lives of respectable citizens, but they were deemed
to be no better than the Anarchists because they schemed to
take away the property of the better classes. The Opportunist
Party had been much relieved when Pope Leo XIII proclaimed
the *Ralliement* in 1893 (a policy of Catholic acceptance of the

Third Republic, if not its policies and politicians)—religious piety being a fine thing now that the working classes seemed determined to universalize the principles of 1789. But should religion fail, then the last defense of order and property would fall to the officer corps. This was the true significance of Dreyfus to the government. "They shrank," said Daniel Halévy, chronicler of the folly abounding, "from strengthening the revolutionary parties by revealing the vile conduct of which certain Army leaders had been guilty."

Jules Méline rose to defend the Army, knowing the impact his rehearsed speech would have on the deputies. From the tribune, the Prime Minister ridiculed the misinformation of Senator Scheurer-Kestner, spoke of secret documents justifying Dreyfus' condemnation, and explained, with the slight exasperation of an objective man whose patience has been strained, that after two meticulous investigations not one shred of proof against Esterhazy existed. The results of the third inquiry would undoubtedly provide irrefutable confirmation in the near future. Then, pausing to obtain the desired dramatic effect, Méline pronounced one of the more memorable blunders ever uttered in the Palais Bourbon—*"il n'y a pas d'affaire Dreyfus"* (there is no Dreyfus Affair). With few exceptions, the deputies gave the Prime Minister a tremendous ovation. Méline's remark would be remembered, for within a few weeks the Dreyfus Affair would achieve the distinction, unique in a nation of affairs beyond number, of becoming known simply as "The Affair."

chapter ten:
J'ACCUSE

As PROMISED, THE GOVERNMENT PROCEEDED
with its own supposedly thorough investigation. General de
Pellieux chose Major A. Ravary, a younger, brasher version
of himself, as the *juge d'instruction* to whitewash Esterhazy after
yet another pretense of sifting the evidence. Major Ravary
went about his business with the arrogance of a billeting officer
in enemy territory. When Mathieu angrily insisted that a letter
in which Esterhazy said he would turn to crime in order to
spare his daughters further suffering be accepted as evidence,
Ravary yielded. But he made it clear that as evidence of treason
the letter counted for little. He laid it aside, shrugging his
shoulders, exclaiming with mock feeling, "How this man loves
his children!" Ravary also dismissed a letter which threatened
Mathieu's own life and that of Monsieur Hadamard, Lucie's
father. Twenty-four hours after Ravary had informed Counterintelligence of the letter's existence, the police agent who had
attempted to trace its source for Mathieu was transferred from
Paris.

Ravary was doing his best to protect the Army, but he ran into stiff resistance from the handwriting experts. Because of the number of documents involved, they were refusing to be stampeded into proving Esterhazy's innocence. Although one of them, Monsieur Charavay, had already told de Pellieux that Esterhazy was not the author of the *bordereau*, he was inclined to agree with his three colleagues that the de Boulancy letters had been written by Esterhazy. And the other three were inclined to ascribe the *bordereau* as well to the real traitor. Esterhazy was disgusted by his protectors' incompetence. In a letter to General de Pellieux he threatened in the guise of seeking advice: "What should I do, seeing that the experts are refusing to draw the conclusions that you were hoping for? . . . How is it that neither Charavay nor Varinard [two of the graphologists], whom you know, has found in my favor? . . . If the experts conclude that the [de Boulancy] writing is mine, it is not impossible to try to prove, for my own defense, that Dreyfus is the author of the *bordereau*"—an unsettling prospect, for the Army's chiefs feared that Esterhazy would lose any countersuit against Mathieu in a civilian court.

In his relations with General de Pellieux Esterhazy confined himself to unctuous insinuations. With Du Paty (now a lieutenant colonel) he was brutally direct. In early December, through his impressionable young nephew Christian, Esterhazy delivered an ultimatum to Du Paty: "If the Major [Esterhazy] is not acquitted of all charges, he will commit suicide." And while Du Paty savored this good news, Christian added that, before killing himself, his uncle would publish Du Paty's correspondence and a full account of their relations.

"This is a case of blackmail! And this is the way in which I am rewarded for having wished to protect Esterhazy against the dangers which threaten him!" Du Paty shrieked. "I shall become the victim of my own good nature—I who am innocent!"

Just as Esterhazy had predicted, Major Du Paty bombarded General de Boisdeffre with urgent letters which became increasingly hysterical. "There are limits to abnegation and patience, and I will not tolerate being dragged through the mud in this manner," he warned the man who had drawn him into the quagmire. If the Chief of Staff would not persuade the Minister of War to protect him, Du Paty vowed to take matters into his own hands; he, too, knew things that were better left in the crammed files of Counterintelligence.* Now there were two blackmail threats for the General Staff to deal with.

So long as the defenders of Alfred Dreyfus (they were now so numerous and so vocal that the term *Dreyfusard* was coined) were led by an aging Senator and a Jewish journalist, Bernard Lazare, the Army remained confident. But while Ravary and de Pellieux struggled with their handwriting experts, the Dreyfusards recruited their most powerful spokesman, an international figure from the world of belles lettres. Émile Zola's articles had been crashing down upon the government and the Army like sledgehammers since Mathieu's charges against Esterhazy. Zola had not witnessed the degradation. At the time he had been in Italy. Unlike the writers Maurice Barrès and Anatole France, he had no disturbing memories of the erect officer in his shredded uniform defiantly shouting his innocence. Furthermore, Zola had recently written a flawed but popular novel, *L'Argent*, based on the Panama Scandal, which was generally considered to be unfriendly to the Jews.

On November 13, 1897, Senator Scheurer-Kestner invited Zola to dinner along with Maître Leblois and Marcel Prévost, the writer. The Senator was risking a great deal. Zola's irascibility was legendary. He championed causes more from spleen than from reason, and he loved France at least as much as he loved himself. Fortunately for the Dreyfusards, what Zola learned that evening first dumbfounded and then electrified him. "It's gripping, it's thrilling! It's horrible! It's a frighten-

---

* Du Paty/Boisdeffre, December 13, 1897. BB 19 82.

ing drama but at the same time how grand it is because of all this!" Zola kept repeating.

Still quivering with excitement when he returned to his home in Médan twenty miles outside Paris, Zola outlined to himself that night the stupendous possibilities of the *Affaire*:

> What I saw in the Affair for literature was this—a trilogy of types: the innocent victim over there with a tempest in his skull; the scot-free traitor here, with his own internal tempest while another man pays for his crime; and the genius of truth, Scheurer-Kestner, silent but active.

The novelist Edmond de Goncourt had often commented on his friend Zola's relish for shocking causes, his "great delight" at being able to dominate Paris "from his modest room." Immense royalties had permitted Zola to exchange the modest room for the egregiously bourgeois house at Médan, but the urge to dominate remained stronger than ever. After November 13 he became, next to Mathieu, the most resolute Dreyfusard in France.

At Durand's restaurant, the chic literary oasis in the Place de la Madeleine, Zola raged against the unconvinced novelists Paul Bourget, Maurice Barrès, and Anatole France, and the poet François Coppée. "It's scientific, it's scientific!" he shouted over and over whenever his friends debated the truth of the Affair. It was impossible to reason with him. Although his two most recent novels, *Lourdes* and *Rome*, had infuriated Catholics, the French Academy was now reconciled to electing him to membership among the forty immortals. Victor Hugo had been dead more than a decade, and Zola was his unquestioned successor. Barrès and Léon Daudet, the son of Alphonse, warned him that he would ruin his candidacy if he defended Dreyfus. It did not matter; Zola intended to begin publishing a series of articles on the Affair immediately. The poet Coppée tried another tack: "*Mais, mon pauvre ami*, you are going to set all your readers against you. You won't sell a single book more."

On November 25 the prestigious *Figaro* published the first of Zola's articles. Just nine days before, *Le Figaro* had published Mathieu's letter to the Minister of War revealing Esterhazy as the traitor. Zola and *Le Figaro* were an explosive combination for the Army. From Berlin the sage Princess Radziwill, by birth a French aristocrat, wrote an Italian friend, "There ought to be some probability of success for it [*Figaro*] to have belled the cat first in this most obscure case."

Zola's first article, "Monsieur Scheurer-Kestner," reviewed the inconsistencies in the evidence against Dreyfus as well as the damning facts against Esterhazy and praised the Alsatian Senator's integrity. He concluded with the words, "Truth is on the march, and nothing will stop it." Ten days later he published "Le Syndicat," an acid parody of the brand of anti-Semitism preached by Drumont:

> We know the concept. Its baseness and simplistic nonsense
> are worthy of those who believe in it. Thus a syndicate is
> created. What that is supposed to mean is that some bankers
> are meeting, creating a pool of funds, exploiting the
> credulity of the public. . . . It is a vast, tenebrous
> enterprise of masked men.

This was the fool's syndicate, Zola snarled. It was an aberration. There was another syndicate, however; a grand cabal of honest men,

> all of them marching along different roads to the same goal,
> going along in silence, searching the earth, and ending
> one glorious morning at the same point. All of them have
> found themselves fatally joined hand in hand at the
> crossroads of truth, at this predestined rendezvous of
> justice.

It was a fine and timely article. Had there been one or two others like it, Theodor Herzl might not have written as he did in *Die Welt* a few weeks later: "Today France is anti-Semitic. About that there can be no doubt." Zola virtually conceded Herzl's point. "I must confess that the sickness is already widespread. The poison has entered into the people even if they are not yet stricken," he wrote for the last time in *Le Figaro*. The people were sufficiently stricken to curtail their purchase of *Le Figaro*. Declining circulation figures compelled the owner de Rodays to cancel Zola's series.

The day after Christmas, the handwriting experts consulted by the Army's investigator, Major Ravary, surrendered. Unanimously, they found that Esterhazy was not the author of the *bordereau*, that the *petit bleu* was a forgery, and that the de Boulancy letters could have been written by someone other than Esterhazy. Now he and the government could safely risk the charade of a full-dress court-martial to clear his name.

What was extraordinary about Major Ravary's exoneration and Esterhazy's forthcoming trial was the attitude of the public. Deceived or confused, many Frenchmen were much more ready to accept the guilt of a Jew than to doubt the integrity of an officer descended from one of Europe's great houses. Especially one who readily explained the plots against him and whose alibis were supported by his superiors. And then, the *bordereau* aside, what had Esterhazy written that was so outrageous after all? The ordinary Frenchman's hatred of Germany and insensate love of his Army disguised an inferiority complex, a fear that France would never settle scores on the battlefield. Hardly a week passed without newspapers railing against the government and its Minister of War because of some alleged compromise of national preparedness, some expedient decision imperiling the nation's defenses. Major Esterhazy had just expressed in the brutal, intimate language intended for his mistress the sour thoughts of many career soldiers—thoughts that tens of thousands of civilians with less spleen kept to themselves.

Despite all the foul play by their enemies, the Dreyfusards continued to fight honorably. In early January 1898, a few days before the court-martial, Mathieu had an opportunity to embarrass Esterhazy's defense. In late December, an Italian journalist living in Paris and a friend of Panizzardi, Enrico

Casella, had offered his services. In exchange for full expenses
and authorization to publish his findings, Casella would ask
Schwartzkoppen in Berlin for all the details of his dealings with
Esterhazy. Mathieu accepted the terms; Casella left for Germany, ingratiated himself with the former military attaché, and
at the end of the first week in January returned to Paris. Punctually, at two in the afternoon, Mathieu presented himself at
Casella's apartment. The domestic explained that her employer
had been unexpectedly called away but would return shortly.
As the minutes passed, Mathieu noticed a large, white envelope
in the center of Casella's desk. By two-fifteen there was still
no Casella and Mathieu scrutinized the envelope more carefully. It was addressed to "Monsieur le Colonel Panizzardi"
and its transparency revealed the large, slow handwriting of
Schwartzkoppen on the paper within.

When Casella arrived at two-thirty, he expressed surprise that
the envelope was unopened. Schwartzkoppen was forbidden to
discuss the Affair in public but he had intended for Mathieu
to intercept this detailed letter to Panizzardi, Casella explained.
For better or worse, Mathieu's morals were not those of the
General Staff. He insisted the letter be handed over to the
Italian military attaché.

The following afternoon, Casella appeared at Mathieu's
apartment unannounced. "It's idiotic, what you've done. I
played the comedian enough for you to understand. Panizzardi
read me a part of that letter. It contains the convincing proof
of Esterhazy's culpability." They had come so close to trapping
him, Casella lamented. The court-martial was only hours away.
By this time a friendly newspaper could have published the
text of Schwartzkoppen's letter; it would have been a calamity
for the Army.

"No, no, it's idiotic!" Casella exploded. "When you've got
to fight against adversaries as unprincipled . . . you haven't
the right to these scruples. They don't have them with you." *

---

* Mathieu Dreyfus, "Souvenirs."

He had done what was necessary, Mathieu insisted. In a fight for justice the means had to be honorable. Yet the man who once had hired a prostitute to seduce a clue from Schwartz-koppen may not have been such a purist from ethical motives alone. Without Schwartzkoppen's public authentication, the value of Casella's letter was, at best, dubious and, at worst, risked an Army accusation against Mathieu of being involved in foreign conspiracy. Mathieu had decided the disadvantages outweighed the possible gain.

On January 10, 1898, Esterhazy went on trial in the same building where, three years before, Alfred Dreyfus had been sentenced to life imprisonment. The same painting of the crucified Christ dominated the upper wall behind the seven military judges. On this occasion, however, it hovered above a judicial carnival rather than a legal persecution. Where Drey-fus had spent weeks in prison awaiting trial, Esterhazy was placed under house arrest until twenty-four hours before the court-martial; only then was he taken to Cherche-Midi prison. For Dreyfus the proceedings had gone on behind closed doors in a nearly empty room. Esterhazy's trial was a performance crammed with sympathizers, many of them women who had stood in line awaiting admission since five o'clock that morning.

Among the twenty-six witnesses, one of the first was the land-lord of Esterhazy's mistress, who related that when Mathieu's accusation was published, Esterhazy had told Mademoiselle Pays he was going to kill himself. Marguerite Pays had matter-of-factly inquired of her landlord whether her lease would expire in the event of her benefactor's death. Mademoiselle Pays bustled to the witness stand to deny the suicide story.

The second day the star witness was Mathieu who forcefully argued the evidence connecting the *bordereau* to the defendant, refusing to be distracted by slander from Esterhazy's attorney. The surprise in Mathieu's testimony came when he read a letter from Esterhazy to Maurice Weil: "I am in such a plight that I can only recover myself by crime."

Esterhazy's turn at the bar was a typical mixture of bravura and irrelevancy. "Of all the infamies of which I am the victim," he orated, "Weil's treason is the most painful to me. I have rendered him services the nature of which I won't state here. I am not a coward or a traitor." The audience applauded. As for the "crime" in the letter to Weil, Esterhazy explained, with a show of reluctance and trembling, that because of his miserable circumstances he had contemplated the killing of himself and his family. Pitilessly pursued by a band of monied miscreants determined to save Dreyfus by discrediting him, he had been saved in the eleventh hour by a mysterious "veiled lady." Who she was and where she came from, Esterhazy did not know, but she had given him the "liberating document"—that super-secret piece of nonexistent evidence whereby he had proven his innocence to the President, the Prime Minister, and the Minister of War; evidence which he had then patriotically surrendered to the proper authorities. The ladies, the soldiers, and the hirelings of Counterintelligence applauded as the *sympathique* Esterhazy stepped down.

The court-martial was not entirely public. Picquart's discussion of the *bordereau* and the *petit bleu* took place only after the audience had been removed. On the pretext of national security, the public was prevented from hearing the sole witness capable of fitting all the pieces together. "The evidence behind closed doors, it is understood, completely crushed Colonel Picquart," the reporter for the New York *Tribune* cabled. That was precisely the misconception the Army intended to create.

The court-martial closed with a several-hours-long argument by the lawyers, a wholly dispensable exercise from the point of view of the judges who took a mere three minutes to return a verdict of acquittal. Esterhazy's greatest danger occurred immediately after the court-martial judgment. He was almost suffocated amidst the pandemonium of his admirers. Ladies wept and fainted; men jostled each other brutally to reach him. Esterhazy graciously waved to his fans from the shoulders of weeping, cheering men who hoisted him above the frenzied

crowd. France had a hero. Women sent him an avalanche of
mail, many claiming to be the veiled lady. Men wrote to thank
him for displaying the martial flamboyance expected of a gentleman and a soldier of France. Philippe, Duc d'Orléans, Pretender
to the throne, was reported to have emerged from his Belgian
sanctuary to embrace Esterhazy on the steps of the court-
martial building. The New York *Tribune* believed "the day's
proceedings have revealed the utter hollowness of the Drey-
fusians' charge against Esterhazy and the flimsiness of the
reasons for their belief in the innocence of Dreyfus."

Outside France, however, very few newspapers concurred
with the *Tribune*. The *Times* of London reported the court-
martial in a tone of frosty disgust. The Vienna *Allgemeine Zei-
tung* observed that "everything connected with the trial and
the manner in which it was conducted was without precedent
and well-nigh incredible." "The Esterhazy trial is finished,"
Budapest's principal newspaper commented, "but the real investigation of the Dreyfus Affair has yet to begin."

The day after his acquittal Esterhazy wrote a personal letter
to General de Pellieux, a more emotional one than the formal
expression of gratitude already posted: "*Mon Général*, I have
just written you in order to express—most inadequately because I cannot find the words to say what I feel—all the gratitude, all the infinite appreciation that I have in my heart for
you." Even though General Billot would soon compel Esterhazy to retire from the Army, the Count had every reason to
be grateful. As he said many years afterwards, "The people
on the General Staff were some very remarkable idiots."

Unaware of these events, although excited by certain hints
in Lucie's December letters, Dreyfus wrote several letters to
the President of France pleading for a retrial. At the end of
the first week in February, he wrote Lucie, "With each day I
expect to learn that the day of justice has finally shone upon us."
But outside his immediate family, there was only one man who
believed Dreyfus might still find justice.

At the height of his career Voltaire had had the courage to stand against the vindictive Louis XV in order to defend the Calases, a Protestant family wrongly convicted of murdering a son to prevent his becoming a Catholic. Voltaire's finest hour had come with the vindication of this family. Émile Zola clung to the idea that Dreyfus could be his Calas Case. When the Esterhazy verdict was announced, he guilelessly confessed to the Deputy Joseph Reinach that he had had "the prima donna's fear that someone would have his idea at the same time . . . and take away his part." That evening Zola locked himself in his study at Médan and wrote until dawn.

There was more to what he wrote than outrage over a heinous judicial error. Zola's ego had been drawn into the Affair at a more personal level. Since his first article in *Le Figaro* seven weeks before, his character and even his patriotism had been defamed in the Nationalist press. Drumont, showing his usual lack of concern for slander, accused Zola of "throwing himself into the melée supported by Jewish stipends." The great naturalistic writer, according to Drumont—"this son of an Italian immigrant"—had revealed "what he was at bottom: the falsest, the most declamatory, the most verbose, the windiest of all the writers of this time." He added, "The day is not far when things will grow warm for Israel and its friends." There was just enough truth in Drumont's barbs and more than enough contumely in his threat to stampede Zola. His indignation had verged on paroxysm three weeks before, when at the funeral of his old friend Alphonse Daudet he was heckled with cries of "Down with Zola! Down with the traitor! Bandit! Sellout!" He knew that Barrès had recently whispered that Zola was an idiot. He was constantly being attacked as a vulgarian, an atheist, a sensationalist, even as a clumsy, turgid writer. But he had never been attacked by butchers, shopkeepers, and workmen. And to be reproached for his Italian lineage was an insupportable indignity. Finishing the long, crackling essay, Zola quickly had a cup of coffee, put on his coat, and headed for the offices of *L'Aurore*, Georges Clemenceau's newspaper.

Reading Zola's essay that morning and recognizing that it might be his golden opportunity for revenge against the Nationalists, Clemenceau agreed to publish it. He mistrusted Jews almost as much as he despised practising Catholics. Later, when Clemenceau met Mathieu, Mathieu "sensed a certain reserve behind the appearance of cordiality on his part as well as that of his entourage. I was the brother of the one whom the country called 'The Traitor'; I was also 'a Jew.' " But, like Zola, Clemenceau had begun to perceive the large personal and historic potential of the Affair. Overturning governments had been the ex-Deputy's principal sport, a pastime he was no longer able to indulge, partly because Drumont had compromised him with the electorate over the Panama Scandal. The fierce-eyed "Tiger" (the sobriquet bestowed upon him as Prime Minister during World War I), whose smooth crown, bushy mustaches, and generous waist gave him the appearance of a eupeptic walrus, was also swayed by the counsel of his friend the politician Arthur Ranc and the favorable reactions to Zola's articles among the intellectuals. Call it *"J'Accuse,"* he suggested when Zola said that he had not been able to think of an appropriate title. The next day, January 13, 1898, *L'Aurore,* with a normal circulation of about thirty thousand, sold nearly three hundred thousand copies.

J'Accuse is a unique document. Like the similar works of Spinoza, Milton, Voltaire, and Hugo, Zola's essay pitted the man of letters against the prejudices of his society when government and public opinion were indifferent or opposed to morality and justice. If not a philosophical treatise, *J'Accuse* was, nonetheless, a magnificent enumeration of specific wrongdoings whose implications were as arresting as anything in the *Aeropagitica* or *Napoleon le Petit.* After *J'Accuse* the role of the man of letters in France and eventually in Western society was irrevocably altered. Addressing the President of the Republic, Zola charged that "a court-martial has but recently, by order, dared to acquit one Esterhazy—a supreme slap at all truth, all justice!"

Since they have dared, I too shall dare. I shall tell the truth
because I pledged myself to tell it if justice, regularly
empowered, did not do so fully, unmitigatedly. My duty is
to speak; I have no wish to be an accomplice. My nights
would be haunted by the spectre of the innocent being,
expiating under the most frightful torture, a crime he never
committed.

In the eyes of the Army, one injustice nullified another.
France must know how absurd and malign was the 1894
travesty against Dreyfus:

Dreyfus, it is shown, knows several languages: crime; he
works hard: crime; no compromising papers are found in
his home: crime; he goes occasionally to the country of
his origin: crime; he endeavors to learn everything: crime;
he is not easily worried: crime; he is worried: crime. And
the simplicity of all these concoctions, pompous assertions
in a vacuum! We were told of fourteen charges in the
accusation; in the end we find only one, that of the
bordereau; and we learn that even the experts were not
unanimous on this, that one of them, M. Gobert, was
roughly handled for not having come to the desired
conclusion. . . . It is a family trial, one is completely among
friends, and it must be remembered, finally, that the
General Staff made the trial, judged it, and has just merely
reaffirmed its judgment.

Zola blamed Lieutenant Colonel Du Paty—"the foggy, complicated ruling spirit, haunted by romantic intrigues"—as the
one "who is first and most of all guilty of the fearful miscarriage of justice." He praised Mathieu, Scheurer-Kestner, and
Picquart for their courage and sense of national honor. Honest
Picquart discovered the real traitor, presented his findings to
his superiors, begged them to act:

These researches lasted from May to September, 1896, and
what must be cried out loud to all is that General Gonse
was convinced of the guilt of Esterhazy, that General Billot

and General Boisdeffre never doubted that the *bordereau*
was the work of Esterhazy; the inquest of Picquart's had
made that conclusion inevitable. But the emotion was
extraordinary, for the condemnation of Esterhazy
involved. . . the revision of the Dreyfus verdict and it was
this of all things that the General Staff wished to avoid at
all cost.

The generals would not act to save an innocent man. Nevertheless, "at Paris, Truth was on the march," indefatigable,
unconquerable. Mathieu Dreyfus and Auguste Scheurer-Kestner
were tightening the noose around Esterhazy. "Witnesses show
him [i.e., Esterhazy] maddened at first, prone to suicide or
flight. Then suddenly, he gambles on a daring front, he amazes
all Paris by the violence of his gestures and attitudes. Help
had come to him."

> Who, people asked in amazement, could be the defenders of
> Major Esterhazy? There is first Colonel Du Paty de Clam;
> there is next, General Boisdeffre, General Gonse, General
> Billot himself, all compelled now to have the Major
> acquitted, since they cannot permit the innocence of Dreyfus
> to be recognized without having the whole War Ministry
> demolished by the public wrath. And the beautiful result
> of this preposterous situation is that the man who is
> supremely honest, who, alone of all men, has done his duty,
> is to be the victim, is to be subjected to derision and
> punishment. . . . This then, Mr. President, is the Esterhazy
> affair: a guilty man who had to be exculpated for "reasons
> of state." For two months past we have been forced to
> look at this fine spectacle, hour by hour. . . . And we have
> seen General Pellieux, then Major Ravary conduct a
> dishonorable investigation from which scoundrels emerge
> purified and honest men besmirched. And then, at length,
> they convoked the court-martial.

Now that the die was cast, that the true nature of their
religious and feudal prejudices had been taken, the chiefs of

the Army must be chastised by the might of republican France. If not, great and liberal France with her rights of man, would expire.

> Such then, Mr. President, is the simple truth. It is the fearful truth. . . . I suspect that you have no power in this matter, that you are the prisoner of the Constitution and of your situation. You have, nonetheless, your duty as a man, on which you will doubtless reflect and which you will fulfill. In any event, I do not despair in the least of ultimate triumph. I repeat with more intense conviction: the truth is on the march and nothing will stop it! It is only today that this affair has begun, since it is only now that sides have definitely been taken; on the one hand, the culprits who want no light at all on this business; on the other, lovers of justice who would lay down their lives for it. I have said elsewhere and I say again, when the truth is buried underground, it grows, it chokes, it gathers such an explosive force that on the day when it bursts out, it blows everything up with it. We shall soon see whether we have not laid the mines for a most far-reaching disaster of the near future.

> But this letter is long, Mr. President, and it is time to conclude.
> *I accuse Colonel Du Paty de Clam* of having been the diabolical agent of the judicial error, unconsciously, I prefer to believe, and of having continued to defend his deadly work during the past three years through the most absurd and revolting machinations.
> *I accuse General Mercier* of having made himself an accomplice in one of the greatest crimes of history, probably through weak-mindedness.
> *I accuse General Billot* of having had in his hands the decisive proofs of the innocence of Dreyfus and of having concealed them, and of having rendered himself guilty of the crime of *lèse* humanity and *lèse* justice, out of political motives and to save the face of the General Staff.
> *I accuse General de Boisdeffre and General Gonse* of being

accomplices in the same crime, the former no doubt through religious prejudice, the latter out of *esprit de corps.*

I accuse General de Pellieux and Major Ravary of having made a villainous inquest, I mean an inquest of the most monstrous partiality, the complete report of which composes for us an imperishable monument of naive effrontery.

I accuse the three handwriting experts, MM. Belhomme, Varinard and Couard of having made lying and fraudulent reports, unless a medical examination will certify them to be deficient of sight and judgment.

I accuse the War Office of having led a vile campaign in the press, particularly in *L'Eclair* and in *L'Echo de Paris* in order to misdirect public opinion and cover up its sins.

I accuse, lastly, the first court-martial of having violated all human right in condemning a prisoner on testimony kept secret from him, and

I accuse the second court-martial of having covered up this illegality by order, committing in turn the judicial crime of acquitting a guilty man with full knowledge of his guilt.

In making these accusations I am aware that I render myself liable to articles 30 and 31 of the Libel Laws of July 29, 1881, which punish acts of defamation. I expose myself voluntarily. . . .

I have one passion only, for light, in the name of humanity which has borne so much and has a right to happiness. . . . Let them dare then to carry me to the court of appeals, and let there be an inquest in the full light of the day!

I am waiting.

The government would have preferred to ignore the challenge. But the clamor within France and the international attention drawn by *J'Accuse* precluded official inaction. Here and there—in French-speaking Canada, in Russia—Zola was denounced and the Army praised. Despite his enlightened political and social policies, the Pope of the Ralliement, Leo XIII, remained silent while allowing the official Jesuit review, *La Civiltà Cattolica*, to inflame Catholic opinion against Jews:

> The Jews have invented the allegation of a judicial error. The
> plot was worked out at the Zionist Congress in Basel, invoked
> ostensibly to discuss the deliverance of Jerusalem. The
> Protestants made common cause with the Jews for the
> creation of a syndicate. . . . The Jews allege a judicial
> error. The real error was that of the Constituent Assembly
> [of 1789] which granted them French nationality.
> That law must be repealed.

But the Jesuits spoke for a minority. The world beyond France
was overwhelmingly pro Zola.

"Zola May Be Cast Into a Dungeon," a worried San Francisco
Examiner informed its readers. The great writer received thirty
thousand telegrams and letters of congratulation from abroad.
Mark Twain wrote in the New York *Herald*:

> Such cowards, hypocrites, and flatterers as the members of
> military and ecclesiastical courts the world could produce
> by the millions every year. But it takes five centuries to
> produce a Joan of Arc or a Zola.

An American novelist's panegyric was less troublesome for the
French government than the Kaiser's Foreign Minister who told
the Reichstag, on January 24, that the German Embassy in Paris
had never had dealings with Captain Dreyfus. A watching world,
an angry Army, and a gleefully vengeful public compelled Prime
Minister Meline to act.

On February 7, 1898, Zola stood trial in the Palais de
Justice on the cautious charge that he had accused the judges
of the Esterhazy court-martial of acquitting the accused on
orders from the government. Although Zola's trial lasted sixteen tumultuous days, it was over before it began. The president of the three-man tribunal, portly Jules Delegorgue, was
the most obsequious of civil servants. The names and addresses of the twelve jurors were published in the Nationalist
press to ensure their intimidation. The courtroom was filled with
uniformed officers under orders to cheer or disrupt the trial
on command. A noted French reporter described the scene:

> For twenty-five years I have attended trials in criminal
> courts but I cannot remember any audience so rough as this
> was. . . . They invaded not only the places reserved for
> the audience but took seats around the judges and jurors,
> sat on windowsills. Some climbed on the stoves. The
> lawyers sat along the walls and on the steps; some young
> men sat on the floor, their legs crossed like Turks in front
> of the jury.

The stunned reporter form the London *Times* agreed:

> Never, even at the most sensational trials of our time, has
> there been such a crowd as that which invaded the Assize
> Court today. In spite of the rigorous restrictions placed
> on admission, there was a perfect crush. Magistrates,
> barristers, journalists, politicians, even a few ladies in
> bright colors had managed to enter by right of favor, and
> half the people had to sit on the floor or the steps or on
> other persons' knees.

Outside the Palais de Justice, only a few steps from Notre
Dame, Nationalist vigilantes glowered at the few Dreyfusards
intrepid enough to come to hail Zola. Henri de Rochefort, the
Nationalist journalist, arrived to *vivats* and a few shouted insults. "It would seem that with four of you at five francs apiece
the Dreyfus Syndicate will not be ruined!" Rochefort shouted
back at his hecklers. Then the mood of the crowd became
uglier. Zola's carriage had arrived. A lone Dreyfusard who cried
"*Vive* Zola!" was set upon and beaten.

Inside, the attorney representing the officers of the Esterhazy
court-martial, Maître Van Cassel, took the measure of Zola's
counsel, Fernand Labori. Van Cassel was known for his vicious
aggressiveness, the giant Labori for his stentorian voice and
dogged debating. Clemenceau's brother, Albert, represented the
indicted editor of *L'Aurore*. Although trained as a physician,
Clemenceau himself, as its owner, insisted on defending the
newspaper.

Zola seemed to be enjoying the preliminaries. Dressed in a
black coat and white vest, he moved about, chatted with journal-

ists, huddled with sympathizers, and read his telegrams. The
flow of telegrams from America, Britain, Japan, Peru, Rumania,
and other countries around the world continued into the second
day. One Belgian telegram contained a thousand names.

The next day, Tuesday, the picayune questions and adversary
feints continued until Labori announced that he intended to
summon Madame Lucie Dreyfus. Judge Delegorgue objected.
The captain's wife could have nothing of interest to tell the
court about the charge. Zola leapt to his feet in protest. "Do
you know article 52 of the Law of 1881?" Delegorgue challenged him. "I don't know the law and I don't want to know
it"—the audience noisily stirred at this—"don't want to know
it at this moment," Zola quickly added above the hubbub.
Madame Zola ostentatiously embraced Madame Dreyfus as she
returned to her seat.

Finally, late in the day, testimony began. Leblois and
Scheurer-Kestner were among the first witnesses. The Senator
spoke at length and cast doubt upon the good faith of Billot.
The white-maned Senator was treated with mute deference by
Judge Delegorgue. Then came the slightly prissy former President of the Republic, Casimir-Périer. "I cannot tell the whole
truth; my duty is not to tell it," he reiterated. Nevertheless, he
took up a good deal of the court's time explaining why he could
explain nothing. It was late evening when the court adjourned.

That morning there had still been a few cheers for Zola.
"There is a foreign accent to those cries which explains their
enthusiasm," Rochefort had told the Chicago *Tribune*'s reporter.
By the end of the day, however, the crowd outside had been
whipped into a murderous state by Drumont's agitators. As
Zola and his friends crossed the courtyard, the Palais de Justice
was stormed by nearly a thousand people screaming for Zola's
blood. At that moment the police closed the gates and vanished,
leaving the writer surrounded by the howling mob. Then there
was a last-minute police charge; the gates reopened, a special
police van appeared, and Zola leapt aboard just in time to
escape being torn to pieces.

Not until February 11, a Friday, did the sessions show any fireworks. The day before, General de Pellieux had stung Zola by calling his conduct a disservice to the nation. Zola insisted on being heard. He reminded the jury that his forty books had been translated into all the major languages, that through him "the language of France has been carried to the whole world. I would ask General de Pellieux if he does not think that there are many ways to serve France?" Zola declaimed. "One can serve it with the sword and with the pen?" And then, his ego overflowing, Zola archly predicted that future generations would remember wobbly, bespectacled Zola long after the trim, positive de Pellieux had gone to his deserved rest. The jury of merchants, toy salesmen, and market gardeners was not favorably impressed.

On Saturday the Army suffered a severe embarrassment. Ever since Scheurer-Kestner had taken an interest in the Affair, the General Staff had made a great deal of its Secret Dossier —its collection of irrefutable proofs of Dreyfus' guilt (in reality, nothing more than Sandherr's original cache which was still being "nourished"). Lieutenant Colonel Henry now claimed again that, while passing Picquart's open door, he had seen Leblois with Picquart examining the Secret Dossier at the beginning of November 1896. He had noticed a portion of the Scoundrel D letter protruding from the large brown envelope, he said. Leblois quickly reminded the court that in previous testimony to Ravary, the witness had said, "The photocopy never left the envelope." It was a difficult moment. Picquart wanted to know what kind of vision could make out the handwriting in a photocopy whose dimensions were less than those of the actual document. "Don't worry; me, I'd recognize it from ten paces," was the rueful and ironically truthful reply. "To that, I oppose the most categorical denial," Picquart disdainfully submitted. Reading skepticism on the faces of the jurors, Henry stepped toward Picquart, stating as provocatively as possible, "This isn't open to discussion—especially when a person is used to seeing a document. I maintain what has been

said and still do. Colonel Picquart has lied about this!" He
offered his cheek and Picquart instinctively raised his arm.
Henry, his bullish neck thrust forward, Picquart flushed and
lowering his arm, the audience silent and hypnotized—it was
Judge Delegorgue who was the first to recover with the serene
understatement, "You two are in disagreement."

Taut, his voice taking on the metallic timbre of restrained
rage, Picquart finally broke through the psychological and professional barriers which had restrained him. For more than an
hour he lectured the court on Dreyfus' innocence, Esterhazy's
treason, and the byzantine deviousness of the General Staff.

By Thursday afternoon, February 17, despite Judge Delegorgue's stringent regulation of testimony, the trial moved onto
the terrain which Zola had cultivated when he wrote *J'Accuse*.
Thanks to General de Pellieux's insistence that Esterhazy could
never have composed so secret and complex a document as the
bordereau, the judges were obliged to let Picquart return to the
bar to discuss the question. Picquart explained that the *bordereau* must have been composed by an officer outside the
General Staff and unfamiliar with artillery expressions. Then
Labori made a final compelling point about the *bordereau*'s
concluding sentence, "I'm off to maneuvers." Dreyfus and all
the Staff apprentices had known since April 1894 that they
were not to attend the Army's annual maneuvers.

This was too much for de Pellieux. The pliant Delegorgue
allowed him to interrupt the defense. Labori, who had learned
the futility of objecting to the unprecedented liberties Delegorgue permitted the generals, promptly took his seat. "I
request to be allowed to speak," de Pellieux declared, "not
about the Dreyfus Case—I won't talk about that. But I shall
repeat the words of Colonel Henry: 'You want the truth—let's
have it!'" The court fell to attention:

At the Ministry of War—and observe, I'm not talking about
the Dreyfus Case—they have had absolute proof of the
guilt of Dreyfus! And I have seen this proof! A letter

arrived at the Ministry of War whose origin cannot be
contested and which says—I'll quote you what's in it—

What de Pellieux recited was the approximate text of the False
Henry, the spurious Alexandrine letter ending, "If anybody
asks you, say just that for nobody must never know what happened with him." Zola and his lawyers exchanged satisfied
glances while Henry did his best to appear impassive. Finally,
the Army was beginning to disclose its vaunted secret evidence.

After de Pellieux's revelation it seemed inevitable that Zola's
trial would turn into a public inquisition of the leaders of the
Army. The government would then have to order the Ministry
of Justice to investigate the evidence against Dreyfus and
Mathieu's charges against Esterhazy. Accompanying Paléologue
from the Palais de Justice that evening, Henry was frightened
and furious. "What a day. What Pellieux did was absurd!
Documents as secret as that should not be discussed in public."
More than anyone else, Henry had cause to dread the adversary
wrath of Maître Labori.

Thus far, the Dreyfus Affair had been a debate over the
supposed miscarriage of justice in the particular case of a
Jewish captain. On the morning of the eleventh day of the Zola
trial, the Chief of Staff magnified the Affair into what it might
otherwise never have become. When General de Boisdeffre
advanced to the witness bar with the stiff gait of a cavalry
officer whose legs had been broken many times in falls, when
he stood before the court in his brilliant dress uniform with
French and foreign medals ashimmer, he proceeded to trans-
mute the question of Dreyfus' innocence or guilt into an issue
of national honor, order, and survival. While he did not actually
demand that Frenchmen abjure their ideals of Liberty, Fra-
ternity, and Civilian Sovereignty, he did peremptorily command
that they accept the supremacy of Order, Expediency, and Military Wisdom. "I shall be brief," de Boisdeffre announced in
clipped tones. He confirmed the truth of General de Pellieux's
claims "on all points," without bothering to discuss their de-

tails. Haughtily, he turned to the jurors for his final, frightening statement:

> Permit me, in closing, to tell you something. You are the jury, you are the nation. If the nation does not have confidence in the chiefs of its Army, in those who have the responsibility for national defense, they are prepared to leave to others this heavy task. You have only to speak. I shall not say another word.

The General excused himself from the bar although Zola's counsel was on his feet to cross-examine.

"You do not have the floor," Judge Delegorgue interrupted. "This incident is closed."

"Excuse me, *Monsieur le Président*, I have some questions to ask," Maître Labori insisted. "This incident is closed," the judge snapped. "Have Major Esterhazy come forward."

Esterhazy's appearance was an anticlimax. The Count arrogantly refused to answer a single question put to him by the defense. Nor did it matter. De Boisdeffre's ultimatum thoroughly cowed the jurors, who were already intimidated by the publication of their names and addresses in *La Libre Parole*.

Zola was charged with stating that the Ministry of War had ordered Esterhazy's acquittal. This he had certainly done, and nothing Zola or his attorneys had said had disproved the veracity of the charge. Legally, Zola's condemnation was ordained by the restricted nature of the indictment. Nevertheless, his address to the court on February 21 was so moving that it seemed just possible that justice might prevail over jurisprudence:

> Dreyfus is innocent, I swear. I vouch for it with my life and honor. In this solemn hour, before this court, before you, gentlemen of the jury, who represent the nation, before France, I swear that Dreyfus is innocent. By my forty years of work, by the respect earned by the work of my life, I swear that Dreyfus is innocent. By all I have gained by the name I have made, and my contribution to the growth of French literature, I swear that Dreyfus is

innocent. May all of this perish, my work fail, if Dreyfus
is not innocent. He is innocent!

But Zola was doomed to win by losing. On February 23 the
jury unanimously found Zola and Georges Clemenceau guilty
as charged. They were fined three thousand francs each; Zola
was sentenced to one year and Clemenceau to four months in
prison—verdicts which their attorneys immediately appealed.

The world press granted front page space to Zola's conviction.
Californians divided their indignation between the sinking of
the battleship *Maine* and the outrage in the Palais de Justice.
The editor of the San Francisco *Examiner* grudgingly praised
"the apostle of dirt in literature," concluding that Zola "has
got more honor out of this case than all his government." On
Chicago's north side the city's plutocracy had devoted February
to blackface *soirées*, talk of Cuba, and the Zola trial. The
Tribune expressed the disgust of Chicago's leading citizens:
"Such a farcical perversion of the methods of justice could not
be conceived as occurring in England or America—probably
in no other country where courts exist except France and
Spain."

Europe agreed. The *Daily News* of London wrote France off
as being "virtually in the hands of a military government."
Budapest's main tabloid, the *Pester Lloyd*, asked, "To what low
depths must the nation have sunk which raises [the journalist]
Rochefort onto a pinnacle and casts Zola into prison?" The
Berliner Tageblatt was severe: "Yesterday the French Army
won its first victory since its defeat in 1870."

But it was an American newspaper published by blacks, the
Bee of the District of Columbia, whose contempt of Zola's
conviction was unexcelled: "French justice seems to have fled
to brutish beasts, for the verdict is simply an expression of
the prejudice and race hate of an uninformed and inferior
mob."

chapter eleven:

"ALL THE CRETINS ARE WITH US"

THE FRANCE THAT BEGAN TO GO MAD AT THE beginning of 1898 had been so brilliant, so reasonable, and so civilized—had been so much the land of light and progress—that those who knew the Great War of 1914 and its grim aftermath nostalgically christened the decade or more after 1890 *la belle époque.* France—Paris—was the world's forcing house of fashion, art, and literature, the source of much science and philosophy and not a little music, and of a luxuriant variety of political creeds and styles of life.

Although the *belle époque* rested on solid achievement, it was an era which celebrated mannered grace and refinement merging with decadence; an era when wit and facile conversation often prevailed over serious thought. Life had come to imitate art with a relish. To the young Englishman Wickham Steed, just arriving from studies in Berlin, "philosophy, as taught at the Sorbonne, sounded sadly thin and casual. Descriptive psychology was little better. Literature, which held, to my mind, an inordinately large place in the university scheme was treated with a care for elegance and a carelessness of earnest thought that shocked me. In fact, nobody seemed earnest." True, Wickham Steed altered his views after he gained admission to some of the capital's more meditative drawing rooms where he found "an enlightened earnestness, an unaffected sincerity such as I had never met before." These qualities were there, but they had to be patiently searched out behind the reigning spirit and style of the aristocracy.

As the numbers of the old aristocracy shrank and its wealth eroded (although not so rapidly as many believed), its titles and tastes became more esteemed. If anything, the ravages of successive revolutions and the infiltrations of the upper-middle classes had made the aristocracy more glamorous and socially more powerful. In that part of Paris known as the Faubourg Saint-Germain, the ancient families, the *gratin* (upper crust), wove an impenetrable residential cocoon in which they relived the past, shuddered at the present, and sedulously set about the endogamous business of perpetuating their own kind.

Money—the want of it—kept the *gratin* from shutting out the vulgar world of the Third Republic altogether. Some of the most gilded dynasties had been straitened even to the point of mongrelization. If the Duc Sosthène de La Rochefoucauld of the Jockey Club had escaped the need to "manure his land" with a monied marriage, he was one of the fortunate. And the Comte Aimery de La Rochefoucauld spoke for the clan and the *gratin* when he sniffed, in relating the unfortunate case of an aristocratic lady who married for love, "a few nights of passion and then a whole lifetime at the wrong end of the table." But the tables were becoming crowded with such people even as the Comte Aimery continued to huff—"they were mere nobodies in the year 1000."

There were not many whose ancestors had served Hugh Capet. The mother of the insufferably haughty Baron Robert de Montesquiou (one of the models for Proust's Charlus) was the heiress of a mere plutocrat. The Marquis Boni de Castellane had married the American heiress, Anna Gould, and was recklessly disregarding the Rothschilds' advice on how to spend her fortune. The Prince Edmond de Polignac rejoiced in the dowry provided by the American parents of Winnareta Singer. The Duc Agénor de Gramont married the daughter of Baron Charles de Rothschild, thus Judaizing one of the realm's noblest lines. Similarly, the grand Caraman-Chimays salvaged their fortune through one union with a rich American family, the Wards, and another with the Dutch banker Greffulhe.

With a few notable exceptions, it was not the old aristocracy who maintained the capital's most brilliant drawing rooms. Instead, the parvenue nobility—only recently entered upon the pages of the *Almanach de Gotha*—was left to fulfill the *gratin's* erstwhile role of artistic and literary patronage. And the ladies of the newer aristocracy performed that function consummately in the *salon*, that glittering, overfurnished drawing room consecrated to gastronomic and verbal excellence.

The Bonaparte Princesse Mathilde was a poor conversationalist with an indifferent kitchen but her "Fridays" in the Rue de Berri were surpassed for the brilliance of her guests only by the Comtesse Greffulhes and those upper-middle class hostesses, Mesdames Lemaire and Straus. Such ladies and their rich husbands served as cultural brokers with an éclat and a generosity rivaling the patrons of the Renaissance. Nobodies in the eleventh century, perhaps; now they compelled even the haughtiest to take notice of them.

It was, then, still a world of *plus ça change*, brilliant, exclusive, in thrall to the titled, leisurely literate. The graceless character of the Third Republic—the monotony of its collapsing, Tweedledum, Tweedledee Cabinets, its recurring larcenous scandals, its blustering egalitarian and anticlerical rhetoric—alienated large numbers of the upper classes, creating the phenomenon of internal *émigrés*—disgusted and nostalgic people, who shut most of the Republic out. As money accumulated behind high tariff walls, part of the Republic's bourgeoisie manufactured pedigrees (almost everyone added a *de* before his name) and affected a haughty manner. Proust expressed the obeisance

of high society to the old nobility through the narrator in
Swann's Way: "And the thought that, if he were seized by a
sudden illness and confined to the house, the people whom his
valet would instinctively run to find would be the Duc de
Chartres, the Prince de Reuss, the Duc de Luxembourg, and
the Baron de Charlus, brought him . . . a certain satisfactory
sense, if not actually of wealth and prosperity, at any rate, of
self-esteem."

In 1898 it seemed that only a misanthrope could wish and
only the rare Marxist could believe that this enchanted world
was about to be disrupted for the sake of an unglamorous Jew.
But it was in the *salons* that the calamity struck with un-
restrained ferocity.

The *crème de la crème* assembled at Madame Émile Straus's
every Sunday. Geneviève Straus was the composer Bizet's
widow; her Jewish second husband maintained a magnificent
residence in the Parc Monceau. There Edmond de Goncourt,
Alphonse Daudet, Stephane Mallarmé, François Coppée, Dumas
fils (until his death in 1895), Guy de Maupassant, Anatole
France, and Marcel Proust represented the world of letters;
Paul Hervieu and Georges de Porto-Riche, the dramatists;
Reynaldo Hahn and Gabriel Fauré, the composers; Caran
d'Ache, Jean Louis Forain, and Jacques Émile Blanche, carica-
turists and illustrators, regularly appeared. On occasion the
British Ambassador would drop in or Prince Albert of Monaco
along with such other titled habitués as the Prince d'Arenberg
or the Princesse Mathilde, niece of Napoleon I. At Madame
Straus' the shadow of Captain Alfred Dreyfus appeared for the
first time in October 1897. "*Mes amis*," Madame Straus announced to her guests after dinner, "Joseph Reinach has a very
important message to give you." Surprised, curious, the company filed into the drawing room where they listened for more
than an hour to Deputy Reinach's didactic discourse on the
bordereau, the irregularity of the Dreyfus court-martial, and
the treason of Major Walsin-Esterhazy.

Joseph Reinach knew that he was embarking upon a course

possibly fatal to his political career. Reinach personified the qualities of assimilated French Jewry. His Alsatian family had embraced France as the Promised Land. Joseph's brother, in his famous *Histoire des Israélites*, was to remind his brethren that "each country has the Jews that it deserves." The Reinachs never doubted that France was worthy of the best, most loyal Jews of Europe. Yet Reinach's patriotism had been troubled, and he had let himself be converted by Bernard Lazare to saving Dreyfus. Now the rotund Deputy was taking a public stand in one of the capital's most exclusive forums. "We heard him with an intense curiosity," the archeologist and historian, Gustave Schlumberger, remembered, "although some of us, myself among them, were already *au courant*."

When Reinach concluded, there was "a moment of silence, almost of stupor, as if all of his listeners were beginning to suspect the frightful noise that this case was going to cause in the world." Schlumberger rose to question "timidly" Reinach's harsh indictment of General Mercier, the former Minister of War, and found himself generally beleaguered. Monsieur Émile Straus was so carried away that he disregarded the role of moderator prescribed for the master of the house and furiously attacked Schlumberger, Alphonse Daudet, Coppée, and several others. It was their last soirée at the Straus home.

The ideological fault line uncovered in the Straus salon soon extended to that of Madame Aubernon de Nerville, an adze-witted lady who had a horror of bores. Two weeks later, in November, the Foreign Ministry's intelligence chief, Maurice Paléologue, dined at the de Nervilles'; Dreyfus monopolized the conversation. "Thus, for the first time at our hostess's table," Paléologue recorded in his diary, "there was talk neither of literature nor of philosophy." As the servants were bringing their coats, one of Madame de Nerville's guests, Paul Hervieu, told Paléologue in sententious tones, "I do not know what is going to come out of this affair but I am certain that I shall see justification—and more than justification—for all that I think of human stupidity and rascality." Charitably, Paléologue spared Hervieu the story of his encounter with Colonel Henry the week before. While strolling along the Seine, Henry had revealed that he had a letter from the Kaiser himself to Ambassador Münster in which the Kaiser openly referred to dealings with Dreyfus.

While hostesses began to compose invitation lists with an eye to their guests' views about Dreyfus and Esterhazy, probably no incident more graphically reflected the bitterness racking France at the beginning of 1898 than the debate on January 22 in the Chamber of Deputies. The leader of the parliamentary Socialists, Jean Jaurès, spoke to the Chamber with withering indignation about the Esterhazy travesty and the manner in which Zola had been indicted. "Are you with the Syndicate?" a royalist Deputy interrupted.

"What did you say, Monsieur de Bernis?"

"I said you must be with the Syndicate, that you are probably the Syndicate's lawyer!" Comte de Bernis shouted.

"Monsieur de Bernis, you are a wretch and a coward!" Jaurès retorted savagely. Even in the excitable Chamber these were unusually harsh words. Pandemonium erupted. A Socialist Deputy ran across the floor and struck de Bernis. As Jaurès left the tribune, de Bernis broke out of the ring of scuffling parliamentarians and chopped Jaurès twice on the back of the neck with his hand.

With the melee in the Chamber, the lengthening roster of duels, and the turbulence of the press in mind, *Psst*, the illustrated satirical review, carried Caran d'Ache's perfect cartoon. In two frames the artist depicted the state of mind, or rather the mindless state, of the French people over the Affair. Assembled before dinner, a typical family of means hears the host decree sternly, "And above all, no talk of the Dreyfus Case!" The second frame shows a scene of mayhem: table cloth torn, dishes shattered and silverware scattered, the butler and the diners pummeling and throttling each other. The caption reads, "They talked about it."

From this time on, thousands of children in Catholic families learned to call the chamber pot a "Zola." Georges Bernanos, Charles de Gaulle, and François Mauriac heard from their parents of the terrible sedition being perpetrated by the Jews and their allies. In an ancient land peopled by mellowed cynics and sophisticates, where what was supposedly new was always *déjà vu* and what appeared to change remained ultimately the same, where logic was Cartesian and passion itself was stylized, the natives went mad. In Bordeaux, Nancy, Nantes, and Rennes mobs roamed the streets sacking Jewish stores and desecrating synagogues in the days after *J'Accuse*. In Algeria the violence required the intervention of the Army.

The woods at Boulogne, Meudon, and Vincennes—even the gardens of suburban villas—echoed the clicks of dueling swords and the reports of pistols fired at regulation paces. In early December the Deputies Joseph Reinach and Alexandre Millerand fired at each other and missed. On January 21, 1898, Jean Ajalbert, a staff member of *L'Aurore*, met Monsieur André Vervoort on the *champs d'honneur*; neither was wounded. Four days later, Pierre Lefevre fought the same Vervoort; again there were no injuries and Vervoort went on insulting Dreyfusards at every opportunity. On February 3 Urbain Gohier, an antimilitarist author, wounded his opponent. On February 26 Georges Clemenceau combatted his old adversary, Drumont, and both walked away unharmed. On March 5 Picquart repaid Henry for his calumny during the Zola trial, wounding Henry in the arm. In mid-June the rich and dandified Marquis Boni de Castellane wounded his Dreyfusard opponent. Three days later the quixotic Nationalist Paul Déroulède tangled harmlessly with his foe. Rochefort was hurt when his turn came, and Barrès injured his fellow writer, Laurent Tailhade, in mid-October. The lunging and blasting went on, gathering in intensity throughout the year. No lives were lost, however, partly because of the ceremonial function which the adversaries knew the duel fulfilled and also because of the corpulence, astigmatism, or incompetence of many of the combatants.

The citadels of the intelligentsia—the cafés, the literary periodicals and the university—felt the quake of the Affair. The experience of one of their members was typical. Léon Blum, an outstanding graduate of the École Normale Supérieure, France's rigorous center for the training of teachers, had been set upon a career as a literary critic. The turning point in his life and that of French Socialism (he would become France's first Socialist and first Jewish Prime Minister) came in early September 1897 when the librarian of the École Normale cycled out to Blum's vacation retreat near Paris.

"Do you know that Dreyfus is innocent?" Lucien Herr wanted to know. But who was this Dreyfus? Blum asked. Herr, whose influence upon *Normaliens* was a phenomenon of two generations, immediately put Blum in the picture. Blum dashed back to Paris to spread the news among his friends at the popular Café des Variétés and at the offices of *La Revue Blanche*, a new magazine on which he, Henri Barbusse, André Gide, Fernand Gregh, Marcel Proust, and several others collaborated with its founders, the three Natanson brothers.

The news was not welcome at first. Most reacted as Proust's friend, Fernand Gregh, did: "The Jews have the misfortune of having a traitor among them and here they are trying to rehabilitate him." Gregh advised Blum that people of the Jewish faith "would do better to let this sad affair sleep forever." Proust listened to Blum, charmingly attentive as always; then excused himself to dress for Madame Straus' salon or Madame Lemaire's without offering an opinion. Blum's closest friend, Pierre Loüys, who had introduced him to Gide and Oscar Wilde, would not even listen. Their friendship abruptly ended. Another intimate, the young diplomat Philippe Berthelot, was so offensive in his anti-Dreyfusard sarcasm that Blum chose principle over affection. Thanks to the influence of Lazare, Herr, Reinach, Zola, and, finally, of the Socialist parliamentarian, Jean Jaurès, the patriotic blinders of Blum's friends began to fall away. But it was a rackingly painful experience. The news of Esterhazy's acquittal finally decided Gregh, along with most of the artists and writers in Blum's circle.

The clarion call of Zola's *J'Accuse* mobilized the young writers of *La Revue Blanche*. They began gathering signatures from prominent artists, academics, and writers condemning the Dreyfus court-martial, the Esterhazy acquittal, and the government's irresponsible conduct in the Affair. By now Proust was anxious to serve the Dreyfusard cause, and he was the ideal Jewish emissary to Madame Arman de Caillavet and Anatole France. He may well have influenced the great writer and his mistress, but it was probably Gregh who actually obtained France's precious signature. The mistress, Madame de Caillavet, was opposed: *"Mais, Monsieur,* you are going to set us at loggerheads with Félix Faure!" Who had signed so far? she demanded to know.

Well, Gregh said, there was Zola.

"Oh! him. He doesn't count, that goes without saying. This sort of thing is his bread and butter."

Trarieux, the former Attorney General, had signed.

"Ah, good, excellent." Madame de Caillavet was satisfied; Trarieux had class.

The *Revue Blanche* petition with its one hundred and four signatures represented something new in modern history, and it was Clemenceau with his uncanny gift who invented the term for it. Offering to reproduce the petition in *L'Aurore* on January 14, he called it the "Manifesto of the Intellectuals". Apparently, this was the first use of the word "intellectual" in this sense. By the end of the year it had achieved the familiarity of an old neologism. A popular book by Albert Reville published shortly afterwards bore the title *Les Étapes d'un Intellectuel* (The Stages of an Intellectual), and contained a quasifictional autobiography of a Dreyfusard conversion.

At first the intellectuals themselves were uneasy with the designation. Émile Durkheim and Lévy-Bruhl dismissed it as pretentious. The militant student leader, Charles Péguy, never accepted it. The distinguished editor of the lofty *Revue des Deux Mondes*, Ferdinand Brunetière, raged to Paléologue: "The mere fact that one has recently created this word . . . proclaims one of the most ridiculous eccentricities of our time. I mean the pretension of raising writers, scientists, professors, and philologists to the rank of supermen." Brunetière remained so upset by the Dreyfusard agitation that he delayed publication of his book on the Calas Case and never permitted a single mention of Dreyfus in *La Revue des Deux Mondes*.

There was truth in Brunetière's statement. Although the tradition of savants and artists engaging in French politics was older than Voltaire and as contemporary as Victor Hugo, politics had never been anything but a temporary digression from their main business. Now, however, as passions exploded over the Affair, the intellectual was emerging as an apostle of justice, insisting that politics was too serious a business to be left to the politicians. Almost overnight the fashionable credo of *l'art pour l'art* was abandoned as the universities, laboratories, cafés, and studios disgorged angry mandarins ready to swap blow for pamphleteering blow (and some real ones) with the Army's defenders. This was the beginning of an era which one of them later described as *"la république des intellectuels."*

Except for the fossils in the French Academy, most of the outstanding academics, artists, and writers converted to Dreyfusism. The cause became a badge of honor, a medal of intellectual and moral righteousness. But those who stood with the Army and the government also deserved commendation for courage. They were honorable men, for the most part, acting according to their best lights. Their revered leader in the Chamber, the very Catholic and very patriotic Comte Albert de Mun (an ex-officer devoted to good works among the proletariat), had expressed the emotions of the anti-Dreyfusards on the occasion of Prime Minister Méline's declaration, "There is no Dreyfus Affair!"

> Here, there are neither friends nor adversaries, neither
> partisans nor enemies of the Cabinet: There are
> representatives of the country, there are Frenchmen anxious
> to keep intact that which is most precious to them, that
> which remains in the midst of our struggles and party

discords the common ground of our invincible hope—the honor of the Army.

De Mun's eloquence and integrity were significant assets in the battle against Zola, but they were inadequate even when added to the literary prowess of Maurice Barrès or the imposing artistic reputation of Edgar Degas. The anti-Dreyfusards felt their inferiority keenly. Approached on the sidewalk by an elderly gentleman who congratulated them incoherently, the artist Forain whispered to Caran d'Ache, "How charming, old chap, all the cretins are with us."

Since *J'Accuse* the Affair had become too much the symbol of all that was revered in the republican tradition to allow for genteel dispute. The "cretins" who had put Dreyfus on his island had to be met head on. The librarian Lucien Herr, the historians Charles Seignobos and Gabriel Monod, the mathematician Henri Poincaré, the director of the Institut Pasteur, Émile Duclaux, the anthropologist Lévy-Bruhl, the sociologist Durkheim, and a whole regiment of writers enthusiastically enrolled under the Dreyfusard banner. Although the grand philosopher, Henri Bergson, never declared himself publicly, he was known to be a sympathizer. Lucien Herr's proselytizing among the university students yielded fateful results. Without much difficulty, Herr won over Charles Péguy.

In Péguy the Dreyfusards acquired their most dynamic young convert. From Orléans, the son of peasants, a reserve officer, Péguy was the prototype of the university student of eighty years later: a brilliant student who had failed his first entrance examination for the École Normale Supérieure and had then left the school in his second year in protest against its extreme academicism. He was a Socialist who was also a Catholic, a religious mystic who was also an intense pagan. Péguy's creed was one of social involvement, of knowledge through action, of *mystique* (a word he made popular) over intellect; it was a creed which foreshadowed existentialism. The coterie he attracted to his bookshop in the Rue Cujas, the narrow street behind the Sorbonne, was to provide the officer corps of the student Dreyfusards—Daniel Halévy, Jacques Maritain, Julien Benda, and others. And through Péguy a much older recruit was won—the retired engineer and self-taught philosopher, Georges Sorel, the father of the General Strike.

Almost no one successfully resisted the madness of 1898. Whether from political opportunism or from a fanatical belief that all that was best in France could be saved only by either damning or saving Dreyfus, Frenchmen behaved in ways they themselves would never have believed possible. Anatole France, for example, had always worshiped the Army. "An army is admirable!" he had rhapsodized in public a dozen years earlier. "Think of it! So many hearts united in a single thought! Such beautiful order!" When Abel Hermant published a novel deriding the Army, Anatole France had been outraged. "A writer," he declared, "cannot be permitted to say everything, every way, in every circumstance, to every sort of person. He is obliged to handle sacred things with respect." Since signing Gregh's petition, however, the great writer had begun to see a jesuitical conspiracy against reason and progress at work in the officer corps.

Romain Rolland, whose multivolume novel, *Jean-Christophe*, later portrayed the Dreyfus era with sensitive justice, was first appalled by the attack on the military leaders. "So much the worse for the intellectuals," he wrote a friend, "if they don't understand at all that, in the Europe of today, national defense is the first duty of the French Army." Rolland accepted the classic argument of the Nationalists:

> I don't hide the dangers from myself. I see the offensive return of Catholicism and militarism. . . . But it's not a matter of what pleases or displeases me. It's a matter of what I believe to be necessary to a nation whose primary interests are superior to the preferences of its individuals.

So spoke the Rolland of early 1898. He could not have been sure of himself, however, because at that moment he was

writing *The Wolves*, a play which would soon be one of the
theatrical *causes célèbres* of the era.

Rolland's play was deftly crafted; the issues of the primacy
of the nation versus the rights of the individual spoke through
the mouths of equally fervent and convincing characters, and,
in the final scene, they were left to the audience to resolve. The
opening night in early May was sold out. As Picquart took his
front-row seat, he was hissed and applauded. During the first
intermission Dreyfusards huddled at safe distances from their
enemies to deplore the unsympathetic portrayel of D'Oryon who
obviously represented their benighted Dreyfus. But they were
fully appeased by the time the curtain descended on the third
and final act. Anti-Dreyfusards fled the theater in dark and
vengeful moods. Shortly thereafter Rolland followed his friend
Péguy into the Dreyfusard camp.

To keep the Dreyfusards from further weakening the confidence of the public, the General Staff aimed to compromise
the character of several key personalities. Despite the Army's
efforts to silence Panizzardi, he was all the more determined
to force the French Army's hand. The Army retaliated at the
end of January; General Gonse invited the Italian Ambassador
to Staff headquarters. There, it seems, he was shown evidence
of Colonel Panizzardi's disreputable moral and professional
conduct. Panizzardi wrote to Schwartzkoppen that Ambassador
Tornielli "has been told that the Syndicate has letters from you
and from me, letters addressed to women in society." (Panizzardi added quickly, "so far as I am concerned they are de-
ceiving themselves.") Very likely the Italian Ambassador was
shown letters to men in society as well, for the Secret Dossier,
today still under lock in the Army's archives, contains a forged
note, the *billet des quatorze armées*, purportedly establishing
the homosexuality of the two attachés. In an angry letter to
Schwartzkoppen, Panizzardi declared open war on the French
generals: "It is no longer a question of saving a man and getting

the real culprit convicted, but a question of *defending our honor* and at the same time giving this Mister Boisdeffre a lesson, putting him in his place and letting everybody—and especially the French—know how this man is lying." Soon, Panizzardi told the horrified British military attaché, Colonel Douglas Dawson, all he knew about the case.

Vice Chief Gonse's next victim was Picquart. The General never quite decided which means of character assassination to direct against the lieutenant colonel. On April 25, 1898, he prepared a report suggesting that Picquart shared the sexual mores of Panizzardi: "In a certain society, Picquart is known under the name of Georgette." Gonse also mentioned a police report supposedly confirming these proclivities, stating that "this report . . . would explain the attitude of Picquart in the Dreyfus Case." Six days later Gonse was advising General de Pellieux in writing to "act on the husband," a reference to the spouse of Picquart's mistress. De Pellieux complied with alacrity, inviting the unsuspecting cuckold to his office, exposing the relationship, and then escorting him to the door with a show of grave empathy. Gonse and de Pellieux probably hoped for a duel or a lawsuit which the scurrilous Nationalist press could feast on. Instead, they succeeded only in breaking up a marriage.

Anxious to tie up the loose ends, Gonse himself created a piece of evidence against Dreyfus. There was a rumor that at the time of the 1894 court-martial Jacques Hadamard, Lucie's brother, had said that he believed his brother-in-law could be guilty. At the end of February Gonse invited the distinguished mathematician Paul Painlevé to recount the story. Though Painlevé categorically denied hearing Jacques Hadamard express such a view, Gonse prepared an official report stating that Professor Painlevé had verified the rumor.* The Vice Chief of Staff, ably assisted by Henry and de Pellieux, had about exhausted his resources.

---

* *Secret Dossier*, No. 96.

Two weeks earlier, however, the General Staff's campaign had received a gratuitous boost when the royalist Deputy Lucien Millevoye publicly quoted the Kaiser's *bordereau* marginalia concerning Dreyfus. The value of this forged annotated *bordereau*, like that of the False Henry, lay in rumors of its existence. After its fabrication, probably in October 1897, Henry himself must have felt the document was too risky, even too preposterous, to circulate. Paléologue had fairly guffawed when Henry mentioned it. Preposterous rumors were another matter and the General Staff had been well served by them. According to one rumor, the original *bordereau* had been forwarded to Berlin and then returned to Colonel von Schwartzkoppen with marginal comments about Dreyfus written in the Kaiser's hand. When it was retrieved by Madame Bastian, French Counterintelligence, in the interests of national security, had made a copy omitting the sensational annotation.

At the time of Panama, Millevoye (who was then a Boulangist) had resigned his seat in the wake of the Chamber's outrage when his evidence that Clemenceau and Rochefort were British agents proved to be forgeries. It was inevitable that a politician like Millevoye would recite the text of the annotated *bordereau*. "Why, yes, of course it exists, citizens," he proclaimed at a public rally. "Do you want to know the contents of it? Here they are! The document says: 'Have this scoundrel Dreyfus send the promised items immediately!'" After Millevoye's February 15 speech, General de Boisdeffre began to plant the story of the annotated *bordereau* in the *salons* and gentlemen's clubs of Paris. Few could imagine that the Chief of Staff, the architect of the Franco-Russian Alliance, a nobleman who once corresponded on the friendliest terms with William II, would perpetrate such an enormity merely to spare the Army the embarrassment of retrying a junior officer. The Kaiser was at his jocular best when he learned of the absurd predicament Millevoye's speech had created for de Boisdeffre. William II amused the Prince and Princess Radziwill by remarking after dinner,

"A gentleman as incompetent as that is not to be feared and my only wish is that they do not remove him." *

The widespread if troubled acceptance by the French upper classes of the existence of an annotated *bordereau* was a measure of the empire of ideology over common sense. Many aristocrats who knew better found themselves trapped by caste. Proust aptly captured this when he made his Duc de Guermantes splutter, "But damn it all, when one goes by the name of Marquis de Saint-Loup, one isn't a Dreyfusard." Princesse Mathilde's situation was somewhat different. Joseph Reinach had practically won her over when General de Boisdeffre appeared. Suddenly, the Princesse began reminding her friends, "I have an officer in my family." Princesse Mathilde strove to keep politics out of her relations with her friends the Strauses as best her blunt simplicity would allow; ultimately she failed. "You, you are among those who believe in the innocence of the other?" she asked Émile Straus one evening.

"I believe in the innocence of people until their guilt has been proven. There are things which inspire doubt in this case," Straus explained. "But," the Princesse exclaimed, "General de Boisdeffre has seen the letters from the German Emperor to Dreyfus."

"My God, Princesse, I don't know kings and emperors as you do, but I am astonished that an emperor would write to a traitor."

Mathilde knew very well that she should know better. With the huffiness of a grande dame long accustomed to making a virtue out of whimsicality, this stout Bonaparte turned on her heel. "*Enfin*," she said, "as strange as it may be, there are letters from William II to Dreyfus."

While all the leaders of society were enrolling in one of the

---

* Annotated *bordereau*: Raoul Allier, *Le Bordereau Annoté* (Paris, 1903); Maurice Paléologue, *Journal* (Paris, 1955), p. 59; Princesse Radziwill, *Lettres* (Bologna, 1932), Vol. II, pp. 134-135; Louis Leblois, *L'Affaire Dreyfus* (Paris, 1929), p. 82.

two camps as if God would judge them on how wisely they had chosen in the Affair, and while the artists, academics, and writers were forming ranks with even greater piety and fervor, the spokesmen for the working classes were seriously divided. In the Chamber of Deputies Jean Jaurès was a solitary voice on the extreme Left crying out for revision—for judicial review and retrial. Jaurès was a man of exceptional intelligence and courage, an inspired historian-turned-politician, whose Socialism owed far more to the historian Jules Michelet than to the writings of Karl Marx.

But even Jaurès was constrained to soft-pedal his Dreyfusism in deference to the Socialist coalition. The largest of the half-dozen Socialist parties, the *Parti Ouvrier Français* (French Labor Party), was violently anti-Dreyfusard, reflecting the deep-seated anti-Semitism of the street vendors, sharecroppers, shopkeepers, railroad employees, and industrial workers who were its constituents. To the proletariat the rich Jews were the generals of capitalism, the people behind the international banking apparatus which exploited them.

Jaurès would have preferred to drive home to the Socialist voters that the economic role of the wealthy Jews was as fossilized as that of the old aristocracy and that economic power was shifting at the very moment the proletariat was being encouraged to attack the Jews through Dreyfus. The new moguls of industry depended upon stock issues, protective tariffs, state subsidies, and the meekest of laws regarding taxation and the rights of employees. Rarely did they rely upon Baron Edmond de Rothschild. Fifty Rothschilds could not have met the economic requirements of France's burgeoning industrial community in the 1890s. Indeed, the great industrialists were neither Jews nor Catholics but Protestants, like Creusot, Schneider, and de Wendel. Instead, Jaurès played for time and signed the anti-Dreyfusard manifesto of the parliamentary Socialists (January 19) stating that the Affair was a civil war between the Jewish bourgeoisie and the clerical bourgeoisie.

While Jaurès withheld his total support of Dreyfusism until

after the elections of May 1898 (significantly, he was opposed
for his seat by the richest industrialist in his *département*), his
future ally, Clemenceau, deplored the shortsightedness of the
Socialists. "Among the chivalrous aristocracy which wishes
death to the Jews, how many are the guests of Monsieur
Rothschild!" he reminded working-class anti-Semites. Could
they not see that upper-class anti-Semitism was generically
different from their own? For the upper classes the "Yid" was
the Jewish baron who had just left the club or the *salon* and
whose invitation to sup or to hunt had been eagerly accepted.
"Alas, it is the same in all the countries of the world," Clemenceau sighed. The common people were always duped into taking
the wrong prejudices much too seriously. Péguy, in an open
letter to a prominent Socialist deputy noted for his political
finesse, threatened the Party with massive student defections:

> *Monsieur,*
>   It's quite simple.
>   We've had enough speeches.
>   We've had too many electoral combinations.
>   If you write another single article in *L'Éclair*, the young
> Socialists will march against you all the way to the Left.
> We want to safeguard Socialist principles not the jobs of
> those who are classed as Socialists on the voting lists.

Still, the Party continued its neutrality.

Léon Blum remembered the spring and summer of 1898 as
a time of heartbreak for Dreyfusards. Even Lucie's letters
began to reflect the emotional toll. "How misfortunes change
one!" she wrote Alfred in early April, three years after his
arrival on Devil's Island:

> One is forced to accept things which seem impossible to bear
> with such resignation. When I say that I accept resignedly,
> that's not true. I make no recriminations because I must
> live and suffer in this way until your complete innocence is
> recognized; but deep inside, my being rebels, becomes

indignant and compressed by these long years of waiting;
it is overflowing with a barely restrained patience.

Lucie had no idea how much more she would have to accept.
It seemed that Frenchmen, intuiting the destructive force of the
Affair, wanted to ballot it away. The national elections of May 8
and 22 avoided the issue except in the largest cities (in Paris
and Algiers especially) where it still was not paramount. Ten days
after the Chamber had adjourned, Prime Minister Méline set
the tone by proclaiming a platform of "neither reaction nor
revolution." The final returns revealed the hostility of the electorate. Jaurès lost his seat. Reinach, who had dared to run on
a revisionist platform and to upbraid his constituents with "it
is we who are defending the honor of the Army," was ousted.
The arch anti-Semite Drumont won a seat from Algiers. When
the new Assembly convened, Scheurer-Kestner was defeated in
the balloting for Vice President of the Senate. It had made no
difference, the depressed Blum saw, that the newly formed
League for the Rights of Man led by Clemenceau, Zola, and
former Attorney General Trarieux had thrown itself into the
struggle. Most of the electorate seemed to share the cynical
opinion of the prominent *littérateur* who told a *Figaro* col-
umnist: "I am indifferent to the Dreyfus Case. If Dreyfus is
innocent, so much the worse for him. Jesus Christ himself was
the victim of a judicial error. When one discovers one of them,
it serves no purpose to make a lot of noise about it because
anybody can make a mistake."

On June 14 Jules Méline, whose government had had a remarkably long life, found himself reversed on a vote of confidence. Thirteen confused days later Henri Brisson became the
new Prime Minister. Brisson, a distinguished republican, belonged to the same Radical Party that Clemenceau had helped
to shape. He was understandably too wary to support the Dreyfusards publicly, but his election was seen as a turning point in
the Affair. This desperate hope vanished in less than a month.
In order to win the necessary votes, Brisson chose as his Minister

of War a civilian who was admired by the Nationalists and respected by the officer corps. Tall, martially erect, Godefroy Cavaignac bore a resemblance to General Mercier. The similarity was not merely physical. Both men were graduates of the École Polytechnique, were close friends, literal-minded and equally arrogant. They shared as well a consuming political ambition. Mathieu Dreyfus knew that Prime Minister Brisson's appointment was a disaster—"Cavaignac was the man of the General Staff."

Brisson's government lost no time declaring its intention to get rid of the Affair. The former Prime Minister had already managed to have Leblois, Picquart's attorney, dismissed as deputy mayor of Paris's fifth *arrondissement* and temporarily barred from practicing law. At the same time Picquart had been dismissed from the Army (February 16). The new Minister of War proceeded to relieve Reinach of his commission in the reserves and to order an investigation against Picquart for divulging secrets. Zola's expulsion from the Legion of Honor would be a matter of time; Cavaignac had only to await the result of Zola's appeal.

In April the Court of Cassation (a rough equivalent of the United States Supreme Court) had reversed Zola's conviction on technical grounds and ordered a retrial. Again it was certain that the novelist would lose. Two days before the inevitable sentence Zola attacked the Prime Minister for his betrayal of revisionism. "You were once the incarnation of republican virtue, you were the lofty symbol of civic honesty," Zola wrote in *L'Aurore*. In jail the novelist would have been invaluable to the Dreyfusards. "Every day in jail and every franc of fine," said the New York *Tribune*, "will add a new leaf to his crown of laurel," and embarrassment to the government. But the Joan of Arc of literature preferred to flee to the damp climate and loneliness of England rather than enter a French cell.

War Minister Cavaignac believed he could bury the Affair forever, save the Army, and relieve the nation of the terrible scandal it was begging to avoid. He had been delighted by the

Dreyfus Secret Dossier when he took over Staff headquarters.
The dossier now contained more than three hundred documents.
(General Billot's son-in-law, a lawyer, had carefully examined
and organized the evidence to protect the General against possible accusations of incompetence and collusion.) With his engineer's eye for discrepancies and overall coherence, Cavaignac
concluded that the Army's case was ironclad. He informed the
Chamber that he would present his conclusions on July 7, 1898.

Some action by the government was urgently needed. The
university students, led by Péguy, were turning the Latin Quarter
into a battleground. A steady stream of newspaper revelations,
such as Casella's account of Schwartzkoppen's and Panizzardi's
earnest declarations that they had never dealt with Dreyfus, were
eroding public confidence. Above all, there was the nuisance of
Esterhazy. Billot, the former Minister of War, had permanently
retired Esterhazy from active duty, but Picquart had brought
formal charges against Du Paty and Esterhazy (or against the
"person or persons unknown," as the charge read) for sending
the "Blanche" and "Speranza" telegrams to Tunisia. The consequences of Picquart's allegations were beginning to alarm the
government.

In early May Esterhazy's nephew, Christian, who had been
living with his uncle and Mademoiselle Pays for several months,
approached Mathieu and Joseph Reinach. He was willing to
testify before the examining magistrate that his uncle was the
author of the two telegrams. Christian was the son of a Bordeaux
notable who had died in 1896 leaving a respectable fortune.
Esterhazy had wasted little time putting himself in contact with
the widow and her son, offering to make his Bordeaux relatives
rich. Because of his role in the infamous *Libre Parole* duels, he
assured them, his old schoolmate Edmond de Rothschild "was
very grateful to me and since that time has helped me most
effectively." Expertly lured, they responded by sending Esterhazy first twenty thousand francs and then another thirty-eight
thousand five hundred francs to be invested with the friendly
Rothschilds. Studying his new booklet entitled *The Art of*

Gaining Money on the Stock Market, Esterhazy banked his booty and sent Christian and his mother several "dividends" subtracted from their own cash. Embezzled and bitter, Christian told the examining magistrate in the telegrams case, Judge Paul Bertulus, everything he knew.

Esterhazy sensed the hostility that was entrapping him. "The maneuvers of the Zola trial were planned at my house," he recalled. Now, de Pellieux, Henry, and Du Paty were much too busy to see him, and his fellow officers publicly spurned him. In an attempt to restore his popularity Esterhazy challenged Picquart to a duel. Wounding Picquart, perhaps even killing him, would earn him the gratitude of France; the telegrams case would be forgotten. But Picquart refused to accept the challenge, preferring the battleground of the courtroom. Esterhazy persevered desperately. In late May, he wrote Picquart:

> I looked for you in vain for several days—you know it. Does your cravenness have a limit, perhaps? If it does, tell me when and where you will dare to meet me face to face in order to receive the chastisement that I promise you. As for me, for the next three days, beginning tomorrow at seven o'clock, I will be walking along the following streets. . . .

Still the lordly Picquart declined to reply. Then, in early June, blind from absinthe, Esterhazy came upon his adversary in a bar and attacked him from behind with his cane. Picquart turned, parried the blows, knocked the cane away, seized Esterhazy by the collar and seat of the pants, and tossed him through the door into the gutter. Obviously, the sooner Cavaignac spoke to the nation through the Chamber, the sooner Esterhazy and Picquart could be silenced.

Lean and severe, the new Minister of War strode to the tribune on the appointed date, July 7. First, he read the document from Counterintelligence in which the letter P had been altered to D—"for D has brought me a lot of interesting things." Next, he produced a Panizzardi-Schwartzkoppen exchange stating, "I have told him that you do not intend to resume relations." Then, after a spirited exegesis of these documents, Cavaignac drily read the decisive proof of Dreyfus' treason— the full text of the letter signed "Alexandrine," the False Henry which Major Henry had so carefully written, retaining Paniz- zardi's salutation and signature. Finally, Cavaignac referred to the affidavit of Dreyfus' confession by Captain Lebrun-Renault of the Garde Républicaine. The Chamber rose to applaud. Méline, the former Prime Minister, had claimed that there was no Affair, but the new Minister of War had demonstrated Dreyfus' treason axiomatically. A motion was overwhelmingly ratified to have the speech printed at public expense and posted in the thirty thousand communes of France. People began to feel that perhaps, after all, there really was no Dreyfus Affair.

For Lucie Dreyfus it was a cruel blow. "When I am feeling too sad and when the burdens of life seem too heavy, too diffi- cult to bear," she wrote Alfred, "I turn away from the present, I conjure up my memories and I find again some strength to keep fighting."

For Léon Blum this was the greatest defeat. He sat with his friends in the office of *La Revue Blanche* immobilized by de- jection. Lucien Herr dropped by, depressed and defeated. No one wanted to speak. Then Jaurès arrived. "Sit down over there and have a cry with us," someone said.

"*Alors*, you too," the ex-Deputy scolded. "But don't you understand that now—and now for the first time—we have the certainty of victory? Méline was invulnerable because he kept quiet. Cavaignac talks, debates—thus, he's already beaten."

Jaurès went home to compose an open letter to the Minister of War which appeared in his newspaper, *La Petite République*, two days later. It was the first of his famous articles later col- lected under the title *Les Preuves* (The Proofs). "Yesterday you committed a criminal and useful work in the Chamber." Criminal because the evidence was forged and proved the il- legality of the 1894 court-martial; useful because the Minister's action afforded thirty million Frenchmen the chance finally to learn the truth.

Jaurès' letter to Cavaignac was published almost simultaneously with one from Picquart to Cavaignac stating that the Alexandrine letter was an invention and that the rest of the War Minister's facts were valueless. Picquart must have known that Cavaignac's reaction would be characteristically swift and severe. On July 12, Cavaignac obtained the Cabinet's permission to bring espionage charges against Picquart and Leblois under the elastic Law of 18 April 1886. The advantage to the government of this law was that those prosecuted under it appeared before a *tribunal de police correctionnel*, a court of summary justice without jury. The following day, the former lieutenant colonel was arrested and imprisoned for divulging official secrets. It was no consolation that at the same time the magistrate investigating Picquart's and Christian Esterhazy's charges against the Count courageously ordered the arrest of Esterhazy on the Tunisian telegrams and the embezzlement charges. After arresting Picquart, Cavaignac moved to have the most prominent Dreyfusards—Scheurer-Kestner, Jaurès, Clemenceau, and Mathieu among them—brought to trial before the Senate. But Prime Minister Brisson's Cabinet was horrified by the proposal; Cavaignac was urged to have an expert reexamine the Dreyfus dossier instead, to be absolutely certain that Jaurès and Picquart were wrong.

To Captain Louis Cuignet, the officer chosen for the investigation, thoroughness was a religion. He took the dossier to his home in the evenings and during weekends, poring over its contents doggedly. At first Cuignet found, as had the Minister of War, that the dossier contained irrefutable evidence against Dreyfus. Then one Saturday evening, scrutinizing the False Henry for the last time, Cuignet suddenly noticed two incredible peculiarities. Shaking the paper under the lamp, he saw that neither the measurement of the lines nor their colors matched. On Sunday afternoon, August 14, Captain Cuignet told Minister Cavaignac that the document was a forgery—that the paper of the center portion did not match the top and bottom. The flabbergasted Minister ordered Cuignet to file

through the dossier again and to reexamine the False Henry—
and to take his time about it. Almost immediately, Cavaignac
boarded a train for General Mercier's headquarters at Le Mans,
two hundred thirty miles northwest of Paris.

chapter twelve:
FROM CALAMITY
TO CALAMITY

WHEN MOISE LEEMAN, ALIAS LEMERCIER-
Picard, was found dangling by the neck from his apartment
windowsill in early March 1898, the Dreyfusards cried that his
suicide had been arranged by the Army. It was true that the
seedy little forger had been too enterprising. After inventing
Counterintelligence documents for small commissions, Henry's
co-conspirator went into business for himself. Toward the end
of 1896 he took a curious note to Mathieu which came to be
known as the "False Otto." It purported to establish that
Esterhazy was trafficking in secrets with the Germans. But
Mathieu had already spent thousands on false leads and, wary
of unsolicited boons, he declined Leeman's offer. However
Moise Leeman died, the Dreyfusard explanation that he was
dispatched because he knew too much was a compellingly
plausible hypothesis. Now, thanks to Captain Cuignet's dili-
gence, the Army was endangered by another forger.

In Cavaignac's much praised speech to the Chamber, the
War Minister had confidently associated his own political as-

pirations and the credibility of the government with quashing the Affair. The False Henry not only exploded Cavaignac's work, it confronted France with the prospect of at least three divisive trials: Dreyfus would have to be spared his slow, certain death on Devil's Island, Henry sent before a court-martial board, and Esterhazy retried. Nor would that be the end of it. Mercier and de Boisdeffre—even Saussier (who had been prescient enough to retire at the beginning of the year)— might have to explain their conduct before a civil tribunal. Until he was certain what to do, the Minister of War ordered Cuignet to stall his investigation.

Later, the Dreyfusards assumed that Cavaignac delayed seeing Henry for two weeks so that he could scheme with the generals. The Prime Minister himself came to share this suspicion because the Minister of War withheld Cuignet's discovery from the Cabinet while he rushed to confer with Mercier. "Would not the consequence of this agreement have been to push you into hiding crucial evidence from the government?" Brisson angrily asked his Minister when he learned the story. It would have been easy to save the author of the False Henry, Cavaignac's defenders pointed out. "I would have had to say only a word to Henry," General Gaudérique Roget, Cavaignac's private secretary, said, "and he would have found a clever alibi." The choice was excruciating, but the generals knew it was better to sacrifice the loyal, uncomplicated Counterintelligence chief than to risk another Lazare pamphlet, an open letter from Mathieu, or revelation by Jaurès.

As Henry was on vacation, Cavaignac decided to delay an interrogation until the end of the month. In the meantime slim hopes were shattered when Captain Cuignet reported, on August 22, 1898, that the forgery was unmistakable and that the evidence against Henry was overwhelming. Henry's session with Cavaignac took place eight days later, at the Invalides, the Army's museum housing the immense tomb of Napoleon I. Generals de Boisdeffre, de Pellieux, Gonse, and

Roget were present. The Minister of War went straight to the point: "The 1894 document contains pieces belonging to another from 1896."

"That strikes me as being impossible," Henry countered, totally surprised.

"There is material proof that certain pieces have been interchanged. How do you explain this fact?"

"How do I explain it—?" Looking about the room for support, reading the cold expressions of Gonse and de Pellieux, Henry faltered, then exploded. "What's being said is that I myself am the one who did the switching! I cannot say that I fabricated a piece that I did not fabricate. I would have had to forge the envelope as well."

"The game of switching the pieces is certain."

"I didn't forge these items." Cavaignac impatiently waved aside this disclaimer. "I arranged a few phrases—'They musn't never know.' But the first sentence is correct. . . . I swear to you that I didn't invent anything."

"You forged the document," Cavaignac insisted.

"I swear that I didn't. I only arranged a sentence in order to make the document more forceful."

"You aren't telling the truth. You forged the second piece using the first as a model."

"I cut off a section of the 1894 document—but not the whole piece."

From that point on, Henry's protestations weakened, contradicted themselves, and finally collapsed. When the Minister of War asked who had put the idea in his head, Henry explained:

> My superiors were worried and I wanted to calm them, to make their minds rest easy. I said to myself: "Let's add just a sentence; if we had a piece of evidence in this situation we're in!" Nobody knew anything about it. . . . I acted solely in the interests of my country.*

---

* BB 19 45 8 3.

An officer was summoned to escort the chief of Counterintelligence to the military prison at Mont Valérien, seven miles west of Paris.

This was the greatest crisis of Henry's life and on the way to prison he reacted with the dull incomprehension of Louis XVI who, on the day the Bastille was stormed, had written "Nothing" in his diary because he was unable to go hunting.

"What do they want?" Henry asked the escorting officer. "It makes you go crazy. My conscience is clear. My poor wife, my poor little boy! Everything has collapsed in a second. I won't make the opening of the hunt. Everybody's expecting me there—what are they going to think?"

At the Invalides, Lieutenant Colonel Henry's superiors were also wondering what to do. For General de Pellieux there was no longer any reason to fight. "As of this moment judicial review is unavoidable," he snapped and strode out of the room to write his resignation at a desk in the Minister's outer office. The letter exuded contempt and fury:

> A dupe of men without honor, having no hope of retaining
> the confidence of my subordinates without which it is not
> possible to wield command, having lost confidence in those
> superiors who caused me to deal in forgeries,
> I have the honor to request that you order my retirement.

Before departing, de Pellieux ordered the resignation carried by an officer to his immediate superior, General Émile Zurlinden, the new Military Governor. The Military Governor soon managed to persuade the general to withdraw his resignation. De Pellieux's letter was so incriminating that Zurlinden and Cavaignac concealed its existence from the Prime Minister.

In the same room General de Boisdeffre composed his farewell:

> I have acquired proof that my trust in Colonel Henry . . .
> was unjustified. That trust was absolute and led me to the
> mistake of declaring a document to be genuine which was

not. . . . In this situation, I must ask you to relieve me
of my duties.

The Minister of War pleaded with the Chief of Staff to reconsider, but de Boisdeffre was adamant; he knew when it was
time to bow out. Cavaignac also pondered his own future.

The news of Henry's arrest swept Europe like a tornado.
On the morning of August 31 Wickham Steed, the London
Times correspondent, interviewed the Italian Prime Minister in
Rome about the Russians' unexpected proposal for an international conference on arms control. The Prime Minister brushed
aside the question. "Henry has been arrested. That is more important than the Czar's circular."

If the French people were not ready to side with the Dreyfusards, overnight it became less tenable, less respectable to
maintain a dogmatic position against revision. "One's first wish
was to believe—as we nearly all believed—in a conspiracy
against the Army," the illustrious Vicomte Eugène Melchior de
Vogüé soon confessed. "Today we have to bow to the evidence:
little by little our General Staff has been dragged down by the
deplorable moral standards of the times, by a false conception
of military status, and has itself become entangled in a network
of lies."

In his cell at Mont Valérien Henry strained to make sense
of his predicament. Sometime before ten on Wednesday morning, August 31, he wrote his adored young wife, Berthe:

> I see that, except for you, everybody has deserted me.
> Nevertheless, you know in whose interests I have acted. My
> letter [the forgery] is a copy and is in no way—absolutely no
> way—a forgery. It merely confirms the verbal instructions
> that were given me. . . . I am absolutely innocent and the
> world will know it a little later, but right now I cannot
> talk.

It was unfortunate that Henry felt he could not tell his wife
the truth.

After he wrote his wife, Henry was calm, according to the prison officials. At eleven-thirty a guard brought him copies of the newspapers as he had requested. The news was not encouraging. The pro-Army *Éclair* denounced his "abominable" crime and *La Libre Parole* was just as severe. At one o'clock Henry declined an offer to walk in the prison yard; instead, he called for a flask of cognac. Drinking small portions of it, he wrote a brief note asking General Gonse to come to the prison. "I absolutely must talk to you," he pleaded. The officer who came at two forty-five to post this letter found Henry morose and uncommunicative. A few minutes later Henry began his last letter, which he left unfinished: "My dearly beloved Berthe, I am almost mad; a terrible pain constricts my brain; I am going to cleanse myself in the Seine." He finished the cognac. At five forty-seven Lieutenant Colonel Henry was found dead in his cell of a razor wound to the throat. He had been dead for more than two hours. At Staff headquarters that night Henry's subordinates, Captains Junck and Lauth, destroyed a large number of documents.

Henry's closest friends doubted that he could have taken his own life. Certainly he would not have done so out of remorse. Some of the guards at Mont Valérien whispered that he died after the visit of an anonymous Staff officer. Captain Junck later formally denied that he was this officer and that he had brought Henry news that the generals could do nothing for him. In any case, there is no record of such a visitor.

In fact, suicide was very likely. Ex-Sergeant-Major Henry, risen from the ranks and assigned to the General Staff by a reforming Minister of War, had become a respected and valuable confidant of gentlemen—a rare achievement for a peasant lad from the dreary eastern village of Pogny. Henry had recently begun reading Marcus Aurelius (in translation) and Montesquieu; his conversation had become elevated, laced with exalted references to honor, duty, fatherland. Within hours after his arrest Henry knew that if he lived, he might do more to destroy the Army he loved than Alfred Dreyfus. Perhaps, as he downed his cognac, Henry remembered that October morning years earlier when he had stood behind a curtain in General de Boisdeffre's office while Captain Dreyfus refused Major Du Paty's revolver. Perhaps he decided then, that owing the Army his life, he must give it.

The Prime Minister and the President had no idea what they should do. The summer recess of the Chamber and Senate enabled them to act without fear of parliamentary intervention, but they seemed too stupefied to take advantage of the opportunity. Prime Minister Brisson was inclined towards judicial review but War Minister Cavaignac insisted that Henry's confession and death changed nothing. He still claimed that the Lebrun-Renault affidavit was sufficient proof against Dreyfus and threatened to resign if the Prime Minister wavered. As Cavaignac saw it—and President Félix Faure agreed—there was now a far more compelling reason to deny Dreyfus a new trial. As the President's aide, General Legrand-Girarde, put it: "Must the external security of the nation be sacrificed to its need for moral peace; must the arrogance of a false triumph be left to the worst enemies of the Army in order to save the peace? Cruel enigma." General Legrand-Girarde never doubted that the right decision was to leave Dreyfus to rot. There were other government advisers who reacted like the heartless lady who said she "hoped Dreyfus is innocent so he will suffer all the more."

But events were overtaking the Prime Minister. On September 3, 1898, the Cabinet received Lucie's formal request for a revision by the Court of Cassation of the 1894 judgment against her husband. Cavaignac resigned, finding himself outnumbered by his colleagues who voted to forward Lucie's request to a six-man special committee. The next day Ferdinand Esterhazy rushed from his train to the Channel steamer which would carry him to sanctuary in England. From that same sanctuary Zola cabled his friends that he was preparing to return.

The Brisson government would have been somewhat less harried if it had not been for Charles-Marie Photius Maurras. A relatively obscure poet and journalist, Maurras had been denied a naval career because of partial deafness. He had written articles in praise of regionalism and joined the Felibrian movement, a society of artists and writers which revered the extinct language and surviving customs of their native Provence. An esthete who was ignorant of sports, Maurras had been sent by his newspaper to Greece to cover the 1896 Olympic Games, the first in modern times. It was the turning point in his life. The contrast between the laggard performance of the "Latins" and the medal-winning feats of the Germans and "Anglo-Saxons" distressed him. Returning home by way of England, he was even more ap·,alled when he observed the maneuvers of Her Majesty's Home Fleet in the Channel. By the autumn of 1898 he had become a feverish militarist and a racist. Convinced that the source of national decline was the contamination of the authentic French race by foreigners—Jews, Protestants, and others—he saw that France could only be great again if she expelled these *"métèques"* (inferior breeds) from her midst. Maurras' ideas owed much to Barrès—but Barrès had been content to denounce only alien cultural influences. Maurras, after a careful reading of Gobineau and Drumont, claimed to have found the cause of French senescence in foreign blood.

Zola and Clemenceau had created the word "intellectual." Barrès and Maurras contributed the term "nationalist" to the glossary of the Affair. When Maurras saw that even *La Libre Parole* was shaken by the False Henry, he wrote a series of incendiary articles—"The First Blood"—for *La Gazette de France*. This half-deaf poet was too intelligent to appeal to the Cartesian reason on which Frenchmen supposedly prided themselves. Instead, he excited the underbelly of Nationalist erogeny. Henry was dead, the victim of the "Syndicate of Treason" (Jews, Protestants, and Freemasons). The first martyr in a holy cause, Henry must be avenged and his memory sanctified. What Henry had done was unimportant; it was the why that mattered. A man who merely forged evidence proving the guilt of a traitorous Jewish officer was certainly not a criminal; he was a great

patriot giving the Zolas, Reinachs, and Picquarts a taste of
their own tactics:

> In the state of confusion in which the national parties find
> themselves, we have not been able to give you the great funeral
> which your martyrdom deserves. We should have flourished
> the bloodstained tunic on our boulevards as well as the
> bloodstained blade, we should have borne the coffin in a
> procession and worshipped the shroud as if it were a black
> flag. It will be to our shame that we did not attempt this. But
> patriotic feeling, although diffused and multiplied against
> itself and still incapable of action, has nevertheless been
> resuscitated.

"The First Blood" succeeded far beyond Maurras' expectations. By the end of the year a reconverted *Libre Parole* was
serving as agent for a national subscription for Madame Henry
and her children. Whatever its doubts within the *salons* about
the Army's cause, outside the aristocracy maintained a nearly
unanimous anti-Dreyfusard cohesion. Week after week *La Libre
Parole* published the names, sums, and squibs of titled Henry
Fund donors. The names of fifteen thousand subscribers (con-
tributing one hundred thirty thousand francs) eventually filled
a seven-hundred-page book, and among the most virulent squibs
those of the clergy were unexcelled:

> A country priest who is making the most ardent vows for the
> extermination of the two enemies of France—the Jew and
> the Freemason. 5 francs.

> An unimportant priest of the Poitevin who will chant the
> Requiem for the last of the Yids with pleasure. 1 franc.

> Abbé Cros, ex-lieutenant, for a floor mat of Yidskin in order
> to trample them under foot morning and evening. 5 francs.

While the special judicial committee considered Lucie's request, Prime Minister Brisson looked for a new Minister of

War. Brisson selected General Zurlinden. He accepted, agree-
ing to support revision of the Dreyfus conviction; two days
later, he told Brisson and the Cabinet that he opposed Lucie's
request and promptly resigned.

Brisson then took the unusual step of asking Mathieu to
recommend a general favored by the family. Mathieu suggested General Paul Darras, the officer who had presided at
his brother's degradation. Darras was known to believe that
the 1894 court-martial had been unjust. Brisson wavered. After
approaching General Darras, he sounded out another officer,
General Charles Chanoine, who accepted without delay. Understandably, Darras was not unrelieved to stand aside.

The choice of Chanoine seemed encouraging, nevertheless.
The new Minister swore that he would nudge the Army into
accepting judicial review. His real intention, however, was to
stop the Dreyfusards. Chanoine knew he could not openly oppose revision in the first hours of his ministry but he believed
he could sabotage it by destroying Picquart. On Chanoine's desk
was his predecessor's last-minute request to the Appellate Court
of the Seine for Picquart's surrender to military authorities to
be court-martialed for the forgery of the *petit bleu*. There were
complications. Picquart was about to be tried by the *tribunal
correctionnel* of the Seine for the Cavaignac espionage accusation. The government's lawyers argued that the nature of the
former Staff officer's crimes vested the military with a prior
and paramount jurisdiction. On September 22, over the furious
objections of Maître Labori, the Appellate Court ordered Picquart transferred from Santé Prison to Cherche-Midi military
prison. Addressing the court, Picquart warned France what
might be in store for him:

> Perhaps this is the last opportunity for me to speak in
> public. . . . I wish everyone to know that if the rope of
> Lemercier-Picard or the razor of Henry should be found in
> my cell, it will mean murder, for a man like myself would
> never commit suicide.

Minister of War Chanoine had acted not a moment too soon for, on September 23, 1898, the Brisson Cabinet voted, by a majority of two and over the objections of the Minister of Justice, to transmit Lucie's appeal to the Court of Cassation—even though the special six-man commission had deadlocked in the matter. The generals held their breaths, expecting the collapse of their case against revision. Although the intellectuals exulted and thousands of university students led by Péguy held rallies under Picquart's window at the Cherche-Midi prison, public opinion remained fairly fixed.

After the acceptance of Lucie's appeal, life in the Hadamard mansion suddenly became much less funereal. For four years Lucie and her children had lived in cloistered fear. "Mother was always very sad," Jeanne remembers. She and her brother wondered when "Papa" would return, but they learned not to press their mother about his mission. At Mathieu's apartment there was less gloom but the same isolation and caution reigned. And there were some painful incidents when the passions engendered by the case penetrated into the apartment itself. The tutor hired by Mathieu came one evening to announce that her regular position as a teacher was being jeopardized; she could no longer continue to give lessons to Marguerite and Émile. Once, from the stairs outside the apartment, little Marguerite was frightened by shouting—"traitors!" "dirty Jews!" Barring the door, her mother told her not to be afraid. They were just a few "Army conscripts passing by who have drunk too much."

By nature and by force of events reticent and retiring, Lucie was now called to be public trustee of her husband's cause. For some time a band of leading Dreyfusards, many of them close friends of Mathieu's, had been regular visitors. Jaurès and Reinach dropped in frequently, bringing messages of encouragement and sometimes lingering to play cards with Jeanne and Pierrot. A kitten arrived from Picquart's prison, one of a litter born at Cherche-Midi. Grateful for the support of her new

friends, Lucie played the unaccustomed part of a celebrity—
but not very successfully. Henriette Psichari, whose brothers
carved *"Vive* Picquart!" on the family piano, noted that Lucie
made many of her female sympathizers feel "ill at ease."
Mademoiselle Psichari's mother (daughter of Ernest Renan)
and several prominent ladies began regularly to visit the Hadamards where Lucie received them in a "sumptuous apartment"
and where "conversation soon faded and the half hour devoted
to sympathy slipped away slowly in the repetition of the same
remarks week after week." Like Alfred, Lucie was incapable
of capitalizing on the melodrama of her situation.

At long last, on September 26, 1898, Lucie was able to write
the letter that she and Alfred had hoped and lived for during a
four-year century:

> My dear Alfred,
>   Today we are overjoyed. I am so deeply happy that I must
> confide my joy to you at once. . . . Finally, this afternoon,
> after suffering much anguish, I learned that the Cabinet had
> submitted the dossier to the Court of Cassation. . . . And
> so we have arrived at the last stage of our journey, at the final
> crisis, which should restore to us what we have been unjustly
> deprived of—our honor.
>   I hope with all my heart that this is the last letter that I
> will send to you in that wretched place. We still have some
> weeks of anguish to pass through but they will be less
> painful now that we feel we are near the end.

The censors let the letter pass, and in early November the
prisoner, whose fate the entire world was watching, replied:

> I want all that lives within me, my thoughts and my heart
> which have not deserted you once these four terrible years,
> to add, if possible, to your joy. . . . When you receive this
> letter, I think that it should all be finished and that your
> happiness and joy will be complete.

Among thinking people the optimism of the Dreyfuses seemed
no more than reasonable. The Prime Minister learned that a

number of prominent generals were eager for the retrial so the Army could recover its honor after the machinations of the General Staff. General de Galliffet, the Army's most respected officer, wanted a second Dreyfus court-martial. Among junior officers there was a growing hostility to the Counterintelligence Service. "What's been placed in question is one bureau of the General Staff," a young officer told a *Figaro* reporter. "They translate, they prod, they photograph, they write in newspapers —they do everything, in a word, except what soldiers do."

When Clemenceau declared in his newspaper, "It is not Dreyfus that we defend—it is France," his logic and morality compelled serious reflection. It seemed public opinion might be returning to the empire of common sense. Of course, the Nationalists could not be expected to abjure their beliefs overnight, and the articles of Maurras in *La Gazette de France* were already providing them with exalted mummery to shore up crumbling prejudices. Still many Catholics migrated to the Dreyfusard side of the barricade. When there was no welcome in the priest-eating League for the Rights of Man, more than two hundred Catholics took membership in the Committee for the Defense of Right and Justice.

But the overwhelming majority of Catholics stood fast behind Comte Albert de Mun who abhorred the Dreyfusards as though they were the Devil. The principal newspaper of the Catholics, *La Croix*, became more shrill in its defense of the Army week by week. They gained support from the respected writer Barrès, whom the Dreyfusard intellectuals were still hoping to win over, but who announced his convictions in *Le Journal* in early October:

> The release of Dreyfus would be, after all, a trivial fact. But if Dreyfus is more than a traitor, if he is a symbol, then the matter is altogether different. . . . The victory of the camp which supports the symbolic Dreyfus would most certainly install in power men who desire the transformation of France according to their own ideas. I, myself, want to preserve France.

The Court of Cassation was divided into three branches; criminal, civil, and petitions. The first was presided over by the incorruptible Justice Louis Loew to whom the case had been referred. The anti-Dreyfusards screamed that Justice Loew was a German Jew and that the criminal branch was suborned by the Syndicate. Ignoring the clamor, Justice Loew selected one of his youngest assistants, Maître Alphonse Bard, to prepare the court's preliminary recommendation. It was the misfortune of the Court of Cassation, the government, the Dreyfusards, and the French people that a series of disasters beset France throughout the winter of 1898–99, a bewildering mixture of domestic and international calamities. The domestic crisis began straightforwardly enough—escalating strikes by laborers. The immediate cause of the international crisis arose from the success of the almost forgotten Marchand mission sent out to cross Central Africa which resulted in the Fashoda Crisis. Everything affected the Affair and the Affair affected everything. Thus, although the strikes and Fashoda emerged independently and were independently resolved, like matter in a solvent they were dispersed by and they colored deeply the Affair.

The beginnings of the Fashoda Crisis went back many years to the "War Scare of 1875," when French politicians feared that the Germans were preparing to mount a war in order to arrest the remarkable recovery of the French Army. Although there was more bluff by the Germans than danger of war, the French believed that the danger had been averted by the intercession of the British and the Russians. In gratitude, the French obligingly closed their eyes in November 1875 when British Prime Minister Disraeli bought with Rothschild money Egypt's 40 percent interest in the French-built Suez Canal. In 1882, to protect their investments, the British temporarily occupied Egypt. In 1883 a British-officered army under General William Hicks was annihilated by the Mahdi, the religious leader of the Sudan. Then, two years later, at the hands of the Mahdi General Gordon achieved his everlasting but diplomatically awkward martyrdom at Khartoum. The British began to behave as though they were committed to perpetual occupation of Egypt. In time, the French became equally obsessed with devising a plan to compel their speedy evacuation.

In the *Chronicles of the Saracenic Empire*, written by El Macin in the thirteenth century, it is said that Prester John of Abyssinia brought the pharaohs to their knees by constructing dikes to divert the Nile at its source. In January 1893 a noted engineer told the Egyptian Institute in Paris that an advanced nation like France would be able to construct a dam in the region of the Nile's headwaters to regulate the river's flow. President Sadi Carnot had been a classmate of this engineer. He invited his Under-Secretary for Colonies, Théophile Delcassé, to the Élysée. "I should like to reopen the Egyptian question," the President announced.

There were the inevitable delays and false starts. It was not until the spring of 1896 that the government decided to send the energetic Captain Jean Baptiste Marchand to the territory adjacent to that of the legendary Prester John, to the region in southern Sudan known as the Bahr al-Ghazal. Marchand was ordered to reach his destination by the most indirect, nearly impossible route—by traveling across the middle of Africa from the west to the east coast. Marchand's mission was to cut the continent in half, to put a French belt across Africa in order to stymie the grand British design of an empire (and a railroad) stretching northeasterly from the South African Cape to Cairo. If Captain Marchand could reach the Nile before the British, moving south from Egypt, conquered the Sudan, France could force the British out of Egypt entirely, or share it, or demand support for French control of Morocco.

On July 10, 1898, after two years and three weeks, the Marchand mission reached the White Nile, hoisted the tricolor at Fashoda, and drank champagne. Marchand deserved a kinder fate than that in store for him. On September 2, the day before Lucie's letter to the government pleading for revision, the Anglo-Egyptian army under the command of General Herbert Kitchener destroyed the forces of the Khalifa, the Mahdi's successor, at Omdurman. Gordon was avenged, the Sudan opened, and the victorious army descended along the Nile in the direction of Fashoda. On September 19 a contingent of the thirty-thousand-man Anglo-Egyptian army encamped before the two hundred-odd African soldiers manning Fashoda. While they waited for instructions from London and Paris, the two commanders observed a strained cordiality. But the French found that even the cordiality of the British was perfidious. A British officer brought Marchand's men copies of recent French newspapers. "One hour after we opened the newspapers, the officers were trembling and weeping," Marchand recalled. "We learned then and there that the terrible Dreyfus Affair had been opened with its dreadful campaign of infamies, and for thirty-six hours not one of us was able to say anything to the others."

There was more to cry about than Lieutenant Colonel Henry's confession and suicide. Queen Victoria's ministers had followed Marchand's odyssey with mounting concern. They had not been certain what to do about France's African strategy until early September. Kitchener's victory at Omdurman made them more determined to refuse to negotiate. Henry's suicide, de Boisdeffre's resignation, and the impending collapse of Prime Minister Brisson's Cabinet convinced the British that France would decline a direct challenge of war. Early in 1898 the beleaguered Gabriel Hanotaux, then the Foreign Minister, had cabled the French Ambassador in London to be firm about Africa: "They perhaps believe that we are being weakened by the Dreyfus Affair. But they are wrong. They see us only through the eyes of the Jewish press." But while Marchand watched Kitchener's army through field glasses throughout September and into October, events belied Hanotaux. France was on the verge of political disintegration, and Britain began to exploit the situation through a policy of truculent diplomacy.

The British Ambassador in Paris, Sir Edmund Monson, nevertheless continued to worry. Monson feared that arrogance born of weakness might lead the French to embrace Fashoda as a *casus belli*. Brisson would never go to war but a Nationalist Cabinet or a government installed through a military coup d'état very well might. Depending on who succeeded Brisson, Ambassador Monson knew that Fashoda and French hatred of Britain could be used to unite the nation and eliminate the Dreyfusard clamor permanently.

For the first time since the climax of General Boulanger's popularity—for the first time in a decade—there was in Paris an odor of insurrection. As ex-Foreign Minister Hanotaux told an English journalist, "If the Army at any time found a leader in any popular general who should become Minister of War, the situation might change, the public might easily become excited." In the Dreyfusard camp there was a fear that General Chanoine, Cavaignac's successor, was just such an officer. Should the new Minister of War be an aspiring Caesar, he was blessed with a ready-made domestic crisis. In mid-September the workers clearing sites for pavilions to house the International Exposition of 1900 went on strike.

While negotiations with the excavators dragged on, the Seine railwaymen's union announced that its members would stop work at the end of the first week in October. Since the bloody days of the Commune of 1871, when General de Galliffet's troops had "saved" France by slaughtering the workers who had seized Paris, the bourgeoisie trembled at the slightest social unrest. In their minds, the bombing of the Chamber of Deputies and the murder of President Sadi Carnot by Anarchists were inspired by working-class designs against order and property. The seventy thousand troops that Chanoine poured into Paris were to save the Republic from another Commune. The bourgeoisie hardly needed to be persuaded that, with the worsening Fashoda Crisis, the striking railwaymen also threatened national security if it became necessary to mobilize the Army against Britain.

As unrest spread throughout Paris by day and the ominous campfires of soldiers burned along the Champs Élysées and on the Champ de Mars by night, reports prepared by security police grew more alarming. "One hears that an enormous Nationalist and anti-Semitic demonstration is being planned for October 25 when the Chamber reconvenes. The rumor is spreading that the troops massed in Paris will serve to enforce rather than to prevent the actions of the Nationalists," one agent wrote on October 13. The Dreyfusards were "extremely uneasy," Mathieu wrote, "because we knew that the General Staff wanted street disturbances. Grave trouble . . . would justify the proclamation of martial law. And once martial law was decreed all power would pass into the hands of the military." The British military attaché was of the same mind. Crossing the Channel almost daily to report, he informed London that the French General Staff intended to exploit both the Affair and Fashoda to galvanize France and to save its own honor.

In America, the weekly magazine *The Outlook* warned of "a desperate plot which involves the turning to revolutionary account of the industrial troubles with which France is just now stirred." In Berlin, London, Rome, and Saint Petersburg the occupants of palaces and ministries, bracing for the coup d'état, thought it was at hand on Tuesday, October 25. As the Chamber reconvened, General Chanoine marched to the tribune and without warning announced his resignation. That was the end of the government of Henri Brisson. The British Ambassador, in his dispatch to Whitehall, stated that the Minister's resignation was an "act of treachery which looks like the first step to a military coup d'état." The Admiralty prepared war orders for the Home, Channel, and Mediterranean fleets. Simultaneously the Italian naval authorities placed the ports of Genoa and La Spezia on alert. Nationalist and anti-Semitic demonstrations did erupt when the Minister of War quit his post, but the orders to seize the capital, which Mathieu had expected, were never issued. The interim government was left to fret over alarming police reports, the generals remained respectful, and the Nationalist and Royalist deputies appeared as concerned to form a constitutional ministry as their Dreyfusard colleagues.

Why Chanoine acted as he did remains a puzzle. Joseph Reinach scoffed at rumors that the Minister of War had accepted the Pretender's offer of a dukedom and a generous annuity to overthrow the regime. Possibly the General's plans were foiled by the usually hopeless staff work of anti-republican plotters. Possibly, at the last moment, he recoiled from the awesome responsibility of the role of a Boulanger. More likely, General Chanoine believed that his timing of Prime Minister Brisson's destruction would dismay and panic his countrymen, that they would rally to the Army, supporting it against the possibility of a Dreyfus revision. But public opinion was not yet ready. The striking workers behaved not as Anarchists or Communards but as workers on strike. There was much concern for Captain Marchand and his two hundred men and great indignation over British truculence, but there was no unanimous sentiment for France to go to war to defend Fashoda, a place very few Frenchmen had ever heard of.

On Thursday, October 27, Sir Edmund Monson met with the interim Minister of Foreign Affairs, Théophile Delcassé. Although he delivered no ultimatum, Monson made it clear that London would discuss terms only after Marchand evacuated Fashoda. After Monson left, Captain Baratier of Fashoda was ushered in. A.-E.-A. Baratier, who had been allowed passage to Alexandria by the British, had steamed to Marseille to present an eyewitness report of the situation at Fashoda. With a military hero in his office, a workers' strike in the capital, and rumors of the officer corps verging on mutiny, Delcassé had reason to conceal his pacific intentions. By the time Baratier returned the next day, Delcassé had heard the Naval Minister's opinion that France would suffer a second Trafalgar in the event of war. As for the glorious Russian ally, in whose primitive economy some five billion gold francs were invested, it had scanned the fine print in the treaty and sent regrets that its obligations did not extend to supporting the French outside Europe. Captain Baratier quit the Quai d'Orsay incensed, disgusted by the lame-duck government and the pettifogging caution of Delcassé. Much of the anti-Dreyfusard press supported Baratier and called for war rather than surrender.

By his resignation General Chanoine had created a situation exactly opposite to what he had wanted; in no way could the Army profit from the Republic's dilemma. Republican France thus barely survived the month of October; on November 1 Charles Dupuy presented his government to the Chamber. Two days later Delcassé, still in command at the Foreign Ministry (and lamenting, "I had no need for the distraction of the Dreyfus Affair"), ordered Captain Marchand to withdraw. Chagrined that they had surrendered rather than fought (but suspecting the consequences), most Frenchmen quickly blotted Fashoda out of their minds. Within a few years, the British, sensitive to France's humiliation, were charitable enough to obliterate the name Fashoda, renaming the fortress Kodok. Even then, the French still would be grappling with the Affair.

chapter thirteen:
A SLIGHT IMPROVEMENT

FOR THREE DAYS IN LATE OCTOBER 1898 MAÎTRE
Bard, the preliminary examiner, presented his findings to the
Court of Cassation's criminal chamber presided over by Justice
Loew. Bard's report was a masterpiece, closely examining every
shred of available evidence, weighing each pro and con before
adducing the truth with inflexible logic and, in the circumstantial areas, unfailingly discerning the probable from the
merely plausible. Bard concluded that Madame Dreyfus' request
for revision was justified. He recommended that the Court of
Cassation's criminal chamber hear the case in plenary session.
The Court agreed and the parade of witnesses began.

The Nationalists went wild. They recalled that Justice Loew
(who, they insisted, was Jewish) had presided at the *Union
Générale* hearings in 1882 as well as at Zola's appeal, two
proceedings whose outcome had greatly annoyed them. They
charged that the criminal chamber had been bought by Rothschild money. *L'Autorité*, Cassagnac's partisan but usually responsible newspaper, warned that if the Court of Cassation
voided the Dreyfus sentence, the nation itself would void the

Court's verdict. Justice Jules Quesnay de Beaurepaire, the president of the civil chamber of the Court of Cassation, noisily resigned at the beginning of the year, accusing his colleague, Justice Loew, of having coached Picquart before his deposition. In fact, de Beaurepaire wanted revenge (against Dupuy and his cohorts) for humiliation he had suffered as Attorney General during the Panama Scandal. The charge was balm to Nationalist spirits and, although at the end of January a judicial commission promptly dismissed Justice de Beaurepaire's allegation (one he continued to make as the new editor of *L'Echo de Paris*, an intemperately Nationalist newspaper), the government was unnerved enough to present a bill before the Chamber of Deputies altering the procedure for appeal in cases of treason.

While the search for justice by the Court of Cassation was being obstructed, the injustices against Picquart continued. Because of public outcry, political maneuvering, and his appeal to the Court of Cassation to rule on the civil or military character of pending charges, Picquart's mid-December court-martial was postponed. He was still in prison and, his friends feared, still in danger for his life. His fate worried the diplomatic community, especially the German and Italian Ambassadors. If the Army's charge of forging the *petit bleu* failed, Germany and Italy would achieve the doubly sweet victory of humiliating the French war machine while appearing to serve justice. There was another potential windfall from helping to clear Picquart—a Franco-German *rapprochement*. Already, in late June, the German Minister of Foreign Affairs, Prince Bernhard von Bülow, and the French Ambassador had discussed such a scheme, whose principal inducement would be a Franco-German cannibalizing of weak Portugal's African colonies. If neither Bülow nor Delcassé took the proposal seriously, others in France and Germany did. The son of the Kaiser's Chancellor, Prince Alexander von Hohenlohe, believed that a few words about the *petit bleu* from Schwartzkoppen could save Picquart, Dreyfus, and European peace. "If at this moment, in this situation, amid a complete turnaround of public opinion," he wrote Schwartzkoppen, "there is anything that we could do to bring the truth to light, would not that have a good effect, would not the great majority of the public in France recognize the honorable nature of our action?" With General Chanoine and Fashoda uppermost in mind, the German and Italian ambassadors to Paris were convinced that the sooner Dreyfus was rehabilitated, the quicker the diplomatic weather would clear.

Prodded by the Prince of Monaco, the German Ambassador took the initiative to help Picquart at the end of November, writing to Schwartzkoppen, "It would be of the utmost importance for the defense to learn *confidentially* whether it is your handwriting, or whether you had it [the *petit bleu*] written." Schwartzkoppen wired his old chief that he had had absolutely nothing to do with the document. Three weeks later a young man in the embassy to whom the *petit bleu* had probably been dictated told Ambassador Münster the truth. This time there were sparks between Paris and Berlin. The old statesman scolded Schwartzkoppen:

> As I must assume from your whole attitude that you wrote that *petit bleu*, as your former chief I demand that you say so candidly and not *deceive* me in the way you unfortunately have been doing in the whole matter. . . . For my part, I have been placed by you in the most uncomfortable situation in the whole Affair; now I am tired of it, and consequently I must demand a *definite explanation*.

In his reply Schwartzkoppen was equivocally contrite. Sincerely regretting the appearance of deception and pleading obedience to orders from a "higher power" to remain uninvolved, he stretched his conflicting loyalties far enough to confide, "I wrote several notes to Esterhazy and it is therefore very possible, even probable, that the one in question comes from me." Unfortunately, the fact that both the *petit bleu* and the note were in an unknown hand rendered this admission valueless. Nor could the Italian Ambassador, Tornielli, do anything to help. Having been rebuffed once, his military attaché,

Panizzardi, could influence the public only if his German colleague broke silence. The well-meaning ambassadors had to tell their French friends that they could not help Picquart. Aggrieved by Schwartzkoppen's duplicity, the upright Münster would have been revolted had he known that his government's secret policy opposed any form of meaningful German assistance in the Affair. On September 29 Foreign Minister Bülow telegraphed his staff from his vacation retreat:

> It is not to be desired that France should immediately win liberal and Jewish sympathies by a quick and scintillating reparation of the Dreyfus Affair. It would be best if the Affair would continue to fester, to upset the Army, and to scandalize all Europe.

Bülow need not have worried about the Affair festering. The French were proving themselves experts in self-mutilation. Even the appearance in late January of Esterhazy's slim book, *Le Dessous de l'Affaire Dreyfus* (The Underside of the Dreyfus Case), admitting again authorship of the *bordereau* but claiming to have acted as Colonel Sandherr's double agent, failed to destroy the Army's case. Frenchmen remembered that Esterhazy's confession had already been reported by the Paris correspondent for the London *Observer*, Rowland Strong. When Strong published the story Esterhazy promptly denied it. It was at least comprehensible, then, that much of the French public concluded that everything attributed to the Count should be disregarded. Among the upper classes a sublime flippancy in the manner of Proust's Duchesse de Guermantes was common. Not even the Devil's Island letters moved her:

> In any case, if this man Dreyfus is innocent, he hasn't done much to prove it. What idiotic letters he writes from that island. I don't know whether Monsieur Esterhazy is any better but he does show some skill in his choice of words and a different tone altogether What a pity for them [the Dreyfusards] there is no way of exchanging innocents.

More indicative of the sentiments of respectable society was the inauguration of the *Ligue de la Patri Française* (League of the French Fatherland) late in January of 1899 under the presidency of Ferdinand Brunetière. An anti-Semitic countess provided the working capital while a majority of the French Academy, along with Barrès, Maurras, Cavaignac, and Major Marchand provided the glamor and political resources.

As the Army entrenched for the final combat, hatred of the Jews became rampant. Dreyfus was a Jew and those who fought his battle were allies of the Jews, opposed to the Army, the Church, and the will of the majority. But such charges did not square with the facts; most Jews did not support Dreyfus. Even after the confession of Henry, the flight of Esterhazy, and the acceptance of the case by the Court of Cassation, there had been no stampede of Jews to enroll in the League for the Rights of Man. The Rothschilds quickly excised the anti-Dreyfusard Schlumberger's name from their guest list, but in the interest of political symmetry they also dropped Joseph Reinach. The elegant Jewish journalist Arthur Meyer, who, if Edmond de Goncourt is to be believed, slept in his pearl gray gloves, conceded that "certain Jews would threaten the universal social order. And regrettably, on this point, Monsieur Drumont is entirely right." There were many friends of the Dreyfus and Hadamard families who approved the caveat of the Jewish editor of *Le Soir*, one of France's largest newspapers:

> Let the Jews take heed. Without Reinach they could count once again upon the protection of the fatherland; if, on the contrary, they persist obstinately in following their evil instinct, the God who protects France will abandon them forever.

Another deity protecting another land was precisely what a small but embarrassingly vocal minority of Jews had in mind. For Joseph Reinach the appearance of Zionism toward the end of 1897 had been the supreme nightmare. He was so horrified that he denounced the movement openly in *Le Figaro*, even at the risk of further publicizing it:

> The sole result of this campaign, which in any case is destined for a pitiful failure, would be to give the impression . . . that those Frenchmen who belong to the Jewish faith are subordinating the idea of the fatherland to I cannot imagine what sort of solidarity which existed in a vague way during barbarous times, which was prevalent no doubt at the origin of civilized societies, but which in modern societies is an anachronism.

But a growing number of influential French Jews were coming to believe that Zionism was not an anachronism but the hope of the community. The First Zionist Congress, held in Basel during the summer of 1897, and also the second in the following year virtually adopted as their themes Bernard Lazare's statement, "Assimilation is not and cannot be a solution." And in distant Baltimore, Maryland, a conference of Jews expressed pleasure at the conduct of the Court of Cassation but was soberly pessimistic. "One hundred years of unquestioned enjoyment of civil rights, one hundred years of loyal devotion to their country did not suffice to save the Jews from the vilest attacks," the conference report observed. "The French Jews are as impotent to silence these attacks as are their fellow sufferers in other places." As the judicial phase of the Affair approached its climax, despite objections such as Reinach's even the cosmopolitan Rothschilds quickened their support of a Jewish homeland.

Although judicial rigor was no more than its duty, under the circumstances the steadfastness of the Court of Cassation's criminal chamber was admirable. It exerted itself to the fullest to corroborate reports of Esterhazy's confession. On January 23, 1899, under a guarantee of immunity from prosecution, Esterhazy came to Paris to defend himself. The self-confident Count's real reason for testifying was to muddle the plainest evidence so that he could profit even from his own confession.

This was the beginning of the myth that Esterhazy had been a double agent in the service of French Counterintelligence and assigned to deal with Schwartzkoppen. "Colonel Henry was one of my comrades," Esterhazy told the Court. "I used to see him quite frequently." What of his confession? Had Rowland Strong of the *Observer* lied? Esterhazy was asked. This was not a matter within the competence of the Court, Esterhazy replied; a court-martial had acquitted him of the authorship of the *bordereau*. The point of law was not quite so clear-cut, the justices insisted. Well, he was not going to discuss the fantasies of an English newsman—Esterhazy paused—"who has as his close friends two very intelligent men with whom he lives in a fairly constant fashion, Lord Alfred Douglas and Sir Oscar Wilde." When he later repeated his confession publicly in March and again in early July, the French authorities merely shrugged their shoulders as they read the English newspapers.

The Court considered Esterhazy's deposition and continued its five-month investigation. Du Paty was questioned closely to bring out the truth about the 1894 telegram sent by Panizzardi to General Marselli, Chief of the Italian General Staff. The still imprisoned Picquart illuminated the vagaries of the Affair with what even his detractors granted was intellect at its Cartesian finest. De Boisdeffre and Mercier filed into court as well as Billot and Gonse, but the first two refused to comment on the secret packet which Du Paty had handed to Dreyfus' judges.

The original Dreyfusards, Forzinetti and Gobert, gave moving depositions, while the testimonies of ex-President Casimir-Périer, ex-Minister of Finance Poincaré, ex-Minister of Foreign Affairs Hanotaux, and Prime Minister Dupuy did nothing to aid the Army. The deposition of Captain Henri Le Rond, once a friend of Esterhazy's, tipped the scales measurably in Dreyfus' favor. An artillery specialist who had been at the Châlons camp in 1894–95, Le Rond recalled Esterhazy's efforts to train at the camp out of turn and his several unauthorized visits. What Madame Marie Chapelon told the Court about the persistent

Lebrun-Renault report of a Dreyfus confession was carefully weighed. Her deceased husband was a friend of Lebrun-Renault and had questioned him about Dreyfus. Lebrun-Renault had told the Chapelons, "Everything the papers said is just imagination! Dreyfus didn't say anything to me."

Martin Freystaetter, a decorated officer in the marine infantry and one of the seven judges in the 1894 court-martial, was an unimpeachable witness. Captain Freystaetter recalled the dramatic impact of Colonel Henry upon the court: "That declaration had a considerable influence upon me." However, he believed now that the verdict had been wrong and he revealed that one of the documents which had decided the judges, the Scoundrel D letter, was never discussed in open court.

While the Court heard evidence in the case, Prime Minister Dupuy introduced the bill on January 28, 1899, to require a verdict by the united branches of the court rather than the criminal chamber alone in cases of treason. The Dreyfusards went berserk; such an action would delay the final decision by months, and they also believed that the majority of the justices of the petitions and civil chambers were opposed to revision. As justification the government cited the lingering suspicions against the criminal chamber stemming from the disproven charges of ex-Justice de Beaurepaire accusing Justice Loew of coaching Picquart. But the real motive was the nearness of national elections. The Minister of Justice had brushed aside the qualms of several colleagues with the advice, "Look to your constituents." By referring Lucie Dreyfus' appeal to the Court of Cassation's forty-nine justices instead of the sixteen in the criminal chamber, Dupuy sought to deny his opponents electoral ammunition while greatly strengthening his position once the Court rendered its verdict. The anguish of the Dreyfusards was indescribable when the government (encouraged, it was widely believed, by President Faure) crowned its perfidy by calling for a vote on the bill the day after the verdict of the criminal chamber. On February 9, 1899, the criminal chamber voided the 1894 conviction of Alfred Dreyfus. On February 10, by a vote of 324 to 207, Prime Minister Dupuy's new law—a retroactive law—passed the Chamber of Deputies. The Dreyfus legal drama now had to be replayed before the entire Court of Cassation.

Suddenly, as if history were on the side of the Dreyfusards, France was thrust into crises which would arouse her common sense. Six days after the Chamber's vote President Faure received Prince Albert of Monaco. As in the past the Prince defended Dreyfus, this time more forcefully and conclusively than ever. Upset by Albert's revelations, Faure repaired to a special room of the Élysée to seek the comfort of his mistress, Madame de Steinheil. Ninety minutes later the hysterical Madame de Steinheil was rushed from a side door of the palace, her nude body covered by a blanket, while the stricken President sank into a fatal coma. Félix Faure died in the late afternoon of February 16. With cruel flippancy Clemenceau wrote in *L'Aurore* the next day that "there is not one less man in France." Two days later the Chamber and the Senate convened at Versailles to elect a successor. They decided upon Émile Loubet, a man proud of his plebeian roots, tainted by the Panama Scandal, and reputedly pro-Dreyfusard.

The extent, if any, of Félix Faure's collusion with the anti-Dreyfusards is unknown, but the Nationalists saw his death and replacement by Émile Loubet as calamitous. Once again plans for a coup d'état were hatched. The day before the President's burial the Duc d'Orléans slipped across the frontier from Belgium and posted himself in the chateau of a faithful nobleman. The Pretender's representatives had had no time to persuade Paul Déroulède, the chief of the League of Patriots, to join the cause of royalism. But the Duc d'Orléans knew that Déroulède intended to overthrow the regime. On the day of the new President's election Déroulède had vowed before the statue of Joan of Arc to sanitize France. "We shall overthrow this Republic to erect a better Rpublic," he adjured his followers. "Long live the better Republic!" The fact that Déroulède hated the royalists even more than the politicians who ran the Republic was dismissed as a manageable inconvenience. The Duc believed that once Déroulède acted, he could rally the generals to his own cause.

After the somber and dignified rites at Notre Dame, Félix Faure's remains were transported to Père Lachaise cemetery under military escort. Déroulède's hopes were pinned on General de Pellieux who commanded this escort. He and his myrmidons waited in the Place de la Nation for the return of the units commanded by the General. But to their surprise, another general was in charge; de Pellieux was home nursing a sudden virus. Even though the general was wrong, it was still the ideal occasion for a coup. Déroulède and his lieutenant grappled for the General's bridle while their few hundred followers bumped against the column of troops shouting, "Onward to the Élysée!" Embarrassed and completely befuddled, the general led his troops to their barracks with Déroulède tangled in his reins, his political proclamation still in his coat pocket. Leaping about the Reuilly barracks, haranguing the tired soldiers, the leader of the League of Patriots stubbornly refused to leave. Reluctantly the officers summoned the civilian police and Déroulède spent the next few months in Santé prison. Philippe Duc d'Orléans rushed back to his Belgian retreat.

Returning to France from South America in the summer of 1898, Ambassador Count Charles de Saint Aulaire noticed the Breton sailors crossing themselves as the ship came within sight of Devil's Island. Were they trying to fend off the evil spirit after whom the island was named? he asked. "Not at all," the captain explained. The ritual had been observed "only since Dreyfus has been there." "In their eyes," Saint Aulaire reflected, Dreyfus "was worse than the devil." The Breton seamen might have taken heart if they had known that the archfiend of the island had been chastised until he was scarcely more than a ghost. Even Lucie might have faltered before recognizing the stooped, palsied, white-haired skeleton as her once self-confident husband. All that had survived against crushing odds was an indomitable will for vindication. As the French Ambassador's ship plowed homeward in the third year of Dreyfus' exile, it remained to be seen whether or not the disgraced officer could survive much longer.

Perhaps it was concern for Dreyfus' survival or perhaps a well-meant but timid desire to defuse the crisis that inspired a daring rescue plan in the spring of 1899. "Dynamite" Johnny O'Brien, a gallant, garrulous, and throughly mendacious soldier of fortune who had fought with the Cubans in the Spanish-American War, agreed to organize a lightning raid on Devil's Island. His contact, a Cuban agent in Jacksonville, Florida, claimed to represent a group of European Jews which was offering half a million dollars to anyone who succeeded in spiriting Dreyfus to the United States. From years of experience in gun-running and smuggling, O'Brien knew the Caribbean like the back of his hand. He told the Cuban agent that the detachment of guards—less than forty, he calculated—could be overwhelmed at night, probably without bloodshed, and that the prisoner would be aboard a swift schooner before the troops on the mainland learned of the attack. O'Brien promised the men, the ship, and a detailed plan by the end of May.*

Speed was essential; it would be impossible to keep the project secret. Already, in Paris, Berlin, and London, there were rumors of an enormous rescue fund. Furthermore, if the rumors persisted, the paranoiac prison commandant, Deniel, would more than likely redouble his already ferocious surveillance. In addition to the machine-gun tower, the trebled guard, and the continual alerts, a telephone cable had been strung from Devil's to the headquarters on Royale. At any hour of the night the sentinels in the guardhouse could expect a call from their chief demanding a complete report on Dreyfus: his last words before going to sleep, the position in which he was lying, whether he appeared calm or feverish, what if anything he

---

* Maurice Baumont, *Aux Sources de l'Affaire* (Paris, 1959), p. 129; Horace Smith, *A Captain Unafraid* (New York, 1912).

murmured in his sleep. The commandant demanded more than unflagging attention from his subordinates. None of them had forgotten the incident on Christmas Day 1897, when one of them had telephoned a comrade on Royale with the jovial message, "Dreyfus wishes you a merry Christmas." Deniel had lifted the receiver instead, and the guard had been severely punished for his levity.

Dreyfus was almost beyond caring. Lucie sensed the dangerous change immediately and wrote letter after letter pleading with Fred to think about his fate and that of herself and the children. He must continue to write, she commanded, no matter how repetitious, how hopeless and insignificant it all seemed. "What was there to say?" he wrote.

> The feelings that are in our hearts, that rule our souls—we know them. Moreover, even we two have finally exhausted the cup of our sufferings. You ask me still, dear Lucie, to talk to you about myself in detail. I cannot! When you suffer as atrociously as this, when you bear such moral miseries, it is impossible to know at the end of one day where you'll be the day after tomorrow.

Somehow, throughout that year and the next, Dreyfus continued to write to his magnificent wife, sometimes lethargically or mechanically, but sometimes with passionate optimism. Even so, his mental powers were steadily decreasing. Doctor Veugmon, the physician who had replaced Delrieu, diagnosed him as a "neuropathic subject." Then a letter from Lucie, written in late September 1898 announced her petition to the government for review of his case. This letter was delivered the first week in November, and three weeks later, for the first time in two years, Deniel allowed Dreyfus to stroll around the island. "I saw the sea again. . . ."

Although Deniel forbade discussion of the Court of Cassation, the minute alterations in the behavior of his guards were unmistakable portents. Dreyfus wrote again to the President of the Republic and to General de Boisdeffre (Dreyfus did not know that he was no longer Chief of Staff). Still nothing seemed to happen. "You cannot imagine how long all these details of procedure take," Lucie wrote at the end of February. It was one of the rare times when her expression was faulty; Alfred, of all people, could best imagine the unjust delays of justice. "It is indeed long," he replied in early April. "The accumulated suffering occasioned by this unending torment is terrible. . . . But the end is everything." Then the end came.

On May 29, 1899, the forty-nine justices of the united Court of Cassation heard the final reports; they stated that the *bordereau* was the exclusive creation of Esterhazy. The reports concluded that the 1894 court-martial had wrongly condemned Captain Alfred Dreyfus. On June 3 the Chief Justice of the Court of Cassation, considering the plea of Lucie's attorney to allow Dreyfus to clear himself before the Army, announced the annulment of the 1894 verdict and remanded the case to the military authorities at Rennes. It was a perfect compromise between civilian justice and military honor. A special ship, the *Sfax*, was sent to bring the prisoner to France.

Two days later, at twelve-thirty in the afternoon, the chief guard handed Dreyfus a cablegram from Paris.

Please make known to Captain Dreyfus immediately.

The Court sets aside and annuls the judgment rendered against Alfred Dreyfus by the first court-martial on December 22, 1894, and sends the accused before the Rennes court-martial board.

He would leave for the mainland on Friday. "Heart and soul with you, children, all," his telegram to Lucie read. "Await with great joy happy moment of embracing you. Kisses all." He had been on Devil's Island for four years, two months, and five days.

In Jacksonville, Florida, Dynamite Johnny O'Brien lost an easy fortune and the United States was spared what would have been one of the greatest diplomatic dilemmas in its history.

On the afternoon of June 4, a Sunday, President Émile Loubet attended the annual steeplechase at Auteuil. Loubet was as different from his predecessor, Félix the Sun President, as Louis XVI from Louis XIV. Devoid of affectation, he was "an ordinary type, quite simple and bluff, totally ignorant of all ostentation and glamor." At the close of his audience with Prince Oskar of Sweden, Loubet had committed the gaffe, unpardonable in presidential majesty, of forgetting to thank the future king for his visit. But, to the Nationalists, his folksiness and lapses in protocol were less reprehensible than his politics. Each week they became more certain that "Panama" Loubet was in league with the Dreyfusards. The decision of the Court of Cassation made them hate him bitterly.

When Loubet took his special box amidst shouts of *"Vive l'Armée! Pa-na-ma! Pa-na-ma!"* he seemed to hear nothing. Nearby a gaggle of young aristocrats alternately cheered their horses and railed at the President for more than two hours while the gendarmes looked on indifferently. When it came to the Affair even the police were partisan, and Prime Minister Dupuy, a cynical and pragmatic politician who coveted the Presidency, may not have seen fit to remind the Prefect of Police of his duty. If the anti-Dreyfusards wanted to blame the President for the Court of Cassation's ruling this only made the Cabinet portfolios more secure. The President of France endured the outrageous hazing while the young noblemen with their white carnation boutonnieres became hysterical. *"Pa-na-ma! Pa-na-ma!"*

Suddenly, one of them leaped into the box, bashing Loubet's top hat and ruffling Madame Loubet before he was immobilized. Savage epithets were one thing but, as one of the President's horrified officers moaned, an act of assault and battery would cause people to say that "once again our cause is compromised by the stupidity of some of our own people." Whatever Frenchmen felt about Dreyfus, only a handful of fanatics approved the caning of the President of the Republic in front of the diplomatic corps.

The Dreyfusards knew that the Auteuil incident was a turning point. The political Left and thousands of ordinary citizens were mobilizing against the threat to republican democracy from the Army, the aristocracy, and the Church. A few days later Radicals, Socialists, and some of the Prime Minister's own supporters combined with mortified Nationalists to vote a motion calling for the defense of republican institutions. Implicitly this move repudiated the government. It was the end of Dupuy. While Dreyfus sailed home aboard the cruiser *Sfax*, the Chamber of Deputies scampered to patch together a new government.

Out of the jockeying for a Prime Minister, a preference emerged for René Waldeck-Rousseau, an enlightened leader of the Opportunist Party. This time a government would be composed of strong personalities who could impose policy upon the almost seditious Army, the disaffected upper classes, and the volatile public. For his Minister of War, Waldeck-Rousseau chose General the Marquis Gaston de Galliffet, Prince of Martigues and permanent member of the Superior War Council. Tall and haughty, Galliffet, like Esterhazy, was an anachronism from the eighteenth century—flamboyant, lucky, and something of a law unto himself. As a junior officer in the ill-fated Mexican campaign, he had once rolled his own intestines into place after a ghastly stomach wound and had staggered to the infirmary more than a mile away. At Sedan Colonel de Galliffet had led the famous "death charge" of the Imperial Cavalry. Republican politicians who could ignore his political arrogance and pride of ancestry were obliged to loathe this Commander in Chief of the troops who had suppressed the Paris Commune of 1871. But many of them trusted a general who had written to Princess Radziwill that Dreyfus "was completely innocent" and who alone seemed capable of bending the Army to the decision of the Court of Cassation.

To balance things, Prime Minister-designate Waldeck-Rousseau astounded the Chamber by offering the Ministry of Commerce to a Socialist deputy, Alexandre Millerand. Lawyer and journalist, Millerand alarmed his bourgeois colleagues because he had authored the Saint-Mandé Program, the official platform of French Socialism that called for gradual nationalization of the principal means of production and exchange. When the vote of confidence came on June 22, 1899, there were many surprised Socialists. Millerand had been one of the most consistent opponents of involvement in the Affair and now he shared the ministerial bench with de Galliffet, the destroyer of the Commune, a member of a government sworn to preside over its liquidation. Still more shocking, the new Minister of Commerce had accepted the position without letting the Party leaders rule on his decision. "Millerandism," Socialist participation in a bourgeois Cabinet, was soon the most divisive ideological issue of European Socialism before the Great War.

As the legendary prisoner of Devil's Island returned, the moods of the French ranged from jubilation through resignation to desperate indignation, with the great majority more resigned than jubilant. None was more enthusiastic than the self-exiled Émile Zola. Comforted by his mistress and their two children in England, Zola had nonetheless written letters that were an outpouring of self-pity. The three graphologists attacked in *J'Accuse* (Belhomme, Couard, and Varinard) had won a libel judgment of thirty-two thousand francs. The contents of Zola's home, including his priceless library, would have fallen under the auctioneer's gavel had not his editor finally arranged to pay the sum. The amount wiped out Zola's accumulated royalties. Depressed by this loss, alienated from the British by his inability to speak their language, physically and spiritually oppressed by the damp winter, and more downcast than ever by the death of his dog Pinpin, Zola was certain he would soon die of heart disease—he suffered from angina pectoris. At last, on June 4, he was able to return home convinced that "henceforth Dreyfus is acquitted." "My soul is elated," he proclaimed in his first article in *L'Aurore* since the judgment,

> but with no feelings of anger or vengeance. If the softness of my heart got the upper hand over my skeptical mind, I would be in favor of a general pardon. . . . As the only penalty for the criminals, I would leave them exposed to eternal public contempt. . . . Still, a public pillory must be erected so that people may finally see and understand. Personally, I leave it to Nemesis to accomplish the work of vengeance. I am not going to lend a hand.

Picquart, after more than three hundred days in Cherche-Midi prison, was released on June 9; four days later the Paris Court of Appeals acquitted him of the charges brought by ex-Ministers Zurlinden and Cavaignac. The world received the news of this liberation enthusiastically. The brilliant lieutenant colonel who had singlehandedly labored to make the ostriches in tunics face the truth and who had stoically endured their persecution was admired from San Francisco to Saint Petersburg.

For one seesawing moment it actually seemed that General Mercier would exchange places with Picquart. The motion to initiate a judicial *instruction* against the former War Minister was hotly debated in the Chamber, but in the end the Deputies postponed the decision until the outcome of Dreyfus' second court-martial. As a result, the second court-martial officers would have to decide not only the freedom of a former captain but the interrelated fate of an ex-Minister and popular General. Still, the Dreyfusards were convinced that the chances for acquittal were favorable.

Meanwhile, the anti-Dreyfusards kept busy. The League of the French Fatherland became more irrational and anti-Semitic. Its hero, Mercier, promised to establish Dreyfus' guilt once and for all "no matter what the cost." The only possible conclusion from this was that he would offer in evidence the unseen, annotated *bordereau*, that legendary document bearing the Kaiser's handwriting. The League's appeal was further enhanced by adopting Marchand. Returning from Africa on June 1, Marchand added glamor. President Loubet grew uneasy over the rising popularity of the soldier-explorer, grumbling to his staff about "the new Boulanger."

By the middle of July the President and Prime Minister were frankly alarmed. A week earlier, at one of the Nationalist revival meetings sweeping the country, General François de Negrier, of the Superior War Council, declared that if the government failed to halt the calumny against the Army, "the members of the Superior War Council are ready to act." At the July Fourteenth anniversary celebration of the 1789 Revolution, the crowds were full of *"Vive l'Armée"* and *"Vive Marchand"*; the customary *"Vive le Président"* was conspicuously absent. The Cabinet ordered reinforced surveillance of suspect officers and civilians.

Even that comedian of coups, Déroulède (recently acquitted in the Reuilly affair), was again doing his best to act as a menace. His League of Patriots had finally joined with the supporters of the Duc d'Orléans—not to restore the monarchy but to bring down the regime. This time the plotters had more money, were better coordinated, and had the support of Jules Guérin's Anti-Semitic League. France's best cryptographer was hustled out of retirement by the government to decipher the telegrams exchanged between the Duc and his followers, some so carelessly encoded that the Pretender had been incapable of making sense of them.

Those anti-Dreyfusards not moved by anti-Semitism, jingoism, or royalism found it simply inconceivable that dozens of the Army's generals and the Ministers of War had behaved criminally, that all of them—Mercier, Billot, Chanoine, Zurlinden, Cavaignac—were wrong about Dreyfus. And if, incredibly, the officers and their evidence were disreputable, should France disavow them for the sake of a single Jewish captain? For people like the archeologist Gustave Schlumberger or the philosopher Pierre Laffitte, the answer was clear. No true Frenchman, Barrès wrote in *Le Journal*, would proclaim his own innocence to the world at the cost of exposing the collective guilt of the Army's *grands chefs*: "If he [Dreyfus] is not a traitor, he will be ashamed of having excited this kind of support."

When the cruiser *Sfax* reached the coast of Brittany in the midst of a storm on the morning of June 30, Captain Dreyfus had been at sea exactly three weeks. The clothes he wore, even his underwear, gifts from Cayenne's black mayor, had been much too light to shield his cadaverous frame against the North Atlantic cold. It was a repetition of the hardship on the *Saint-Nazaire* more than four years before. The shock of the cold weather set off a spasm, but he was so ecstatic during the hours the *Sfax* lay at anchor offshore that pain almost ceased to matter. In his autobiography he wrote:

> After five years of martyrdom, I was returning to seek justice. The horrible nightmare was ending. I believed that men realized their mistake. I was expecting to see my loved ones and after them my comrades waiting with arms wide open and tears in their eyes.

His fevered imagination conjured up a gala evening in dress uniform with Mercier, de Boisdeffre, and Du Paty de Clam gallantly competing for the *mot juste* with which to regret their part in the greatest miscarriage of justice since the Calas Case. But there was to be no family or tearfully embracing comrades waiting ashore. Instead, at nine that evening a rowboat pulled alongside the ship. Dreyfus, feverish and unsteady, was ordered to jump into it. Somehow he remained conscious and landed just inside the lurching boat, his legs skinned and seriously bruised. A few minutes later he was told to make ready to climb aboard a coastal steamship. "Suffering from the wounds," he clambered up the rope ladder. After more than an hour on the steamer he was dropped into a second rowboat

which took him to the fishing village of Port Haliguen, a spot
so small and remote that it was unconnected by telegraph or
telephone with the rest of France. A horse-drawn carriage and
three silent gendarmes took him to the railroad station where a
special train was waiting. At six the next morning Dreyfus
arrived at the military prison in the city of Rennes.

"Instead of finding men united in a common idea of justice,"
he was finding "only anxious faces, minute precautions, a mad
debarkation in the middle of the night into a raging sea. It
was fortunate that during the long and bitter months of my
imprisonment I had learned to impose upon my morale, my
nerves, and my body a tremendous power of control." At nine
o'clock on his first morning at Rennes he had just washed off the
caked blood, his legs still stabbing with pain from the rowboat
accident, when an officer informed him that his wife was waiting in the room adjoining his cell. At a few minutes past nine
on a Saturday morning, October 15, 1894, Dreyfus had been
taken away from Lucie, and at a few minutes past nine on
Saturday, July 1, 1899, they were reunited. Hands entwined,
mute, they cried. Their feelings were "too intense to be expressed by human speech," Dreyfus said simply. Because
embracing was forbidden, an infantry lieutenant stood by to
enforce the rules.

On Monday morning his attorneys, the placid Demange and
the demonstrative Labori, came to fill Dreyfus in on the developments of the last five years. Of all the literate inhabitants
of the planet, Dreyfus was probably the most ignorant of the
Affair. From Demange he heard the name Esterhazy for the
first time. He learned of Picquart's discovery of the *petit bleu*
and the Army's attempt to conceal the document. He strained
to understand Zola's tempestuous intervention, Henry's suicide,
and de Boisdeffre's resignation. He was told of the army of
intellectuals and politicians mustered in his defense, of overthrown Cabinets, Nationalist and royalist conspiracies, of the
verbal and actual violence between the leagues of the Left and
the Right, and of the worldwide passion excited by his case.

Now, on the threshhold of victory, the symbol of France's honor could mumble through missing teeth, "All my beliefs in justice, all my illusions have collapsed. I who never doubted justice." He hated Lebon and Deniel for their rank sadism, had lost respect for Mercier, and pitied de Boisdeffre; still he was seized with "an immense sorrow, a great sadness, for this Army that I loved." Barrès had guessed shrewdly in saying that Dreyfus would be "ashamed of having excited this kind of support." He had not remained half alive on his desolate rock for more than four years for the sake of his honor, his commission, and his family to become the symbol of a political movement which, among other heterodoxies, was dedicated to humiliating generals and housebreaking the Army.

The immediate concern, however, was not the state of national politics but Dreyfus' health. Although Mathieu found his brother "very calm, quite serene, extraordinarily confident" at their first meeting on Monday afternoon, the changes were deplorable. The brisk Staff officer now "spoke with pronounced slowness—it was clear that he hadn't completely regained the power of speech," Mathieu later observed. What was true of speech was also true of his mental faculties. It was hardly surprising that Dreyfus, stricken by blackouts and attacks of amnesia, tended to forget much of what he was told and to scramble the little he retained. The malaria, the anemia, the injured legs, the recurrent nightmares made recovery in the Rennes prison almost as punishing as sheer survival on Devil's Island had been. He went on a diet of eggs and milk and counted on that last bit of resilience to pull him through.

In the weeks that followed, thousands wrote to Dreyfus. On Tuesday, July 4, Anatole France welcomed him home: "You were sustained, I know, by the consciousness of your innocence and the hope of seeing it recognized one day. This hope will not be betrayed." Two days later Zola posted his plain-speaking letter to Rennes. "Ah! This heroic brother," he wrote of Mathieu, "he has been devotion, bravery, and wisdom. For eighteen months we have protested your innocence."

Now your great task is to bring us tranquility with justice . . .
to complete our work of atonement by showing the man for
whom we fought and in whom we have embodied the triumph
of human solidarity. When the innocent man rises, France
will become again the land of equity and goodness.

Zola also saw the dilemma that was certain to disturb Dreyfus,
the fear that he was being entrapped in a plot for political
vengeance. "You will also save the honor of the Army, this
Army that you loved so much and in which you placed your
whole ideal." Then, with Italian warmth, Zola closed: "My
heart is overflowing; I can but suffer with you for what you
have suffered and for what your valiant wife has suffered. I
embrace you affectionately."

Eleanora Duse cheered, "Lose not courage nor patience!"
George Sand's daughter said that if her mother were alive,
"her voice would be raised among those of the defenders of
justice." Mark Twain, concerned about Dreyfus' health, sent
Lucie a somewhat wacky testimonial of the "miraculous heal-
ing power of Mr. Kellgreu, 49 Eaton Square, SW, London."
Showing the American knack for combining business with
sympathy, the president of Havana Hand-Made Cigars, Mr. L.
Lampert of Chicago, dispatched a box of his finest to the Paris
Embassy for consignment to Dreyfus. The same shrewd business eye prompted Olen W. Kennedy, editor of the Star Publishing Company of Muncie, Indiana, to write the American
consul general in Paris that "Indiana people are anxious to hear
your opinion. . . . We realize that you are placed in a peculiar
position to say anything, but you may find a way to give the
people of this state a few words about this most interesting
case."

While Dreyfus convalesced, the opening date of the court-
martial, August 7, was approaching. Throughout the Affair,
however excited, outraged, or moral they became, neither
the parliamentarians nor the justices ever forgot the importance
of timing and staging. The speed of the Court of Cassation's
final investigation and decision insured a court-martial held

while most Frenchmen were on vacation and the Chamber of Deputies was in recess. The selection of Rennes as the stage was certainly not without significance. This remote, ancient, spotlessly clean, Breton city straddling the Vilaine River, with its shabby-genteel nobility, frugal, pious tradespeople, and hardy women in little flat, white-lace caps, impressed an envious English Dreyfusard as "the town of a people that has long since learned, as we shall never, to make its first business the agreeable living of life." But the citizenry of Catholic Rennes did not find the international notoriety of a miscreant Jewish officer's trial at all agreeable.

chapter fourteen:
MILITARY JUSTICE

T HROUGHOUT THE FIRST WEEK IN AUGUST trains from Paris disgorged platoons of foreign dignitaries and journalists. At the Hotel Moderne fronting the Vilaine River, there were so many reporters that tables squeezed through the dining room onto the terrace, spilled onto the sidewalk and across the street, and continued multiplying up to the river bank. It was not surprising that almost no foreign correspondents took the Army's side. What was remarkable was the Dreyfusard conversion of the French press. "The entire press with a few rare exceptions is now won over to the Dreyfus cause," General Legrand-Girarde of the Élysée staff wrote indignantly:

> He is no longer just a martyr, a victim, he's the most glorious officer in our Army. They go into ecstasies on the beauty of his feelings, on the profundity of his opinions. It's not any longer his rehabilitation they're after; they're preparing his apotheosis.

The Dreyfusard bias of the press was so strong that Maurice Barrès sneered that the city was overrun with the hirelings of "the Syndicate." When the dandified Arthur Meyer entered the Hotel Moderne, he was accosted in the lobby. Meyer, the anti-Semitic Semite, had to scurry off with what remained of his composure to demand police protection.

Throughout Rennes elaborate security precautions were imposed. Hotel registration forms were scrutinized daily. Plainclothesmen checked arrivals at the station against their list of leaguers and provocateurs, especially those belonging to the Anti-Semitic League. Cavalry and infantry patrolled the city. As the agreeable nature of the Renneois became maledictory, hard cider and harder words streamed with such force in the working-class districts that an English newsman cabled his paper of the imminent danger of a Dreyfusard massacre. Britain's Lord Chief Justice had found such passions unfathomable at first. When he remarked matter of factly to a cab driver taking him to the court-martial that Dreyfus was surely innocent, the driver risked his gratuity to growl, "Well then, are the generals guilty?" Only then did the Lord Chief Justice begin to understand the faulty equation compromising the logic of Europe's most logical race.

Outnumbered and unwelcome, Parisian Dreyfusards squeezed into an attractive inn, Les Trois Marches, on the outskirts of the city, just across the road from an estate placed at General Mercier's disposal by a local aristocrat. Except for Lucie and the Laboris, all the important Parisian revisionists found their way to Les Trois Marches: Mathieu; Picquart; Jaurès; Demange; Gabriel Monod, the historian; P.-V. Stock, the publisher; Séverine, the well-known woman journalist; and a score more. Lucie, wanting to stay closer to Alfred, was given lodging in the home of a Madame Godard, not a Dreyfusard but nevertheless sympathetic to Lucie's position. Meanwhile, Nationalists of every description poured into the city and were made to feel at home by landladies and tavern keepers. When ex-Minister of War Godefroy Cavaignac arrived, he was met by cheering citizens who carried his luggage the short distance to the Hotel de France.

There were no volunteers to carry luggage for the foreign visitors, almost all of whom believed in Dreyfus' innocence. The people of Rennes resented their presence—especially the Americans and the English "armed with Kodaks" and "lurking about the city." Their resentment must have been attenuated somewhat by the lodging fees collected; "the most primitive sleeping accommodations command exorbitant prices varying from eight dollars to ten dollars a night," an unhappy American newsman cabled. The local military authorities encouraged the resentment.

The Army imagined that the court-martial could be held in a seven-and-a-half-foot-high attic, the windows of which exposed it on all sides to the hot August sun. But the press roared, witnesses and spectators objected to the endless stairs, and those with a fine sense of historic drama worried about the "acoustic properties" of the trial room. In the final hours before the court-martial the Army relented; the proceedings were moved to the city's high school.

On Monday, August 7, and for thirty-two days thereafter, the globe spun from its temporary axis at Rennes. In Omaha, Nebraska, the headline "It Begins Today" was self-explanatory for the *World-Herald*'s readers. At a few minutes past seven in the morning, bewhiskered Colonel Albert Jouaust, the elderly president of the tribunal, announced, "The session is open. Bring in the accused." Few in the overcrowded auditorium had ever laid eyes on Alfred Dreyfus. Forty-five minutes earlier, when he had marched the short distance from the prison to a guarded room in the school, the Avenue de la Gare had been sealed by cavalry. Two ranks of infantry, their backs opposite each other, had formed a passage across the road through which Dreyfus had to pass. Even if those who held the special courtroom pass had been allowed to approach, they could not have glimpsed the prisoner. They now waited utterly silent. When Dreyfus entered, there was a gasp.

Hugo's Jean Valjean, Dumas' Count of Monte Cristo, or Stendhal's Fabrizio might have lived up to their expectations—brave and cunning victims who emerged from prison none the worse for wear and enormously prepossessing. But beyond the realm of fiction few human beings could have survived Dreyfus' ordeal and satisfied the romantic expectations in the Rennes courtroom. "There came in a little old man—an old, old man of thirty-nine" who had the "gait of an Egyptian mummy," one of the journalists recorded. But Barrès saw another figure: "Oh, how young he seemed to me at first, this poor little man who, loaded down with so many descriptions, moved with a prodigious rapidity." It was a moment so poignant that Mathieu "did not have the courage to watch. I closed my eyes. I heard 'Be seated!' I opened my eyes."

Most of the reporters wrote that Dreyfus "walked quickly, with an elastic step." But what of the voice and mannerisms? Again, all was filtered through the lens of partisanship. "He did not give the impression of a soldier," Arthur Meyer shrugged. Opening his eyes, Mathieu was pleased by his brother's seated posture, "upright and stiff, turned toward the judges." He knew what will Dreyfus must have mustered to walk to the platform, mount, salute, and identify himself in a steady voice. Again Barrès saw things differently. All this briskness and self-control proved that Dreyfus "by an intonation or by a simple movement is afraid of letting his secret escape." Although they would never admit it, the Dreyfusards from Les Trois Marches and the reporters from the Hotel Moderne were disappointed, even a little repelled by their symbol.

Dreyfus sat on a platform erected for the occasion in front of the auditorium stage. At its center was a long table covered by a dark blue cloth behind which the seven Army judges were seated. Besides Colonel Jouaust, only two of them were to take an active part in the proceedings, Lieutenant Colonel Brogniart and Captain Beuvais. The third ranking officer, Major Merle, was to be remembered for his occasional facial expressions. At the right end of the platform there was a table for Maîtres Demange and Labori. At a second table to the left sat Major Carrière, the aged and imperturbably dull prosecutor, and his assistants. Finally, there was a witness bar constructed of light oak on the platform. Four chairs for witnesses were at the base of the platform and in front of them another cluster for dignitaries. In this section sat former President Casimir-Périer, flanked by Generals Billot and Chanoine; in the row behind were Mercier, Cavaignac, and Zurlinden. A row of soldiers with bayoneted rifles separated this section from the public gallery. Among its spectators was an unidentified female Dreyfusard, always present and always dressed in white—the mysterious *"Dame Blanche."* Along the far sides, running the length of the hall, were pine tables reserved for the press. Above the stage, even more disturbing than the cadaverous defendant, was a life-size crucifix, an alabaster Christ impaled upon a black cross.

The opening session nearly fizzled. There was a recitation of the charges, followed by a lengthy reading of excuses from absent witnesses. Among those too ill to attend were Maurice Weil and Du Paty de Clam. There was no surprise that Esterhazy and Mademoiselle Pays had failed to reply to their summonses. The court retired for thirty minutes to deliberate the question of absenteeism. When the judges returned, the president ordered the reading of the 1894 d'Ormescheville report. Had Dreyfus been embalmed, he could not have been more still as the hearsay, innuendo, and distortions compiled by d'Ormescheville droned into the auditorium. His self-control was vulnerable at one point only—his complexion. Barrès and Jules Lemaître were highly amused by the spectrum of colors, the shades of pink, yellow, and beige which revealed his reactions.

A sergeant handed Dreyfus the original *bordereau* and Colonel Jouaust began the brutal interrogation that was to be his approach throughout the court-martial. The civility of a title was never accorded; the defendant remained "Dreyfus"

or "You" and always with an edge of enmity in the voice. Had
he written the *bordereau,* the president asked? No. It was not
in his handwriting nor could he have said some of the things in
it. Furthermore, Dreyfus added calmly, the Court of Cassation
had determined that the *bordereau* had been written by another
officer.

What the Court of Cassation had decided was none of the defendant's business, Jouaust interrupted. What about the hydro-
pneumatic brake on the 120-mm. cannon? What about the
firing manual? "It is not impossible that you could have written
about these things," Jouaust insisted. Composedly, Dreyfus answered, "Colonel, there is no impossibility about any of these
conditions." Why had his hand trembled during Du Paty's
dictation and why had he confessed on the day of the degradation? The composure crumbled. Swaying in his chair, his voice
breaking, Dreyfus exploded: "It's iniquitous to condemn an
innocent man! I never confessed anything! Never!" The
auditorium jumped and fell silent for a few seconds until the
defendant recovered and the president resumed his questioning. This was the only excitement on the first day. Jouaust continued to badger Dreyfus with the discredited evidence of the
1894 court-martial, in arrogant disregard of the findings of
the High Court, until court adjourned at eleven in the morning.

The public and press were barred from the auditorium on
Tuesday, Wednesday, Thursday, and Friday while the documents in the Secret Dossier were examined. During the first
closed session Labori's sharp eye saw the officer in charge of
the Secret Dossier, a General Chamoin, add a sheet to the
dossier placed before Colonel Jouaust. When the defense objected, Chamoin was ordered to explain. It was the old mis-
translation of the Panizzardi telegram that he had tried to add
at Mercier's request. With characteristic forbearance Jouaust
declined to reprimand the ex-Minister. What the Rennes tribunal
discovered was not that the Secret Dossier offered up at long
last proofs of treason, but gossip, abuse, irrelevance, duplica-
tion, and one or two forgeries. When the Affair was finally re-

solved, a portion of the Secret Dossier vanished into a special cabinet in the Army's archives at the Chateau de Vincennes where it remains to this day, sixty-eight years after the last judicial decision.

After the closed sessions were adjourned on Friday, a frightened General Chamoin drew Labori aside in the courtyard. Whether blackmail was his idea or Mercier's is unknown, but Chamoin revealed that he had a compromising letter written by Esterhazy about Labori's hot-blooded daughter. When this was shrugged off, Chamoin became desperate. Labori told him that his friend P.-V. Stock was boarding the afternoon train for Paris to give the Prime Minister a complete report on his courtroom trick. Praying that he had not irreparably compromised his chances for another star, General Chamoin surrendered the Esterhazy note, admitting that it also had been given him by General Mercier, and headed for the station.

Chamoin could not have guessed that the government would refuse to take notice of the attempt to slip in inadmissible evidence. Prime Minister Waldeck-Rousseau coldly informed Labori's friend that intervention in the matter was out of the question. But without firmness from the government, Stock protested, there was no way to make the generals or the officers of the court behave correctly. At least Chamoin ought to be placed under arrest. The Minister of War had announced that if Chamoin were censured he would resign and proclaim Dreyfus guilty. The Prime Minister told Stock, "I will not have Chamoin arrested—make sure you tell your friends that good and well." "Mister Prime Minister," Stock predicted at the close of the audience, "Dreyfus is going to be convicted again."

The second public session on Saturday, August 12, had the éclat the spectators wanted. The second witness, Maurice Paléologue of the Ministry of Foreign Affairs, rehearsed the facts surrounding the conflicting texts of the 1894 Panizzardi telegram. When he finished, this matter should have been dismissed, for Paléologue proved that the text in Sandherr's files was impossible because of the nature of the Baravelli code in which it was written. Nevertheless, when it was his turn at the bar, General Mercier would unabashedly refer to the Sandherr version—"Dreyfus arrested, our emissary alerted"—as if the court had been told nothing. The third witness, former President Casimir-Périer, was expected to reveal the truth about the Lebrun-Renault confession. But that was not what the high-strung ex-President wanted to talk about.

In 1894 there had been rumors that, as President of the Republic, Casimir-Périer had promised the Dreyfus family a public court-martial. Furthermore, he had seen a letter signed by the accused asserting the existence of such a promise. The court now learned that Casimir-Périer bore a grudge against the defendant over this bit of forgotten gossip. For a few minutes Colonel Jouaust was able to bring the ex-President to the question of Dreyfus' confession as reported by Lebrun-Renault, but the testimony was equivocal. Casimir-Périer knew nothing of it. He and Prime Minister Dupuy had simply brought the officer to the Élysée to admonish him for gossiping to the press about the degradation. In the next breath the ex-President returned to his grudge. He was not going to leave the bar until "they know who has lied here." The Nationalists applauded, but it was Dreyfus who was to be admired. With sincere and dignified concern he replied, "The words . . . in a letter whose terms I no longer recall have most certainly been twisted. I understand very well the indignation of Monsieur Casimir-Périer." The elder statesman stepped down, fully satisfied that this implausible rumor so annoying to his dignity was quashed. The fate of Alfred Dreyfus did not concern him.

The clerk called General Auguste Mercier. With Colonel Henry dead, the nearest semblance of a Nationalist hero was the original War Minister in the case, and the General did his best to play the role. Mathieu, his usual charity strained by tension, saw him as something of a monster, "horribly ugly—an ugliness caused by a disaster—with sea-green eyes half covered by thick, creased eyelids." Still, even in his brilliant undress uniform adorned with the order of Grand Officer of the

Legion of Honor, Mercier did show the ill effects of the Affair.
Having begun his career a staunch republican, one of the few
in the Army, he was now, approaching retirement, a prisoner
of his royalist supporters. His friend General Legrand-Girarde,
visiting the Mercier home a few months before the court-martial,
found it congested with the "dregs of all the gossips and bigots.
Listening to them, it seemed to me to be the end of the last
century on the eve of the Revolution."

Two items commanded the attention of the courtroom as
Mercier took the stand: his dazzling crimson and gold képi
which he placed on the shelf attached to the witness stand and
a black leather portfolio bulging with documents. The clerk
read the General's lengthy deposition which had been presented
before the Court of Cassation. Then slowly, almost inaudibly,
Mercier began. At first he intoned banalities about the circumstantial reasons for suspecting Dreyfus. His testimony was
déjà vu and the court's attention more respectful than ex-
pectant as he droned on. However, when Mercier paused,
emptied his water glass, and announced, "I no longer have
reason to keep silent, I am going to accomplish what I consider my duty," the court came alive. "In 1894 the diplomatic
situation was perilous." If there had been haste or technical
irregularities in the conviction of Dreyfus, he said, these must
be understood against the backdrop of German complicity at
the highest level.

Mercier explained that the Kaiser himself was actively interested in espionage, and "in certain exceptional cases the
chiefs . . . in such centers as Paris, Brussels, and Strasbourg
used to correspond even directly and personally with the
Kaiser." The court was invited to infer that the defendant had
been a master spy so invaluable that he was the penmate of
William II. Mercier even hinted that Counterintelligence had
intercepted a note to Dreyfus from the mighty Hohenzollern.
The General added that on two occasions, "two historic nights,"
France and Germany had even been on the verge of war over
Dreyfus. On the night of December 12, 1894, Mercier told the

court, Ambassador Münster had threatened to close the German
Embassy and return to Berlin. While the audience absorbed
this enormity, the General pressed his advantage. On the
evening of January 6 (the day after the degradation), apparently furius over Dreyfus' harsh punishment, the German
government had saber-rattled anew. "For four and a half hours
we were uncertain whether war or peace would emerge from
the exchange of communications." There were hisses from the
Dreyfusards, and former President Casimir-Périer shook his
head violently from side to side. A ten-minute recess was
called.

Precisely at ten o'clock Mercier recommenced. He dredged
up rumors of confessions and repeated the discredited texts of
the Panizzardi telegram and the Scoundrel D letter without
objection from Colonel Jouaust. It was obvious by now that
the panel of Army officers was temperamentally and profes-
sionally incapable of treating a three-star general sternly. Only
once did Jouaust press Mercier for clarification. Why, if
Mercier believed Lebrun-Renault, had he made only the most
perfunctory effort to establish the veracity of Dreyfus' confession? Why had he not made certain that the President of
the Republic and the Prime Minister had thoroughly grilled
this officer? And why was Dreyfus not confronted with the
story of his own confession before being sent to Devil's Island?
"Ah," the General exclaimed with the merest hint of unreadi-
ness, "I might have done so but at the time it did not seem
important enough."

Mercier droned on, mechanically removing document after
document from his leather portfolio for the clerk to read to the
court. Finally, after filling some thirty pages more of soporific
testimony, he delivered his concluding statement. "I have not
arrived at the age I am without having learned from sad experience that what is human is subject to error. Moreover,
if I am weak-minded, as Monsieur Zola has said, at least I
am an honest man and the son of an honest man. If the slightest
doubt had touched my mind, I would be the first to tell you

and to say in front of you to Captain Dreyfus: 'I was honestly mistaken.' "

"That's what you ought to say!" Dreyfus screamed, taking a step in Mercier's direction before a guard restrained him. The mummy, the automaton, was alive after all and capable of visceral anger. Startled journalists, witnesses, spectators recovered and applauded. For one moment the moral fervor which everyone had expected actually prevailed.

"I would say to Captain Dreyfus," Mercier responded haughtily, this time looking directly at the defendant, "I made an honest mistake. I would admit it with the same honesty and I would do all that is humanly possible in order to make good a horrible mistake."

"It's your duty!" Dreyfus shouted.

"*Eh bien, non,*" Mercier whispered. Never once since 1894 had he doubted the absolute culpability of Alfred Dreyfus. It was the turn of the Nationalists to applaud. A little after eleven the session ended.

Rennes went to lunch and then to sleep until the afternoon heat subsided. But before the last carafe of wine was downed, the guests and citizens of the city speculated on the judicial tournament less than forty-eight hours away—the Monday meeting of Labori and Mercier. That very Saturday Labori had received a letter from Clemenceau who was nursing his health at Carlsbad. "At this point I am for a resolute offensive," the ex-politician encouraged. "Our objective is to be winners *as far as public opinion goes.* That's all that matters. The judges will follow if our victory is decisive enough." Labori agreed completely. Whereas Demange, like Dreyfus, believed in the basic decency of the Army, Labori felt that the battering ram was Dreyfus' only hope. He would strike Mercier in his own falsehoods and specious logic and shatter his insufferable self-righteousness.

While Rennes thought of nothing but the Dreyfus trial, Paris had its own diversion. By the second week in August Prime Minister Waldeck-Rousseau decided that the Nationalist and royalist conspiracies were grave enough to require a roundup of the key plotters. Most, including Déroulède, were apprehended, many fled across the border, but one, Jules Guérin, neither fled nor surrendered. Instead, with a handful of followers, the leader of the Anti-Semitic League barricaded himself in a house in Paris not far from the Gare de l'Est. At first the Prime Minister wanted the police to storm Guérin's house in the Rue de Chabrol, but when the Cabinet resisted, Waldeck-Rousseau relented. Parisians have always favored a man who makes the authorities look ridiculous, and Guérin's plan was to do just that—to show France how spineless was the Dreyfusard government of Waldeck-Rousseau. By the weekend working-class men and women, and not a few bourgeois, were good-naturedly jostling through police lines with loaves of bread and sausages which they hurled up to Guérin's men. "Fort Chabrol" defied the government for five raucous weeks. While the Prime Minister wondered what to do, Guerin and his friends decided to liquidate Labori. Evidence indicates that an officer of the General Staff, Major Rollin, conspired with them.*

It was a little after six on Monday morning, August 14, when Labori, his wife, Picquart, and Monsieur Gast, Picquart's cousin, set out for the courtroom and the eagerly awaited confrontation with General Mercier. They had not gone far when Madame Labori realized she had forgotten her purse and returned for it. As the rest of the party turned to cross the bridge over the Vilaine River, a slender, red-haired man, not quite thirty, wearing a short black coat and white cap, approached from the rear and fired a single shot. Picquart sprinted after him shouting to bystanders for assistance. But the assailant cried out, "I have killed the traitor's lawyer! Make way for a patriot!" and was allowed to pass. Eventually the gunman escaped into a wooded area on the city's outskirts.

Picquart returned to the fallen Labori just in time. Another

---

* Marguerite Labori, *Labori, Ses Notes, Manuscrites, Sa Vie* (Paris, 1947), pp. 230–234.

young man, pretending to help, was trying to pry the lawyer's
satchel from beneath him. When news reached the court, the
session was suspended. Mercier himself hurried to the lawyer's
house. By a millimeter the bullet had missed the spine and
stopped just short of the lung. The physician's prognosis was
that Labori would be able to return to the courtroom in two
weeks.

When the moment was psychologically right to demand an
adjournment of the court-martial, when the shocking news of
Labori's near-assassination paralyzed the tribunal, Demange was
satisfied to request an hour's recess. A few days later it was
too late. A panel of local physicians submitted affidavits stating
that the wounded attorney might need months to recover.
Jouaust decided to carry on. Some Dreyfusards suspected that
Demange was not unhappy to be rid of his colleague.

Thereafter, matters increasingly worsened for Dreyfus. On
the opening day of the court-martial he had smiled and shaken
hands with his attorneys. Only once again did he smile: when
Bertillon befuddled the court with his sworling calligraphic
diagrams, impenetrable formulas, and yeasty arguments. No
one appreciated Bertillon's testimony, except Mercier, who
had put the zany anthropometrist to proving that the *bordereau*
had, in effect, written itself. According to Bertillon, mathe-
matical equations demonstrated that the document was an imi-
tation of Dreyfus imitating Esterhazy. In a more serious vein,
the court heard both Hanotaux and Casimir-Périer swear that
Mercier's "historic nights," with France and Germany on the
verge of war and Generals de Boisdeffre and Saussier waiting
for mobilization orders, were fabrication. (Mercier off-handedly
said he might be mistaken about the dates.) Unfortunately there
was no Labori to hammer away at the lie perpetrated by the ex-
Minister. Demange was content to make a courtly gesture of
disgusted incredulity.

Mercier recognized that the judges might not be willing to
ignore completely the guidelines laid down by the Court of
Cassation, so he invented new evidence. Dreyfus had given the

Germans the secret of the Robin shell, France's newest artillery projectile. The gravity of this charge impressed the court when Army experts testified that a shell recently developed by the Germans was based upon the Robin device. Next it was asserted that Dreyfus had given the Germans his lecture notes taken at the War College. Finally, he was accused of giving the secret formula of the Turpin melinite explosive to the Germans.

Demange tried to refute the charges. There was no similarity between the Robin and the German shell; they, in fact, worked on entirely different principles. The betrayal of the melinite formula had occurred several years before Dreyfus could have known of it. As for the lecture notes introduced in evidence, the Germans had transcribed them from a notebook covering War College courses given after Dreyfus' graduation. But Mercier and three generals had made these charges; how could a lawyer assisted by mere majors and captains reason against them?

In lockstep behind Mercier came Captains Junck and Lauth of Counterintelligence and others who repeated the old canards of d'Ormescheville—that the defendant gambled, fornicated, spoke ill of France, and asked too many questions of his superiors. Dreyfus, when asked to comment on these charges, replied drily, "If Captain Junck's ideas of honor allow him to divulge private conversation, mine do not." For chivalric Frenchmen this was the wrong note to strike. There were men on both sides of the Affair who thought ill of a husband who did not spring theatrically to his feet to defend his wife's honor.

As far as hard evidence was concerned, the witnesses for the defense consistently excelled. Picquart acted the dazzling pedagogue for the fourth or fifth time. Judge Bertulus (who investigated the telegram charges against Esterhazy) astonished the court with his story of Lieutenant Colonel Henry's collapse in his office and his all-but-total admission of a plot against Dreyfus. When Madame Henry leapt from her seat shouting "Judas!" Bertulus handed the judges a note addressed to him, Bertulus, which stated that the attractive widow had been coached to erupt at the end of his testimony. Once again Monsieur Gobert, the handwriting expert, described the pressure put on him by Vice Chief Gonse in October 1894. His colleague Charavay retracted his earlier testimony. He was now absolutely certain that the *bordereau* had been written by Esterhazy. More testimony from young officers (and even a general) showed that Dreyfus knew that his turn at maneuvers had been canceled and therefore would not have concluded a document with "I'm off to maneuvers." General after general had insisted that the *bordereau* items were classified beyond access to all but a few officers and were too technical even to be comprehended by most. Former President Casimir-Périer returned to say that Mercier had assured him the *bordereau* items were "without great importance."

From Dreyfus there were periodic flashes of impatience with the libelous statements of the generals and the casual sifting of evidence by the judges. "We must be precise and not play around with words," he scolded Colonel Jouaust when the maneuvers question was being debated. "In August 1894 the second-year trainees knew definitely that they would not attend maneuvers." Again it was Dreyfus who reprimanded his judges for letting the trial meander between hearsay and hypothesis. "I have only one observation to make," he told them. "I am astonished when anyone comes here publicly to affirm convictions based on an untruth, that anyone comes today still advancing arguments which the Court of Cassation has adjudicated." It was a good legal point—it was *the* point, in fact— but it made not the slightest difference.

On Tuesday, August 22, eight days after his near-assassination, Labori returned. Jouaust made a brief, graceful statement of sympathy and welcome, but by then the psychological edge had been blunted. During his absence Mercier had preempted the role of the prosecutor from the passive and barely competent Major Carrière. When the General wished to speak, he did so without bothering to ask the court's permission. Uninvited, he sat at the end of the judges' table, summoning witnesses and cross-examining with impunity. Was anybody willing to listen to his side, Dreyfus had begged at one point. "All these days I have been listening to speeches for the prosecution. I cannot defend myself."

Immediately Labori struggled to rebuild the defense. Newspapers reported that the hour of Mercier's reckoning had come. The "good, invincible giant" of a lawyer treated the General with the same hot and cold abuse that had been reserved until then for Dreyfus. Using Mercier's sworn testimony, Labori should have been able to destroy him. Many of the spectators and the journalists believed that the attorney succeeded. Mercier waffled the business of the "historic nights," refused to say whether or not a document bearing the Kaiser's marginalia existed, and lamely explained that he had destroyed the 1894 commentary which Du Paty secretly communicated to Dreyfus' judges because it was "his personal property." Labori reminded Mercier that communication of trial documents without the knowledge of the defense was a crime. The ex-Minister explained that he had not ordered the judges to examine them in his capacity as a general and as the Minister of War but as a citizen; his order had been a "moral" one. In fact, Mercier managed to be so inconsistent and evasive that the booming, aggressive Labori never quite achieved the dramatic breakthrough the Dreyfusards were expecting. Mercier was roughly handled and his stature much reduced, but he survived the ordeal.

There were a few moments of high drama yet to come at Rennes. The report of the medical officer on Devil's Island caused audible sobbing in the auditorium when it was read by the clerk. Even in the section occupied by the Nationalists, newsmen noted the embarrassed agitation of handkerchiefs. Whatever he lacked in charm and flair, Frenchmen learned that Alfred Dreyfus possessed an endurance that was incomparable. When the report was finished, Jouaust asked hoarsely if the defendant wished to speak. "No, Colonel," Dreyfus replied in a full, even voice. "I am here to defend my honor. I do not wish to speak here of the atrocious sufferings, physical and moral, which I, a Frenchman and an innocent man, was subjected to on Devil's Island for five [sic] years." The correspondent for the London *Times* wrote dithyrambs about how "Anglo-Saxon" Dreyfus was; but once again, for the volatile, verbal French, the defendant's stoicism seemed more peculiar than heroic.

The Gallic flair that Dreyfus lacked was present in every gesture of Georges Picquart, and Labori tried to show the judges what insidious steps the General Staff had taken to ruin this good man for the sake of a criminal. Disregarding the Court of Cassation once again, Colonel Jouaust had allowed testimony denouncing the *petit bleu* as a forgery perpetrated by Picquart. Labori revealed that during the first judicial inquiry into this charge against Picquart, the Army had made much of the heavier ink in which Esterhazy's name was written, suggesting that the original name on the document had been replaced. In truth, Labori thundered, photographic analysis disclosed that in different and heavier ink the name Esterhazy had been traced over the name Esterhazy. How did General Zurlinden explain this? He was not sure, Zurlinden mused, but it was likely that an officer had accidentally smudged the *petit bleu* and fearing a reprimand had rewritten the name. In that case, the document must be authentic, Labori asserted sarcastically. No, Picquart was a forger, Zurlinden replied dogmatically.

A few days later it was the prosecution's turn to jolt the court by presenting an exotic surprise witness named Edler von Cernuszki, a self-styled former Austrian officer who claimed to be of Serbian royal blood. This remarkable and talkative refugee swore he had seen incontrovertible proofs in Vienna that the defendant was the master spy of the Triple Alliance (Germany, Austria, Italy) in France. There was more than a hint of desperate indigence about Cernuszki, and under Labori's hammer blows both his character and his memory proved shaky. Nevertheless, he could not be dissuaded from his allegations. Cernuszki's testimony was more than shocking; it was an extreme example of the Army's bad faith. A tacit accord existed between defense and prosecution to limit argument to French evidence. Outraged, not stopping to consult his colleague, client, the family, or the Dreyfusards, Labori dispatched a telegram to the German government requesting the appearance of Schwartzkoppen at Rennes. Demange, the Dreyfuses, and their allies were more upset by Labori's telegram than by Cernuszki. The Army was permitted to use testimony of a seedy Slav, but the possibility of the Kaiser's former attaché appearing in court was deplored as an unpatriotic miscalculation. It became Labori's second wound. Nevertheless, the Kaiser was sufficiently compassionate to have the *Reichs-Anzeige* publish a categorical denial that Germany had ever sought or received the services of Captain Dreyfus.

As both sides prepared to give their final arguments, not a single foreign observer thought the stream of unmonitored testimony could be called reputable judicial proceedings. Very few of the foreigners understood that in France no rules govern hearsay or irrelevant testimony. Witnesses are encouraged to challenge one another on the theory that their inexpert confrontations may lead to truth. As one observer put it, "Obviously what is lacking in this justice is a strict defintion, as exists in England, of the word *witness*, requiring the judge to dismiss facts irrelevant to the charge." And the haphazardness of this "justice" was miserably compounded at Rennes, as it had been in 1894, by seven Army officers who were ignorant of the law.

During the last days of the court-martial, the Dreyfusards busily weighed the chances for an acquittal verdict. Word had reached them of a note sent to the Prime Minister by General de Galliffet suggesting that "it would be charitable to advise more gentleness to Monsieur Labori. The news I have makes me fear that he is hurting his client." They had also heard that the Minister of War had sent a confidential telegram to Major Carrière, the incidental prosecutor, recalling the verdict and guidelines of the Court of Cassation. Prime Minister Waldeck-Rousseau's hope that the generals could be persuaded that ac-

quittal of Dreyfus was, in the long run, the best course for
everyone had begun to crumble. The leaders of the League for
the Rights of Man demanded that the government take steps to
guarantee acquittal, failing which, Waldeck-Rousseau knew, he
would be confronted by a revolt of the Left when the Chamber
reconvened.

The Prime Minister decided to ask the German Ambassador
to seek a deposition from Schwartzkoppen. The Kaiser's reaction was to write in the margin of Münster's request, "Am I
the Kaiser of France?" The German government reminded
Waldeck-Rousseau that Germany had already categorically
denied dealings with Alfred Dreyfus. Ambassador Münster was
thoroughly saddened. His ambassadorship was also finished,
for within a few days the Kaiser was raging through the cor-
ridors of Potsdam Palace over the revelation at Rennes of
Madame Bastian's espionage at the German Embassy.

With the Prime Minister and the Minister of War finally
beginning to exert influence, the Dreyfusards believed there
was a real possibility of acquittal if they could prevent Labori
from having the last word. Jaurès was designated executioner.
Over breakfast, on Friday, September 8, he and a friend joined
the lawyer. "My dear Labori, I am going to the point straightaway," the Socialist leader announced. "Acquittal is certain if
you renounce speaking. At present, the most reliable information is that acquittal is assured by at least three votes and
probably four." Labori agreed instantly. There would be no
raising of the voice, no gestures, no flourishes of language.
Labori had wanted to rub the court's nose in Esterhazy's guilt,
to show the travesty of Zola's trial, to point up the logic of
Henry's pitiful suicide, to slap the judges and spectators with
the various editions of Esterhazy's confessions. Demange would
elect to speak of the lack of proof against his client, of the
well-meant errors of patriotic soldiers, and of the soldierly
character of the defendant.

When the final hour came, Maître Demange rose to address
the court. "It was known that he would speak all day," the

reporter from the London *Times* groaned, "and I for one looked forward to it with gloom. . . . Not one word did he say whereby the fiercest partisans against Dreyfus could be offended." Had the prosecution established beyond the least doubt that Captain Alfred Dreyfus was guilty of treason? Demange demanded. If not, the seven judges were obliged to vote for acquittal. Maître Demange's peroration was judically correct, eloquent, and equable. Colonel Jouaust asked Dreyfus to address the court for the last time. "Colonel," the atonal voice replied, "I am innocent."

On September 9 the tribunal's verdict was proclaimed. By a vote of five to two Dreyfus was once again found guilty of high treason with extenuating circumstances. Instead of life, the court imposed a sentence of ten years' confinement, five of which the defendant had already served. Immediately, demonstrations were mounted in Berlin, London, New York, and Vienna.

chapter fifteen:

IF DREYFUS HAD NOT BEEN DREYFUS

"A THRILL OF HORROR AND SHAME RAN through the whole civilized world," the London *Times* editorial reported twenty-four hours after the Rennes verdict. Only among French Canadians and in Russia (where the Saint Petersburg *Novoie Vremia* bannered *"Vive la France!"*) was the outcome praised. The rest of the world fairly howled disgust. There were spontaneous demonstrations in Florence and Naples. The attorney general of Nova Scotia called for a boycott of the Paris Exposition of 1900. In Budapest and Vienna the crowds before the French Consulate and Embassy were hostile and hard to control. "All the newspapers, Nationalist and Liberal, appearing this morning published articles against France and our Army," cabled the French chargé d'affaires from Berlin. In London nearly fifty thousand marched from Hyde Park to the French Embassy, where speakers excoriated not only the verdict but the nation responsible for it.* At the same hour the

---

* *Documents Diplomatiques Français*, Vol. 15, especially pp. 324–453 for reports of foreign reactions to Rennes.

canon of Saint Paul's Cathedral intoned, "A nation is on trial. France stands at the judgment bar." In an unciphered telegram from Balmoral Castle, Queen Victoria told her Prime Minister she was "too horrified for words at this monstrous, horrible sentence. . . . If only all Europe would express its horror and indignation! I trust there will be a severe retribution."

Across the land Americans stood outside newspaper offices awaiting the cable from Rennes. Although the Hearst papers had warned, "That Captain Dreyfus will be condemned is almost the universal opinion heard in Rennes tonight," people were appalled by the decision. There were meetings and demonstrations from New York to San Francisco. "What dreadful news is this from Rennes," William James wrote. "I am glad I belong to a Republic [forgetting that officially so was France]." The attorney general of Montana sententiously advised that "missionary work could be profitably performed in France as well as in the unexplored regions of Central Africa." Colonel Henry Watterson of Kentucky, distinguished for both his military and international experience, thought that it was already too late to save France. Interviewed in New York at the Waldorf-Astoria, he said sadly, "I love the French people but I can't help thinking that the Latin races are doomed. Spain is dead, Italy is dying, and France is down with an incurable disease." Ex-Senator William Washburn of Minnesota was less kind: "I feel as every white man must, and think that France ought to be called down by the entire civilized world."

Congressman-elect Jefferson M. Levy of New York said he would offer a resolution when Congress reconvened, calling for American withdrawal from the Paris Exposition of 1900. Congressman Levy added that his resolution had the backing of Tammany Hall, a fact which the New York City Council's resolution condemning the vedict soon confirmed. In Louisville committees of influential citizens organized to urge President McKinley to intercede with President Loubet. The Merchant Exchange of St. Louis and the San Francisco Chamber of Commerce voted unanimously to boycott the Paris Exposition.

The people of Chicago were the most adamant. A total boycott of French products was self-imposed by the citizenry, and when Mr. D. B. Wright fired six of his construction workers for being French, the act was widely praised. An editorial in the *Daily Tribune* exactly expressed Chicagoans' views: "The French General Staff stands impeached already before the civilized world, and the nation that has winked at the perjury and iniquity of these officers has marked itself with the brand of degeneracy and the contempt of nations."

"Justice has been done. Dreyfus has been condemned. As Frenchmen we rejoice over it. As Catholics we praise God for it," gloated *La Croix*, the ultra Catholic newspaper. The majority of the French were embarrassed by such virulence but many tried to believe their country was being victimized by self-righteous Americans and perfidious Englishmen to the glee of the mortal enemy across the Rhine. "Well, what about the Negroes in the South?" spluttered General Legrand-Girarde of the Élysée staff, when he heard that the United States might withdraw from the Exposition. There was also the Turks' recent massacre of Christian Armenians and the Russians' unrelenting persecution of Jews. Most Frenchmen understood (even if they did not admit it) why such facts seemed meaningless when measured against the enormity of Rennes. "*Mon cher*," Anatole France told Clemenceau, "they have just committed an unpardonable blunder. It's all over for us." Clemenceau put this sentiment into his editorial for *L'Aurore*:

> France is now a country with no security either for the
> liberty, the life or the honor of her citizens. A horde ganged
> up on us, a praetorian guard, a host of monks who have
> savagely burnt all that forty centuries of human effort have
> accomplished.

In their autobiographies, memoirs, and posthumous papers nearly all the members of the French government contrived to appear outraged in the wake of Rennes. Each wrote that he had been ready to have the case resubmitted to the Court of

Cassation and to vote for freeing Dreyfus until the impaneling of a third court-martial board. If such a plan existed, it was rapidly abandoned. "A third court-martial would convict Dreyfus unanimously," Minister of War de Galliffet assured the President and Prime Minister; and if they tried to impose such a policy, he would resign. No one observed that this time the Court of Cassation might annul the verdict outright. Nor was it suggested that de Galliffet could be replaced by a civilian if the generals went on strike.

It was the political philosopher, Georges Sorel, who told Frenchmen the truth about Rennes: "The conviction of Dreyfus was the least unpleasant solution for the government." A regime that had quaked before Guérin and his rowdies in the Rue de Chabrol had no stomach for prosecuting General Mercier. France—even much of Dreyfusard France—was exhausted by the Affair. Furthermore, most Frenchmen flattered themselves that, whatever the Anglo-Saxons and the rest of the world might think, France had not acquitted herself too badly. Already the *gratin* were smugly repeating the quip of the German Foreign Minister who, when told that Dreyfus had been sent to Devil's Island because he was a Jew, retorted, "I don't know about that, but I know that if he hadn't been Jewish he wouldn't have returned." The majority believed that the ideal dénouement was clemency for Dreyfus, a moratorium on debate, and a general amnesty in time for the Paris Exposition.

Less than twenty-four hours after the verdict, Joseph Reinach informed Mathieu that the rumors of a pardon were accurate. That Sunday evening, September 10, a conclave of Dreyfusard leaders met at Mathieu's apartment in Paris. Reinach and Bernard Lazare urged Mathieu to persuade his brother to accept. France needed peace badly, the former argued. Without the pardon "a cry of horror will be raised not only against the criminals who caused your brother's conviction but against France herself." It was clear that, with the exception of embarrassing Zionists, Reinach and Lazare were speaking for French Jewry. Alexandre Millerand, the Socialist Minister of

Commerce, sketched the likely chaos if General de Galliffet quit. Jaurès wanted to continue the fight but wavered when Mathieu spoke of his brother's deplorable medical condition. The physicians suspected that he had incipient cancer of the spine. Clemenceau alone was intractable, arguing that a pardon would sacrifice the "grandeur of the moral battle."

On Monday Mathieu, Clemenceau, and the others hurried to the Ministry of Commerce in response to Millerand's telephone call. They had to decide quickly, the Minister said. Clemency would become more awkward after the inevitable rejection of an appeal by the Court of Military Review. Moreover, it was his opinion as a lawyer that the Court of Cassation would have to remand the case to a court-martial because there were no new facts; there was only the technicality that Colonel Jouast had failed to stipulate the conditions of Dreyfus' incarceration. Strolling in the Ministry gardens after the meeting, Mathieu swore to Clemenceau, "I will not separate myself from you; if you persist in wanting the pardon refused, I agree." "Yes," the cantankerous ex-politician sighed, "but if I were your brother, I'd accept."

It remained to be seen whether Dreyfus would allow himself to be pardoned. The previous Sunday he had brushed aside the idea. Having survived Devil's Island for the sake of honor, he vowed to Lucie and Mathieu, he would not trade honor now for tainted freedom. Knowing how slim his chances were of surviving another revision, he asked Lucie to send for Pierrot and Jeanne. The children already sensed the climax of a great drama. They had witnessed the commotion in the Valabrègue household when their cousins, Marguerite and Émile, attempted to set out secretly from Carpentras on foot for Rennes, 638 miles away. But Pierrot and Jeanne were never to start their journey. Dreyfus quickly decided that the memory of their father in prison would be an intolerable legacy.

Then, later alone with Mathieu, Dreyfus confessed his greatest fear: "I will never stand a new degradation. I won't put on my uniform. It won't be soiled a second time. I'll make them drag me; they'll have to carry me by force. Not that, never, never!"

But the politicians had proposed an entirely different degradation—pardon. On Tuesday, at six in the morning, Mathieu came again to discuss the proposal. Dreyfus hesitated, "for I had no need whatsoever of clemency. I was thirsting for justice."

> But, on the other hand, my brother told me that my seriously undermined health left me little hope of holding up for long in the conditions in which I was going to be placed, that freedom would allow me to pursue much more easily the redress of the atrocious judicial mistake of which I was still the victim. . . . Mathieu added that the withdrawal of my appeal was advised and approved by men who had been the principal defenders of my cause. Finally, I thought of the suffering of my wife, my relatives, my children.
> Consequently, I agreed to withdraw my appeal but with the flat stipulation of my absolute and irrevocable intention to pursue the legal revision of the Rennes verdict.

At the last moment President Loubet temporized. Worried about the Army's reaction, he wanted to postpone signing the pardon until key generals had been informed. Now it was Millerand's turn to threaten resignation. Loubet yielded. On September 19, 1899, Alfred Dreyfus was a free man. "The Government of the Republic has given me my liberty," his written statement to the press said. "Liberty is nothing to me without honor. From this day forward I shall continue to seek amends for the shocking judicial wrong of which I am still the victim."

Picquart wrote Dreyfus what was for him a warm letter: "What remains to be done is no more than a formality, for you have been vindicated as no one else ever has been before—by the entire world."

Prime Minister Waldeck-Rousseau recommended that Dreyfus should retire to the Isle of Jersey off the English coast in order to avoid "incidents" in France. Resenting the Prime Minister's

nervous advice, the family went instead to Bordeaux where they
were joined by the first Dreyfusard, Forzinetti, now in the
employ of Monaco. Prince Albert of Monaco wanted Alfred
and Lucie to be his guests, Forzinetti said, and presently an
official invitation arrived. But to leave France would have been
to admit shame or lack of courage. As for the Army, on September 21 General de Galliffet promulgated an *ordre du jour*
decreeing, "The incident is closed."

"No one wanted to understand my father," Jeanne Dreyfus
insists with an inflection of injured surprise even now. "We
Alsatians were taught never to show emotion in public." A few
men understood and admired. Joseph Reinach, who had not
been to Rennes and had probably never seen Dreyfus before,
met the ex-captain at Carpentras in the fall. Only the unusually
bright blue eyes revealed the profundity of Dreyfus' emotion,
when he said simply, "*Merci.*" "I was proud to believe [this
response] equally worthy of him and of me," Reinach remarked.
In *La Revue Blanche*, one of France's most iconoclastic phi-
losophers, the young Julien Benda, extolled Dreyfus:

> By the sobriety of his conduct, by the austerity of his
> attitude, by the drily scientific character of his defense and
> even of his indignation, by that famous atonality of his voice,
> by the absence of all that which certain people call "charm"
> —in a word, by the lack of all those means appropriate for
> exciting sentimentality—Captain Dreyfus has come to
> symbolize naturally and in all its purity the cause of
> justice.

For the rest of Dreyfusard France, however, Dreyfus was at
best a neutral hero; at worst, an egocentric ingrate. As second
thoughts about the pardon emerged, it was Benda's friend
Charles Péguy whose irony was to become gospel: "We might
have died for Dreyfus, but Dreyfus would not have died for
Dreyfus"—which was a variation of Theodore Herzl's "One
can't even guarantee that he would have been on the side of the
victim if someone else had suffered the same fate in his place."

When asked how much Dreyfus understood of his case, Clemenceau replied, "Nothing at all."

There were several months of low-key hostilities while adversaries regrouped and reconnoitered. In January the Left gauged its strength in the senatorial elections. It won eighty of the ninety-nine contested seats, though one of the new senators was Auguste Mercier, recently retired from the Army. The doyen of the Senate and of the Dreyfusards, Auguste Scheurer-Kestner, had recently died. On the eve of the Rennes court-martial he had written contentedly to his daughter, "How many men are there who, after they have sacrificed themselves to a just cause, witness the triumph of that cause?"

In May, the Paris Municipal Council would be elected and the Left was confident of a majority there as well. For the present, except for extremists of both camps, the French were too busy with the Exposition to argue the Affair, at least in public. With the instincts of the lawyer and the enlightened elitist, Prime Minister Waldeck-Rousseau sought to lead France into the twentieth century free of the rancor of the immediate past. On January 1, 1900, he introduced a general amnesty bill in the Chamber denying litigation on current and future cases to do with the Affair. On April 1 he opened the great International Exposition.

The theme of the grandiose *L'Exposition Universelle* was *"le bilan du siècle"*—the achievements of the century. Two hundred eighty acres stretching along both banks of the Seine, from the Eiffel Tower to the Place de la Concorde, were occupied by spectacular palaces devoted to Arts and Letters, Agriculture, Civil Engineering, Education, Electricity, Housing, Hygiene, Mechanics, Metallurgy. Monaco's pavilion was larger than Great Britain's, and Germany's (the first since 1870) possessed a martial ponderousness made almost forbidding by guards sporting exaggerated Wilhelmine mustaches. Because of the pardon Congressman Jefferson Levy of New York had not introduced his bill and America participated. The most popular

pavilion was the Russian, containing a gigantic map of France
in marble and jasper with cities represented in precious stones.
Paris contributed several grand monuments—the flamboyantly
baroque Grand Palais and its sister the Petit Palais. Near the
Place du Trocadéro were other monuments to French civilization—the pavilions of Algeria and several other colonial posses-
sions. The celebration of *la belle époque*, of which France was
the genius, seemed not only complete to Frenchmen in the
spring of 1900 but a gala confirmation of an international leadership as splendid and as immortal as the French language itself.
But there was no edifice devoted to the achievements of Honor
or Justice.

Prime Minister Waldeck-Rousseau knew he would have to
pay a price for his amnesty bill to those who wanted to break
the forces of Altar, Chateau, and Sword still crippling France.
In return for not denouncing the amnesty bill, the Radical and
Socialist politicians demanded an attack upon the Catholic religious orders. In the national elections of 1898 the edgy
cooperation of Liberal Catholic and Opportunist politicians had
been mutually disastrous. The faithful had fought the Ralliement
with a violent disobedience unrivaled in recent history; the
Pope himself had been accused of heresy by a learned French
prelate.* It made political sense now for the Prime Minister to
comply with Radical and Socialist demands. In early January
1900 the police raided the offices of the newspaper *La Croix*
(published by the Assumptionist order), seizing nearly two
million francs and documents allegedly proving the fathers had
plotted to overthrow the regime. The Assumptionist as well as
the Augustinian congregations were shortly dissolved by government decree. Having nipped the Assumptionist plot, the Left-
wing militants proceeded to make a great deal of the founding
of the Action Française, the most aggressive and enduring of
the reactionary leagues, headed by Charles Maurras.

---

* Abbé Emmanuel Barbier, *Histoire du Catholicisme Libéral et Social en
France* (Bordeaux, 1924). 5 vols.

In May the Paris municipal elections voted in a Nationalist majority to the surprise of the Left. The Radicals and the Socialists demanded an official response. Against his best judgment Waldeck-Rousseau again complied. On October 28, a few days before his amnesty bill was to be voted on in the Chamber, he announced that certain religious orders were poisoning the spiritual life of France and promised that once they were dissolved, the "billion francs of the congregations" would fall to the electors. The Prime Minister introduced forthwith a bill for their dissolution.

The Dreyfuses were bewildered by what was happening. On the one hand, Waldeck-Rousseau's moderate republicans were clearly anxious to obliterate the Affair by amnesty. On the other hand those opposing amnesty were equally committed to using the Rennes verdict to destroy Catholic power and to exploit anti-clericalism for electoral purposes. Waldeck-Rousseau claimed that Dreyfus' acceptance of clemency terminated the Affair. Clemenceau and Jaurès dismissed the pardon as a temporary medical and political concession. The Dreyfuses had no desire to be swept up in some historic combat between spokesmen for France of the *ancien regime* and Jacobin France; above all they dreaded a battle in which religious hatred inspired the opponents. Having played his role in stirring France as she had never before been stirred, Mathieu believed with Zola that an interval of calm and compromise was essential for his brother's ultimate exoneration. And, Mathieu believed, France needed rest as much as Alfred Dreyfus.

In the interest of harmony Dreyfus obligingly retired from Carpentras with Lucie and the children to a villa on Lake Geneva a few days after President Loubet officially opened the Exposition in April. The Villa Hauterive, with the mountains of the Jura behind and the lake nearby, was ideal for Dreyfus' recovery. Soon, with the aid of a cane, he was walking without becoming exhausted. The malaria seizures abated under heavy dosages of quinine. But for the rest of his life, the nightmares

of the degradation, the days aboard the *Saint-Nazaire*, his hut
on Devil's Island, and the shackles would trouble him. Four
years of enforced silence made ordinary conversation exceedingly difficult, even with Lucie. They had already said everything a thousand times in letters; so they sat in the shade
"exchanging silent glances" while Pierrot and Jeanne played
nearby.

The retreat to Switzerland improved Dreyfus' health only
somewhat more than it troubled and irritated many sympathizers and allies. Before leaving for Switzerland, Dreyfus
had written to the chairman of the Senate's amnesty committee
protesting legislation which "extinguishes prosecutions and suits
from which I had hoped revelations, perhaps confessions, would
result." He continued:

> The bill thus deprives me of my most cherished hope, that of
> having my innocence legally proclaimed. . . . This amnesty
> will redound to the exclusive profit of General Mercier, the
> principal author of the crime of 1894.

This was his second written protest against the amnesty proposal and, like the first, it was unavailing. But beyond letters
to the government there was little he felt he could do. As for
the mounting irritation of the Parisian Dreyfusards, Mathieu
was there to reason with the Radical politicians, the chiefs of
the League for the Rights of Man, and the members of the
newly formed Trois Marches Society (membership limited to
the veterans of Rennes), explaining why Dreyfus could not be
the official leader of their cause; why, although opposing the
amnesty, he refused to break publicly with the Prime Minister.
One thing Mathieu could not explain was the intuition of the
Jews that for them, at least for a time, the Affair could only
yield diminishing returns and grave risks. Sir Edmund Monson,
the British Ambassador, correctly explained to his anxious
Queen: "The calculation probably made by Dreyfus and his
advisers may be that it will be more advantageous to wait for

a more dispassionate condition of public opinion before taking any steps for definite rehabilitation."

By the end of the year the Dreyfusards were exasperated with the Dreyfuses. "Your brother has remained silent for a year," Labori scolded Mathieu. "You only concern yourself with your brother's skin. That's your right and that of your family's but you are forgetting the country. You're forgetting your friends." Labori insisted that the Dreyfuses owed Picquart the loyalty of denouncing the amnesty and of even publicly reproving the Prime Minister. They narrowly missed coming to blows and Mathieu left the attorney's office vowing, "Everything is over between us."

In early December the Prime Minister's amnesty speech to the Chamber stated that the Rennes judgment had been "correctly rendered" and that Dreyfus' acceptance of clemency had been unconditional. Once passed, the amnesty would not only nullify Du Paty's indictment and the charges against Esterhazy and Mercier but would also deny Picquart and Zola the right of judicial exoneration. For Zola, world opinion was vindication enough. But for Picquart, disgraced by charges of forgery and betrayal of duty, being an international hero was less consoling.

A few days before Christmas 1900 Dreyfus returned to Paris for one of the most painful encounters in a life already uniquely charged with agony. In Labori's office, shaking Picquart's hand for the first time since his arrest, Dreyfus rambled on about the new cityscape created for the Exposition. Communication between the rigid Dreyfus and the regal Picquart would have been strained however comfortable the occasion. This meeting was doomed from the start. *Monsieur le Capitaine* understood the requirements of honor, Picquart ventured coldly. His own opinion of the pardon had not been sought, but he insisted that his views on the amnesty be heard. Dreyfus pleaded with Picquart and Labori to understand. Mathieu had told him that outright opposition to the government was impossible; "We would have the whole republican party against us." They had nothing to say to each other, Picquart interrupted. Dreyfus removed his pince-nez and rose, his arm extended. The former Lieutenant Colonel refused the gesture. "But to separate like this would be abominable," Dreyfus pleaded. Picquart, thoroughly disgusted, managed a frigid "Good-bye, sir." When he reached Labori's reception room, Dreyfus fainted.

On December 27 the amnesty bill was approved by the Chamber.

The Dreyfuses and the Dreyfusards parted company. Clemenceau and Picquart repeatedly rebuffed Mathieu's attempts to repair their relations. Dreyfus himself retired from the scene, dividing his time between Carpentras and Geneva while he finished the manuscript *Five Years of My Life*, an international best seller. If many French readers found his prose stilted and the letters repetitious, Americans, Englishmen, Germans, Russians, and Japanese read and wept. When Dreyfus' French publisher mailed the proofs to Geneva in March 1901, the Swiss customs officer enclosed a personal note in the packet: "Yesterday as I was examining publishers' shipments, I read the sincere and moving story of your Calvary. I am taking the liberty of sending you the sincere expression of my deep sympathy, of my firm belief in your innocence, and of my hope for your very early vindication." Among militant Dreyfusards *Five Years of My Life* was one more example of the family's ingratitude. P-V. Stock, whose firm had once risked bankruptcy for the Dreyfusards, was not even informed of the contract with another publisher.

France's inability to digest the Affair was again underscored in autumn 1902. Zola and his wife had returned to Paris from their country place at Médan. There was a chill in the air. Before retiring, the writer ordered a fire lit in the bedroom hearth. Sometime during the early morning of September 29, he stumbled from bed. "I feel sick. My head is splitting," he told his wife. A few minutes later Zola struggled to reach the silken cord to summon the domestics. Later that morning, after repeatedly knocking and shouting, the servants smashed the door lock and found their master dead, head down in a pool of vomit on the floor; his wife was still alive but unconscious. They had been poisoned by carbon monoxide flowing back into the room from a blocked flue. The previous day several anti-Dreyfusard masons working on the roof of an adjacent house had sealed one of Zola's chimneys. The next day they returned and secretly removed the obstruction.

Madame Zola recovered in time for her husband's funeral. His restored membership in the Legion of Honor entitled the writer to military rites and the new government of Prime Minister Émile Combes ordered lavish burial preparations. The plans for the obsequies pleased the widow save in one important detail. She was afraid of what might happen if Dreyfus attended. Ironically, Zola's greatest rival had the final word. Anatole France informed Madame Zola that he would refuse to deliver the funeral oration unless she withdrew her objections to Dreyfus' presence, which she did.

"Everything begins in *mystique* and finishes up in politics," Péguy wrote of the Affair. It was a legitimate reproach, but much of the responsibility for politicizing Dreyfusism belonged to Péguy himself. Not since the early 1880s had anticlericalism so dominated national life. Wages, working conditions, and the prices of meat and bread were important in the balloting of April–May 1902, but the Radicals and the Socialists won a majority in the new Chamber by promising to tame the priests and their aristocratic co-conspirators. A sure sign of the times was that Jaurès returned to the Chamber and Clemenceau, a few weeks earlier, entered the Senate. For moderates, conservatives, and royalists, the national elections were a disaster. Prime Minister Waldeck-Rousseau foresaw the advent of politics which he disdained but for which he bore responsibility: "The present Cabinet no longer responds to the demands of the present situation." Offering poor health as an additional reason to step down, Waldeck-Rousseau departed on June 1, 1902, although his government still had the Chamber's confidence.

The new Prime Minister, Émile Combes, was a provincial physician who had spent his early adulthood as a seminarian and a professor of logic and the rest of it hating the Church. Senator Combes believed that his mission was to smite the Catholic Church and purge the officer corps of the Army and Navy. Announcing his opposition to a "program of appeasement" before the Chamber, the "Little Father" attacked. Three thousand Catholic primary schools run by female congregations were shut. In March 1903 Combes struck again. Under a new law all Catholic male congregations were ordered to apply for government authorization. Six were approved and fifty-four rejected. Troops were used against peasants seeking to protect monks from expulsion; officers resigned their commissions; several lives were lost; even Waldeck-Rousseau protested. Undaunted, Combes pressed harder. By October 1903 sixteen thousand Catholic schools, hospitals, monasteries, and commercial establishments had been closed. Belgium and Britain swarmed with dazed French priests and nuns. From the *département* of the Hautes-Pyrénées thousands of messages begged the government to let the grotto of Lourdes remain open.

Over the Navy Combes placed a civilian who seldom granted interviews to admirals. The new Minister of War, General Louis André, went about his business with zeal worthy of his superior. Officers' careers slowed or advanced according to political and religious data in the secret files of the anti-Catholic Freemasons. "Attended his son's first communion," one colonel's card read. It was placed in the "Carthage" file, limbo for Catholic officers; only officers in "Corinth" received promotions. André's domination of the Army was strong enough so that in the spring of 1903 he could agree to have the Rennes verdict reconsidered.

The Dreyfusards had planned carefully for this day. To bring the case before the Court of Cassation again, Dreyfus' attorneys had to present a significant new fact. In England Esterhazy had confessed again, but the French court demanded proof of the accused's innocence rather than of the culprit's guilt. Mathieu

heard rumors that Colonel Jouaust and Major Merle were dissatisfied with the Rennes verdict and that Jouaust had voted to
acquit. But Jouaust refused to discuss the case. In late October
of 1902 Mathieu went to Montpellier to find that Major Merle
already regretted any remarks he had made. Still, the trip was
not a total loss. Mathieu was certain that Merle had spoken of
the annotated *bordereau*, the document supposedly bearing the
Kaiser's marginalia. Believing that somehow Mercier had influenced the judges with yet another forgery subsequently destroyed, Mathieu, Leblois, and Reinach discussed the matter
with Jaurès. Here was, if not a new fact, a significant new
hypothesis.

Jaurès timed his unveiling of "evidence" carefully, conferring
with Prime Minister Combes, General André, and former Prime
Minister Brisson. His speech to the Chamber began on April 6,
1903. Ostensibly the Socialist leader rose to argue against
the right of a young Nationalist deputy to take his seat in the
Chamber. The Affair came alive again as Jaurès retold the
cabals of the generals, the ministers, the leagues, and the clergy.
A current of exaggerated shock (possibly on cue by Left-
wing deputies) passed through the Chamber when he spoke
of the deceased General de Pellieux's resignation letter protesting against the "forgeries" of his superiors on the occasion of
Henry's arrest. "Excuse me for my interruption," Brisson exclaimed. "I was Prime Minister at that time and I declare that
the government of which I was the leader had no knowledge
of that letter." Every head turned in the direction of the former
Minister of War, Godefroy Cavaignac, now an emaciated figure
dying of cancer. Jaurès asked for a vote to reopen the Affair
on grounds that the annotated *bordereau* was undoubtedly
among the forgeries alluded to in de Pellieux's letter. Jaurès
had mounted a stunning assault. The Chamber voted to have
General André review the evidence and make the final decision.

While the government harried monks and nuns and studied
the Rennes court-martial, the Dreyfusard intellectuals churned
out propaganda literature. Anti-Dreyfusard propagandists, they

wrote, had invented a Jewish Syndicate which financed a fifth column of anarchists and traitors. The Dreyfusards retaliated with a religious conspiracy—the cabal of monarchists and Nationalists financed by the Jesuits. Some of the Dreyfusard literature, like Zola's earlier *Lettre à la France*, was sober and noble: "France, you are heading back to the Church; you are returning to the past, to the intolerant and theocratic past which your eminent sons have fought with their skill and their blood." Much of it, like passages in Reinach's 1903 volume of his *Histoire de l'Affaire Dreyfus*, was pure politics: "In every profession, even in the civil service—and especially in the Army—being recommended (secretly) and supported by the [Jesuit] Fathers is a priceless advantage." Knowing that propaganda is enhanced by a hissable villain, Reinach and others offered the public the garrulous Father du Lac, a busybody Jesuit principal of an exclusive military high school in Paris and alleged confessor of General de Boisdeffre. From the "little cell of Father du Lac, so plain, a crucifix on the bare wall and the ever open and annotated Army Directory on the desk," Reinach traced the principal conspiracies against French democracy and justice. And some Dreyfusard propaganda, like Jean Ajalbert's *The Black Forest* and Anatole France's *Penguin Island*, matched the intolerance of the enemy. Whether noble, partisan, or crude, the messages of the Dreyfusards were highly credible not only because of the well-known anti-Semitism and anti-Republicanism of Catholic religious orders in France, but because of the culpable silence of the Vatican.

It was also fortunate for the Dreyfusards that General André, the Minister of War, was thorough in his investigation of the evidence used to convict Dreyfus. Since the archivist Gribelin needed his pension, the Minister squeezed a confession from him: Gribelin stated that Henry had ordered him to swear that he had seen Picquart give his attorney classified documents. Checking the finances of Counterintelligence, General André discovered a twenty-five-thousand-franc discrepancy which he interpreted as payment of a sizable bribe to the self-styled

Serbian nobleman, Cernuszki. Several officers were arrested. Next, André's staff confirmed that the document alleging "D . . . has brought me a number of interesting things" should have read "P." Similarly, he proved that one of the Secret Dossier pieces signed "Alexandrine" had had its date altered from 1895 to 1894.

Approved by André, a report favoring review was submitted to the Minister of Justice and, in March 1904, the criminal branch of the Court of Cassation convened to reconsider the Dreyfus conviction. Suddenly the anti-Dreyfusards counterattacked. On November 4 royalist deputies offered proof to the Chamber of General André's spy network made up of Freemasons. The Combes government would probably have been overthrown had the Minister of War not been struck twice in the face by a young royalist as he left the tribune. Eleven days later, however, this brilliant political General resigned in disgrace. Still, the anti-Dreyfusard salvo had come too late to stop the second revision.

While the High Court deliberated, the agony of priest-eating ran its course. France, the eldest daughter of the Church, formally severed diplomatic ties with Rome on July 29, 1904. In that same month, a special parliamentary committee submitted its report favoring separation of Church and State. Diderot of the Enlightenment had proclaimed, "Men will never be free till the last king is strangled with the entrails of the last priest." Prime Minister Combes, desperate to finish Diderot's great mission—"It is the only reason I took office," he had said—asked for a vote on his separation bill a few days after André's resignation. By now, however, the savage humiliation of the two great pillars of ancient France, the Army and the Church, was beginning to backfire. Before his enemies and turncoat friends mustered the votes to throw him out, Prime Minister Combes resigned at the beginning of 1905. At the end of the year the Chamber finally voted 341 to 233 an amended Combes bill for separation of Church and State.

Meanwhile, the Court of Cassation plodded through the mound

of documents and the regiment of surviving and newly recruited witnesses. Nearly all repeated verbatim the testimonies given before. Gribelin, the archivist, told a new tale. Major Cuignet of False Henry fame, now a member of Action Française and quite deranged, created a few research problems for the justices, as did Bertillon who was even more deranged. Du Paty de Clam sincerely regretted the role of villain that circumstances had foisted upon him. Under the stern encouragement of the justices he surrendered the original draft of the Dreyfus commentary prepared for Mercier in 1894. Slippery as ever, Senator Mercier swore again that Dreyfus was guilty but sloughed over the annotated *bordereau* as "a completely inexact fable."

Madame Bastian added color. What had happened to a few generals and ministers was negligible when compared to what Dreyfus had done to her. Thanks to him she had lost her job at the German Embassy and the extra wages from the wastebaskets, she complained. Spain's former military attaché categorically denied ever having said that Dreyfus was spying for Germany. There was a poignant moment when Émile Straus recounted the death-bed recantation of Princess Mathilde and her reconciliation with his wife. Generals Gonse and Zurlinden reiterated their gospel of guilt. General Billot recalled again his early suspicions about the False Henry. Maurice Weil paid dearly for his friendship with Saussier and Esterhazy. The role of his wife as liberal bedmate and his own role as Jewish confidence man were exposed. Finally, Jaurès and Picquart hypnotized the justices with their eloquence and passion.

The criminal chamber had completed its work, and in accordance with the politically inspired law of 1899 the full Court of Cassation was ready to consider the Rennes verdict. Beset by international and domestic crises, the new Prime Minister, Maurice Rouvier, prevailed upon the Court to delay its Dreyfus decision. While the Germans were challenging French expansion in Morocco, the Prime Minister was saddled with grass-roots reaction to the law separating Church and State. In Brittany peasants were arming. Army officers were surrendering their swords rather than expel monks and nuns from their cloisters. In May national elections would take place and were likely to reflect a backlash against government religious policies. Two months before the elections the Prime Minister was voted out of office over the fatal shooting of a Catholic demonstrator in northeastern France. The new government, headed by Ferdinand Sarrien, appointed Georges Clemenceau as Minister of Interior. Shortly afterwards the national elections resulted in a clear victory for the coalition of left-wing parties, and Minister of Interior Clemenceau emerged as the government's dominant personality. Appropriately, the Court of Cassation was encouraged to render its verdict on the Affair.

On Thursday, July 12, 1906, Chief Justice Ballot-Beaupré announced the decision of the united Court of Cassation: the Rennes verdict was annulled and Dreyfus declared innocent of all charges by unanimous vote; by majority vote there was to be no referral of the case to a military tribunal. What was ironic, if not bizarre, was the finding that no conclusive proof existed that a crime had ever been committed. The *bordereau* by itself could not be deemed sufficient without a confession that secret documents had been passed to a foreign power. Eleven and a half years after his first conviction, Alfred Dreyfus was cleared of all charges.

Twenty-four hours after the verdict Prime Minister Sarrien's government demanded a vote in the Chamber on a special bill reintegrating Dreyfus and Picquart into the Army with rank of major and brigadier general, respectively. The bill was passed 473 to 42. Shouting down Mercier's objection that the Court of Cassation had taken its decision *in camera*, the Senate simultaneously voted enactment. But the mixing of justice with politics was the second nature of the government even on this historic day. The fine print of the reintegration law discriminated against Dreyfus. It was stipulated that Picquart should enjoy a seniority in rank of one day more than all general officers serving at the time of his dismissal, February 16, 1898. Noth-

ing was said about Dreyfus' seniority, however, and he became,
in a sense, the last major in the Army, a status which encouraged his retirement. As the law makers went about right-
ing the wrongs done the living, they also remembered the dead.
A law was passed to have Zola's ashes transferred to the Panthéon, the enormous shrine of France's great which towers over
the Latin Quarter. Two years later, attending the Zola ceremony
at the Panthéon, Major Dreyfus would be shot in the arm by
a Nationalist fanatic who was apprehended at the scene, duly
tried, and unanimously acquitted by a Paris jury.

On July 20, with Lucie watching from one window and General Picquart from another, Major Dreyfus was inducted into
the Legion of Honor and ceremonially reintegrated into the
Army in a small courtyard adjacent to the one where, eleven
years earlier, he had been degraded. He had requested the
smaller courtyard because of his terrible memories of the one
facing the Place Fontenoy. "*Vive* Picquart! *Vive* Dreyfus!"
some of the small crowd shouted, but the atonal voice shouted
back, "*Non, messieurs, non*, I beg of you. *Vive la France!*"
On October 15, exactly twelve years after his arrest, Dreyfus
reported for duty at the Vincennes garrison.

The great drama had not ended, but the part Alfred Dreyfus
had been forced to play was finished. "It is all over, and so
much the better," Halévy wrote in his "Apology for Our Past":

> We shall keep our memories which bring us honor and which
> will never disgrace us: we shall even honor the crisis which
> was brutal but not unhealthy and which will make us continue
> our efforts, but we will NOT BOAST OF BEING VICTORIOUS for
> the issue was confused.

That Péguy could never concede. He declared in *Our Youth*:
"More simply, we were heroes. More precisely, French heroes.
We shall be on half pay all our lives perhaps."

But they had not destroyed the enemy. Battered and reformed,
the *ancien régime*, the France of Altar and Sword survived,
also with its myths and its heroes. Persecuted, relatively im-

poverished, the clergy of France rebuilt from the shambles of its former power a lean and more modest but far sturdier religious edifice. The Separation Law proved an unforeseen boon. Neo-royalism—Facism in evolution—and the gospel of Jewish guilt for national calamities became the preoccupations of reactionary France. But these developments belong to chapters of French history in which Dreyfus played only a symbolic role.

Dreyfus retired from the Army on July 26, 1907. He told his family that the politicians had been more uneasy than his fellow officers about his return to active duty. To the soldiers and officers of the Vincennes garrison, he was still a first-rate officer; that was all that mattered. The Dreyfuses began to take annual trips to Switzerland and Italy. In Florence, while the family visited the Uffizi, he preferred to sit in the Piazzale Michelangelo ruminating the past. At the beginning of the Great War in 1914 Dreyfus returned to active duty as a lieutenant colonel serving on the same front at Verdun as his officer son. Pierrot survived the war in which the sons of Mathieu, Joseph Reinach, and Lieutenant Colonel Henry were slaughtered. Then came Dreyfus' permanent retirement as colonel.

Dreyfus' last years passed quietly. His name was a symbol of justice throughout the globe. But Dreyfus the man declined to assume the mantle of a Dreyfusard. "I was only an artillery officer whom a tragic mistake prevented from pursuing his career," he told a friend. "Dreyfus the symbol of justice—that's not me. It's you who created that Dreyfus." On one memorable occasion the man and the symbol united. In August 1927, he appealed to Massachusetts to spare the lives of the anarchists Sacco and Vanzetti: "[Their execution] would be the greatest moral disaster of many years, fraught with terrible consequences to American justice." Dreyfus added that, "when doubt exists, it is fighting providence to commit the irreparable." *

---

* "Dreyfus Appeals for Sacco Stay," New York *World*, August 22, 1927, p. 1. Dreyfus' detractors have had the last word, however. The account of Pierre Van Paassen, *Days of Our Youth* (New York, 1940), p. 172, that Dreyfus refused to endorse clemency has received wide acceptance.

A brilliant officer but a limited spirit, Alfred Dreyfus had achieved the three ambitions of his life: restoration to the Army, vindication, and participation in the successful struggle to avenge the rape of Alsace-Lorraine. In September 1899 General de Galliffet had proclaimed prematurely, "The case is closed." After July 1906 Dreyfus behaved in total obedience to de Galliffet's *ordre du jour*. He retreated into himself, living "an intense inner life," his son wrote, "but scarcely knew any longer how to communicate his emotions to others. He had simply lost the habit of expressing them."

In June 1930 General von Schwartzkoppen's widow sent Dreyfus an advance copy of her husband's account of the Affair. In her enclosed letter Madame von Schwartzkoppen explained, "It had always been his desire to testify in the outrageous case of which you were the principal figure and the victim. For various reasons which his memoirs clearly indicate, it was impossible for him to do so during his lifetime." Schwartzkoppen's book stirred renewed debate, and had Dreyfus possessed the slightest literary and political imagination, he would at least have composed the preface for the French edition. Instead, he confined himself to a note of thanks to Madame von Schwartzkoppen. "But if he had had an imagination," François Mauriac wondered in his own preface to the most recent edition of *Five Years of My Life*, "if he had had an imagination would he have survived?"

After a long illness following surgery, Colonel Dreyfus gripped his son's hand, "closed his eyes, and quietly passed away" at about five in the afternoon of July 12, 1935, the twenty-ninth anniversary of the law restoring him to the Army.

After the rehabilitation Mathieu and his family returned to Mulhouse where he devoted himself to the factory with the intensity formerly given his brother. Mathieu, the extroverted tactician whom Zola had praised as "*ce frère héroique*," became disillusioned after the pardon. There were the clever aspersions on Dreyfus' reserve and apolitical behavior; there were the deceptions by trusted associates who exploited the fight for justice for political gain; and there was the bitter reality that Drey-fusards—and most of France—cared so little about Dreyfus the human being that they took only formal notice of the rehabilitation ceremony and, thereafter, forgot the man.

Mathieu's deepest regret was the loss of Clemenceau's and Picquart's friendship. "I shall do my duty when that is required, but you will permit me to remain aloof," Clemenceau had written, refusing Mathieu's dinner invitation to celebrate Jaurès' annotated *bordereau* speech. But later Clemenceau acceded to much more than the imperative of duty; after the rehabilitation, he returned to the affection and respect for Mathieu of their heroic years. To Mathieu's children he confessed, "Your father is the one man who has ever been able to influence me."

But Georges Picquart remained unforgiving to the end. Advancing toward him with outstretched hand as the audience applauded the 1906 verdict, Mathieu saw Picquart abruptly march from the courtroom.

Mathieu returned to Paris shortly before the Great War. If friends had disappointed him, his children, Marguerite and Émile, were an abundant compensation. Both were spirited and unscarred by the Affair. Through her second husband, Ernest Mercier, Marguerite Dreyfus would have an influence which was not negligible upon the politics of the Third Republic. Her first husband was Joseph Reinach's son, Adolphe, one of France's most gifted young archaeologists. In 1914 Lieutenant Reinach vanished in action during the First Battle of the Marne. The following year Lieutenant Émile Dreyfus died in the Champagne offensive. In February 1931 Mathieu died in Paris.

Most of the other celebrities in the Affair had long since de-parted: Anatole France, Joseph Reinach, Jaurès, assassinated by a Nationalist fanatic a few hours before Germany declared war on Russia on July 31, 1914. General Picquart, having served as Minister of War under Prime Minister Clemenceau, was thrown from his horse in the first month of the terrible year of 1914 which destroyed *la belle époque*. He refused medical attention and lost consciousness the next day while working at his desk. His friend, General Lallemand, heard Picquart's last words: "The sooner it is finished, the better."

General von Schwartzkoppen, commander of a division on the Russian front, died of wounds in a Berlin hospital, deliriously shouting that Dreyfus was innocent. First Lieutenant Charles Péguy died leading his company in a charge in the First Battle of the Marne, a fitting close to a life dedicated to a philosophy of action. The Marquis Du Paty de Clam also fell at the head of his battalion.

Senator Mercier lived out the war as a pariah to the Left and a petted relic of the Right. The last heard from him was on a dismal evening at the height of General Erich Ludendorff's final offensive in 1918, when he came to the offices of Maurras' newspaper. The offensive could not succeed, he told the staff. "Suppose the political circumstances were different," Daudet fantasized, "another regime and Mercier the Minister of War of the King of France. We would have had another Louvois [Louis XIV's Minister of War]." Three years later the imperturbable Mercier was dead. The elegant de Boisdeffre had preceded him by two years. The ambassadorship to Russia that he craved eventually went to Maurice Paléologue.

A principal character in the Affair lived on in fair prosperity until 1923. During the war he wrote newspaper articles under the pseudonym Fitzgerald. Mr. Fitzgerald's articles on French military strategy were so disconcertingly wise that Paris, fearing a leak at Army headquarters, asked the British authorities to investigate the journalist's sources. The journalist was Esterhazy; his information derived from the Paris press and his ever-fecund imagination. During the remainder of his life in exile Esterhazy, alias the Count of Voilemont, went monthly to the Harpenden post office to collect a retainer mailed from France. While in England, he also sired an illegitimate son by his attorney's wife. Today, that son lives in Paris not far from

Mathieu's daughter, and should they ever meet, the two would agree completely about the knavery of the Count of Voilemont. Though Reinach's research suggested Esterhazy was not really a Frenchman but a migrant Slav, the Count insisted until the end that he was not only French but loyal. "I never betrayed my country," he wrote to *La Libre Parole* a few days before the final verdict of the Court of Cassation. The documents he had given the Germans were not restricted; a foreign power could have obtained them simply by asking the General Staff's liaison officer assigned to foreign military attachés. It was all a tragicomedy, Esterhazy believed. "I have said and I repeat," he wrote to his French attorney, "that the Dreyfus Affair was the triumph of the most disgusting cowardice of both sides."

That was an interpretation to which not a few jaded Dreyfusards could subscribe. But Esterhazy had a more personal interpretation of the Affair, which he shared with his French attorney in the final hours of the drama. "You will be surprised to receive this letter," he wrote Maître Robinet de Cléry in the summer of 1904. "Nevertheless, I beg you to be kind enough to read it to the end. It will show you, in any case, what senseless causes determine human destiny—and that of nations." The victory of Dreyfusism meant the end of France as they knew her, he continued. "None of this would have happened if the conservatives had had a bit of spirit and intelligence. But they would not even have had need of it if the ups and downs of life had not made me marry Mademoiselle de Nettancourt." So much for the destiny of nations; they depend upon adequate doweries and happy unions.

Lucie survived Alfred by ten years, graying but erect and alert until the end. For her the Affair was the nightmare shuttered in the past. The letters were locked away and whatever pertained to the Affair was painstakingly collected and filed as the years went by; she almost never spoke of it. Her daughter, Jeanne, became the wife of a prominent physician

and had two daughters, Simone and Madeleine, and two sons,
Louis and Étienne. Pierre's marriage produced four daughters.
He was deeply devoted to his father and, after his death, to
his memory. In late December 1946 Pierre was killed in an air
crash on his way to New York.

Lucie was mistaken, however, in thinking that the terrible
chapter was closed. The year before Dreyfus died, the Third
Republic had only survived because of two or three determined
police charges. On the infamous day of February 6, 1934, the
currents set in motion by the Stavisky Scandal (the suicide of
a well-connected Jewish embezzler) swept forty thousand extremists into the Place de la Concorde to battle the police defending the Chamber of Deputies. Sixteen people were killed
and six hundred and fifty-five wounded. It was the first re-
hearsal for takeover by Maurras' Action Française and the
para-military leagues.

The year after Alfred's death the forces of the Left united
in a Popular Front against the totalitarian menace, and Léon
Blum was elected Prime Minister. The government outlawed
the leagues, reduced the autonomy of the Bank of France,
granted the workers a forty-hour week with paid vacations, and
guaranteed the right to collective bargaining. Then Léon Blum
called for a "pause" in social reform and the Right counterattacked. The Popular Front was disbanded and the slogan
"Better Hitler than Blum" was heard everywhere.

Alfred's "first sad impression" had been the sight of German
troops occupying Mulhouse after the debacle at Sedan. In May
1940, after another debacle at Sedan, Lucie Dreyfus watched
as her husband's world was destroyed once more. But this time,
after the German blitzkrieg, a French rebirth did not seem
likely. For Charles Maurras, however, the death of eighty
thousand French soldiers in two weeks and the suicide of the
Third Republic were evidence of a "divine miracle"—a unique
opportunity to reconstruct France in the image of *Travail,
Famille, Patrie*, the words of Vichy replacing those of *Liberté,*

Egalité, Fraternité. The anti-Semitism which was both cause and consequence of the Affair had found ultimate and terrible expression in German National Socialism and in the Fascism of Marshal Philippe Pétain's État Français.

In the summer of 1940 Lucie moved with her family to Montpellier in the South of France, in the zone unoccupied by the conquering Germans. There they remained even after November 1942 when the Wehrmacht invaded Vichy territory. As French Jews, they were relatively secure so long as they minded their politics. But Lucie's granddaughter, Madeleine Lévy, joined the Resistance. She died in Auschwitz shortly before the camp was liberated. Lucie died on December 14, 1945, nearly a year and a half after the liberation of Paris.

For a time there was a street in Mulhouse named after Alfred Dreyfus—the only public monument in all France—but not so long ago this street was widened and renamed. While riding in a taxi with the daughter of Mathieu Dreyfus, the writer began to ask about the street in Mulhouse. "Shush, Monsieur," she interrupted, "please speak English—the driver, you know."

Selected Sources and Bibliography

I. Archives, Libraries, Services
   Archives de la Préfecture de Police (Paris)
   Archives Municipales de Mulhouse
   Archives Nationales de France
   Archives of the United States of America
   Bibliothèque Historique de la Ville de Paris
   Bibliothèque Nationale
   British Museum (Colindale Newspaper Library)
   Fogg Museum, Harvard University
   Houghton Library, Harvard University
   Library of Congress
   Nicholas Murray Butler Library, Columbia University
   Service Historique de l'Armée Française, Archives.
   Société Française du Microfilm.

The Adolphe Ochs Collection in the Bibliothèque Historique de la Ville de Paris is the most complete privately assembled Dreyfus collection in existence, and rarely used.

The Archives de l'Armée, Section Historique, Chateau de Vincennes, Paris, contain the final Secret Dossier, never previously examined by a foreign historian and unavailable to most French scholars. The Secret Dossier comprises documents withheld by the Ministry of War when the Army's Dreyfus file was transferred to the Archives Nationales. Reasons for withholding: forgeries of Military Counterintelligence, patent irrelevancies, evidence (forged?) of sexual idiosyncrasies of several principals in the Affair.

Archives Nationales de France: Serialized under BB 19, the Dreyfus documents are voluminous. Portions remain unexamined closely and surprises still await patient researchers.

Lee M. Friedman Collection of Judaica, the Houghton Library, Harvard University: Under FC9 D 862 is catalogued the largest Dreyfus collection in the United States. Rarely used.

Salle des Manuscrits, Bibliothèque Nationale: Among its extensive holdings on the Affair are the uncatalogued papers of Ferdinand Esterhazy and the catalogued memoirs and notes of Mathieu Dreyfus and Auguste Scheuer-Kestner.

326

The logbook at the Archives of the United States lists reports from the American military attaché, Paris. These interesting titles cause deepest regret that the reports were destroyed early in this century. The Italian Archivi Storici dei Ministeri degli Esteri e della Difesa and the Archivio Centrale della Stato contain nothing relative to the Affair. German documents on the Affair are believed to have been destroyed or lost at the end of World War II. The Archives de la Prefecture de Police (BA/107) are valuable not for hard evidence but for reflecting official concerns during the period. The Public Record Office (United Kingdom) contains a fairly large amount of Dreyfus material but no surprises and virtually all of it accessible in a variety of published works. A final, unexplored repository of potential value may be the Archives du Palais de Monaco. Unfortunately the author was unable to obtain permission to use them from His Serene Highness Prince Rainier III.

II. Primary Sources
Listed below and briefly described are sources that are new, rarely used, or indispensable. Other sources, many equally eligible, have been relegated to the general list of primary works.

Autobiographies, Memoirs, Papers, Interviews

Barrès, Maurice. *Mes Cahiers, 1896–1923*. Paris: Plon, 1963.
————. *Scènes et Doctrines du Nationalisme*. Paris: Plon, 1925. Anti-Dreyfusard classic by a major participant. Accuracy intentionally subordinated to ideology.
Blum, Léon. *Souvenirs sur l'Affaire*. Paris: Gallimard, 1935. A Dreyfusard classic by a major participant. Contains a number of factual inaccuracies.
Daudet, Léon. *Au Temps de Judas: Souvenirs des Milieux Politiques, Littéraires, Artistiques et Médicaux*. Paris: Nouvelle Librarie Nationale, 1920. Anti-Dreyfusard classic by a participant. Accuracy intentionally subordinated to bigotry.
Dreyfus, Alfred. *Cinq Annés de Ma Vie, 1894–1899*. Paris: Fasquelle, 1962 [originally published 1901]. Contains most of the extant correspondence of Alfred and Lucie. Five letters to Dreyfus (two from Anatole France, one from Georges Clemenceau, another from Georges Picquart, and one from Émile Zola) are appended. There is also an illuminating preface by François Mauriac and a valuable "Vie du Capitaine Dreyfus" by Dreyfus' grandson Jean-Louis Lévy.
Dreyfus, Mathieu. "Souvenirs sur l'Affaire Dreyfus." Bibliothèque Nationale: Typewritten MS, N. Fr. 14379. This memoir covers the period 1894–1906 and offers invaluable insights into personalities and internecine Dreyfusard disputes. An abbreviated and generally unavailable published

text exists: Robert Gauthier, *Dreyfusards! Souvenirs de Mathieu Dreyfus et d'Autres Inédits* (Paris: Julliard, 1965).

Dreyfus, Pierre. *The Man Alfred Dreyfus.* Trans. by Donald C. McKay. New Haven: Yale University Press, 1937. Preface by Pierre Dreyfus, Alfred's son, and notes to Dreyfus correspondence by McKay are particularly useful.

Esterhazy, Ferdinand. "Papiers." Bibliothèque Nationale: uncatalogued. Voluminous collection; small portion covering the period 1898–1903 examined with special permission.

Labori, Ses Notes, Manuscrites, Sa Vie. Labori, Marguerite, ed. Paris: Victor Attinger, 1947. Indispensable, although raising a number of questions about Labori's relation with the Dreyfus family and about his near assassination at Rennes.

Leblois, Louis. *L'Affaire Dreyfus: L'Iniquité, La Réparation, Les Principaux Faits et Les Principaux Documents.* Paris: Aristide Quillet, 1929. Leblois died before completing this careful reconstruction of intimate details of the Affair.

Legrand-Girarde, Félix. *Au Service de la France.* Paris: Presses Littéraires de France, 1954. Probably the best reflection of the attitude of general officers, enhanced in value because Legrand-Girarde was a member of the Élysée military staff under President Félix Faure and Émile Loubet.

Lévy, Jeanne Pierre-Paul. Daughter of Alfred Dreyfus. Provided several hours of tape-recorded recollections and lent family photographs and documents. Madame Lévy is custodian of Dreyfus correspondence and had never previously discussed the Affair outside the family.

Mercier, Marguerite. Daughter of Mathieu Dreyfus. Possesses vivid memory, trove of memorabilia, and provided hours of tape-recorded recollections. Madame Mercier's unpublished memoir, "Petites Images d'un Passé Vivant," is of considerable value.

Paléologue, Maurice. *An Intimate Journal of the Dreyfus Case.* New York: Criterion Books, 1957 [*Journal de l'Affaire Dreyfus.* Paris: Plon, 1955]. A mine of anecdotal political and social information. Long awaited for its revelations, Paléologue's posthumous work is seriously flawed by thesis that an unknown general (the real traitor) manipulated events in order to avoid discovery. It is the source of the flourishing "third man" theory to explain the Affair.

Proust, Marcel. *Jean Santeuil.* Trans. by Gerard Hopkins. New York: Simon & Schuster, 1955 [originally published 1952]. Neither strictly autobiographical nor historical but not entirely fiction, Proust's dry run for *À la Recherche du Temps Perdu* exposes the social psychology of the Affair with the veracity of art.

Reinach, Joseph. "Lettres et Papiers." Bibliothèque Nationale: Deuxième Série, N. a. fr. 24901–24902. Vols. II, III. Invaluable but perilous collection containing forged and dubious pieces relative to Esterhazy and Henry as well as authentic material on Esterhazy's military and political connections in France and his years in England.

Renard, Jules. *Journal, 1887–1910.* Paris: Nouvelle Revue Française, 1960 [originally published 1927]. Moderately useful account of the ferment in the artistic and intellectual circles.

Scheurer-Kestner, Auguste. "Papiers." Bibliothèque Nationale: N.a. fr. 12711 & 23819. Disappointing but not without value for details of preliminary skirmishing among Dreyfusards and the politicians.

Schwartzkoppen, Maximilian von. *The Truth About Dreyfus.* New York: G. P. Putnam's Sons, 1931. Like Paléologue's, another testament expected to dispose of the troublesome aftermath of the Affair. Flawed by Schwartzkoppen's lie about the *bordereau.*

Stock, P.-V. *Mémorandum d'un Éditeur: L'Affaire Dreyfus Anécdotique.* Paris: Stock, 1938. Appropriate title: an anecdotal account valuable for its Dreyfusard prejudices and for its frequently fascinating gossip.

Waldeck-Rousseau, Pierre Marie René. "Papiers Personnels." *Le Matin*, February–March 1911. Serialized over the objections of the Prime Minister's widow.

Histories

Dardennes, Henriette. "L'Affaire Dreyfus, Crise de Conscience Nationale." Bibliothèque Nationale: Typewritten MS, N. a. fr. 13497–500. Written by daughter of Minister of War Godefroy Cavaignac, this detailed account presents the classic Nationalist argument for Dreyfus' guilt.

Dutrait-Crozon, Henri. *Précis de l'Affaire Dreyfus avec une Répertoire Analytique.* Paris: Nouvelle Librairie Nationale, 1909 & 1924. The indispensable source for Anti-Dreyfusards. Purports to prove Dreyfus' guilt.

Reinach, Joseph. *Histoire de l'Affaire Dreyfus.* Paris: Charpentier & Fasquelle, 1900–11. 7 vols. This fundamental work by one of the key participants is a literary and documentary tour de force; but it is marred by Reinach's misinformation about Esterhazy's past, the manner of the discovery of the *bordereau*, the prejudices against Sandherr, and the certainty of Esterhazy's and Henry's collusion in treason.

Documents

Conseil de Guerre de Rennes. Le Procès Dreyfus devant le Conseil de Guerre de Rennes, 7 Août–9 Septembre 1899: Compte Rendu Sténographique 'in extenso.' Paris: Stock, 1900. 2 vols. Transcript of Rennes court-martial.

Documents Diplomatiques Français, 1871–1914. First, Second,

Third Series. Paris: Commission de Publication des Documents Relatifs aux Origines de la Guerre de 1914, 1950.

The Dreyfus Case, a Documentary History. Louis L. Snyder, ed. New Brunswick: Rutgers University Press, 1973. First fairly complete compendium in translation of the documents of the Affair. Serious chronological inaccuracies.

Instruction Fabre et les Décisions Ultérieurs. Paris: Éditions du Siècle, n.s. Judicial proceedings against Picquart resulting from charges brought by Minister of War Cavaignac.

Lettres d'un Coupable. Henry Leyret, ed. Paris: Stock, 1898. Excellent Esterhazy source if used cautiously.

Procès Dautriche: Compte Rendu Sténographique. Paris: Société Nouvelle de Librairie et d'Édition, 1905. Transcript of court-martial of Captains Dautriche, Rolland, *et al.,* for unauthorized expenditure of secret funds of Military Counterintelligence.

Procès Zola devant la Cour d'Assises de la Seine et la Cour de Cassation (7 Février-23 Février; 31 Mars-2 Avril 1898): Compte Rendu Sténographique 'in extenso' et Documents Annexes. Paris: Stock, 1898. 2 vols. Transcripts of trial and appeal of Émile Zola.

Report of Proceedings of the Second Annual [Zionist] Conference, June 18–19, 1899. Baltimore. 1899.

Révision du Procès Dreyfus à la Cour de Cassation: Compte Rendu Sténographique 'in extenso.' Paris: Stock, 1898. Report and recommendation of Maître Bard, investigating magistrate for the criminal chamber of the Court of Cassation, reviewing the 1894 Dreyfus court-martial verdict.

Révision du Procès Dreyfus: Enquête de la Cour de Cassation. Paris: Stock, 1899. 2 vols. Depositions, proceedings, verdict of the criminal chamber; depositions and proceedings of the United Court of Cassation reviewing the 1894 Dreyfus court-martial judgment.

Révision du Procès Dreyfus: Débats de la Cour de Cassation, Rapport de Mᵉ. Ballot-Beaupré, Conclusions de M. le Procureur Général Manau, Mémoire et Plaidoirie de Mᵉ. Mornard. Arrêt de la Cour. Paris: Stock, 1899. Windup of arguments and judgment annulling the 1894 Dreyfus court-martial verdict with order for a second court-martial at Rennes.

Révision du Procès de Rennes: Débats de la Cour de Cassation. Audiences de 3, 4, et 5 Mars 1904. Paris: Société Nouvelle de Librairie et d'Édition, 1940. Transcript of first phase of Dreyfus' second appeal.

Révision du Procès de Rennes, 15 Juin–12 Juillet 1906: Mémoire de Mᵉ. Mornard. Paris: Ligue Française pour la Défense des Droits de l'Homme et du Citoyen, 1907. Transcript of final sessions and verdict in the Affair by the Court of Cassation.

Secret Dossier. Archives de l'Armée, Section Historique.

III. Primary Sources, General
      Books
      Albalot, Antoine. *Trente Ans de Quartier Latin*. Paris: Société
        Française d'Édition Littéraire et Technique, 1930.
      Allier, Raoul. *Le Bordereau Annoté: Etude de Critique His-
        torique*. Paris: Société Nouvelle de Librairie et d'Édition,
        1903.
      André, Louis. *Cinq Ans de Ministère (Fragments de Mém-
        oires)*. Paris: Stock, 1906.
      Bac, Ferdinand. *Intimités de la III*e *République: La Fin des
        'Temps Délicieux*.' Paris: Hachette, 1935.
      ———. *La Princesse Mathilde, Sa Vie et ses Amis*. Paris:
        Hachette, 1928.
      Barbier, Abbé Emmanuel. *Histoire du Catholicisme Libéral
        et Social en France*. Bordeaux, 1924.
      Barrès, Maurice. *Le Roman de l'Énergie Nationale: Les
        Déracinés, L'Appel au Soldat, Leurs Figures*. Paris: Plon,
        1897, 1900, 1902.
      Beauvoir, Simone de. *Memoirs of a Dutiful Daughter*. Trans.
        by James Kirkup. London: Weidenfeld & Nicolson, 1959
        (Originally published 1958).
      Benda, Julien. *Dialogues à Byzance*. Paris: Revue Blanche,
        1900.
      ———. *The Treason of the Intellectuals*. Trans. by Richard
        Aldington. New York: Norton, 1969 [originally published
        1928].
      Blum, Léon. *Souvenirs sur l'Affaire*. Paris: Gallimard, 1935.
      Blunt, Wilfrid Scawen. *My Diaries: Being a Personal Narra-
        tive of Events, 1888–1914*. New York: Knopf, 1921. 2 vols.
      Bonnamour, Georges. *Le Procès Zola*. Paris: A. Pierret, 1898.
      Boussel, Patrice, ed. *L'Affaire Dreyfus et la Presse*. Paris:
        A. Colin, 1960.
      Braibant, Charles M. *Un Bourgeois sous Trois Républiques*.
        Paris: Buchet Khostel, 1961.
      Brisson, Henri. *Souvenirs: L'Affaire Dreyfus avec Documents*.
        Paris: Cornély, 1908.
      Bruchard, Henry de. *Petits Mémoires du Temps de la Ligue,
        1896–1901*. Paris: Nouvelle Librairie Nationale, n.d.
      Brulat, Paul. *L'Affaire Dreyfus: Violence et Raison*. Paris:
        Stock, 1898.
      Caillaux, Joseph. *Mes Mémoires*. Paris: Plon, 1942. 3 vols.
      La Caricatura nell' Affare Dreyfus. Milano: Tipografico Edi-
        trice Verri, 1899.
      Clemenceau, Georges. *Contre la Justice*. Paris: Stock, 1900.
      Cocheris, Jules, *Situation Internationale de l'Egypte et du
        Soudan*. Paris, Plon, 1903.
      Combarieu, Abel. *Sept Ans à l'Élysée, avec le Président
        Émile Loubet, de l'Affaire Dreyfus à la Conférence Al-
        gésiras, 1899–1906*. Paris: Hachette, 1932.
      Combes, Émile. *Mon Ministère: Mémoires, 1902–1905*. Paris:
        Plon, 1956.

Conybeare, Frederick C. *The Dreyfus Case*. London: George Allen, 1899.

Cornély, Joseph. *Notes sur l'Affaire Dreyfus*. Paris: Société Française d'Édition et d'Art, 1903.

Cuignet, Louis. *Souvenirs de l'Affaire Dreyfus: Le Dossier Trarieux-Tornielli-Reinach*. Paris: Ligue Française Antimaçonique, 1911.

Daudet, Léon. *Paris Vécu*. Paris: Gallimard, 1969 [originally published 1928].

———. *Quand Vivait Mon Père*. Paris: B. Grasset, 1940.

Dawson, Douglas. *A Soldier-Diplomat*. London: John Murray, 1927.

Débidour, Antonin. *L'Église Catholique et l'État sous la IIIe République, 1870–1906*. Paris: F. Alcan, 1969. 2 vols.

De Haime, E. *Affaire Dreyfus: Les Faits Acquis*. Paris: Stock, 1898.

Desachy, Paul. *Bibliographie de l'Affaire Dreyfus*. Paris: E. Cornély, 1905.

Drumont, Edouard. *La France Juive: Essai d'Histoire Contemporaine*. Paris: Flammarion, 1886. 2 vols.

France, Anatole. *Crainquebille*. Trans. by Jacques Leclerq. New York: Heritage Press, 1949 [originally published 1901].

———. *L'Église et la République*. Paris: Éditions d'Art, 1905.

———. *Penguin Island*. Trans. by A. W. Evans. New York: Gabriel Wells, 1924 [originally published 1908].

France, Jean. *Ligues et Complots: Trentes Ans à la Rue des Saussaies*. Paris: Gallimard, 1931.

Freycinet, Charles de. *Souvenirs, 1878–1893*. Paris: Delagrave, 1913.

Gohier, Urbain. *L'Armée Contre la Nation*. Paris: Revue Blanche, 1898.

Goncourt, Edmond and Jules. *Journal: Mémoires de la Vie Littéraire, 1891–1896*. Paris: Fasquelle et Flammarion, 1956 [originally published 1887–96].

Grand-Carteret, J. *L'Affaire Dreyfus et l'Image*. Paris: Flammarion, 1898.

Gregh, Fernand. *L'Age d'Or: Souvenirs d'Enfance et de Jeunesse*. Paris: Grasset, 1947.

Guyot, Yves. *Les Raisons de Basile: L'Affaire Dreyfus*. Paris: Stock, 1899.

Halévy, Daniel. *Luttes et Problèmes*. Paris: Payot, 1911.

———. *Charles Péguy et les Cahiers de la Quinzaine*. Paris: Payot, 1918.

Harding, William. *Dreyfus: The Prisoner of Devil's Island*. New York: Associated Publishing, 1899.

Herzl, Theodore. *L'Affaire Dreyfus*. Paris: Fédération Sionniste de France, n.d.

———. *Complete Diaries*. New York: Herzl Press, 1940.

Hess, Jean. *A l'Ile du Diable: Enquête d'un Reporter aux Iles du Salut et à Cayenne*. Paris: Nilson, n.d.

Jaurès, Jean. *Oeuvres, Textes Rassemblés, Presentés et An-notés par Max Bonnefous.* Paris: Rieder, 1931. 4 vols.

Jouvenel, Robert de. *La République des Camarades.* Paris: Grasset, 1914.

Lazare, Bernard, *Une Erreur Judiciaire: La Verité sur l'Affaire Dreyfus.* Brussels, 1896.

The Letters of Queen Victoria, a Selection from Her Majesty's Correspondence and Journal Between the Years 1886 & 1901. Third Series. London: John Murray, 1932. 3 vols.

Marie, Paul. *Le Petit Bleu: Étude Critique.* Paris: Stock, 1899.

Mauclair, Camille. *Servitude et Grandeur Littéraire.* Paris: Ollendorff, 1922.

Maurras, Charles. *Au Signe de Flore: Souvenirs de Vie Politique, Affaire Dreyfus, la Fondation de l'Action Française, 1898–1900.* Paris: Les Oeuvres Représentatives, 1931.

Mende, Elsie Porter, and Whittier, Henry Greenleaf. *An American Soldier and Diplomat, Horace Porter.* New York: Frederick A. Stokes, 1927.

Meyer, Arthur. *Ce Que Je Peux Dire.* Paris: Plon, 1912.

————. *Ce Que Mes Yeux Ont Vu.* Paris: Plon, 1911.

————. *Forty Years of Parisian Society [Ce Que Mes Yeux Ont Vu].* London: E. Nash, 1912.

Péguy, Charles. *Temporal and Eternal.* Trans. and abr. by Alexandre Dru. New York: Viking, 1958 [originally published as *Notre Jeunesse*, 1910].

————. *Oeuvres en Prose, 1909–1914.* Paris: Pléiade, 1957. [especially *L'Argent, L'Argent suite*].

Proust, Marcel, *Swann's Way.* Trans. by C. K. Scott Moncrieff. New York: Random House, 1956 [originally published 1913].

————. *Guermantes Way.* Trans. by C. K. Scott Moncrieff. New York: Random House, 1952 [originally published 1920].

————. *The Past Recaptured.* Trans. by Frederick A. Blossom. New York: Random House, 1959 [originally published 1927].

Psichari, Henriette. *Des Jours et des Hommes, 1890–1961.* Paris: Grasset, 1962.

Quillard, Pierre. *Le Monument Henry, Liste des Souscripteurs Classé Méthodiquement et Selon l'Ordre Alphabétique.* Paris: Stock, 1899.

Radziwill, Princess Marie Dorothéa. *Lettres de la Princesse Radziwill au Général de Robilant, 1889–1914.* Bologna: Niccolo Zanichelli, 1933. 4 vols.

Reville, Albert. *Les Étapes d'un Intellectuel, Apropos de l'Affaire Dreyfus.* Paris: Stock, 1898.

Rolland, Romain, et Lugné-Poe. *Correspondance, 1894–1901.* Paris: L'Arche, 1957.

————. *The Wolves.* Trans. by Barrett H. Clark. New York: Random House, 1937 [originally published 1898].

Saint-Aulaire, Auguste Félix Charles de. *Confession d'un*

Vieux Diplomate. Paris: Flammarion, 1953.

Schlumberger, Gustave. *Mes Souvenirs, 1844–1928.* Paris: Plon, 1934.

Simond, Émile. *Histoire de la IIIe République de 1894 à 1896.* Paris: H.C.-Lavauzelle, 1921.

Sorel, Georges. *La Révolution Dreyfusienne.* Paris: Marcel Rivière, 1909.

Steed, Wickham. *Through Thirty Years, 1892–1922: A Personal Narrative.* New York: Doubleday, 1924. 2 vols.

Stevens, G. W. *The Tragedy of Dreyfus.* New York: Harper, 1899.

Tharaud, Jérome and Jean. *Notre Cher Péguy.* Paris: Plon, 1926.

———. *Mes Années Chez Barrès.* Paris: Plon, 1928.

———. *La Vie et la Mort de Déroulède.* Paris: Émile-Paul, 1914.

Thibaudet, Albert. *Les Idées de Charles Maurras.* Paris: La Nouvelle Revue Française, 1920.

———. *Trente Ans de Vie Française: La Vie de Maurice Barrès.* Paris: La Nouvelle Revue Française, 1921.

Van Paassen, Pierre. *Days of Our Years.* New York: Hillman-Curl, 1940.

Vasili, Paul [Juliette Adam]. Ed. and trans. by Raphael Ledos de Beaufort. *Society in Paris. A Series of Letters from Count Paul Vasili to a Young French Diplomat.* London: Chatto & Windus, 1890.

Villemar, H. *Dreyfus Intime.* Paris: Stock, 1898.

Vizetelly, Ernest. *Republican France, 1870–1912: Her Presidents, Statesmen, Policy, Vicissitudes and Social Life.* London: Holden and Hardingham, 1912.

Weill, Georges. *Histoire du Catholicisme Libéral en France, 1828–1908.* Paris: F. Alcan, 1909.

Zévaès, Alexandre. *Le Cinquantenaire de J'Accuse.* Paris: Fasquelle, 1948.

———. *Histoire de la IIIe République.* Paris: Éditions de la Nouvelle Revue Critique, 1946.

———. *Le Scandale de Panama.* Paris, 1931.

Zola, Émile. *L'Affaire Dreyfus, la Vérité en Marche.* Paris: Garnier-Flammarion, 1969 [originally published 1899].

———. *Oeuvres Complètes.* Vol. 14. Paris: Cercle de Livre Précieux, 1970.

Articles

Baldwin, Elbert. "A Day in Paris." *The Outlook*, November 26, 1898, pp. 767–70.

———. "The Dreyfus Case Again." *The Outlook*, September 10, 1898, pp. 101–2.

———. "The Danger in France." *The Outlook*, October 1, 1898, pp. 207–72.

————. "Plotters Against France." *The Outlook*, October 22, 1898, p. 461.

————. "The Chances of War." *The Outlook*, October 29, 1898, p. 509.

————. "The Dreyfus Trial." *The Outlook*, September 9, 1899, pp. 1–5.

————. "The Dreyfus Affair." *The Outlook*, September 23, 1899, p. 186.

————. "A Significant Silence." *The Outlook*, November 11, 1899, pp. 624–25.

Brisson, A. "The Degradation of Dreyfus." *Living Age*, February 12, 1898, pp. 432–33.

Chevrillon, André. "Huit Jours à Rennes." *La Grande Revue*, February 1900, pp. 280–336.

Conybeare, Frederick C. "General Picquart." *Cornhill Magazine*, August 1914, pp. 167–73.

Coppée, François. "Lettres Inédites (1878–1908)." *La Revue de France*, February 1936, pp. 427–66.

Lebon, André. "La Mission Marchand et le Cabinet Meline." *Revue des Deux Mondes*, March 15, 1900, pp. 274–96.

Morse, John T. "The Dreyfus and Zola Trials." *Atlantic Monthly*, May 1898, pp. 589–602.

Newspapers

The Bee (Washington, D.C.) : March 5, 1898, p. 4; September 3, 1898, p. 4; September 2, 1899, p. 4.

Daily Tribune (Chicago) : January 11, 1898, p. 7; January 12, 1898, p. 1; January 14, 1898, p. 6; January 16, 1898, p. 3; September 1, 1898, p. 1; August 6, 1899, p. 1; August 13, 1899, p. 1; September 1, 1899, p. 1; September 9, 1899, p. 1; September 10, 1899, p. 1; September 11, 1899, p. 1.

The Enquirer (Philadelphia) : January 1, 1898, p. 3; January 14, 1898, p. 3; February 8, 1898, p. 1; February 24, 1898, p. 1; September 1, 1898, p. 1; September 2, 1898, p. 2.

The Examiner (San Francisco) : January 1, 1898, p. 3; January 14, 1898, p. 3; February 8, 1898, p. 1; February 24, 1898, p. 1; September 1, 1898, p. 1; September 2, 1898, p. 2.

The Examiner and the Moree General Advertiser (Moree, Australia) : August 12, 1899, p. 2; August 19, 1899, p. 2.

Le Figaro (Paris) : January 3, 1895, pp. 1, 2; January 5, 1895, p. 1; January 6, 1895, pp. 1, 2; August 31, 1898, p. 1; September 2, 1898, p. 1; July 1, 1899, p. 1; July 2, 1899, p. 1; July 31, 1899, p. 3.

Le Journal des Débats (Paris) : September 2, 1898, p. 1.

La Libre Parole (Paris) : Throughout 1893–94.

Le Matin (Paris) : February 5–March 13, 1911 (Waldeck-Rousseau papers).

Morning World Herald (Omaha, Nebraska) : September 1, 1898, p. 1; September 3, 1898, p. 4; August 7, 1899, p. 1; September 1, 1899, p. 1; September 4, 1899, p. 1; September 10, 1899, p. 1; September 11, 1899, p. 1.

Le Petit Journal (Paris): April 1894.
Le Siècle (Paris): August 8, 1899, p. 1; August 12, 1899, p. 1; August 13, 1899, pp. 1, 2; August 19, 1899, p. 2; August 26, 1899, p. 1; August 27, 1899, p. 1; August 28, 1899, p. 1; August 30, 1899, p. 1.
Le Temps (Paris): November 3, 1894, p. 2; January 6, 1895, p. 1; October 31, 1894, p. 2.
The Times (London): January 11–15, 1898; February 8, 9, 24, 1898; September 1, 2, 1898, p. 3; August 7, 8, 14, 15, 23, 24, 26, 28, 1899, all p. 3; September 5, 8, 10, 12, 1899, all p. 3.
The Tribune (New York): January 11, 12, 14, 16, 1898, pp. 7, 1, 6, 3; September 1, 1899, p. 1; August 6, 13, 1899, p. 1; September 1, 9, 10, 11, 1899, all p. 1.
Le Voltaire (Paris): September 1, 1892, p. 2.

IV. Secondary Sources

Books

Ambler, John S. *Soldiers Against the State: The French Army in Politics.* Garden City, N.Y.: Doubleday, 1968.
Andrew, Christopher. *Théophile Delcassé and the Making of the Entente Cordiale.* New York: Macmillan, 1968.
Arendt, Hannah. *The Origins of Totalitarianism.* New York: World, 1964 [originally published 1951].
Auclair, Marcelle. *La Vie de Jean Jaurès ou la France d'Avant 1914.* Paris: Seuil, 1954.
Baumont, Maurice. *Aux Sources de l'Affaire, L'Affaire Dreyfus, d'après les Archives Diplomatiques.* Paris: Productions de Paris, 1959.
Beau de Loménie, E. *Les Responsabilités des Dynasties Bourgeoises.* Paris: Denoël, 1943–63. 4 vols.
Bibliographie Sommaire de l'Affaire Dreyfus depuis 1924. Paris: Cahiers Naturalistes, 1957, vol. III.
Boisdeffre, Pierre de. *Métamorphose de la Littérature de Barrès à Malraux.* Paris: Éditions Alsatia, 1950. 2 vols.
Bourgeois, E. *History of Modern France, 1852-1913.* Trans. by G. W. Prothero. Cambridge: University Press, 1919. 2 vols.
Bouvier, Jean. *Le Krach de l'Union Générale (1878–1885).* Paris: Presses Universitaires, 1960.
———. *Les Rothschilds.* Paris: A. Fayard, 1967.
Brogan, D. W. *The Development of Modern France, 1870–1939.* London: Hamish Hamilton, 1959.
Brombert, Victor. *The Intellectual Hero: Studies in the French Novel, 1880-1955.* Chicago: University of Chicago Press, 1961.
Brown, Roger G. *Fashoda Reconsidered: The Impact of Domestic Politics on French Policy in Africa, 1893-1898.* Baltimore: Johns Hopkins, 1969.
Bruun, Geoffrey. *Clemenceau.* Cambridge, Mass.: Harvard University Press, 1944.

Burnand, Robert. *La Vie Quotidienne en France de 1870–1900*. Paris: Hachette, 1947.

Buthman, William C. *The Rise of Integral Nationalism in France, With Special Reference to the Ideas and Activities of Charles Maurras*. New York: Octagon, 1970 [originally published 1929].

Byrnes, Robert F. *Antisemitism in Modern France: The Prologue to the Dreyfus Affair*. New Brunswick, N.J.: Rutgers University Press, 1950.

Capéran, Louis. *L'Anticléricalisme et l'Affaire Dreyfus, 1897–1899*. Toulouse: Imprimerie Régionale, 1948.

Castillon du Perron, Marguerite. *La Princesse Mathilde*. Paris: Librairie Académique Perrin, 1963.

Challener, Richard D. *The French Theory of the Nation in Arms, 1866–1939*. New York: Russell & Russell, 1965.

Chapman, Guy. *The Dreyfus Case: A Reassessment*. London: Rupert Hart-Davis, 1963.

———. *The Third Republic of France: The First Phase, 1871–1894*. London: Macmillan, 1962.

Charensol, Georges. *L'Affaire Dreyfus et la Troisième République*. Paris: Éditions Kra, 1930.

Charpentier, Armand. *Historique de l'Affaire Dreyfus*. Paris: Pasquelle, 1933.

Chastenet, Jacques. *Histoire de la Troisième République*. Paris: Hachette, 1952–63. 7 vols.

Colton, Joel. *Léon Blum: Humanist in Politics*. New York: Knopf, 1966.

Compère-Morel. *Jules Guesde: Le Socialisme Fait l'Homme*. Paris: Quillet, 1938.

Dansette, Adrien. *Histoire Religieuse de la France Contemporaine: L'Église Catholique dans la Mêlée Politique et Sociale*. Paris: Flammarion, 1965.

———. *Histoire des Presidents de la République de Louis-Napoléon Bonaparte à Vincent Auriol*. Paris: Amiot-Dumont, 1953.

David, R. *The French Legal System: An Introduction*. Dobbs Ferry, N.Y.: Oceana Press, 1958.

Dimont, Max. *Jews, God and History*. New York: Simon & Schuster, 1962.

Dolléans, Edourd. *Histoire du Mouvement Ouvrier (1830–1959)*. Paris: A. Colin, 1957–60. 3 vols.

Druck, David. *Baron Edmond Rothschild: The Story of a Practical Idealist*. New York, 1928.

Eubank, Keith. *Paul Cambon, Master Diplomatist*. Norman, Okla.: University of Oklahoma Press, 1960.

Fiechter, Jean-Jacques. *Le Socialisme Français: De L'Affaire Dreyfus à la Grande Guerre*. Geneva: Droz, 1965.

Fosca, François. *Histoire des Cafés de Paris*. Paris: Firmin-Didot, 1934.

La France de l'Affaire Dreyfus à Nos Jours. Bibliothèque du Centre de Documentation Juive Contemporaine. Paris: 1964.

Gimpel, Jean. *The Cult of Art: Against Art and Artists*. New York: Stein & Day, 1969.

Giscard d'Etaing, Henri. *D'Esterhazy à Dreyfus*. Paris: Plon, 1960.

Goguel, François. *Politique des Partis sous la Troisième République*. Paris: Seuil, 1958.

Goldberg, Harvey. *The Life of Jean Jaurès*. Madison, Wisc.: University of Wisconsin Press, 1962.

Gorce, Paul-Marie de la. *The French Army: A Military-Political History*. Trans. by Kenneth Douglas. New York: Braziller, 1963.

Griffiths, Richard. *The Reactionary Revolution: The Catholic Revival in French Literature, 1870–1914*. London: Constable, 1966.

Guillemin, Henri. *L'Énigme Esterhazy*. Paris: Gallimard, 1962.

Haas, Jacob de. *Theodore Herzl: A Biographical Study*. New York: The Leonard Co., 1927.

Halasz, Nicholas. *Captain Dreyfus: The Story of a Mass Hysteria*. New York: Simon & Schuster, 1955.

Halpern, Rose A. "The American Reaction to the Dreyfus Case." Unpublished M.A. thesis, Columbia University, 1941.

Harding, James. *The Astonishing Adventure of General Boulanger*. New York: Scribners, 1971.

Hay, Malcolm. *The Foot of Pride: The Pressure of Christendom on the People of Israel for 1900 Years*. Boston: Beacon, 1950.

Hemmings, F. W. J. *Émile Zola*. New York: Oxford, 1970.

Herzog, Wilhelm. *From Dreyfus to Pétain: "The Struggle of a Republic."* Trans. by Walter Sorell. New York: Creative Age Press, 1947.

Hertzberg, Arthur. *The French Enlightenment and the Jews: The Origins of Modern Anti-Semitism*. New York: Columbia University Press, 1968.

Howard, Michael. *The Franco-Prussian War: The German Invasion of France, 1870–1871*. London: Rupert Hart-Davis, 1961.

Hubert, Renée R. *The Dreyfus Affair and the French Novel*. Boston: Eagle Enterprises, 1951.

Iiams, Thomas M., Jr. *Dreyfus, Diplomatists and the Dual Alliance: Gabriel Hanotaux at the Quai d'Orsay (1894–1898)*. Geneva: Droz, 1962.

Jackson, John Hampden. *Clemenceau and the Third Republic*. London: Hodder & Stoughton, 1946.

Jefferson, Carter. *Anatole France: The Politics of Skepticism*. New Brunswick, N.J.: Rutgers University Press, 1965.

Johnson, Douglas. *France and the Dreyfus Affair*. London: Blandford, 1966.

Josephson, Matthew. *Zola and His Time*. New York: Macaulay, 1928.

Jussem-Wilson, Nelly. *Charles Péguy*. New York: Hillary House, 1965.

Kahn, David. *The Codebreakers: The Story of Secret Writing*. New York: Macmillan, 1968.

Kayser, Jacques. *L'Affaire Dreyfus*. Paris: Gallimard, 1946.

Kedward, H. R. *The Dreyfus Affair: Catalyst for Tensions in French Society*. London: Longmans, 1965.

Langer, William L. *The Diplomacy of Imperialism, 1890–1902*. 2d ed. New York: Knopf, 1960.

Laqueur, Walter. *A History of Zionism*. New York: Holt, 1972.

Larnac, Jean. *Comtesse de Noailles, Sa Vie, Son Oeuvre*. Paris: Sagittaire, 1931.

Laski, Harold. *Authority in the Modern State*. New Haven: Yale University Press, 1927.

Manévy, Raymond. *La Presse Française de Renaudot à Rochefort*. Paris: J. Fôret, 1958.

———. *La Presse de la Troisième République*. Paris: Corréa, 1955.

Maritain, Raissa. *Les Grandes Amitiés*. New York: Éditions de la Maison Française, 1941. 2 vols.

Marrus, Michael R. *The Politics of Assimilation: A Study of the French Jewish Community at the Time of the Dreyfus Affair*. Oxord: Clarendon Press, 1971.

Martin du Gard, Roger. *Jean Barois*. Trans. by Stuart Gilbert. New York: Viking, 1949 [originally published 1913].

Massis, Henri. *Maurras et Notre Temps*. Paris: Palatine, 1951. 2 vols.

Mauriac, Claude. *Marcel Proust par Lui-meme: Images et Textes*. Paris: Seuil, 1953.

Maurois, André. *Marshal Lyautey*. Trans. by Hamish Miles. London: The Bodley Head, 1931.

Mazel, Henri. *Histoire et Psychologie de l'Affaire Dreyfus*. Paris: Boivin, 1934.

Miguel, Pierre. *L'Affaire Dreyfus*. Paris: Presses Universitaires de France, 1961.

Mitterand, Henri. *Zola Journaliste: De l'Affaire Manet à l'Affaire Dreyfus*. Paris: A Colin, 1962.

Moorehead, Alan. *The White Nile*. New York: Harper, 1961.

Mounier, Emmanuel. *La Pensée de Charles Péguy*. Paris: Seuil, 1935.

Noland, Aaron. *The Founding of the French Socialist Party, 1893–1905*. Cambridge: Harvard University Press, 1956.

Nolte, Ernst. *Three Faces of Fascism: Action Française, Italian Fascism, National Socialism*. Trans. by Leila Venneurtz. New York: Holt, 1966 [originally published 1963].

Osgood, Samuel M. *French Royalism Under the Third and Fourth Republics*. The Hague: Martinus Nyhoff, 1960.

Painter, George. *Marcel Proust: A Biography*. London: Chatto & Windus, 1961, 1965. 2 vols.

Perry, Ralph Barton. *The Thought and Character of William James as Revealed in Unpublished Correspondence and Notes, Together with his Published Writings*. Boston: Little, Brown, 1936.

Persil, Robert. *Millerand, 1859–1943*. Paris: Societé d'Éditions Françaises, 1941.

Peyrefitte, Roger. *L'Exilé de Capri*. Paris: Club des Éditeurs, n.d.

Porter, Charles W. *The Career of Théophile Delcassé*. Philadelphia: University of Pennsylvania Press, 1936.

Quennell, Peter, ed. *Marcel Prouse, 1871–1922: A Centennial Volume*. New York: Simon & Schuster, 1971.

Remond, René. *The Right in France, 1815 to the Present*. Trans. by James M. Laux. Philadelphia: University of Pennsylvania Press, 1966 [originally published Paris, 1954].

Rudorff, Raymond. *The Belle Epoque: Paris in the Nineties*. New York: Saturday Review Press, 1973.

Sanderson, G. N. *England, Europe and the Upper Nile, 1882–1899*. Edinburgh: University Press, 1965.

Sartre, Jean-Paul. *Réflexions sur la Question Juive*. Paris: Paul Morihien, 1946.

Seager, Frederic H. *The Boulanger Affair: The Political Crossroad of France, 1886–1889*. Ithaca, N.Y.: Cornell University Press, 1969.

Sedgwick, A. *The Ralliement in French Politics, 1890–1898*. Cambridge: Harvard University Press, 1965.

Schechter, Betty. *The Dreyfus Affair: A National Scandal*. London: Victor Gollancz, 1967.

Sée, Henri. *Histoire de la Ligue des Droits de l'Homme*. Paris: Ligue des Droits de l'Homme, 1927.

Shapiro, David, ed. *The Right in France, 1890–1919*. Carbondale, Ill.: Southern Illinois U. Press, 1962.

Shattuck, Roger. *The Banquet Years: The Origins of the Avant Garde in France, 1885 to World War I*. New York: Harcourt, Brace, 1955.

Shirer, William L. *The Collapse of the Third Republic: An Inquiry into the Fall of France in 1940*. New York: Simon & Schuster, 1969.

Silverman, Dan P. *Reluctant Union: Alsace-Lorraine and Imperial Germany, 1871–1918*. University Park, Pa.: Pennsylvania State University Press, 1972.

Silvera, Alain. *Daniel Halévy and His Times: A Gentleman-Commoner in the Third Republic*. Ithaca, N.Y.: Cornell University Press, 1966.

Simon, Maron J. *The Panama Affair*. New York: Scribner's, 1971.

Smith, Horace. *A Captain Unafraid: The Strange Adventures Of Dynamite Johnny O'Brien*. New York: Harper, 1912.

Soltau, Roger H. *French Parties and Politics, 1871–1921*. New York: Russell & Russell, 1965 [originally published 1930].

———. *French Political Thought in the 19th Century*. New York: Russell & Russell, 1959 [originally published 1931].

Steinheil, Walther. Trans. by Raymond Johnes. *Dreyfus*. London: Allen & Unwin, 1930.

Suffel, Jacques. *Anatole France*. Paris: Éditions du Myrte, 1946.

Swart, Konraad W. *The Sense of Decadence in Nineteenth Century France*. The Hague: Martinus Nijhoff, 1964.

Thibaudet, Albert. *French Literature from 1795 to Our Era*.

Trans. by Charles Lam Markmann. New York: Funk & Wagnalls, 1967 [originally published 1938].

Thomas, Louis. *Le Général de Galliffet, 1830–1909*. Paris: Aux Armes de France, 1941.

Thomas, Marcel. *L'Affaire sans Dreyfus*. Paris: A. Fayard, 1961.

Tint, Herbert. *The Decline of French Patriotism, 1870–1940*. London: Weidenfeld & Nicolson, 1964.

Tuchman, Barbara W. *The Proud Tower: A Portrait of the World Before the War, 1890-1914*. New York: Macmillan, 1966.

Vandervelde, E. *Jaurès*. Paris: F. Alcan, 1929.

Watt, Richard M. *Dare Call It Treason*. New York: Simon & Schuster, 1963.

Weber, Eugen. *Action Française; Royalism and Reaction in Twentieth Century France*. California: Stanford University Press, 1962.

Weil, Bruno. *L'Affaire Dreyfus*. Paris: Gallimard, 1930.

Weill, Georges. *Histoire du Catholicism Libéral en France, 1828–1908*. Paris: F. Alcan, 1909.

Weinstein, H. *Jean Jaurès: A Study of Patriotism in the French Socialist Movement*. New York: Columbia University Press, 1936.

Werth, Alexander. *The Twilight of France, 1933–1940*. New York: H. Fertig, 1966 [originally published 1942].

Wormser, Georges. *La République de Clemenceau*. Paris: Presses Universitaires de France, 1961.

Willard, Claude. *Les Guesdistes: Le Mouvement Socialiste en France, 1893–1905*. Paris. Éditions Sociales, 1965.

Williams, Roger L. *Henri Rochefort, Prince of the Gutter Press*. New York: Scribner's, 1966.

Wilson, Edmund. *Axel's Castle*. New York: Scribner's, 1931.

Articles

Grossman, James. "The Dreyfus Affair Fifty Years Later, The Captain Who Became A Case." *Commentary*, January 1956, pp. 25–31.

Kayser, Jacques. "Émile Zola et l'Opinion Publique." *La Nef*, December 1948, pp. 48–58.

Pawlowski, G. de. "A Propos de l'Affaire Dreyfus." *Les Annales Politiques et Littéraires*, August 15, 1930, pp. 155–57.

Peter, J.-P. "Dimension de l'Affaire Dreyfus." *Annales (Economies, Sociétés, Civilizations)*, November-December 1961, pp. 1141–67.

Schwarzschild, Steven. "The Marquis de Morès, The Story of a Failure." *Jewish Social Studies*, January 1960, pp. 3–26.

Silberner, Edmund. "French Socialism and the Jewish Question, 1864–1914." *Historia Judaica*, April 1954, pp. 3–38.

Szajkowski, Zosa. "The Growth of the Jewish Population of France." *Jewish Social Studies*, July & October 1946, pp. 179–96, 297–315.

Index